World Directory of Environmental Organizations
Third Edition

A Handbook of National and International Organizations and
Programs—Governmental and Non-Governmental—Concerned
with Protecting the Earth's Resources

Edited by
Thaddeus C. Trzyna
with the assistance of Ilze M. Gotelli

California Institute of Public Affairs
in cooperation with the
Sierra Club
and
IUCN—The World Conservation Union

Published and sold by the

California Institute of Public Affairs
P.O. Box 10
Claremont, California 91711, USA
Telephone (1 714) 624-5212

Orders and all other correspondence concerning this book should
be sent to the above address.

Who's Doing What Series No. 2 (Third Edition)

Cover design: Linda Ware, Ware Graphics, Claremont

The entries in this directory are based on information provided by the organizations
listed and from other sources purporting to be accurate. Listing does not imply
endorsement by the sponsoring organizations. Descriptions and interpretations are
those of the editor and do not necessarily represent the views of the sponsors.
Designations of geographic entities do not imply any expression of opinion on the
part of the sponsors about the legal status of any country, territory, or area, or of
its authorities, or concerning the delimitation of boundaries.

First Edition published 1973 by the Sierra Club, San Francisco; Second Edition
published 1976 by Public Affairs Clearinghouse, a program of the Center for
California Public Affairs (former name of the California Institute of Public
Affairs); Third Edition published 1989 by the California Institute of Public Affairs.

Library of Congress Catalog Card No. 75-38124
ISBN 0-912102-87-X
ISSN 0092-0908

CONTENTS

HOW TO USE THIS BOOK

■ Take a minute to study the table of contents. It shows how the book is structured.

■ If you are looking for information about a particular organization, start with the index at the back of the book. However, most *national* organizations are not indexed; check in the country listings in Part 7.

■ If you are looking for organizations concerned with a particular subject, see Part 2, Who's Doing What: Problems, Resources, and Biomes.

■ If you are looking for organizations concerned with a particular region of the world, see Part 3, The World Regions: Key Organizations.

■ If you want to learn about the global movement to protect the environment, look through the entries. This is not only a reference book but a profile of the field; it is meant to be read. And, as one reviewer of an earlier edition wrote about the *World Directory*, it "helps readers and researchers to see instantly that they are not alone in the struggle for world survival."

PLEASE HELP US

The *World Directory of Environmental Organizations* is not a commercial venture but a collaborative effort of three non-profit organizations to provide a service to the world conservation community. Please help us update and improve the book by sending us new information and suggestions for other organizations that should be included (keeping in mind the general criteria given in the introduction). These should be sent to: Editors, *World Directory of Environmental Organizations*, P.O. Box 10, Claremont, California 91711, USA. We would greatly appreciate your assistance.

FOREWORD

By Michael McCloskey, Chairman, Sierra Club

Environmentalism today is a truly universal phenomenon. While environmental issues have traditionally been seen as a preoccupation of rich countries, interest has swelled in the developing world. Environmentalism is on the rise in North and South, East and West. In the Sudan, environmentalists work with reporters to expose scandals in the ivory trade; Mexican activists lobby their government and appear nightly on television; Soviet environmentalists march to protest nuclear contamination; indigenous peoples in Sarawak block logging trucks.

While the historical roots of environmentalism go back more than a century, the sheer number of organizations included in the *World Directory* reflects a rising tide of interest. The *Directory* gives quick access to groups and agencies involved in environmental issues around the world.

Citizens' groups and independent activists are central to this movement. Their members are motivated by anxiety over threats to their habitat, threats which endanger not only the human species, but all living species. Humans have subdued most of the earth. Our increasing numbers put stress upon the quality of soil, air, and water. Chemicals introduced into ecosystems often result in irreversible damage. Citizens worldwide are protesting this lack of human restraint and the way we have "fouled our nest."

Environmentalism is not a movement built along conventional lines of politics, for it does not directly involve the distribution of economic gains and the control of production. Instead, environmentalists unite to guide the production process in order to protect environmental values.

So far, few of the world's major political parties have taken environmental interests very seriously. But as environmentalists in developing countries seek ways of being heard by government, they are finding that the emerging world focus on environmental issues is eliminating some barriers to their progress.

Almost overnight, it seems, environmental activists worldwide are learning practical means of moving governments to respond. Political sophistication is growing as environmentalists realize that merely "making a statement" is not enough. In the process, they often forge new trails as they seek ways of participating in governments unused to accommodating public intervention. Accustomed to traditional parties and pressure groups, government leaders often don't know quite what to make of citizens who don't pursue economic rewards.

Some have suggested that environmentalism may be in the vanguard of social issues that will fundamentally reorganize politics in the next century. With persistence, ingenuity, and confidence we are finding ways to break through the wall of resistance and indifference. And as we do, we are empowering citizens to participate in the governance of their countries. For the first time, many citizens feel that they are not just spectators or victims; they can play a role in shaping their future. And with this participation, governments that were less than responsive to their citizens are becoming more so. There is a trend toward democracy.

The non-governmental organizations in this book are often small and finding their way, but they may have a staggering impact in making this planet habitable for generations to come.

The Sierra Club is pleased to have a continuing role in the *World Directory of Environmental Organizations*.

INTRODUCTION

The *World Directory of Environmental Organizations* is a handbook of organizations and programs concerned with protecting the environment and managing natural resources. It covers national and international organizations, both governmental and non-governmental, in all parts of the world.

The book is divided into six parts. Part 1, Introduction, explains the purposes of the *Directory* and how to use it. Part 2, Who's Doing What: Problems, Resources, and Biomes, is designed to help users identify key organizations concerned with some fifty topics of interest, such as air quality, wildlife, or wetlands. Part 3, The World Regions: Key Organizations, lists the countries in each major world region, along with the main international organizations concerned.

Part 4, United Nations System, describes environmental activities of UN organizations and specialized agencies. Part 5, Other Intergovernmental Organizations, describes international agencies outside the UN system. Part 6, International Non-Governmental Organizations, covers citizens', professional, and other non-governmental organizations which have a substantial membership from more than one country or are governed by an international board.

Part 7, Country and Area Listings, lists countries and areas of the world in alphabetical order. Under each country heading are arranged: (a) national directories of environmental organizations that are known to us; (b) governmental agencies; and (c) other organizations (including government-affiliated groups devoted primarily to research or education). At the end of the book are a list of directories and databases related to environmental protection, and an index of organizations and major programs.

The causes of environmental problems and their solutions cut across many fields of endeavor. Recognizing this, we include leading organizations in several related areas: agriculture, appropriate technology, conflict resolution, development, energy, future studies, indigenous peoples, population, tourism, and transportation. These entries cover international organizations and key national groups. International scientific organizations in fields related to environmental protection and resource management are included; however, only the principal national scientific organization is listed for each country.

In deciding what kinds of non-governmental organizations to include in Part 7, we use somewhat different criteria for developing, socialist, and Western countries. Our main goal is to identify groups that influence policy or are major sources of information. In the West, citizens' groups, independent foundations, and professional societies are usually most prominent in this way, but in socialist states and many Third-World countries, research institutes often play a leading role in shaping environmental policy.

Listings of non-governmental organizations in Part 7 are limited to major national NGOs, groups that have international programs, and groups that can serve as a resource on a special problem or topic. The large number of NGOs listed for the United Kingdom and the United States reflects the number of groups in those countries that work internationally (e.g., the Antarctica Project in Washington) or have special expertise (e.g., the Association for the Reduction of Aircraft Noise in London). Names of organizations are given in the national language, when available, followed by an English translation (which is often our own, rather than an official, translation).

The first edition of the *World Directory of Environmental Organizations* was issued by the Sierra Club in 1973. The second edition was published for the Sierra Club by the California Institute of Public Affairs in 1976. Both editions were produced in cooperation with the International Union for Conservation of Nature and Natural Resources (IUCN-The World Conservation Union). No comprehensive global directory has been published since. To fill the need, we plan to issue revisions much more frequently. The book is now a project of the California Institute in cooperation with the Sierra Club and IUCN.

This third edition was completely rewritten. The information was gathered from numerous sources. Virtually all of the material given for the international organizations described in Parts 4, 5, and 6 was provided directly by the organizations themselves. Whenever possible, we quote from and paraphrase the information sent to us. (Quotations have been converted to a uniform style of U.S. English, although British forms such as "centre" have been kept in names of organizations, programs, and publications.) The information for the listings of national organizations in Part 7 was obtained from contacts in the various countries, IUCN files, material provided by international organizations, and various directories and periodical publications.

When the source of our information was more than two years old, the date of our source is given in brackets, e.g., [85]. For some countries, our information was dated and far from complete. We hope to rectify this in the next edition by circulating the book widely with a request for comments and additions.

We appreciate the help given to us by the many organizations and individuals who contributed to this edition of the *Directory*. Special thanks are due to Delmar Blasco, Liz Hopkins, and Jeff McNeely of the IUCN Secretariat, Gland; Zbigniew Karpowicz, World Conservation Monitoring Centre, Cambridge; Martina E. Vandenberg, California Institute of Public Affairs; Peter Jacobs, Université de Montréal; Jannis Klein, Canadian Nature Federation, Ottawa; and Michael McCloskey, Sierra Club, Washington. The editors assume all responsibility for errors and omissions.

ABOUT THE SPONSORS

The **California Institute of Public Affairs**, founded in 1969,
is an independent organization affiliated with the Claremont Colleges. It
organizes collaborative policy forums, conducts research, and publishes
reference books on California issues, primarily in the field of the
environment and natural resources. CIPA also works to foster an
awareness of the world as an interdependent system and of California's
special role as social laboratory and bellwether. Its international activities
include producing the *World Directory of Environmental Organizations*
and other information guides, including an international dimension in
many of its policy projects, and participating in the program of the IUCN
Commission on Sustainable Development. Address: P.O. Box 10,
Claremont, California 91711, USA.

The **Sierra Club**, founded in 1892, is a citizens' environmental
organization with over 500,000 members in 57 chapters throughout the
United States and Canada. It works to explore, enjoy, and protect the
wild places of the earth; to practice and promote the responsible use of
the earth's ecosystems and resources; and to educate and enlist humanity
to protect and restore the quality of the natural and human environment.
Its International Program focuses primarily on the policies and actions of
the U.S. government, both at home and abroad, and the multilateral
development banks. The Club also forges links with non-governmental
organizations in other countries through its cooperative Earthcare
Network. Address: 730 Polk Street, San Francisco, California 94109,
USA.

IUCN-The World Conservation Union, formally known as the
International Union for Conservation of Nature and Natural Resources,
was founded in 1949. It is an independent alliance of 600 sovereign
states, governmental agencies, and non-governmental organizations
representing 120 countries. Uniting on equal terms, members of IUCN
tackle shared challenges in environmental and natural resources
conservation, using the *World Conservation Strategy* as an agreed basis for
setting priorities for action. IUCN's Secretariat receives technical support
from a worldwide fellowship of more than 3,000 experts who serve on six
Commissions. IUCN supplies and redirects information, coordination,
detailed guidance, and start-up action in pursuit of a global program of
applied conservation that is adopted every three years by its governing
General Assembly. Address: Avenue du Mont-Blanc, CH-1196 Gland,
Switzerland.

GLOSSARY

Some Commonly-used Abbreviations, Acronyms, and Initialisms

CIDIE, Committee of International Development Institutions on the Environment

CITES, Convention on International Trade in Endangered Species of Wild Fauna and Flora (administered by UNEP)

DIESA, Department of International Economic and Social Affairs (of the UN Secretariat)

DTCD, Department of Technical Co-operation for Development (of the UN Secretariat)

EC, European Community

ECA, Economic Commission for Africa (UN)

ECE, Economic Commission for Europe (UN)

EEC, European Economic Community

ESCAP, Economic and Social Commission for Asia and the Pacific (UN)

ESCWA, Economic and Social Commission for Western Asia (UN)

FAO, Food and Agriculture Organization of the United Nations

Habitat, UN Centre for Human Settlements

IAEA, International Atomic Energy Agency (UN)

ICSU, International Council of Scientific Unions

IFAD, International Fund for Agricultural Development (UN)

IIED, International Institute for Environment and Development

ILO, International Labour Organization (UN)

IMO, International Maritime Organization (UN)

Infoterra, International Register for Sources of Environmental Information (part of UNEP)

INSTRAW, International Research and Training Institute for the Advancement of Women (UN)

INTECOL, International Association for Ecology

IOC, Intergovernmental Oceanographic Commission (Unesco)

IUBS, International Union of Biological Sciences

IUCN, International Union for Conservation of Nature and Natural Resources

MAB, Man and the Biosphere Programme (of Unesco)

NGO, Non-governmental organization

OAS, Organization of American States

OECD, Organisation for Economic Co-operation and Development

Ramsar Convention, Convention on Wetlands of International Importance especially as Waterfowl Habitat

SCOPE, Scientific Committee on Problems of the Environment (of ICSU)

TRAFFIC, wildlife trade monitoring units of WWF

UN, United Nations

UNCTAD, United Nations Conference on Trade and Development

UNDP, United Nations Development Programme

UNDRO, United Nations Disaster Relief Co-ordinator

UNEP, United Nations Environment Programme

Unesco, United Nations Educational, Scientific and Cultural Organization

UNFPA, United Nations Population Fund

UNIDO, United Nations Industrial Development Organization

UNITAR, United Nations Institute for Training and Research

UNSCEAR, UN Scientific Committee on the Effects of Atomic Radiation (under UNEP)

UNSO, United Nations Sudano-Sahelian Office (UNDP/UNEP)

UNU, United Nations University

USAID, United States Agency for International Development

WCED, World Commission on Environment and Development

WFC, World Food Council (UN)

WFP, World Food Programme (UN)

WHO, World Health Organization (UN)

WMO, World Meteorological Organization (UN)

WWF, World Wide Fund for Nature (or World Wildlife Fund)

SOME LANDMARK EVENTS

We present the following as a tentative list of key events since 1945 in the emergence of an international system for protecting the global environment - and a consciousness of the interrelationships among environment, resources, population, development, economics, and politics.

1948 IUCN: The International Union for the Protection of Nature is founded at Fontainebleau, near Paris; in 1956 it will be renamed the International Union for Conservation of Nature and Natural Resources. IUCN-The World Conservation Union, a unique partnership of governments and non-governmental organizations, will become a keystone of the global environmental community

1949 Lake Success: The United Nations Scientific Conference on the Conservation and Utilization of Resources is held in Lake Success, New York. It is the first major UN meeting on natural resource problems

1958 Law of the Sea: The First UN Conference on the Law of the Sea, Geneva, approves draft conventions on environmental protection; the UNCLOS meetings will continue for decades

1961 WWF: The World Wildlife Fund, now the World Wide Fund for Nature, is created at Morges, Switzerland; it will become a leading non-governmental actor in international conservation

1962 Silent Spring: Rachel Carson's book *Silent Spring* is published in the United States; her warning of worldwide pollution from DDT and other chemicals receives wide attention

1966 First Photos of "Spaceship Earth": The U.S. Lunar Orbiter takes the first photographs of the earth from the vicinity of the moon, revealing the finite and frail nature of the biosphere. As Fritjof Capra has written, these pictures "became a powerful new symbol for the ecology movement and may well be the most significant result of the whole space program"

1967 Torrey Canyon: A tanker carrying 118,000 tons of crude oil, the *Torrey Canyon,* is wrecked off Land's End, England. This is the largest oil spill to date and raises public awareness of hazards to the environment

1968 Swedish initiative: The Swedish government places an item called "the human environment" on the agenda of the UN Economic and Social Council; this will eventually lead to the 1972 Stockholm Conference

1968 Unesco Biosphere Conference: The Intergovernmental Conference of Experts on the Scientific Basis for Rational Use and Conservation of the Resources of the Biosphere is held in Paris under Unesco auspices; it is a turning point in the emergence of an environmental perspective in the community of international organizations

1970 **Earth Day:** In the United States, 20 million people across the country participate in peaceful demonstrations and teach-ins on Earth Day (April 21); this marks the birth of the modern environmental movement in that country

1971 **MAB:** The Man and the Biosphere program is founded by Unesco

1971 **Founex Report:** A meeting at Founex, Switzerland, called to prepare for the 1972 Stockholm Conference, results in the first major exposition of the links between development and environmental protection in the Third World

1972 **Blueprint for Survival:** A manifesto signed by 36 of Britain's leading scientists and thinkers is published in Teddy Goldsmith's journal *The Ecologist*. Entitled "Blueprint for Survival," it warns of the "extreme gravity" of the global situation and the "breakdown of society and irreversible disruption of life-supporting systems on this planet" and calls for a steady-state society

1972 **The Limits to Growth:** The Club of Rome, a group of leaders and thinkers from 40 countries, issues this report written by Donella and Dennis Meadows. Based on a pioneering U.S. project of computerized global modeling, it argues that if present population, food, pollution, and resource trends continue, the limits to growth on the planet will be reached within the next 100 years; like the "Blueprint," it calls for a state of global equilibrium and stirs much controversy

1972 **Stockholm Conference:** The United Nations Conference on the Human Environment is held in Stockholm, Sweden; it results in creation of United Nations Environment Programme (UNEP); Maurice Strong of Canada chairs the conference and will be appointed UNEP's first Executive Director. A simultaneous Environment Forum is an important step in recognizing the key role of non-governmental organizations, and sets a precedent for future international environmental conferences

1974 **CITES:** The Convention on International Trade in Endangered Species of Wild Fauna and Flora is opened for signature in Washington; this is an important step in controlling illegal commerce in ivory, furs, and other products of endangered species

1974 **Bucharest Population Conference:** The first World Conference on Population is held under UN auspices in Bucharest, Romania; 1,250 delegates from 135 countries participate

1974 **Cocoyoc Declaration:** A symposium in Cocoyoc, Mexico, identifies maldistribution of resources as a key factor in environmental degradation. The meeting, sponsored by UNEP and UNCTAD and chaired by economist Barbara Ward, results in a declaration calling for development action focused on filling basic human needs

1974 **Rome Food Conference:** The World Food Conference is held in Rome; this UN meeting lays the groundwork for an overall strategy to attack the world food problem and results in creation of the World Food Council and World Food Programme

1975 **Dag Hammarskjöld Report:** Sweden's Dag Hammarskjöld Foundation brings together leading thinkers to produce an influential report,

What Now: Another Development, which builds on the Founex and Cocoyoc documents and calls for Third-World development that is need-oriented, endogenous, self-reliant, ecologically sound, and based on self-management and participation

1976 Habitat Conference: In Vancouver, Canada, Habitat: The United Nations Conference on Human Settlements, focuses world attention on the plight of cities, especially in the Third World, and results in establishment of a new Habitat Centre in the UN system

1977 Desertification Conference: The United Nations Conference on Desertification, held in Nairobi, Kenya, raises awareness of desertification - the destruction of the biological productivity of the land which ultimately leads to a desert-like condition - and produces an international plan of action

1977 Water Conference: The United Nations Water Conference, held in Mar del Plata, Argentina, results in the UN setting a goal of providing clean water and adequate sanitation to all in the world by 1990; this will prove to be far from realistic, but the meeting points attention to the central role of water in public health and environmental planning

1979 Greenhouse Effect: A World Climate Conference in Geneva, organized by the World Meteorological Organization, concludes that the "greenhouse effect" from increased buildup of carbon dioxide in the atmosphere demands urgent international action. With few exceptions, government leaders and the press will not take this seriously until the late 1980s

1980 Brandt Commission Report: The Independent Commission on International Development Issues, chaired by former West German Chancellor Willy Brandt, issues its report, *North-South: A Program for Survival*, which recommends a massive increase in aid to developing countries and also calls for environmental impact assessments to be applied to development proposals

1980 World Conservation Strategy: The *World Conservation Strategy* is released by IUCN, UNEP, and WWF. Bold in its purpose and scope, it calls for "global coordinated efforts" for sustainable development, based on "will and determination"

1980 Global 2000: The *Global 2000 Report to the President*, commissioned by U.S. President Jimmy Carter, is widely publicized; it projects what the world might be like if present trends continue and calls for "vigorous and determined new initiatives" to deal with global environmental deterioration of "alarming proportions." It is followed the next year by *Global Future: Time to Act*, which recommends U.S. government responses

1982 Charter for Nature: The UN General Assembly adopts a World Charter for Nature prepared by IUCN

1984 Bhopal: A leak of deadly methyl isocyanate at a Union Carbide pesticide plant in Bhopal, India, kills some 2,800 people and injures tens of thousands of others, many mortally; it is the world's worst industrial accident to date

1986 **Chernobyl:** An accident at the Chernobyl Nuclear Power Station in the Soviet Ukraine spreads radioactive material throughout the Northern Hemisphere; it is the worst nuclear accident to date

1986 **Ottawa:** The Conference on Conservation and Development: Implementing the World Conservation Strategy is held in Ottawa, Canada, to evaluate progress in implementing the 1980 *Strategy* and consider proposals for revising it; sponsors are IUCN, the Canadian Government, and others

1987 **Brundtland Report:** The World Commission on Environment and Development issues its report, *Our Common Future.* The Commission, created by the UN and chaired by Norwegian Prime Minister Gro Harlem Brundtland, calls for "a new era of economic growth, one that must be based on policies that sustain and expand the environmental resource base"

1987 **Montreal Protocol:** A protocol designed to reduce depletion of the ozone layer is negotiated in Montreal under UNEP auspices; it sets limits on production and consumption of certain chlorofluorocarbons and halons and will enter into force at the start of 1989. UNEP Executive Director Mostafa K. Tolba states that "This is the first truly global treaty that offers protection to every single human being on this planet"

Part 2
Who's Doing What: Problems, Resources & Biomes

This part of the *World Directory* directs you to organizations concerned with specific environmental problems, natural resources, or biomes (such as wetlands and grasslands). Headings are listed in the table of contents on pages 3-4. See the index to locate the descriptions of organizations in Parts 4, 5, 6, and 7. Abbreviations are explained in the glossary. Note that this part of the directory is not meant to be a complete index of subjects by organization but rather a guide to key actors in each field.

BROAD CONCERNS

See also: Future Studies. Listed here are organizations with broad interests in environmental protection and natural resource management.

UN system: The UN Environment Programme plays the central role in environmental affairs in the UN system. Other UN entities with broad interests in the environment and natural resources include: Economic and Social Council (and the regional economic commissions); UN University; Food and Agriculture Organization of the UN; UN Educational, Scientific, and Cultural Organization; World Bank Group.

Other intergovernmental organizations: Commonwealth Secretariat; Council for Mutual Economic Assistance; Council of Europe; European Community; Organization for Economic Co-operation and Development.

International NGOs: IUCN-The World Conservation Union and the World Wide Fund for Nature are the leading international NGOs. The Centre for Our Common Future carries forward the work of the World Commission on Environment and Development. The Environment Liaison Centre International builds ties among environmental NGOs around the world and represents their interests with UNEP. Some other key groups with broad concerns are the Institute for European Environmental Policy, the International Council of Scientific Unions and its Scientific Committee on Problems of the Environment, the International Institute for Environment and Development, and the International Association for Ecology.
Major activist organizations at the international level include Friends of the Earth International and Greenpeace International (both of whose national units are listed in Part 7). Other international NGOs with broad interests include: Common Property Resource Network; Commonwealth Human Ecology Council; Europa Nostra; European Environmental Bureau (a clearinghouse for NGOs in EEC countries); Foundation for Environmental Conservation (publisher of the important quarterly *Environmental Conservation*); International Foundation for the Survival and Development of Humanity (a joint US-USSR effort); International Geographical Union; International Institute for Applied Systems Analysis; International Network of Resource Information Centers (Balaton Group); International Organization for Standardization (quantitative standards related to environmental protection); International Organization of Consumers Unions; International Professional Association for Environmental Affairs; International Society for Ecological Modelling; International Union of Biological Sciences; International Union of Geodesy and Geophysics; International Union of Pure and Applied Chemistry; Society for Ecological Restoration and Management; Society for Ecology (German-language).

Leading national organizations with broad interests that work internationally: *United States:* Leading groups are the Smithsonian Institution; Conservation Foundation; East-West Center; Friends of the Earth; National Audubon Society; National Wildlife Federation; Natural Resources Defense Council; New York Zoological Society (Wildlife Conservation International); Resources for the Future; Sierra Club; World Resources Institute; and Worldwatch Institute. Others include: Center for Field Research (Earthwatch); Conservation International; Rocky Mountain Institute; Scientists' Institute for Public Information; Society for Conservation Biology; Threshold; University of Michigan, School of Natural Resources; Yale University, School of Forestry and Environmental Studies.

AGRICULTURE AND ENVIRONMENTAL PROTECTION
See also: Appropriate Technology; Biotechnology; Grasslands; Pest Management; Soil; Toxic Materials; Water Resources.

UN system: UN Development Programme; World Food Council; World Food Programme; Food and Agriculture Organization of the UN; International Fund for Agricultural Development.

Other intergovernmental organizations: CAB International; Inter-American Institute for Cooperation on Agriculture; Tropical Agricultural Research and Training Center.

International NGOs: The Consultative Group on International Agricultural Research, affiliated with the World Bank, supports and coordinates 13 specialized centers, which are listed in the CGIAR entry. Others: International Alliance for Sustainable Agriculture; International Commission of Agricultural Engineering; Inter-Union Commission on the Application of Science and Technology to Agriculture, Forestry, and Aquaculture; International Federation of Organic Agriculture Movements.

National: Many of the national organizations listed in Part 7 are concerned with agriculture. The following are particularly interested in promoting sustainable agriculture. *Netherlands:* Delft University of Technology, Information Center for Low External Input Agriculture. *Norway:* Agricultural University of Norway, Norwegian Center for International Agricultural Development. *United Kingdom:* Bio-Dynamic Agricultural Association; British Organic Farmers; Farm and Food Society; Henry Doubleday Research Association; Permaculture Association; Soil Association. *United States:* American Farmland Trust; Institute for Alternative Agriculture.

AIR QUALITY
See also: Climate; Health and the Environment; Occupational Safety and Health; Toxic Materials.

UN system: UN Environment Programme; World Health Organization; World Meteorological Organization; Economic Commission for Europe (Convention on Long-Range Transboundary Air Pollution); International Civil Aviation Organization.

International NGOs: Air Pollution Action Network; European Association for the Science of Air Pollution; International Association of Meteorology and Atmospheric Physics; International Union of Air Pollution Prevention Associations.
National: *Japan:* Japan Air Cleaning Association. *Sweden:* National Swedish Environment

Protection Board (disseminates information about acid rain); Swedish NGO Secretariat on Acid Rain. *United Kingdom:* National Society for Clean Air. *United States:* Acid Rain Information Clearinghouse; Acid Rain Foundation; Air and Waste Management Association; American Lung Association.

APPROPRIATE TECHNOLOGY
See also: Pest Management. Listed here are a few key organizations that develop and promote appropriate technology, that is, technology that is need-oriented, self-reliant, and ecologically sound.

UN system: UN Children's Fund; UNITAR/UNDP Centre on Small Energy Resources; UN Educational, Scientific, and Cultural Organization (Unesco Information Programme on New and Renewable Sources of Energy).

International NGOs: International Research Centre on the Environment 'Pio Manzù'; Mesoamerican Center for the Study of Appropriate Technology.

National: *Netherlands:* Socially Appropriate Technology Information Services (SATIS). *Sweden:* Institute for Environmentally Sound Technologies. *Switzerland:* Swiss Center for Appropriate Technology. *United Kingdom:* Intermediate Technology Development Group. *United States:* Office of Appropriate Technology (Congress); TRANET.

ARID LANDS

UN system: Centre for Science and Technology for Development; Economic and Social Commission for Asia and the Pacific (Regional Network of Training and Research Centres of Desertification Control); UN Sudano-Sahelian Office; UN Environment Programme; Food and Agriculture Organization of the UN; UN Educational, Scientific, and Cultural Organization (MAB Arid and Semi-Arid Zones Network); International Fund for Agricultural Development.

Other intergovernmental organizations: League of Arab States (Arab Centre for the Studies of Arid Zones and Dry Lands); Permanent Interstate Committee for Drought Control in the Sahel.

International NGOs: International Center for Agricultural Research in the Dry Areas.

National: Numerous national organizations are interested, particularly those in countries with arid regions. A few examples: *Argentina:* Argentine Institute of Arid Zone Research. *Bahrain:* Arabian Gulf University, Desert and Arid Zones Sciences Program. *China:* Chinese Academy of Sciences, Institute of Desert Research. *Israel:* Ben Gurion University of the Negev, Jacob Blaustein Institute for Desert Research. *Namibia:*

Desert Ecological Research Unit. *Saudi Arabia:* King Saud University, Center for Desert Studies. *USSR:* Academy of Sciences of the Turkmen SSR, Desert Institute. *United Kingdom:* Green Deserts; University College of North Wales, Centre for Arid Zone Studies. *United States:* Association of Arid Land Studies; Texas Tech University, International Center for Arid and Semiarid Land Studies; University of Arizona, Office of Arid Lands Studies.

BIOTECHNOLOGY
Biotechnology, or genetic engineering, offers great potential for good but also great potential for long-term damage to the environment. Following are some key organizations concerned with the environmental implications of this new technology.

UN system: The leading agencies concerned are the UN Environment Programme, UN Industrial Development Organization; and UN Educational, Scientific, and Educational Organization.

Other intergovernmental organizations: European Community; Organisation for Economic Development and Co-operation.

International NGOs: The International Council of Scientific Unions has a Scientific Committee on Biotechnology. The International Union of Pure and Applied Chemistry has a Commission on Biotechnology.

National: The pioneering groups in this field are the *(United States)* National Institute of Health, which has a Recombinant DNA Advisory Committee, and the *(United Kingdom)* Advisory Committee on Genetic Manipulation, part of the Health and Safety Executive. *(Sweden's)* Dag Hammarskjöld Foundation has been interested in the impacts of biotechnology on developing countries.

CAVES
See also: Natural Areas, Parks, and Wilderness.

International NGOs: International Union of Speleology; Speleological Federation of Latin America and the Caribbean.

National: *United States:* American Cave Conservation Association; National Speleological Society.

CLIMATE
See also: Air Quality. The following list includes key organizations working on the impacts of global climate change.

UN system: Center for Science and Technology for Development; UN Environment Programme (Earthwatch; Intergovernmental Panel on Climate Change); Food and Agriculture Organization of the UN; United Nations Educational, Scientific, and Cultural Organization; World Meteorological Organization.

Other intergovernmental organizations: Inter-African Committee for Hydraulic Studies.

International NGOs: Committee on Climatic Changes and the Ocean; ICSU-WMO Joint World Climate Research Programme; International Association of Meteorology and Atmospheric Physics; Special Committee for the International Geosphere-Biosphere Programme; International Society of Biometeorology.

National: *Canada:* Canadian Climate Centre. *Sweden:* Beijer Institute. *United Kingdom:* University of East Anglia, Climate Research Unit. *United States:* Department of Energy (Oak Ridge National Laboratrory); Climate Institute; National Center for Atmospheric Research; Pacific Institute for Studies in Development, Environment, and Security; University of Minnesota, Humphrey Institute of Public Affairs.

COMMUNICATIONS MEDIA
See also: Education and Training.

UN system: Economic and Social Commission for Asia and the Pacific (Asian Forum for Environmental Journalists).

International NGOs: Better World Society; European Centre for Environmental Communication; Panos Institute.

National: *United Kingdom:* Television Trust for the Environment. *United States:* Environmental Media Association.

CONFLICT AND THE ENVIRONMENT
The most serious threat to the environment is the "nuclear winter" that would result from large-scale nuclear war. Many peace and conflict-resolution organizations not listed in this directory are concerned with the environmental dimensions of conflict. Those listed in this book include the following:

UN system: The UN Environment Programme has a program area on the arms race and the environment.

Other intergovernmental organizations: University for Peace.

CULTURAL HERITAGE
See also: Human Settlements.

UN system: UN Educational, Scientific, and Cultural Organization.

International NGOs: Europa Nostra; International Council on Monuments and Sites.

National: Some of the national conservation groups listed have a dual interest in natural and cultural heritage. Of particular note: *Greece:* Greek Society. *Israel:* "Hai-Bar" Society for the Establishment of Biblical National Wildlife Reserves. *Italy:* Ministry of Cultural Heritage; Our Italy. *United Kingdom:* National Trust.

DEVELOPMENT AND THE ENVIRONMENT
The relation between environmental problems and economic and social development, particularly in the Third World, has had increasing attention, particularly since publication of the 1987 report of the World Commission on Environment and Development, *Our Common Future.*

UN system: The following UN entities are concerned with environment-development issues: Administrative Committee on Coordination (Task Force on Rural Development; Task Force on Science and Technology for Development); Department of International Economic and Social Affairs (Development Information System); Department of Technical Cooperation for Development (including its Natural Resources and Energy Division and the Centre for Science and Technology for Development); UN Centre for Regional Development; UN Children's Fund; UN Development Programme; UN Environment Programme; UN Research Institute for Social Development; Food and Agriculture Organization of the UN; International Fund for Agricultural Development; UN Industrial Development Organization; World Bank.

Other intergovernmental organizations: African Development Bank; Arab Bank for Economic Development in Africa; Arab Fund for Economic and Social Development; Asian Development Bank; CAB International; Caribbean Development Bank; Central American Bank for Economic Integration; Commonwealth Fund for Technical Cooperation; European Community; European Investment Bank; Inter-American Development Bank; Islamic Development Bank; Nordic Investment Bank.

The Committee of International Development Institutions on the Environment encourages multilateral development banks to pay more attention to protecting the environment. The Development Assistance Committee of the Organisation for Economic Co-operation and Development is a forum for donor countries to consult on assistance to developing countries.

International NGOs: Bank Information Center (concerned with activities of multilateral development banks); Centre for Our Common Future (following up on the work of the World Commission on Environment and Development); Confederation of International Scientific and Technological Organizations for Development; Development Innovations and Alternatives; Environment and Development in the Third World; European Association of Development Research and Training Institutes; Independent Commission of the South

on Development Issues; the former Independent Commission on International Development Issues (Brandt Commission); International Biosciences Network; International Coalition for Development Action; International Council of Scientific Unions, Committee on Science and Technology in Developing Countries; International Council of Voluntary Agencies; International Foundation for Development Alternatives; International Institute for Environment and Development; IUCN-The World Conservation Union (particularly its Commission on Sustainable Development); Oxfam; Panos Institute; Society for International Development; Third World Academy of Sciences; Third World Forum; the former World Commission on Environment and Development (Brundtland Commission).

National: The following agencies and NGOs in donor countries provide development assistance or are concerned with the relationship between development and environmental protection: *Australia:* Department of Foreign Affairs. *Austria:* Ministry of Foreign Affairs. *Belgium:* Secretary of State for Development Cooperation; Belgian Development Assistance Organization. *Canada:* Canadian International Development Agency; Institute for Research on Public Policy; International Development Research Centre; North-South Institute. *Denmark:* Ministry of Foreign Affairs. *Finland:* Finnish International Development Agency. *France:* Ministry of Cooperation; French Institute of Scientific Research for Development Cooperation. *Federal Republic of Germany:* Ministry for Economic Cooperation. *Holy See:* Pontifical Council "Cor Unum." *Ireland:* Department of Foreign Affairs. *Italy:* Ministry of Foreign Affairs; Association for Soil and Water Conservation and Re-Equilibrium of Ecosystems. *Japan:* Japan International Cooperation Agency; Asian Community Trust. *Kuwait:* Kuwait Fund for Arab Economic Development. *Netherlands:* Ministry of Foreign Affairs; BothENDS (under the Netherlands National Committee for IUCN). *New Zealand:* Ministry of Foreign Affairs. *Norway:* Ministry of Development Cooperation. *Saudi Arabia:* Saudi Fund for Development. *Sweden:* Swedish International Development Authority; Swedish Agency for Research Cooperation with Developing Countries; Dag Hammarskjöld Foundation. *Switzerland:* Federal Department of Foreign Affairs. *United Arab Emirates:* Abu Dhabi Fund for Economic Development. *United Kingdom:* Overseas Development Administration; Centre for World Development Education; Institute of Development Studies; Overseas Development Institute. *United States:* African Development Foundation; Agency for International Development; Inter-American Foundation; Peace Corps; Ashoka; Conservation Foundation; Conservation International; Coordination in Development; East-West Center; Environmental Defense Fund; International Development Conference; National Research Council (Board on Science and Technology for International Development); Natural Resources Defense Council; Overseas Development Council;

World Resources Institute.

ECONOMIC ASPECTS
See also: Development and the Environment; Industry and Environmental Protection.

UN system: UN Conference on Trade and Development; General Agreement on Tariffs and Trade.

International NGOs: International Society for Ecological Economics.

National: *United Kingdom:* Center for Economic and Environmental Development; Schumacher Society. *United States:* Resources for the Future.

EDUCATION AND TRAINING
See also: Communications Media.

UN system: The UN Environment Programme and The UN Educational, Scientific, and Cultural Organization (Unesco) have a joint International Environmental Education Programme. Unesco has other educational activities related to the environment.

Other intergovernmental organizations: ASEAN Council for Higher Education in Environment; Council of Europe (Committee on Environmental Education and Training); Training Centre on Environmental Matters for Small Local Authorities in the EEC Mediterranean Countries; University for Peace.

International NGOS: Foundation for Environmental Education in Europe; International Council for Environmental Education in French-Speaking Countries; International Society for Environmental Education; Commission on Education and Training of IUCN-The World Conservation Union.

National: *United Kingdom:* International Centre for Conservation Education; National Association for Environmental Education. *United States:* Coolidge Center for Environmental Leadership (target is university students from abroad); Green Library (sets up libraries abroad);

ENERGY, GEOLOGY, AND MINING
See also: Appropriate Technology; Nuclear Energy and Radiation. The following are concerned with the environmental dimensions of energy, the earth sciences, and mining.

UN system: UN Revolving Fund for Natural Resources Exploration; UNITAR/UNDP Centre on Small Energy Resources; UN Development Programme; UN Environment Programme; UN Industrial Development Organization; Food and Agriculture Organization of the UN; International Atomic Energy Agency; UN Educational, Scientific, and Cultural Organization (Unesco Information Programme on New and Renewable Sources of Energy); World Bank Group.

International NGOs: Asian Institute of Technology, Regional Energy Resources Development and Management Program; Association of Geoscientists for International Development; Convention on Regulation of Antarctic Mineral Resources (listed in Part 7 under Antarctica); International Association of Engineering Geology; Inter-Union Commission on the Lithosphere.

National: Many of the national organizations listed are concerned with energy issues. Of special note: *United Kingdom:* National Energy Efficiency Forum. *United States:* International Institute for Energy Conservation; Rocky Mountain Institute.

FISH AND FISHERIES
See also: Lakes, Rivers, and Waterways; Oceans, Coastal Zones, and Islands; Wetlands.

UN system: Food and Agriculture Organization of the UN (Fisheries Department).

Other intergovernmental organizations: Commission for the Conservation of Antarctic Marine Living Resources; Commission for the Convention on Future Multilateral Cooperation in North-East Atlantic Fisheries; Inter-American Tropical Tuna Commission; International Association of Fish and Wildlife Agencies; International Baltic Sea Fishery Commission; International Commission for the Conservation of Atlantic Tuna; International Commission for the Southeast Atlantic Fisheries; International Council for the Exploration of the Sea; North Atlantic Salmon Conservation Organization; Northwest Atlantic Fisheries Organization; Joint Danube Fishery Commission (listed under "River, Lake, and Boundary Commissions" in Part 5); South Pacific Forum (Fisheries Agency).

International NGOs: Asian Fisheries Society; Atlantic Salmon Federation; Gulf and Caribbean Fisheries Institute; International Center for Living Aquatic Resources Management; International Institute of Fisheries Economics and Trade; Inter-Union Commission on the Application of Science and Technology to Agriculture, Forestry, and Aquaculture.

National: *United Kingdom:* Fisheries Society of the British Isles. *United States:* American Fisheries Society.

FORESTS AND FORESTRY
See also: Natural Areas, Parks, and Wilderness; Plants; Tropical Ecosystems.

UN system: UN Non-Governmental Liaison Service (International Tree Project Clearinghouse); Food and Agriculture Organization of the UN (Forestry Department).

Other intergovernmental organizations: African Timber Organization; CAB International; International Tropical Timber Organization; Arab Forestry Institute.

International NGOs: Commonwealth Forestry Association; European Youth Forest Action Foundation; Green Belt Movement; International Council for Research in Agroforestry; International Union of Forestry Research Organizations; International Union of Societies of Foresters; Inter-Union Commission on the Application of Science and Technology to Agriculture, Forestry, and Aquaculture; Men of the Trees; Nordic Forestry Federation; Union of European Foresters.

National: The following national organizations have international interests: *United Kingdom:* University of Oxford, Oxford Forestry Institute. *United States:* Children of the Green Earth; Nitrogen-Fixing Tree Association; Society of American Foresters; Winrock International Institute; World Forestry Center.

FUTURE STUDIES
Environmental and natural resource questions have been at the center of the future studies movement, which started in the 1960s and focuses on long-range projections, possibilities, and policy alternatives. Some of the movement's key organizations are listed here.

International NGOs: Association Internationale Futuribles; Club of Rome; International Federation of Institutes for Advanced Study; World Future Studies Federation.

National: *Ireland:* Irish Futures Society. *United States:* Institute for Alternative Futures; Institute for 21st Century Studies; World Future Society.

GRASSLANDS

International NGOs: European Grassland Federation.

National: *Australia:* Australian Rangeland Society. *New Zealand:* Tussock Grasslands and Mountain Lands Institute. *United Kingdom:* British Grassland Society; Grassland Research Institute. *United States:* Grassland Heritage Foundation; Society for Range Management.

HEALTH AND THE ENVIRONMENT
See also: Air Quality; Biotechnology; Nuclear Energy and Radiation; Occupational Safety and Health; Toxic Materials; Water Quality.

UN system: The UN Environment Programme and the World Health Organization are the main bodies concerned.

Other intergovernmental organizations: Caribbean Environmental Health Institute; Pan American Health Organization; Pan American Center for Sanitary Engineering and Environmental Sciences.

International NGOs: International Association for Medicine and Biology of Environment.

National: National environmental health organizations are listed in Part 7. Of special note: *United States:* A leading research center is the National Institute of Environmental Health Sciences, listed under Department of Health and Human Services; two important professional societies are the American Medical Association and National Environmental Health Association.

HUMAN SETTLEMENTS
See also: Land Use.

UN system: The UN Centre for Human Settlements (Habitat) is the focal point in the UN system.

Other intergovernmental organizations: Latin American Housing and Human Settlements Development Organization.

International NGOs: ASEAN Association for Planning and Housing; Athens Centre of Ekistics; Commonwealth Association of Architects; Commonwealth Association of Planners; Coordination Group of Non Governmental Organizations in the Field of Man-Made Environment; Eastern Regional Organization for Planning and Housing; European Council of Town Planners; Habitat International Coalition; International Federation for Housing and Planning; International Institute for Environment and Urban Planning; International Union of Architects; World Society for Ekistics.

National: *United Kingdom:* Groundwork Foundation (urban fringes); London Green Belt Society; Royal Town Planning Institute; Town and Country Planning Association. *United States:* American Planning Association; National Institute for Urban Wildlife.

IMPACT ASSESSMENT

Intergovernmental organizations: Working Group on an International Commission for Impact Assessment.

International NGOs: International Association for Impact Assessment.

National: *United Kingdom:* The University of Aberdeen's Center for Environmental Management and Planning is a leading center in this field.

INDIGENOUS PEOPLES AND TRADITIONAL ECOLOGICAL KNOWLEDGE

Two important issues arise here: how to protect the interests of indigenous peoples when their areas are to be developed or given a protected status (such as in a national park); how to use the knowledge of traditional peoples in managing resources more effectively.

Intergovernmental organizations: Inter-American Indian Institute.

International NGOs: Anti-Slavery Society; International Work Group for Indigenous Affairs; Inuit Circumpolar Conference; Minority Rights Group; World Council of Indigenous Peoples.

National: *Canada:* Department of Indian and Northern Affairs; Inuit Tapirisat of Canada. *India:* Chipko Movement. *Mexico:* Friends of Sian Ka'an. *Panama:* Study Project for Management of Wild Areas of the Kuna Yala. *United Kingdom:* Survival International. *United States:* Bureau of Indian Affairs (under the Department of the Interior); Association on American Indian Affairs; Cultural Survival; South and Central American Indian Information Center.

INDUSTRY AND ENVIRONMENTAL PROTECTION

See also: Economic Aspects.

UN system: UN Environment Programme (UNEP Industry and Environment Office); UN Industrial Development Organization.

International NGOs: International Chamber of Commerce and its International Environmental Bureau.

National: *United Kingdom:* Business and Industry Panel for the Environment; Center for Economic and Environmental Development. *United States:* INFORM; World Environment Center.

LAKES, RIVERS, AND WATERWAYS

See also: Fish and Fisheries; Natural Areas, Parks, and Wilderness; Water Resources; Wetlands.

Intergovernmental organizations: *See* "River, Lake, and Boundary Commissions" in Part 5.

International NGOs: Center for the Great Lakes (Canada-U.S.).

National: *Egypt:* Suez Canal Authority. *United Kingdom:* Inland Waterways Protection Society. *United States:* Panama Canal Commission; American Rivers; North American Lake Management Society.

LAND USE

See also: Human Settlements; Landscape Architecture. The following organizations are particularly concerned with the planning and regulation of privately-owned lands:

International NGOs: European Association for Country Planning Institutions; International Society of City and Regional Planners; Inter-American Planning Society.

National: Many of the national organizations listed in Part 7 have an active interst in land use. Of special note: *United States:* Trust for Public Land.

LANDSCAPE ARCHITECTURE

See also: Human Settlements; Land Use.

International NGOs: European Committee of Landscape Architects; International Federation of Landscape Architects.

National: *United Kingdom:* Landscape Institute. *United States:* American Society of Landscape Architects.

LAW AND LEGAL ACTION

International NGOs: European Council of International Law; Inter-American Bar Association; International Association for Water Law; International Bar Association; International Centre of Comparative Environmental Law; International Council of Environmental Law; International Law Association; International Nuclear Law Association; Commission on Environmental Policy, Law, and Administration and Environmental Law Center of IUCN-The World Conservation Union; Law Association for Asia and the Pacific.

National: *Canada:* Canadian Environmental Law Association. *France:* French Society for Environmental Law. *Mexico:* Mexican Academy of Environmental Law. *United States:* American Bar Association; Environmental Law Institute; University of New Mexico, School of Law, Natural Resources Center.

MOUNTAINS

UN system: UN Environment Programme; UN University; UN Educational, Scientific, and Cultural Organization (including the MAB Alpine Network, focused on Europe).

Other intergovernmental organizations: Association of the Central Alps; International Centre for Integrated Mountain Development (Himalayas).

International NGOs: International Commission for the Protection of Alpine Regions (focused on Europe); International Mountain Society; International Union of Alpinist Associations.

NATURAL AREAS, PARKS, AND WILDERNESS

See also: Arid Lands; Caves; Cultural Heritage; Forests and Forestry; Grasslands; Human Settlements; Lakes, Rivers, and Waterways; Mountains; Oceans, Coastal Zones, and Islands; Tourism Impacts; Tropical Ecosystems; Wetlands.

UN system: UN Educational, Scientific, and Cultural Organization (Man and the Biosphere Programme).

Other intergovernmental organizations: Council of Europe (European Committee for the Conservation of Nature and Natural Resources).

International NGOs: Federation of Nature and National Parks of Europe; International Wilderness Leadership Foundation; Commission on National Parks and Protected Areas of IUCN-The World Conservation Union; Latin American Committee on National Parks; World Wide Fund for Nature.

National: This is a focus of many of the national conservation groups listed in Part 7.

NOISE

See also: Health and the Environment; Occupational Safety and Health.

UN system: International Civil Aviation Organization.

International NGOs: European Association Against Aircraft Noise; International Association Against Noise.

National: *Japan:* Aircraft Nuisance Prevention Association. *United Kingdom:* Association for the Reduction of Aircraft Noise; Noise Abatement Society. *United States:* Acoustical Society of America.

NUCLEAR ENERGY AND RADIATION

UN system: Secretariat of the UN Scientific Committee on the Effects of Atomic Radiation; International Atomic Energy Agency.

International NGOs: International Committee on Radiological Protection; International Nuclear Law Association; International Radiation Protection Association; Nordic Society for Radiation Protection.

National: *United Kingdom:* Society for Radiological Protection. *United States:* Safe Energy Communication Council.

OCCUPATIONAL SAFETY AND HEALTH

See also: Air Quality; Biotechnology; Health and the Environment; Noise; Nuclear Energy and Radiation; Toxic Materials; Water Quality.

UN system: International Labour Organisation; UN Industrial Development Organization; World Health Organization.

International NGOs: International Commission on Occupational Health; International Federation of Chemical, Energy, and General Workers' Unions.

National: A leading national research center is the *(United States)* National Institute for Occupational Safety and Health, listed under Department of Health and Human Services.

OCEANS, COASTAL ZONES, AND ISLANDS

See also: Fish and Fisheries; Lakes, Rivers, and Waterways; Natural Areas, Parks, and Wilderness; Polar Zones; Water Quality; Wetlands; Wildlife.

UN system: Office for Ocean Affairs and the Law of the Sea; UN Environment Programme (Regional Seas Programme); International Maritime Organization; UN Educational, Scientific, and Cultural Organization (Intergovernmental Oceanographic Commission; Coastal Marine Programme).

Other intergovernmental organizations: Baltic Marine Environment Protection Committee; Bonn Commission (North Sea); International Commission for Scientific Exploration of the Mediterranean Sea; International Council for the Exploration of the Sea; League of Arab States (Red Sea and Gulf of Aden Environment Programme); Oslo Commission (Northeast Atlantic); Paris Commission (Northeast Atlantic); Permanent South Pacific Commission (Southeast Pacific); Regional Organization for the Protection of the Marine Environment (Arabian or Persian Gulf); Secretariat for the Protection of the Mediterranean Sea; South Pacific Commission; South Pacific Forum.

International NGOs: Advisory Committee on Pollution of the Sea; Engineering Committee on Oceanic Resources; Greenpeace International; International Committee on Coral Reefs; Scientific Committee on Oceanic Research; International Ocean Institute; International Oceanographic Foundation; World Underwater Federation.

National: See the listings for island countries and territories in Part 7. The following are of special note: *Canada:* International Ocean Development Centre. *Ecuador:* Charles Darwin Foundation for the Galapagos Islands. *Federal Republic of Germany:* Alfred Wegener Institute. *United Kingdom:* Marine Biological Society; Marine Conservation Society. *United States:* American Littoral Society; Center for Marine Conservation; Coastal Society; Cousteau Society; Marine Technology Society; National Coalition for Marine Conservation; Oceanic Society; University of California, Scripps Institution of Oceanography; Woods Hole Oceanographic Institution. *Virgin Islands of the U.S.:* Island Resources

Foundation.

PEST MANAGEMENT
See also: Agriculture and Environmental Protection; Appropriate Technology; Toxic Materials.

UN system: Food and Agriculture Organization of the UN (Agriculture Department).
Other intergovernmental Organizations: CAB International Institute of Biological Control.

International NGOs: International Association for Biological Control of Noxious Animals and Plants.

National: *United States:* Bio-Integral Resource Center.

PLANTS
See also: Forests and Forestry; Natural Areas, Parks, and Wilderness.

UN system: UN Environment Programme (Secretariat for the Convention on International Trade in Endangered Species of Wild Fauna and Flora).

International NGOs: International Board for Plant Genetic Resources; International Association of Botanic Gardens; Latin American Plant Sciences Network; Organization for Flora Neotropica; Organization for the Phyto-Taxonomic Investigation of the Mediterranean Area; Seed Action Network.

National: *Guatemala:* Guatemalan Orchid Association. *United Kingdom:* Royal Botanic Gardens, Kew; National Council for the Conservation of Plants and Gardens; Sacred Trees Trust; World Tree Trust. *United States:* American Association of Botanical Gardens and Arboreta; Center for Plant Conservation.

POLAR ZONES

International NGOs: Arctic Institute of North America; Arctic International Wildlife Society; Comité Arctique International; Inuit Circumpolar Conference.

National: See the listings in Part 7 under the following countries and areas: Antarctica; Canada; Falkland (Malvinas) Islands; Greenland; Iceland; Finland, Norway, South Georgia and the South Sandwich Islands; Sweden; USSR; USA (including Alaska listings which follow the main USA entries). *See also:* Scott Polar Research Institute, listed under United Kingdom.

International NGOs: Arctic Institute of North America; Arctic International Wildlife Range Society; Comité Arctique International; Inuit Circumpolar Conference.

POLITICS AND POLICY

Intergovernmental organizations: Inter-Parliamentary Union.

International NGOs: Commission on Policy, Law, and Administration and Commission on Sustainable Development of IUCN-The World Conservation Union.

National: *Germany (Federal Republic):* Social Science Research Center, Berlin. *United Kingdom:* Ecology Party; Green Alliance; Liberal Ecology Group; Socialist Environment and Resources Association. *United States:* Americans for the Environment (political skills training); California Institute of Public Affairs (work on policy-making); Institute for Resource Management (conflict resolution); International Studies Association (policy research); Keystone Center (conflict resolution); League of Conservation Voters (election committee); Program on Negotiation at Harvard Law School (conflict resolution).

POPULATION AND GROWTH MANAGEMENT

UN system: Population Division; Economic Commission for Latin America and the Caribbean (Latin American Demographic Centre); UN Population Fund.

International NGOs: International Planned Parenthood Federation; International Union for the Scientific Study of Population; IUCN-The World Conservation Union (which has a population program).

National: *United Kingdom:* Population Concern. *United States:* Population Council; Population Crisis Committee; Population Institute; Population Reference Bureau; Population Resource Center; Stanford University, Morrison Center for Population and Resource Studies; World Population Society; Zero Population Growth.

PSYCHOLOGY AND SOCIAL SCIENCE

UN system: Center for Social Development and Humanitarian Affairs; UN Research Institute for Social Development; UN Educational, Scientific, and Cultural Organization.

International NGOs: Association for the Study of Man Environment Relations; International Association of Applied Psychology; International Union of Anthropological and Ethnological Sciences; People and Physical Environment Research.

National: *Japan:* Man-Environment Research Association. *United States:* American Psychology Association.

RELIGION, THE HUMANITIES, AND ENVIRONMENTAL PROTECTION

Intergovernmental organizations: Islamic Development Bank.

International NGOs: The World Wide Fund for Nature has been a leader in this field. Others: Buddhist Perception of Nature; International Development Ethics Association; Islamic Academy of Sciences; World Council of Churches.
National: *Holy See:* Pontifical Council "Cor Unum"; Pontifical Academy of Sciences. *United Kingdom:* Buddhist Ecology Network; Christian Ecology Group; Findhorn Foundation; Sacred Trees Trust. *United States:* American Society for Environmental History; Cornell University, Center for Religion, Ethics, and Social Policy.

SOIL
See also: Agriculture and Environmental Protection; Arid Lands; Energy, Geology, and Mining; Forests and Forestry; Grasslands; Tropical Ecosystems; Water Resources.

UN system: Food and Agriculture Organization of the UN (Agriculture Department).

International NGOs: African Soil Science Association; International Board for Soil Resources and Management; International Society of Soil Science; International Soil Reference and Information Centre; Latin American Society of Soil Science; World Association of Soil and Water Conservation.

National: *United Kingdom:* Soil Association. *United States:* Soil and Water Conservation Society of America.

SOLID WASTE AND RESOURCE RECOVERY
See also: Toxic Materials.

International NGOs: Clean World International; International Solid Wastes and Public Cleansing Association.

National: *United Kingdom:* Keep Britain Tidy Group. *United States:* Air and Waste Management Association.

TOURISM IMPACTS

Intergovernmental organizations: CAB International; World Tourism Organization.

International NGOs: International Association of Scientific Experts in Tourism; World Leisure and Recreation Association.

TOXIC MATERIALS
See also: Agriculture and Environmental Protection; Air Quality; Health and the Environment; Industry and Environmental Protection; Nuclear Energy and Radiation; Occupational Safety and Health; Pest Management; Solid Waste and Resource Recovery; Water Quality.

UN system: UN Environment Programme (International Register of Potentially Toxic Chemicals); World Health Organization (International Programme on Chemical Safety).

Other intergovernmental organizations: Organisation for Economic Co-operation and Development (Environment Committee).

International NGOs: European Committee for the Protection of the Population Against the Hazards of Chronic Toxicity; European Institute of Ecology and Cancer; International Coalition for Justice in Bhopal; No More Bhopals Network; Pesticide Action Network; World Institute of Ecology and Cancer.

National: *United States:* Air and Waste Management Association; National Coalition Against the Misuse of Pesticides.

TRANSPORTATION AND ENVIRONMENTAL PROTECTION
See also: Human Settlements; Noise.

UN system: International Civil Aviation Organization.

National: *United Kingdom:* Pedestrians Association.

TROPICAL ECOSYSTEMS

UN system: UN Educational, Scientific, and Cultural Organization (MAB Tropical Forests Network).

Other intergovernmental organizations: International Tropical Timber Organization; Tropical Agricultural Research and Training Center.

International NGOs: International Center of Tropical Agriculture (Colombia) and International Institute of Tropical Agriculture (Nigeria), listed under Consultative Group on International Agricultural Research; International Society for Tropical Ecology; International Society of Tropical Foresters; Rain Forest Action Network; Regional Mangrove Information Network .

National: See the listings for tropical countries and territories in Part 7 (Hawaii listings follow the main USA entries). The following are of special note: *Brazil:* Institute of Amazonian Studies. *Costa Rica:* Tropical Science Center; Organization for Tropical Studies. The following organizations outside the tropics have a special interest in tropical ecosystems: *France:* Tropical Forestry Technical Center. Also note under the *United States:* Institute of Pacific Islands Forestry (Hawaii), listed under Department of Agriculture; Smithsonian Institution; International Society for the Preservation of the Tropical Rainforest; Tropical Forests Working Group; Yale University,

Tropical Resources Institute.

WATER QUALITY
Note: Organizations generally concerned with water are listed under Water Resources, below. *See also:* Oceans, Coastal Zones, and Islands; Lakes, Rivers, and Waterways; Soil; Solid Waste and Resource Recovery; Toxic Materials.

UN system: UN Development Programme (International Drinking Water Supply and Sanitation Decade); UN Environment Programme; World Bank; World Health Organization.

International NGOs: Asian Institute of Technology, Environmental Sanitation Information Center; European Federation for the Protection of Waters; European Water Pollution Control Association; International Association on Water Pollution Research and Control.

National: The following national organizations work internationally on water problems: *United Kingdom:* International Society for the Prevention of Water Pollution; WaterAid. *United States:* Clean Water Action Project; Water Pollution Control Federation.

WATER RESOURCES
See also: Lakes, Rivers, and Waterways; Oceans, Coastal Zones, and Islands; Water Quality; Wetlands.

UN system: Administrative Committee on Coordination (Intersecretariat Group for Water Resources); UN Environment Programme (Environmentally Sound Management of Inland Waters); International Fund for Agricultural Development; Food and Agriculture Organization of the UN; UN Educational, Scientific, and Cultural Organization (International Hydrological Programme); World Meteorological Organization (Hydrology and Water Resources Programme).

Other intergovernmental organizations: CAB International; Interafrican Committee for Hydraulic Studies.

International NGOs: Central American Regional Water Resources Committee; European Institute for Water; European Mediterranean Commission on Water Planning; International Association for Water Law; International Association of Hydrological Sciences; International Commission on Irrigation and Drainage; International Commission on Large Dams; International Council of Scientific Unions, Committee on Water Research; International Institute for Land Reclamation and Improvement; International Institute for Water; International Irrigation Management Institute; International Reference Centre for Community Water Supply and Sanitation; International Training Centre for Water Resources Management; International Water Resources Association; International Water Supply Association; Islamic Network of Water Resources Management;

World Association of Soil and Water Conservation.

National: *United States:* American Water Resources Association; Soil and Water Conservation Society of America.

WETLANDS
See also: Lakes, Rivers, and Waterways; Natural Areas, Parks, and Wilderness; Oceans, Coastal Zones, and Islands; Water Resources.

Intergovernmental organizations: Ramsar Convention Bureau.

International NGOs: International Waterfowl and Wetlands Research Bureau.

WILDLIFE
See also: Fish and Fisheries; Pest Management. The following is organized mainly by subject:

UN system: UN Environment Programme (Secretariat for the Convention on International Trade in Endangered Species of Wild Fauna and Flora, and Secretariat of the Convention on the Conservation of Migratory Species of Wild Animals).

Other intergovernmental organizations: Commission for the Conservation of Antarctic Marine Living Resources; Council of Europe (European Committee for the Conservation of Nature and Natural Resources); International Association of Fish and Wildlife Agencies; International Whaling Commission; North Pacific Fur Seal Commission.

International NGOs (broad interests): Beauty without Cruelty International; International Association of Zoo Educators; International Council for Game and Wildlife Conservation (hunting group); International Foundation for the Conservation of Game (hunting group); International Fund for Animal Welfare (animal protection); International Union of Directors of Zoological Gardens; IUCN-The World Conservation Union (Species Survival Commission and World Conservation Monitoring Centre); Nordic Council for Wildlife Research; Seed Action Network (genetic resources); Wildlife Preservation Trust International; World Blue Chain; World Society for the Protection of Animals; World Wide Fund for Nature.

Leading national organizations working internationally (broad interests): *United Kingdom:* Fauna and Flora Preservation Society. *United States:* Smithsonian Institution; RARE; Wildlife Society; Monitor.

Mammals: *Intergovernmental organizations:* International Whaling Commission; North Pacific Fur Seal Commission. *International NGOs:* Bat Conservation International; European Association for Aquatic Mammals; European Cetacean Society; European Committee for the Protection of Fur

Animals; International League for the Protection of Cetaceans; International Primate Protection League; International Primatological Society; Sea Shepherd Conservation Society (marine and terrestrial mammals). *United Kingdom:* Whale Conservation Society. *United States:* Marine Mammal Commission; American Cetacean Society; Cetacean Society International; International Snow Leopard Trust; Pacific Whale Foundation; Society for Marine Mammalogy; Whale Center.

Birds: *International NGOs:* The leading organization is the International Council for Bird Preservation. Others: International Association for Falconry and Conservation of Birds of Prey; International Waterfowl and Wetlands Research Bureau; World Pheasant Association. *United Kingdom:* Wildfowl Trust. *United States:* Ducks Unlimited.

Reptiles and Amphibians: *International NGOs:* Caribbean Conservation Corporation (marine turtles); European Herpetological Society. *United States:* Chelonia Institute (marine turtles).

Fishes: *See* major heading above, "Fish and Fisheries," above.

Insects: *International NGOs:* Xerces Society (butterfly protection). *: Mexico:* Monarch Butterfly. *United Kingdom:* Joint Committee for the Conservation of British Insects.

WOMEN AND THE ENVIRONMENT
See also: Education and Training.

International NGOs: International Council of Women; WorldWIDE.

National: *Kenya:* Green Belt Movement (part of the National Council of Women).

YOUTH AND THE ENVIRONMENT

UN system: UN Children's Fund.

International NGOs: European Youth Forest Action Foundation; International Youth Conference on the Human Environment; International Youth Federation for Environmental Studies and Conservation; Latin American Federation of Young Environmentalists; World Organization of the Scout Movement.

Part 3
The World Regions: Key Organizations

This part of the *World Directory* directs you to organizations concerned with the major regions of the world: Antarctica and the Southern Ocean, Africa, Australia and Oceania, Latin America and the Caribbean, North America, East Asia, West Asia, and Europe. See the index to locate descriptions of organizations in Parts 4, 5, 6, and 7.

ANTARCTICA AND THE SOUTHERN OCEAN

See the following listings in Part 7: Antarctica, Falkland Islands (Islas Malvinas), South Georgia and the South Sandwich Islands.

AFRICA

UN system: UN Non-Governmental Liaison Service (Sahel Information Service); Economic Commission for Africa; UN Conference on Trade and Development (Special Program on Least-Developed Countries focuses on Africa); UN Sudano-Sahelian Office; UN Research Institute for Social Development (Programme on Strategies for the Future of Africa); UN University (UNU Institute for Natural Resources in Africa).

The UN Environment Programme has a regional office in Nairobi, Kenya, and regional seas programs for East Africa and West and Central Africa. The Food and Agriculture Organization of the UN has a Regional Forestry Commission for Africa.

Other intergovernmental organizations: African Development Bank; African Ministerial Conference on the Environment; African Timber Organization; Arab Bank for Economic Development in Africa; Club of Friends of the Sahel; Interafrican Committee for Hydraulic Studies; International Commission for Scientific Exploration of the Mediterranean Sea; Permanent Interstate Committee for Drought Control in the Sahel; Secretariat for the Protection of the Mediterranean Sea; Southern African Development Coordination Conference. *See also* "River, Lake, and Boundary Commissions" in Part 5.

International NGOs: African NGOs Environment Network; African Soil Science Association; East African Natural History Society; East African Wildlife Society; Environment and Development in the Third World; International Foundation for the Survival and Development of Humanity (a new USA-USSR group which will focus attention on African development); International Institute of Tropical Agriculture; International Livestock Center for Africa; Organization for the Phyto-Taxonomic Investigation of the Mediterranean Area; Pan-African Council for Protection of the Environment and for Development; SOS Sahel International; West Africa Rice Development Association.

National organizations outside the region: *United States:* African Wildlife Foundation; Friends of Africa in America.

National organizations in the region: *See* the following listings in Part 7: Algeria, Angola, Benin, Botswana, Burkina Faso, Burundi, Cameroon, Cape Verde, Central African Republic, Chad, Comoros, Congo, Côte d'Ivoire, Djibouti, Egypt, Equatorial Guinea, Ethiopia, Gabon, Gambia, Ghana, Guinea, Guinea-Bissau, Kenya, Lesotho, Liberia, Libya, Madagascar, Malawi, Mali, Mauritania, Mauritius, Mayotte, Morocco, Mozambique, Niger, Nigeria, Reunion, Rwanda, St. Helena and Dependencies, Sao Tome and Principe, Senegal, Seychelles, Sierra Leone, Somalia, South Africa, Sudan, Swaziland, Tanzania, Togo, Tunisia, Uganda, Zaire, Zambia, Zimbabwe. *See also:* Atlantic Ocean; Indian Ocean.

AUSTRALIA AND OCEANIA

UN system: The UN Environment Programme has a regional sea program for the South Pacific.

Other intergovernmental organizations: South Pacific Commission; South Pacific Forum.

International NGOs: Asia-Pacific People's Environment Network; Pacific Science Association; University of the South Pacific, Institute of Natural Resources.

National organizations in the region: *See* the following listings in Part 7: America Samoa, Australia, Christmas Island, Cook Islands, Fiji, French Polynesia, Guam, Johnston Atoll; Kiribati, Marshall Islands, Micronesia, Midway Islands; Nauru, New Caledonia, New Zealand, Niue, Norfolk Island, Northern Mariana Islands, Palau, Papua New Guinea, Pitcairn Islands, Solomon Islands, Tokelau, Tonga, Tuvalu, United States (see East-West Center; also see Hawaii entries after main listings); Vanuatu, Wake Island; Wallis and Futuna, Western Samoa. *See also:* Indian Ocean, Pacific Ocean.

LATIN AMERICAN AND THE CARIBBEAN

UN system: Economic Commission for Latin America and the Caribbean. The UN Environment Programme has a regional office in Mexico City and an office for the Caribbean in Kingston, Jamaica; it has regional sea programs for the Caribbean and the Southeast Pacific. The Food and Agriculture Organization of the UN has a Regional Forestry Commission for Latin America.

Other intergovernmental organizations: The Organization of American States is the key regional organization. Others: Caribbean Community; Caribbean Development Bank; Central American Bank for Economic Integration; Inter-American Development Bank; Inter-American Tropical Tuna Commission; International Association of Fish and Wildlife Agencies; Latin American Housing and Human Settlements Development Organization; Pan American Center for Sanitary Engineering; Permanent South Pacific Commission (Southeast Pacific); Tropical Agriculture Research and Training Center. *See also* "River, Lake, and Boundary Commissions" in Part 5.

International NGOs: Caribbean Conservation Association; Caribbean Conservation Corporation; Central American Federation of Non-Governmental Conservation Associations; Central American Water Resources Committee; Eastern Caribbean Institute for Agriculture and Forestry; Gulf and Caribbean Fisheries Institute; Inter-American Association of Sanitary and Environmental Engineering; Inter-American Bar Association; Inter-American Planning Society; Latin American Association for the Promotion of Habitat, Architecture, and Urbanism; Latin American Committee on National Parks; Latin American Federation of Young Environmentalists; Latin American Network of Environmental NGOs; Latin American Society of Soil Science; Mesoamerican Center for the Study of Appropriate Technology; Organization for Flora Neotropica; Pacific Science Association; Regional Network of Non-Governmental Conservation Organizations for Sustainable Development in Central America; Speleological Federation of Latin America and the Caribbean.

National organizations outside the region: *United States:* Conservation International; Nature Conservancy.

National organizations in the region: *See* the following listings in Part 7: Anguilla, Antigua and Barbuda, Argentina, Aruba, Bahamas, Barbados, Belize, Bolivia, Brazil, Cayman Islands, Chile, Colombia, Costa Rica, Cuba, Dominica, Dominican Republic, Ecuador, El Salvador, French Guiana, Grenada, Guadeloupe, Guatemala, Guyana, Haiti, Honduras, Jamaica, Martinique, Mexico, Montserrat, Netherlands Antilles, Nicaragua, Panama, Paraguay, Peru, Puerto Rico, St. Christopher and Nevis, St. Lucia, St. Vincent and the Grenadines, Suriname, Trinidad and Tobago, Turks and Caicos Islands, Uruguay, Venezuela, Virgin Islands (British), Virgin Islands (U.S.). *See also:* Atlantic Ocean, Pacific Ocean.

NORTH AMERICA

UN system: The Economic Commission for Europe includes Canada and the USA. The UN Environment Programme has liaison offices at UN headquarters, New York, and in Washington. The Food and Agriculture Organization of the UN has a Regional Forestry Commission for North America.

Other intergovernmental organizations: Inter-American Tropical Tuna Commission; International Association of Fish and Wildlife Agencies; North Atlantic Treaty Organization; Organization of American States; Pan American Center for Sanitary Engineering. *See also* "River, Lakes, and Boundary Commissions" in Part 5.

International NGOs: Arctic Institute of North America; Arctic International Wildlife Range Society; Canada-United States Environmental Council; Center for the Great Lakes; Inter-American Association of Sanitary and Environmental Engineering; Inter-American Bar Association; Inter-American Planning Society; International Arctic Committee; International Foundation for the Survival and Development of Humanity (USA-USSR); Inuit Circumpolar Conference; Pacific Science Association.

National organizations: *See* the following listings in Part 7: Bermuda, Canada, United States of America, St. Pierre et Miquelon. *See also:* Arctic Ocean, Atlantic Ocean, Pacific Ocean.

EAST ASIA

UN system: Economic and Social Commission for Asia and the Pacific. The Food and Agriculture Organization of the UN has a Regional Forestry Commission for Asia. The UN Environment Programme has a regional office in Bangkok, Thailand, and a regional sea program for East Asia.

Other intergovernmental organizations: Asian Development Bank; Association of Southeast Asian Nations; International Centre for Integrated Mountain Development (Himalayas); South Asia Cooperative Environment Programme; South Asian Association for Regional Cooperation. *See also* "River, Lake, and Boundary Commissions" in Part 5.

International NGOs: ASEAN Association for Planning and Housing; Asian Ecological Society; Asian Environmental Society; Asian Fisheries Society; Asian Institute of Technology; Asia-Pacific People's Environment Network; Buddhist Perception of Nature; Eastern Regional Organization for Planning and Housing; International Arctic Committee; International Coalition for Justice in Bhopal; International Society for Tropical Ecology; Inuit Circumpolar Conference; Law Association for Asia and the Pacific; No More Bhopals Network; Pacific Science Association; Regional Mangrove Information Network.

National organizations outside the region: *United States:* East-West Center.

National organizations in the region: *See* the following listings in Part 7: Bangladesh, Bhutan, British Indian Ocean Territory, Brunei, Burma, Cambodia, China, Cocos (Keeling) Islands, Hong Kong, India, Indonesia, Japan, Korea (Democratic People's Republic), Korea (Republic), Laos, Macau, Malaysia, Maldives, Mongolia, Nepal, Philippines, Singapore, Sri Lanka, Taiwan, Thailand, USSR (Siberia), Viet-Nam. *See also:* Indian Ocean, Pacific Ocean.

WEST ASIA

UN system: Economic and Social Commission for Western Asia. The UN Environment Programme has a regional office in Manama, Bahrain, and regional sea programs for the Mediterranean, the Arabian or Persian Gulf, and the Red Sea. The Food and Agriculture Organization of the UN has a Regional Forestry Commission for Asia.

Other intergovernmental organizations: Arab Bank for Economic Development in Africa; Arab Fund for Economic and Social Development; Cooperative Council for the Arab States of the Gulf; Federation of Arab Scientific Research Councils; International Centre for Integrated Mountain Development (Himalayas); International Commission for Scientific Exploration of the Mediterranean Sea; Islamic Development Bank; League of Arab States; Regional Organization for the Protection of the Marine Environment (Arabian or Persian Gulf); Secretariat for the Protection of the Mediterranean Sea; South Asia Cooperative Environment Programme; South Asian Association

for Regional Cooperation.

International NGOs: Asian Environmental Society; Asian Fisheries Society; Islamic Network of Water Resources Management; Islamic Academy of Sciences; Organization for the Phyto-Taxonomic Investigation of the Mediterranean Area.

National organizations: *See* the following listings in Part 7: Afghanistan, Bahrain, Iran, Iraq, Israel, Jordan, Kuwait, Lebanon, Oman, Pakistan, Qatar, Saudi Arabia, Syria, Turkey (Anatolia), United Arab Emirates, Yemen Arab Republic, Yemen (People's Democratic Republic). *See also:* Indian Ocean.

EUROPE

UN system: The Economic Commission for Europe has an active interest in environmental problems; it is the only major European intergovernmental body that includes both Eastern and Western Europe (Canada and the USA are also members). The UN Environment Programme has a regional office in Geneva, Switzerland, and an office for the Mediterranean in Athens, Greece. UNEP has a regional sea program for the Mediterranean. The Food and Agriculture Organization of the UN has a Regional Forestry Commission for Europe.

Other intergovernmental organizations: The Council of Europe has a key role in exchange of information about national environmental activities. Other organizations: Association of the Central Alps; Baltic Marine Environment Protection Committee; Bonn Commission; Council for Mutual Economic Assistance; European Community; European Investment Bank; International Baltic Sea Fishery Commission; International Commission for Scientific Exploration of the Mediterranean Sea; Nordic Council; Nordic Council of Ministers; Nordic Investment Bank; North Atlantic Treaty Association; Secretariat for the Protection of the Mediterranean; Training Centre on Environmental Matters for Small Local Authorities in the EEC Mediterranean Countries. *See also* "River, Lake, and Boundary Commissions" in Part 5.

International NGOs: The European Environmental Bureau is a clearinghouse of environmental information for the EEC countries. The Institute for European Environmental Policy is also a key group in the region. IUCN-The World Conservation Union has a special program on Eastern Europe. Other organizations: Europa Nostra; European Association Against Aircraft Nuisance; European Association for Aquatic Mammals; European Association for Country Planning Institutions; European Association for the Science of Air Pollution; European Association of Development Research and Training Institutes; European Centre for Environmental Communication; European Cetacean Society; European Committee for the Protection of Fur Animals; European Committee for the Protection of the Population Against the Hazards of Chronic Toxicity; European Committee of Landscape Architects; European Council of Town Planners; European Council of Environmental Law; European Federation for the Protection of Waters; European Grassland Federation; European Group for the Ardennes and the Eifel; European Herpetological Society; European Institute for Water; European Institute of Ecology and Cancer; European Mediterranean Commission on Water Planning; European Water Pollution Control Association; European Youth Forest Action Foundation; Federation of Nature and National Parks of Europe; Foundation for Environmental Education in Europe; International Arctic Committee; International Commission for the Protection of Alpine Regions; International Foundation for the Survival and Development of Humanity (USA-USSR group); International Friends of Nature; Inuit Circumpolar Conference (includes Greenland); Nordic Council for Ecology; Nordic Council for Wildlife Research; Nordic Forestry Federation; Nordic Society for Radiation Protection; Organization for the Phyto-Taxonomic Investigation of the Mediterranean Area; Society for Ecology (German-language group); Union of European Foresters.

National organizations outside the region: *United States:* German Marshall Fund of the U.S.

National organizations in the region: *See* the following listings in Part 7: Albania, Andorra, Austria, Belgium, Bulgaria, Cyprus, Czechoslovakia, Denmark, Faroe Islands, Finland, France, German Democratic Republic, Germany (Federal Republic), Gibraltar, Greece, Greenland, Holy See, Hungary, Iceland, Ireland, Italy. Liechtenstein, Luxembourg, Malta, Monaco, Netherlands, Norway, Poland, Portugal, Romania, San Marino, Spain, Svalbard, Sweden, Switzerland, Turkey (in Europe), USSR, United Kingdom, Yugoslavia. *See also:* Arctic Ocean, Atlantic Ocean.

Part 4
The United Nations System

Note on the United Nations:

The United Nations and its various programs and specialized agencies carry on numerous activities related to environmental protection and natural resource management. The United Nations Environment Programme (UNEP) is at the center of these activities. However, most of the UN's environmental work is carried out without direct UNEP involvement. It can be difficult to track down specific environmental activities within the UN system. They are scattered throughout many agencies and are often carried out jointly by several groups. To search for particular topics or programs, two reference books are especially helpful: The *ACCIS Guide to United Nations Information Sources on the Environment,* issued in 1988 by the UN Advisory Committee for the Co-ordination of Information Systems (ACCIS), focuses primarily on information resources but also provides considerable detail on programs. The *Annual Report of the Executive Director* of UNEP contains numerous references to the UN activities supported by UNEP or with which it collaborates. The standard reference on the UN is the *Yearbook of the United Nations;* unfortunately, it is usually several years out of date. UN documents are indexed in *UNDEX: United Nations Documents Index,* available in major libraries. For a general checklist of UN books and periodicals, contact the UN office in your country or write to: United Nations Publications, New York, New York 10017, USA; or Palais des Nations, CH-1211 Geneva 10, Switzerland.

A. THE UNITED NATIONS

United Nations Secretariat
Includes the following units concerned with environmental matters:
■ Administrative Committee on Coordination (ACC), Room S-3720, United Nations, New York, NY 10017, USA. Works to ensure that the activities of the UN and its specialized agencies are coordinated. One of its responsibilities is to submit to the Governing Council of UNEP an annual report on international cooperation in the field of the environment. The preparatory process for the ACC discussions on environment is undertaken by the Executive Director of UNEP. Subsidiary bodies of ACC that are concerned with the environment include the Intersecretariat Group for Water Resources; Task Force on Rural Development; and Task Force on Science and Technology for Development. ACC also includes the Advisory Committee for the Co-ordination of Information Systems (ACCIS). Pub: *ACCIS Guide to United Nations Information Sources on*

the Environment (1988).

■ Office for Ocean Affairs and the Law of the Sea, Office of the Secretary General, United Nations, New York, NY 10017, USA. Established in 1987 to consolidate UN marine affairs activities. Provides information, advice, and assistance to governments, international organizations, scholars, and others on the legal, political, and economic aspects of the UN Convention on the Law of the Sea, as well as advice on overall ocean policy. The Convention, negotiated in 1982 and by 1988 signed by 144 countries, covers many aspects of protection, management, and utilization of marine resources. Pub: *Law of the Sea Bulletin* (irregular); legal materials; bibliographies.

■ Department of International Economic and Social Affairs (DIESA), United Nations, New York, NY 10017, USA. Includes:

The Population Division, which collects and disseminates a large amount of information on world population questions. Pub: *Population Bulletin of the United Nations* (biennial); *Population Studies* (irregular).

DIESA's Information Systems Unit, which maintains the Development Information System (DIS). This contains over 10,000 bibliographic references to unpublished studies from several UN offices, and produces the bimonthly *Development Information Abstracts*.

■ Department of Technical Cooperation for Development, United Nations, New York, NY 10017, USA. Includes:

The Natural Resources and Energy Division. Coordinates UN programs in natural resources and energy for developing countries.

Centre for Science and Technology for Development (CSTD), One United Nations Plaza, New York, NY 10017, USA. T: (1 212) 963-860. Tx: 422 311. Fax: (1 212) 963-4116. Established by the 1979 UN Conference on Science and Technology for Development. Implements the Conference action plan, which calls for strengthening the science and technology capabilities of developing countries; restructuring the existing pattern of international scientific and technological relations; and strengthening the role of the UN system in this field. Two of CSTD's major areas of concentration are directly related to the environment: applying science and technology to the combat of drought and desertification, and the effects of global climate change on development. Other areas of interest include, for example, dumping of plastic waste at sea; energy options for developing countries; alternative technology; and biotechnology. Pub: *Update* (quarterly newsletter); bulletins on new technologies.

■ UN Non-Governmental Liaison Service (NGLS). Maintains offices in New York (United Nations, New York, NY 10017, USA. T: (1 212) 963-3125); and Geneva (Palais des Nations, CH-1211 Geneva 10, Switzerland. T: (41 22) 798 58 50. Tx: 289620. Fax: (41 22) 98 75 24.) The New York office helps NGOs in the U.S. and Canada locate resources within the UN system and organize programs related to the UN development agenda. The Geneva office does the same for NGOs in Europe, Japan, Australia, and New Zealand. NGLS includes the International Tree Project Clearinghouse (ITPC), a worldwide service which coordinates international information collection and dissemination for NGOs involved in forestry-related activities. It also maintains the Sahel Information Service (SIS), a computerized network which links NGO consortia in several West African countries. Pub: *United Nations Development Education Directory*. ITPC issues a periodic newsletter, directories of NGOs concerned with forestry (by world region), research papers, and NGO manuals.

■ Centre for Social Development and Humanitarian Affairs (CSDHA), United Nations Office at Vienna, P.O. Box 500, A-1400 Vienna, Austria. T: (43 222) 2631-0. Tx: 135612. C: UNATIONS. Program includes conducting research and information dissemination on social aspects of environmental problems (e.g., popular participation theories; programs to improve the rural environment; rural-urban migration). Pub: Research reports.

■ United Nations Centre for Regional Development (UNCRD), Marunouchi 2-4-7, Naka-ku, Nagoya 460, Japan. Concerns include environmental planning and management. Pub: *Regional Development Dialogue; UNCRD Newsletter; UNCRD Bulletin;* monographs, bibliographies, research reports, and conference proceedings.

Economic and Social Council (ECOSOC)
The 5 regional economic commissions listed below promote intergovernmental cooperation and conduct studies and training in economic and social affairs, including natural resource management and environmental protection.

■ Economic Commission for Africa (ECA), P.O. Box 3001, Addis Ababa, Ethiopia. T: (251 1) 44-72-00. Tx: 21029. C: ECA. Established 1958. Maintains a Division of Natural Resources. ECA administers the African Institute for Economic Development and Planning (B.P. 3186, Dakar, Senegal), and has programming and operational centers in Cameroon, Morocco, Niger, Rwanda, and Zambia, as well as a liaison office in New York.

■ Economic Commission for Europe (ECE), Palais des Nations, CH-1211 Geneva 10, Switzerland. T: (41 22) 734 60 11. Tx: 289696. C: UNATIONS. ECE's region includes the USA and Canada. The Commission has an Environment and Human Settlements Division and an active interest in environmental matters, focusing on general policy and management issues, environmental impact assessment, air pollution problems, low-waste technology, waste management, and water management, as well as flora, fauna, and their habitats. ECE also provides the secretariat for the Convention on Long-range Transboundary Air Pollution. Maintains a liaison office in New York. Pub: Numerous technical reports.

The Six-Year Environment Program of the United Nations, 1990-95

Note: Not to be confused with UNEP, the United Nations Environment Programme, the six-year
program outlined here cuts across the entire UN system, laying out a coordinated plan for individual agencies
for implementing their various environmental projects. It is a useful guide to UN priorities and where various
environmental interests lie within the UN System (see also Part 2 of this directory: "Who's Doing What").
This program was approved by UNEP's Governing Council in 1988. Agency abbreviations shown here are included in the
glossary and in the listings of UN agencies in this part of the directory. A more detailed outline of the six-year
program is available from UNEP.

(1) Atmosphere

(a) Atmospheric composition, processes, and pollution: To be implemented by IAEA, ICSU, UNEP, WHO, WMO
(b) Climate and climatic change: ECA, FAO, ICSU, UNEP, Unesco, Unesco-IOC, WMO

(2) Water

(a) Water resources and freshwater ecosystems: DTCD, ECE, FAO, IAEA, ICSU, IFAD, ILO, UNDP, UNDRO, UNEP, Unesco, World Bank, WHO, WMO
b) Drinking water supply and sanitation: ATRCW, DIESA, DTCD, ECA, ILO, INSTRAW, UNICEF, World Bank, UNDP, UNEP, Unesco, UNIDO, WHO, WMO

(3) Terrestrial Ecosystems

(a) Soils: ECA, FAO, IAEA, IFAD, UNEP, Unesco, WMO
(b) Arid lands and desertification: DTCD, ESCWA, FAO, IFAD, ILO, UNDP, UNDRO, UNEP, Unesco, UNIDO, UNSO, World Bank, WFP, WMO
(c) Tropical forest and woodland ecosystems: ECA, FAO, IFAD, ILO, IUCN, UNCTAD, UNEP, Unesco-MAB, UNU, WMO
(d) Temperate and cold zone ecosystems: ECE, FAO, UNEP, Unesco, WMO
(e) Mountain and highland ecosystems: FAO, UNEP, Unesco, UNU, WMO
(f) Biological diversity and protected areas: FAO, IAEA, UNEP, Unesco, WW
(g) Microbial resources and related biotechnologies: ECE, FAO, IAEA, ILO, UNDP, UNEP, Unesco, UNIDO, UNU, WHO, WMO
(h) Agricultural lands and agrochemicals: ECA, ESCAP, FAO, IAEA, ILO, UNDP, UNEP, Unesco, UNIDO, WHO, WMO

(4) Coastal and Island Systems

(a) Management and rehabilitation: DIESA, DTCD, ECA, ESCAP, FAO, Habitat, IMO, UNEP, Unesco, UNIDO, UNU, WHO

(5) Oceans

(a) Regional marine environments: DTCD, FAO, IAEA, ILO, IMO, UNEP, Unesco, Unesco-IOC, WHO, WMO
(b) Global marine environment: FAO, DTCD, IAEA, ILO, IOC, IMO, UNEP, Unesco, UN, UNIDO, WHO, WMO
(c) Living marine resources: FAO, UNEP, Unesco, Unesco-IOC

(6) Lithosphere

(a) Mineral resources and disaster mitigation: DIESA, DTCD, ECA, IAEA, UNDRO, UNEP, Unesco, WMO

(7) Human Settlements and the Environment

(a) Human settlements planning and management: ECE, Habitat, ILO, UNDP, UNEP, Unesco, UNIDO, World Bank, WHO
(b) Community preparedness for natural and man-made disasters: ECA, ECE, Habitat, ILO, IOC, UNDP, UNDRO, UNEP, Unesco, UNIDO, World Bank, WMO

(8) Health and Welfare

(a) Hazards of pollution: DIESA, ECE, FAO, IAEA, IARC, ILO, UNDP, UNEP, UNIDO, UNSCEAR, WHO

(b) Environmental aspects of communicable diseases: FAO, UNEP, WHO

(c) The working environment: IAEA, ILO, UNIDO, WHO, WMO

(9) Energy, Industry, and Transportation

(a) Energy and environment: DIESA, ECE, FAO, IAEA, ILO, UNDRO, UNDP, UNEP, UNIDO, UNU, World Bank, WHO, WMO

(b) Industry and environment: ECA, ESCAP, ECE, ILO, UNDP, UNEP, UNIDO, World Bank, WHO

(c) Transportation: DIESA, ECE, FAO, Habitat, IAEA, ICAO, ILO, IMO, IOC, UN, UNDP, UNEP, Unesco, UNIDO, World Bank, WMO, WHO

(10) Peace, Security, and Environment

(a) Environmental impacts and consequences: DPSCA, DTCD, FAO, Peace Research Institute Oslo, UNEP, UNSCEAR, UNITAR, WMO

(11) Environmental Assessment

(a) Scientific and technical information for environmental impact assessments: DIESA, FAO, Habitat, IAEA, ILO, IMO, UN UNDP, UNEP, Unesco, Unesco-IOC, UNIDO, World Bank, WHO, WMO

(b) Monitoring and environmental data/assessment: UN system

(12) Environmental Management Measures

(a) Environmental aspects of development planning and cooperation: DIESA, DTCD, ECE, FAO, IFAD, ILO, International Monetary Fund, UNCTAD, UNCTC, UNDP, UNFPA, UNEP, Unesco, UNIDO, UNITAR, UNU, World Bank, WFC, WFP

(b) Environmental law and institutions: ECE, FAO, IAEA, International Council of Environmental Law, ILO, IMO, UN, UNCTAD, UNDP, UNEP, UNITAR, WHO, World Intellectual Property Organization, WMO

(13) Environmental Awareness

(a) Environmental education and training: ILO, UNEP, Unesco, UNDP, UNFPA, UNICEF, UNIDO, UNU, WHO

(b) Public information (increasing public awareness of policy issues): ESCAP, UNEP

■ Economic Commission for Latin America and the Caribbean (ECLAC) (Comisión Económica para América Latina y el Caribe) (CEPAL), Casilla 179-D, Santiago, Chile. T: (56 2) 485051. Tx: 240077. C: UNATIONS. Established 1948. A Development and Environment Unit was established as a joint ECLAC-UNEP activity in 1980; it conducts studies and training, advisory, and technical cooperation projects. Major concerns have included impacts of large water development projects, urbanization, and expansion of agricultural frontiers, as well as generally promoting the concept of integrating environmental considerations in development planning. ECLAC includes the Latin American Institute for Economic and Social Planning (ILPES). Maintains the Latin American Demographic Centre (CELADE) in Mexico City, a subregional headquarters in Trinidad and Tobago, and offices in Washington, New York, Argentina, Brazil, Colombia, and Uruguay. Pub: *CEPAL Review;* newsletter; research reports (most in Spanish; some in English).

■ Economic and Social Commission for Asia and the Pacific (ESCAP), United Nations Building, Rajdamnern Avenue, Bangkok 10200, Thailand. T: (66 2) 2829161-200. Tx: 82392 escap th. C: ESCAP. Fax: (66 2) 2829602. Established 1947. Has an Environmental Co-ordinating Unit, which promotes integration of environmental considerations into national development plans and projects, as well as the Commission's own work. This is done through research, technical assistance, training, conferences, developing management plans, and cooperating with other international organizations. Promotes the Asian Forum of Environmental Journalists. Sponsors the Regional Network of Training and Research Centres of Desertification Control. Marine and coastal environments have received special attention. ESCAP maintains a liaison office in New York. Pub: *ESCAP Environment News* (quarterly); research reports, conference proceedings, and manuals.

■ Economic and Social Commission for Western Asia (ESCWA), P.O. Box 27, Baghdad, Iraq. T: 95068. Tx: 213468 unecwa ik. C: ESCWA. (Mail to P.O. Box 5749, New York, NY 10163, USA.) Established 1973. ESCWA has an Environmental Co-ordination Unit, which is concentrating on identifying problems and formulating alternatives in the areas of desertification, urban waste management, water pollution, industrial pollution, and transfer of environmentally-sound technology. It is also preparing an environmental perspective for the ESCWA Region to the year 2000. Maintains a liaison office in New York. Pub: Research reports.

United Nations Centre for Human Settlements (Habitat) (UNCHS)
P.O. Box 30030, Nairobi. T: (254 2) 333930. Tx: 22996. C: UNHABITAT. Fax: (254 2) 520724. Established 1978. UNCHS, also known as Habitat, assists governments in making affordable and effective improvements in human settlements policies, planning, and conditions, especially for the developing countries. It also initiates, promotes, and coordinates human settlements activities in the UN system. Habitat's research and development program concentrates on 8 priority areas: settlements policies and strategies; settlements planning; shelter and community services; development of the indigenous construction sector; low-cost infrastructure for human settlements; land; mobilization of finance for human settlements; and human settlements institutions and management. Field projects are conducted in many developing countries (e.g., implementing a low-cost housing program in Burundi; infrastructure development in rural areas in Benin; demonstrating low-cost sanitation technologies in rural Jordan; development of a land information data base in Singapore). UNCHS maintains an office in New York. Pub: *Habitat News* (3 times a year); *Shelter Bulletin; Project Information Report,* annual; technical reports, training materials, and films (catalog available).

United Nations Children's Fund (UNICEF)
3 United Nations Plaza, New York, NY 10017, USA. T: (1 212) 326-7000. Tx: 239521. C: UNICEF. Fax: (1 212) 888-7465. Established 1946. Conducts humanitarian and development programs of long-range benefit to children of developing countries. UNICEF's "basic services strategy" is "an alternative to that of relying on the slow spread of conventional health, education, and social services to meet the urgent needs of children and mothers." Regarding the environment, one of the Fund's major program areas is water supply and sanitation, emphasizing installation of simple, low-cost water supply and excreta disposal systems. Such projects are undertaken in over 90 countries. Another UNICEF program area is appropriate technology, which includes promotion of fuel-efficient cookstoves, bio-gas plants, community woodlots, and waste recycling. About 75% of UNICEF's income comes from voluntary contributions from governments; the remainder is from fund-raising efforts, including greeting-card sales. There are UNICEF national committees in some 30 industrialized countries and field offices in Geneva and throughout the Third World. Pub: *UNICEF News,* quarterly; *Ideas Forum,* newspaper for NGOs; *State of the World's Children,* annual report; annual reports for country programs; films; public information materials (catalogs available).

United Nations Conference on Trade and Development (UNCTAD)
Palais des Nations, CH-1211 Geneva 10, Switzerland. T: (41 22) 734 60 11. Tx: 289696. C: UNATIONS. Established 1964. UNCTAD promotes international trade, particularly that of developing countries, with a view to accelerating economic development. Regarding the environment, the UNCTAD Special Program on Least-Developed Countries has been concerned with the effects on external trade of the drought in Africa. Maintains an office in New York. Pub: *Least-Developed Countries,* a series of annual reports, includes brief information on environmental problems in the LDCs.

United Nations Development Programme (UNDP)
1 United Nations Plaza, New York, NY 10017, USA. T: (1 212) 906-5000. Tx: 125 980. C: UNDEVPRO. Established 1965. UNDP is the world's largest grant development assistance organization, drawing on the expertise of some 35 specialized and technical UN agencies to work in over 150 countries in virtually every sector of development. UNDP provides grant assistance to build skills and develop resources in areas such as agriculture, industry, health, education, economic planning, transportation, and communications. It is active in environmental protection in 3 basic ways: (1) It provides program support in middle-income countries for large-scale projects directly concerned with combating various forms of pollution and other kinds of ecological damage. (2) More numerous are UNDP-supported projects that are designed to prevent or limit any environmental side-effects caused by development of large dams, formation of man-made lakes, massive irrigation schemes, and widespread use of chemical fertilizers and pesticides. (3) There are extensive UNDP-assisted projects directed at helping low-income countries improve the utilization of forests, soils, and water resources. Moreover, many UNDP-supported projects for large-scale urban planning and renewal contain major environmental components, with special emphasis on sanitary engineering, sewerage, and location of industrial plants with a view to minimizing air and water pollution. UNDP is the lead agency for the International Drinking Water Supply and Sanitation Decade (1981-1990), a joint effort of several UN agencies to provide low-cost water and sanitation technologies worldwide. UNDP maintains a European Office in Geneva and field offices in over 100 developing countries. Pub: *World Development* (general magazine); *Cooperation South* (magazine about technical cooperation

among developing countries); films; numerous program reports and public information materials (catalog available).

UNDP associated funds (same address) include:

■ United Nations Revolving Fund for Natural Resources Exploration (UNRFNRE), which provides financing for high-risk exploration projects for mineral and geothermal resources in developing countries.

■ United Nations Sudano-Sahelian Office (UNSO), a joint activity of UNDP and UNEP, which is primarily concerned with projects to combat drought and desertification in 22 countries of the Sudano-Sahelian region of Africa.

Office of the United Nations Disaster Relief Co-ordinator (UNDRO)
Palais des Nations, CH-1211 Geneva 10, Switzerland. T: (41 22) 731 02 11. Tx: 28 148 undr ch. C: UNDRO. Concerns include research and collecting and disseminating information about environment-related disasters (e.g., landslides resulting from deforestation; oil spills; industrial accidents). Maintains a liaison office in New York. Pub: *UNDRO News*, bimonthly; guides to disaster management.

United Nations Environment Programme (UNEP)
P.O. Box 30552, Nairobi, Kenya. T: (254 2) 333930 or 52000. Tx: 22068 or 22173. C: UNITERRA. Fax: (254 2) 520711.
■ Regional Office for Africa, at Headquarters
■ Regional Office for Asia and the Pacific, ESCAP, Rajadamnern Avenue, Bangkok 10200, Thailand. T: (66 2) 829161-200. Tx: 82392 th. C: UNITERRA.
■ Regional Office for Latin America, Edificio Naciones Unidas, Presidente Mazaryk 29, Apartado Postal 6-718, Mexico 5, D.D., Mexico. T: (52 5) 2501555. C: CEPAL.
■ Regional Co-ordination Unit (Caribbean), 14-21 Port Royal Street, Kingston, Jamaica. T: (1 809) 92 29 269. Tx: 2340 unlos ja.
■ Regional Office for West Asia, P.O. Box 10880, Manama, Bahrain. T: (973) 27 60 72. Tx: 7457 unep bn. C: UNEPROWA.
■ Regional Office for Europe, Pavillons du Petit-Saconnex, 16, avenue Jean Trembley, CH-1209 Geneva, Switzerland. T: (41 22) 798 84 00. C: UNITERRA.
■ Co-ordinating Unit for the Mediterranean Action Plan, Leoforos Vassileos Konstantinou 48, Athens 501/1, Greece. T: (30 1) 72 44 536. Tx: 222 611 medugr.
■ New York Liaison Office, Room DC2-0816, New York, NY 10017, USA. T: (1 212) 963-8138. C: UNATIONS.
■ Washington Liaison Office, 1889 F Street, NW, Washington, DC 20006. T: (1 202) 289-8456. Tx: 89-606 uninfocen wsh.
Established 1972, following the UN Conference on the Human Environment, held in Stockholm. UNEP's role is one of coordinating, catalyzing, and stimulating environmental action, primarily--but not exclusively--within the UN system. UNEP also works with and through the international scientific community, research centers, intergovernmental organizations, and NGOs. "The great majority of environmental activities being implemented by the UN system are carried out with little or no direct participation of UNEP. Within their specialized mandates, ILO, FAO, WHO, Unesco, WMO, UNIDO, and others have long been executing environmental projects, some of which predate the establishment of UNEP." UNEP works to "identify gaps where nothing or too little is being done and to stimulate and catalyze the necessary action; and to pinpoint overlaps in the UN system's efforts to protect and improve the environment and to seek to coordinate those efforts both inside and outside the system."

UNEP's activities are divided into 10 programs:

Environment and development: UNEP encourages the formulation and application of methodologies that promote systematic consideration of environmental concerns in policy-making and planning (e.g., cost-benefit analysis; integrated physical planning). It has a special interest in promoting such methods in development cooperation activities. Projects focus on energy, environmental law, and industry and transportation (the latter through the UNEP Industry and Environment Office in Paris; see listing below).

Environmental awareness: UNEP and Unesco jointly conduct the International Environmental Education Programme, "the major international vehicle for the promotion of environmental education at the local, national, regional, and global levels." UNEP sponsors both general and specialized environmental training through workshops and postgraduate courses, as well as by organizing regional training networks. It produces numerous publications, audio-visuals, and press releases. INFOTERRA, UNEP's International Environmental Information System, is "the world's largest environmental information system"; it facilitates the exchange of expert knowledge through a network of national focal points, 6 regional service centers, and some 25 special sectoral sources.

Earthwatch: UNEP's environmental assessment arm is Earthwatch. This includes the Global Environment Monitoring System (GEMS), which coordinates the collection of data worldwide on such trends as climate change, soil degradation, and air quality. The Global Resource Information Database (GRID) was established within GEMS to make basic environmental data on soils, forests, hydrology, vegetation, land use, climate, and pollution more readily available to national and international decision-makers; it makes extensive use of satellite imagery and computer technology. Also within Earthwatch are the World Climate Impact Studies Programme (WCIP), and the Monitoring and Assessment Research Centre (MARC).

Oceans: UNEP focuses its work on the marine environment on trends in the global marine environment; living resources; and protection of 10 regional seas programs (the Mediterranean, [Arabian or Persian] Gulf, West and Central Africa region, Southeast Pacific, Red Sea, Caribbean, Eastern Africa region, South Pacific, East Asia region, and South Asia region).

Water: The main focus of work in this field is a program for the Environmentally Sound Management of Inland Waters (EMINWA), which concentrates on promoting cooperation in water matters among countries sharing a common river basin (e.g., the Zambezi River Basin; the Lake Chad Basin). There are related projects in training and in formulating guidelines and improving methods of analysis and decision-making in water management.

Terrestrial ecosystems: Activities are concerned with soils, tropical forests, other ecosystems, management of agricultural chemicals and residues, genetic resources, the lithosphere, and wildlife and protected areas. In the latter field, UNEP provides the secretariats for the CITES and CMS conventions, both of which are described separately below.

Arid and semi-arid lands ecosystems and desertification control: UNEP maintains a Desertification Information System (DESIS), participates in desertification control projects in some 15 countries, and sponsors training courses and media projects. It co-sponsors the UN Sudano-Sahelian Office (UNSO) with UNDP.

Health and human settlements: UNEP works closely with WHO, FAO, and other international agencies on environmental health and occupational safety and health problems. The International Register of Potentially Toxic Chemicals (IRPTC) facilitates the international exchange of information on hazardous chemicals. Activities related to human settlements include publishing guidelines, training courses, and public education.

The arms race and the environment: Work in this field includes research and symposia on the practical links between conflict resolution and environmental protection.

Pub: *UNEP News* (bimonthly magazine); *The Siren* (quarterly newsletter of the Regional Seas program); *Infoterra Bulletin* (bimonthly); *Annual Report of the Executive Director* (includes a detailed description of activities); *The State of the World Environment,* annual; *Infoterra World Directory of Environmental Expertise; Infoterra International Directory of Sources;* Environment Briefs Series (on topics such as water, hazardous chemicals, and tropical forests); Industry and Environment Series; newsletters of regional offices and individual programs; numerous guidelines, reports, books, and papers (a list of publications is included in the UNEP annual report).

UNEP activities located elsewhere include:

■ Intergovernmental Panel on Climate Change (WMO-UNEP). Described under the World Meteorological Organization, below.
■ UNEP Industry and Environment Office, Tour Mirabeau, 39-43 Quai André Citroën, F-75739 Paris Cedex 15, France. T: (33 1) 45 78 33 33. Tx: 650273. Fax: (33 1) 45 78 32 34.
■ Secretariat of the United Nations Scientific Committee on the Effects of Atomic Radiation (UNSCEAR), Vienna International Centre, P.O. Box 500, A-1400 Vienna, Austria. T: (43 222) 26310. C: UNATIONS.
■ Secretariat for the Convention on International Trade in Endangered Species of Wild Fauna and Flora (UNEP/CITES), 6 rue du Maupas, Case Postale 78, CH-1000 Lausanne 9, Switzerland. T: (41 21) 20 00 81. Tx: 24584 ctes ch. C: CITES. Established 1975. Administers the Convention, which was drawn up in 1973 to protect wildlife against over-exploitation and prevent international trade in species threatened by extinction. Trade has become a "major factor in the decline of species as improvement in transport facilities has made it possible to ship live animals and plants and their products anywhere in the world...The wildlife trade is a highly lucrative business and involves a wide variety of species, both as live specimens and as products. Millions of live animals and plants are shipped around the world each year to supply the pet trade and to meet the demand for ornamental plants. Furskins, leather, ivory, and timber, and articles manufactured from these materials, are all traded in large quantities." Member countries act by banning commercial trade in an agreed list of currently endangered species and by regulating and monitoring trade in others that may become endangered.

Appendix I of the Convention lists species threatened with extinction which are, or may be, affected by trade. So as not to endanger them, no permits are issued for international trade in these species unless there are exceptional circumstances. Among those listed are all apes, lemurs, the giant panda, many South American monkeys, great whales, cheetah, leopards, tiger, Asian elephant, all rhinoceroses, many birds of prey, cranes, pheasants and parrots, all sea turtles, some crocodiles and lizards, giant salamanders, and some mussels, orchids, and cacti.

Appendix II of the Convention lists species which might become endangered if trade in them is not controlled and monitored "in order to avoid utilization incompatible with their survival." To prevent threatened species from being traded under the guise of non-threatened species similar in appearance, some non-threatened species are also included in this appendix. International trade in Appendix II species is permitted with proper documentation issued by the government of the exporting country. The list includes, among others, all species in the following groups which are not already in Appendix I: primates, cats, otters, whales, dolphins, and porpoises, birds of prey, tortoises, crocodiles, and orchids, as well as many other species such as the African elephant, fur seals, the black stork, birds of paradise, the coelacanth, some snails, birdwing butterflies, and black corals. In addition, countries may enforce even stricter control than required by CITES if they wish to give special protection to a listed species, or they may even ban trade in all their wildlife.

Biennial meetings review the working of the Convention and discuss changes to the lists of protected species. Species may be moved from one appendix to another or entered or removed with the agreement of the Conference. Enforcement of CITES is the responsibility of member states, who are required to establish management and scientific authorities for the purpose. In most countries, customs officers are given the responsibility of enforcing CITES regulations. Governments are also required to submit reports, including trade records, to the CITES Secretariat.

To ensure effective enforcement, the Secretariat acts as a clearing house for the exchange of information and liaison between the member states and with other authorities and organizations. On behalf of the CITES Secretariat, data on world trade in wildlife are collected and analyzed by the Wildlife Trade Monitoring Unit (WTMU) of the World Conservation Monitoring Centre in Cambridge, England (a joint venture of IUCN, UNEP, and WWF). Apart from the trade statistics submitted by governments, WTMU also receives information from the WWF/IUCN TRAFFIC offices in several countries. Members are the governments of over 85 countries which are signatories to CITES.

■ Secretariat of the Convention on the Conservation of Migratory Species of Wild Animals (UNEP/CMS), Wissenschaftszentrum, Ahrstrasse 45, D-5300 Bonn 2, Federal Republic of Germany. T: (49 228) 302 152. Tx: 855-420 wz d. Fax: (49 228) 302 270. Administers the Convention, adopted in 1973 in Bonn, which aims to protect migratory species of animals that migrate across or outside national boundaries. As of the beginning of 1989, 28 countries and the EEC had become signatories.

United Nations Population Fund (UNFPA)
220 E. 42nd Street, New York, NY 10017, USA. T: (1 212) 850-5631. C: UNATIONS. Established 1969. UNFPA is the "largest internationally-funded source of population assistance worldwide. Its allocations are about US $150 million annually. More than a quarter of population assistance to developing countries goes through UNFPA. The Fund works "to build up the capacity to respond to needs in population and family planning; to promote awareness of population problems in both developed and developing countries and possible strategies to deal with them; to assist developing countries at their request in dealing with their population problems, in the forms and means best suited to the individual country's needs; and to play a leading role in the UN system in promoting population programs, and to coordinate projects supported by the Fund." Pub: *Populi* (quarterly magazine); *UNFPA Newsletter* (monthly); *State of*

World Population Report, annual; policy statements; issue reports; needs assessment reports; country studies; films (publication and film catalog available).

United Nations Institute for Training and Research (UNITAR)
801 United Nations Plaza, New York, NY 10017, USA. T: (1 212) 963-8621. Tx: 220379 unitr ur. C: UNINSTAR. Established 1963. UNITAR provides training at various levels to people, particularly from developing countries, who are being assigned to the UN or its specialized agencies, or for assignments with their own governments that are connected with the work of the UN and related organizations. It also conducts research related to the objectives and functions of the UN family of organizations. UNITAR maintains offices in Geneva, Rome, Santiago, and Lima. Includes:
■ UNITAR/UNDP Centre on Small Energy Resources, Via Panama 12, I-00198 Rome, Italy. Established 1984. Co-sponsored by UNITAR and the UN Development Programme. Promotes the development of small energy resources, particularly for the benefit of rural populations of developing countries, through seminars and exchange of technical information.

United Nations Research Institute for Social Development (UNRISD)
Palais des Nations, CH-1211 Geneva 10, Switzerland. T: (41 22) 98 84 00. Tx: 28 96 96. C: UNATIONS. Established 1963. Conducts research into problems and policies of social development and its relation to economic development. Projects related to the environment have included studies of food security. UNRISD administers the Programme on Strategies for the Future of Africa (B.P. 3501, Dakar, Senegal). Pub: *Research Notes* (bulletin); research and program reports.

United Nations University (UNU)
Toho Seimei Building, 15-1 Shibuya 2-chome, Shibuya-ku, Tokyo 150, Japan. T: (81 3) 499-2811. Tx: J25442. C: UNATUNIV. Fax: (81 3) 499-2828. Established 1973. The UNU is not a degree-granting institution with traditional students and a faculty, but rather "an international community of scholars" enjoined to work on "pressing global problems of human survival, development, and welfare." Most of its work is carried out through research and training centers created by the UNU or through formal associations with existing institutions and contract researchers. The centers include the United Nations University Institute for Natural Resources in Africa (INRA) at Yamoussoukro, Côte d'Ivoire.

One of the UNU's 5 major program areas is "Global Life Support Systems," which attempts to "measure the stresses of deforestation, acid rain, ocean pollution, and carbon dioxide increase, and the threat of such problems to life on this planet. in particular, the UNU is attempting to add the perspectives of international scientists from a variety of disciplines and cultures on topics such as the geosphere, the biosphere, energy, and endogenous ecosystems." Other program areas focus on peace, development, and democracy; the global economy; alternative rural-urban configurations; and science, technology, and global learning. The University maintains offices in New York and Paris. Pub: *Work in Progress* (newspaper); numerous books, research reports, and conference proceedings (catalog available).

World Food Council (WFC)
Via delle Terme di Caracalla, I-00100 Rome, Italy. T: (39 6) 57971. Tx: 610181 fao i. C: FOODAGRI. Acts as "advocate, catalyst, and coordinator in stimulating governments and the international community to adopt the policies and programs necessary to alleviate world hunger and improve the global food system; and a political overview body that serves as the eyes, ears, and conscience of the UN system regarding food issues." The Council decided in 1988 to include ecological issues affecting food security in its future work program, and has embarked on a special joint effort with UNEP to explore this. WFC maintains an office in New York. Pub: Reports of meetings; public information materials.

World Food Programme (WFP)
Via Cristoforo Colombo 426, I-00145 Rome, Italy. T: (39 6) 57971. Tx: 626675. C: WORLDFOOD. Fax: (39 6) 57975652. Established 1961. A joint program of the UN and FAO. WFP provides food aid, that is, aid in the form of food, rather than cash or technical assistance. Since WFP often supplies food as an incentive to development self-help projects--as part wages in labor-intensive projects of many kinds, particularly in rural development--it is an important actor in the international development community. (It also provides food relief to poor people, and food aid in cases of natural disasters and to refugees.) Pub: *World Food Programme News* (quarterly); public information materials; program reports.

B: SPECIALIZED AGENCIES OF THE UNITED NATIONS

Food and Agriculture Organization of the United Nations (FAO)
Via Terme di Caracalla, I-00100 Rome, Italy. T: (39 6) 57971. Tx: 610181. C: FOODAGRI.
■ FAO Regional Office for Africa, P.O. Box 1628, Accra, Ghana. T: 66851. Tx: 2139. C: FOODAGRI.
■ FAO Regional Office for Asia and the Pacific, Maliwan Mansion, Phra Atit Road, Bangkok 10200, Thailand. T: (66 2) 281-7844. Tx: 82815. C: FOODAGRI.
■ FAO Regional Office for the Near East (Provisional Office at FAO Headquarters)
■ FAO Regional Office for Europe, at FAO Headquarters
■ FAO Regional Office for Latin America and the Caribbean, Casilla 10095, Santiago, Chile.

T: (56 2) 462061. Tx: 340279. C: FOODAGRI.
■ Liaison Office for North America, 1001 22nd Street, NW, Suite 300, Washington, DC 20437, USA. T: (1 202) 653-2400. Tx: 64255. C: FOODAGRI.
■ FAO Liaison Office with United Nations Headquarters, Room DC1-1125, United Nations, New York, NY 10017, USA. T: (1 212) 963-6036. Tx: 236350. C: FOODAGRI. Fax: (1 212) 888-6188.
■ Office of the FAO Representative to the United Nations Organizations in Geneva, Palais des Nations, CH-1211 Geneva 10, Switzerland. T: (41 22) 734 60 11. Tx: 289375. C: FOODAGRI.
Established 1945. FAO carries out a major program of technical advice and assistance for the agricultural community on behalf of governments and development funding agencies; collects, analyzes, and disseminates information; advises governments on policy and planning; and provides opportunities for governments to meet and discuss food and agricultural problems. Pub: (also see below): *Ceres* (bimonthly review; publication temporarily suspended); *The State of Food and Agriculture* (annual review); numerous yearbooks, reports, and educational materials (catalog available).

Major FAO units concerned with environmental and natural resource problems are:
■ Interdepartmental Working Group on Environment and Energy. Responsible for FAO's Environment and Energy Programs Coordinating Centre. Pub: *Environment & Energy* (newsletter); *Management of Natural Resources for Food and Agriculture: FAO and the Environment; FAO's Activities in Combating Desertification.*
■ Forestry Department. FAO is "the world's leading international agency for the collection and analysis of information on all aspects of forestry and forest industry. This information is disseminated to governments, institutions, and individuals throughout the world through publications, meetings, training courses, study tours, and by the technical assistance and expertise of the FAO forestry field program in developing countries." FAO is "deeply involved" in the implementation of the Tropical Forestry Action Plan (TFAP), a cooperative effort initiated by FAO and others in 1985 as a vehicle for harmonizing international assistance in tropical forest conservation and development. The basic objective of FAO's forestry programs is to help developing countries manage and use their forest resources on a sustainable basis with increasing social, economic, and environmental benefits to national development goals. The Forestry Department includes a Forest Resources Division (responsible for development and conservation of forest resources; and development of forestry institutions, including training, education, research, policy, and legislation); a Forest Industries Division (responsible for helping countries develop forest-based enterprises); the Forestry Policy and Planning Service (which provides a continuing information basis for monitoring issues and trends); and an

Operations Service (which implements some 240 FAO-assisted forestry projects around the world). Forest Department concerns include wildlife management, watershed management, agroforestry, desertification, national parks and protected areas, protection of forest genetic resources, and control of pollution from the pulp and paper industries. Pub: *Unasylva* (forestry quarterly).

■ Fisheries Department. Includes a Fisheries Resources and Environment Division, a Fisheries Industry Division, and a Fishery Policy and Planning Division. Concerns include controlling overfishing, developing small-scale fisheries, aquaculture development, the international trade in fish and fish products, promotion of the role of fisheries to alleviate malnutrition, water quality as it affects fisheries, depletion of marine mammals, and fish genetic resources.

■ Agriculture Department. Environmental concerns of this department include soil conservation, desertification, land-use planning, fertilizer use, organic recycling, water resource development problems, control of vector-borne diseases, crop and animal genetic resources, pesticides, and food and feed contamination.

■ Regional commissions and technical committees. Regional Forestry Commissions have been established for Africa, Latin America, the Near East, North America, Asia, and Europe. They promote and coordinate forest policies resulting from FAO recommendations. Other regional and specialized groups set up under FAO are numerous; they include, for example, the Indian Ocean Fisheries Commission and panels of experts on such topics as tuna research and integrated pest control.

General Agreement on Tariffs and Trade (GATT) 154 rue de Lausanne, CH-1211 Geneva 21, Switzerland. T: (41 22) 39 51 11. Tx: 28787. C: GATT. Fax: (41 22) 31 42 06. Established 1947. Lays down agreed rules for international trade; works to reduce trade barriers. Regarding the environment, GATT research has included studies of the relation between pollution control and the structure of international trade.

International Atomic Energy Agency (IAEA) P.O. Box 100, A-1400 Vienna, Austria. T: (43 222) 2360. Tx: 1 12645. C: INATOM. Established 1957. Seeks to "accelerate and enlarge the contribution of atomic energy to peace, health, and prosperity throughout the world" and to "ensure so far as it is able, that assistance provided by it or at its request or under its supervision or control is not used in such a way as to further any military purpose." IAEA provides countries with technical assistance in areas related to nuclear power. Regarding environmental protection, it is particularly concerned with all aspects of radiation safety, and has established regulations for safe transport of radioactive materials, which have been adopted as legal standards by many governments. IAEA has adopted codes for the safe operation of nuclear power plants and research reactors, and advises governments on nuclear reactor siting. It has determined princi-

ples for limiting the introduction of nuclear wastes into the sea. It maintains an international register of releases of radioactive material that cross national boundaries. A major function of the Agency is to establish and administer safeguards to ensure that nuclear materials and equipment intended for peaceful uses are not diverted to military purposes. Members of IAEA are the governments of over 100 countries. The Agency maintains liaison offices in New York and Geneva. Pub: *IAEA Bulletin,* bimonthly; *Atomic Energy Review,* quarterly; proceedings, technical reports, and bibliographies (catalog available).

International Civil Aviation Organization (ICAO) 1000 Sherbrooke Street West, Montreal, Quebec H3A 2R2, Canada. T: (1 514) 285-8219. Tx: 05-24513. C: ICAO. Fax: (1 514) 288-4772. Established 1947. Works to develop the principles and techniques of international air navigation and to foster the planning and development of a safe, efficient, and regular international air transport system. ICAO responsibilities related to the environment include control of aircraft noise and engine emissions; air transport of dangerous goods; and aeronautical meteorology (in cooperation with WMO). Members of ICAO are the governments of 157 countries. ICAO has offices in Paris, France; Bangkok, Thailand; Cairo, Egypt; Mexico City; Lima, Peru; Nairobi, Kenya; and Dakar, Senegal.Pub: Technical documents; training materials (catalogs available).

International Fund for Agricultural Development (IFAD) Via del Serafico 107, I-00142 Rome, Italy. T: (39 6) 54591. Tx: 620330. C: IFAD. Fax: (39 6) 5043463. Established 1977 at the UN World Food Conference. IFAD "was created to be different from most institutions" because it addresses hunger and malnutrition by alleviating rural poverty, "the root cause of these scourges." It works to alleviate such poverty "through promoting equity and cost-effective measures rather than through welfare." Over its first decade, IFAD channeled over US $10 billion to projects in 89 developing countries. Two key areas of focus for loans and grants are small-scale irrigation and rural credit. Other areas of emphasis include the training, organization, and support of rural women; environmental protection; the strengthening of delivery institutions for the poor; and traditional crop development. The "IFAD style" is "reflected in its grassroots approach and its NGO focus."

In regard to the environment, some 55% of IFAD's projects include environmental components such as water conservation, erosion control, and afforestation. These components "stress a participatory approach because smallholders are the most effective front-line defense of their own natural resource base." "The Fund appreciates that there is a positive as well as a negative link between rural poverty and the environment. The link is negative in that impoverished populations struggling for survival will necessarily wrest it from marginal soils, deplete forests and water supplies, and otherwise degrade the environment to do so. The positive link is that as rural poverty is relieved... smallholders will themselves participate in efforts to improve the...resources on which they depend. IFAD seeks to break the negative link by reinforcing the positive one." In the Fund's Orissa Tribal Development Project in India, for example, close communal ties and indigenous expertise in mixed cropping, hoe cultivation, and agroforestry are being drawn on to restore marginal lands. Members of IFAD are the governments of 143 countries. IFAD maintains liaison offices in New York and Washington.

International Labour Organisation (ILO)
4, route des Morillons, CH-1211 Geneva 22, Switzerland. T: (41 22) 799 61 11. Tx: 22-271 bit ch. C: INTERLAB. Fax: (41 22) 98 86 85.
■ ILO Liaison Office with the United Nations, 300 E. 44th Street, 18th Floor, New York, NY 10017, USA. T: (1 212) 697-0150. C: LABORINTER. Fax: (1 212) 883-0844.
■ ILO Regional Office for Africa, P.O. Box 2788, Addis Ababa, Ethiopia.
■ ILO Regional Office for Latin America and the Caribbean, Apartado Postal 638, Lima 1, Peru. T: (51 14) 40-48-50.
■ ILO Regional Office for Asia and the Pacific, P.O. Box 1759, Bangkok, Thailand. T: (66 2) 282-9161.
Established 1919. The general purpose of ILO is to raise working and living standards worldwide. The major environmental concern of the Organisation is the protection of workers against the effects of a harmful working environment and pollution of the workplace. Workers' housing is also a concern. ILO has prepared a Model Code of Safety Regulations for Industrial Establishments. It has a Working Conditions and Environment Department. ILO's International Occupational Safety and Health Information Centre (CIS) has an extensive data base. ILO also administers the International Centre for Labour Studies in Geneva. Pub: *Safety and Health at Work: ILO-CIS Bulletin*, bimonthly; numerous other publications (catalog available).

International Maritime Organization (IMO)
4 Albert Embankment, London SE1 7SR, England. T: (44 1) 735 7611. Tx: 23588. C: INTERMAR. Established 1948 (as the Inter-Governmental Maritime Consultative Organization). Initially concerned primarily with promoting safety at sea, IMO soon became active also in dealing with the threat of marine pollution from ships. The Marine Environment Protection Committee (MEPC) has responsibility for this area and maintains a Sub-Committee on Bulk Chemicals. IMO administers the International Convention for the Prevention of Pollution of the Sea by Oil (1954), the International Convention for the Prevention of Pollution from Ships (1973), and a number of related agreements. It also administers the Convention on the Prevention of Marine

Pollution by Dumping of Wastes and Other Matter (1972 London Dumping Convention), which controls incineration, as well as dumping, at sea. In addition to these formal treaty instruments, IMO has adopted several hundred recommendations dealing with a wide range of environmental subjects, e.g., carrying of dangerous chemicals and liquefied natural gas; safety for nuclear merchant ships; construction of offshore drilling units. Technical assistance and training is provided to national authorities, particularly in developing countries. It operates the World Maritime University at Malmö, Sweden. Members of IMO are the governments of some 133 countries. Pub: Conventions, codes of regulations, recommendations, manuals, and conference proceedings (catalog available).
■ Joint Group of Experts on the Scientific Aspects of Marine Pollution (GESAMP). Office at IMO headquarters. A joint group of IMO, FAO, Unesco, WMO, WHO, IAEA, UN, and UNEP. Provides scientific advice on ocean pollution to the sponsoring organizations and their member states and to the International Oceanographic Commission; prepares periodic reviews of the state of marine pollution and problems requiring special attention. Holds annual meetings. Maintains 21 working groups (e.g., Consequences of the Human Perturbation of the Ocean Floor; Review of the Health of the Oceans; Principles for Developing Coastal Water Quality Criteria). Pub: Reports of annual sessions and studies of working groups.

United Nations Educational, Scientific and Cultural Organization (Unesco)
7, place de Fontenoy, F-75700 Paris, France. T: (33 1) 45 68 10 10. Tx: 270 602. C: UNESCO. Established 1945. Unesco fosters international cooperation in education, science, and culture. All of its programs place heavy emphasis on education, training, exchange of information, and promotion of research and advancement of knowledge. It has Regional Offices for Science and Technology in Nairobi, Kenya; Montevideo, Uruguay; Amman, Jordan; New Delhi, India; Jakarta, Indonesia; and Beijing, China. There are Regional Offices or Centres for Education in Dakar, Senegal; Santiago, Chile; Caracas, Venezuela; Amman, Jordan; and Bucharest, Romania. There are liaison offices in New York and Geneva. Pub: *Unesco Courier* (monthly magazine); numerous books, reports, and educational materials (catalog available).
The main Unesco programs related to environmental and natural resource management are:
■ Man and the Biosphere Programme (MAB). Initiated in 1970, MAB is a "nationally-based, international program of research, training, demonstration, and information diffusion aimed at providing the scientific basis and the trained personnel needed to deal with problems relative to rational utilization and conservation of resources and resource systems and to human settlements. The MAB Programme emphasizes research for

solving problems: It thus involves research by multi-disciplinary teams on the interactions between ecological and social systems, field training, and the application of a systems approach to understanding the relationships between the natural and human components of development and environmental management." MAB has field projects in over 100 countries under the auspices of MAB National Committees. It is governed by the MAB International Coordinating Council (ICC). *Research:* Four broad research orientations were approved by the MAB Council in 1986. These are: ecosystem functioning under different intensities of human impact; management and restoration of human-impacted resources; human investment and resource use; and human response to environmental stress. *Education and training:* Many of MAB's field projects include educational components (e.g., a seminar on environmental impacts of tourism development on islands). There are also several continuing training courses (e.g., an annual program on integrated pastoral management in the Sahel; an annual postgraduate course in integrated study and rational use of natural resources in France). *Biosphere Reserves:* MAB is also responsible for a worldwide system of Biosphere Reserves, in which protected areas of representative terrestrial and coastal environments are recognized for their value in conservation and in providing the scientific knowledge, skills, and human values to support sustainable development. Over 260 such areas, which must fit strict criteria, have been designated in 70 countries. *MAB Networks:* MAB supports several international networks, informal groups that share information and resources. These include the Northern Science Network (high latitudes); the Network on Smaller Mediterranean Islands; the Alpine Network (European Alps); the Humid and Sub-Humid Tropical Forests Network; the Arid and Semi-Arid Zones Network; and the International Biosphere Reserve Network. Pub: *Nature and Resources* (quarterly journal); *InfoMAB* (newsletter, 3 times a year); biennial report; *MAB Bibliography;* MAB Book Series; MAB Technical Notes; MAB Report Series (Green Reports); MAB Information System; audio-visuals (catalog available).

■ World Heritage List. Under the 1972 Convention for the Protection of the World's Natural and Cultural Heritage, Unesco is responsible for maintaining the World Heritage List of natural and cultural properties that are of universal importance, transcending political and geographic boundaries. The List so far includes over 280 sites in 65 countries, and includes such places as the Grand Canyon, the Taj Mahal, Machu Picchu, and Auschwitz. Decisions on including properties in the List are made by Unesco's World Heritage Committee, which is advised by IUCN on natural sites and by the International Council on Monuments and Sites (ICOMOS) on cultural sites. Pub: Map and list.

■ International Environmental Education Programme (IEEP), a joint effort of Unesco and UNEP, promotes exchange of information about environmental education worldwide. Pub: *Connect* (quarterly newsletter); *Directory of Institutions Active in the Field of Environmental Education.*

■ Other Unesco programs. Several other intergovernmental programs in the science sector of Unesco relate to environmental and natural resource problems. These include the International Hydrological Programme (IHP), the Intergovernmental Oceanographic Commission (IOC), the International Geological Correlation Programme (IGCP), and the Coastal Marine Programme (COMAR), and the Unesco Information Programme on New and Renewable Sources of Energy.

United Nations Industrial Development Organization (UNIDO)
P.O. Box 300, Vienna International Centre, A-1400 Vienna, Austria. T: (43 222) 2631-0. Tx: 135612. C: UNIDO. Established 1965. Provides technical assistance and training and conducts research on promoting industry in developing countries. Its environmental concerns include health and safety in workplace environments, and environmental impacts of industrial development. UNIDO is now systematically integrating environmental considerations into its technical assistance projects; these include, for example, air and water pollution control measures and reduction of industrial hazards. The main UNIDO unit responsible is the Section for Integrated Industrial Projects of the Department of Industrial Operations. UNIDO maintains liaison offices in New York and Geneva. Pub: *Environmental Protection within the Context of the Work of UNIDO;* technical documents (e.g., *Industrial Water Use and Treatment Practices; Environmental Assessment and Management of the Fish Processing Industry*).

Universal Postal Union (UPU)
Case Postale, CH-3000 Berne 15, Switzerland. T: (41 31) 43 22 11. Tx: 912761. C: UPU. Fax: (41 31) 43 22 10. Established 1874. Promotes efficient operation of postal services. Among its publications directed to postal managers is *Saving Energy and Raw Materials.*

World Bank Group
1818 H Street, NW, Washington, DC 20433, USA. T: (1 202) 477-1234. Tx: 64145. C: INTBA-FRAD. Fax: (1 202) 477-6391. The World Bank Group is composed of the World Bank (International Bank for Reconstruction and Development), the International Development Association, and the International Finance Corporation. These institutions assist in the development of member countries through direct loans as well as the promotion of investments by private investors. In 1987, the Bank announced a reorganization that will include more attention to resource conservation and environmental aspects of development projects. A new Environment Department, overseen by the Vice President for Policy, Planning, and Research, reviews and evaluates economic development projects proposed

for financing from the standpoint of its potential effects on the environment, and to incorporate such environmental safeguards as are appropriate. In addition, a 5-year assessment of the most severely-threatened environments in 30 developing countries will be carried out; funding for forestry project will be increased; and the Bank will cooperate with Mediterranean countries to protect the Mediterranean Sea. The Bank has Regional Missions in Nairobi, Kenya; Abidjan, Côte d'Ivoire; and Bangkok, Thailand; as well as offices in New York, Paris, and Geneva.

World Health Organization (WHO)
20 avenue Appia, CH-1211 Geneva 27, Switzerland. T: (41 22) 791 21 11. Tx: 27821. C: UNISANTE. Fax: (41 22) 91 07 46. Established 1946. WHO's overall objective is "the attainment by all peoples of the highest possible level of health." Its Division of Environmental Health works to strengthen environmental health programs in governmental agencies. It assists countries in carrying out extensive health-related environmental monitoring and analysis of the data collected. WHO has programs in community water supply and sanitation; environmental pollution control, including chemical safety; public health aspects of housing and urban development; food safety; human resources for environmental health; and promotion of research. A number of activities in these fields are carried out jointly with other international organizations (e.g., the International Programme on Chemical Safety is a joint UNEP/ILO/WHO endeavor; there are Joint FAO/WHO Expert Committees on Food Additives; and the Health-Related Monitoring Program of the Global Environmental Monitoring System is a joint WHO/UNEP effort). WHO has regional offices in Brazzaville, Congo; Alexandria, Egypt; Copenhagen, Denmark; New Delhi, India; and Manila, Philippines, as well as liaison offices in New York and Addis Ababa, Ethiopia. It administers the International Agency for Research on Cancer in Lyon, France. The WHO Regional Office for the Americas/Pan American Sanitary Bureau is a joint organization of WHO and the Organization of American States. Pub: *World Health* (monthly, of general interest); *Bulletin of the World Health Organization* (semiannual scientific journal); Environmental Health Criteria Series; numerous manuals, training documents, and scientific studies, and other publications (catalogs available).

World Meteorological Organization (WMO)
Case Postale 5, CH-1211 Geneva 20, Switzerland. T: (41 22) 34 64 00. Tx: 23260. C: METEO-MOND. Fax: (41 22) 34 23 26. Established 1951 as successor to the International Meteorological Organization founded in 1878. WMO facilitates international cooperation in establishing networks of stations and centers to provide meteorological and hydrological services and observations; promotes the establishment and maintenance of systems for the rapid exchange of meteorological and related information; promotes standardization of meteorological and related observations and ensures the uniform publication of observations and statistics; furthers the application of meteorology to aviation, shipping, water problems, agriculture, and other human activities; promotes activities in operational hydrology and furthers close cooperation between meteorological and hydrological services; and encourages research and training in meteorology and related fields.

Global climate change is a major concern of WMO. Its World Climate Programme monitors climate variations and changes in order to be able to warn governments of climate impacts that may significantly affect human welfare and activities. The research component of the Programme is carried out jointly by WMO and the International Council of Scientific Unions (ICSU) and is described under ICSU in Part 5 of this book. Climate impact studies are coordinated by UNEP.

The WMO Hydrology and Water Resources Programme is concerned with qualitative and quantitative assessments and forecasts of water resources; standardization of all aspects of hydrological observations; and organized transfer of hydrological techniques in many areas, including forecasts and mitigation of floods related to tropical cyclones, severe storms, and rapid snowmelts. Technical assistance and training are provided to developing countries.

Members of WMO are the governments of 160 countries and territories. WMO maintains regional offices in Bujumbura, Burundi; and Asunción, Paraguay. Pub: *WMO Bulletin,* quarterly; *Meteorology and the Human Environment; Climate Variations, Drought, and Desertification; Man and the Composition of the Atmosphere;* numerous manuals and technical documents (catalog available).
■ Intergovernmental Panel on Climate Change (IPCC). This group, co-sponsored by WMO and UNEP, had its first meeting in 1988. It is charged with addressing knowledge gaps in science, impacts, and policy choices associated with global warming.

World Tourism Organization (WTO)
See listing in Part 5.

Part 5
Other Intergovernmental Organizations

African Development Bank (AfDB or ADB)
B.P. 1387, Abidjan 01, Côte d'Ivoire. T: (225) 32
07 11. Tx: 23717. C: AFDEV. Established 1963.
The regional development bank for Africa, with
some 50 African and 25 non-African member
states. A Socio-Environmental Policy Division is
the focal point for environmental matters, giving
guidance on policies and operational procedures,
coordinating technical tasks, reviewing projects,
developing guidance tools, and organizing training
activities. A detailed Programme for Environmental Activities, adopted in 1967, is the framework for further strengthening the role of AfDB
in the field of environment and development.
Pub: *ADB News* (monthly) *ABD Quarterly Review.*

**African Ministerial Conference on the
Environment**
Bureau of the Conference, care of UNEP Regional Office for Africa, P.O. Box 30552, Nairobi,
Kenya. T: (254 2) 333930. Tx: 22068. C:
UNITERRA. Fax: (254 2) 520711. Established
1985. Administers a cooperative, region-wide
program in environmental rehabilitation. Maintains six African environment networks: on
monitoring, soils and fertilizers, energy, water,
and environmental education and training.

African Timber Organization (ATO)
B.P. 1077, Libreville, Gabon. T: (241) 73 29 28.
Works for "cooperation in matters of forestry
management and timber marketing. Its object is
to allow member countries to study and coordinate
the ways and means of ensuring an optimum
development of their forest and timber products.
In order to reach these goals, the ATO sets for
itself the following objectives: (a) to ensure among
member countries a continuous exchange of
information and mutual support concerning their
forestry management, timber marketing, and
industrialization policies; and (b) to coordinate the
commercial policies of the member countries,
particularly in regard to prices, product designations, terminology and gradings, standardization
of conditioning and quality control, and tax
matters." Also concerned with "technological and
industrial research, particularly on unknown or
little-known tree species"; harmonizing "policies of
reforestation, and forestry and environmental
management"; and related matters. Members are
the governments of 12 African countries.

Arab Bank for Economic Development in Africa
(ABEDA)
P.O. Box 2640, Khartoum, Sudan. T: 73646.
Tx: 22248 sd. C: BADEA. Established 1974.
Development finance institution for non-Arab
countries in Africa; major areas for support are
economic infrastructure, agriculture, and industry.
According to CIDIE, an environmental specialist
has not been appointed to the BADEA staff.
Members are the governments of 17 Arab
countries.

Arab Fund for Economic and Social Development
(AFESD)
P.O. Box 21923, Safat, Kuwait. T: (965) 2451580.
Tx: 22153. C: INMARABI. Established 1968.
Regional development finance institution for the
Arab states.

Arab League
See League of Arab States

Asian Development Bank (ADB)
P.O. Box 789, 1099 Manila, Philippines. T: (63 2)
711-3851. Tx: 23103. C: ASIANBANK. Fax: (63
2) 741-7961. Established 1966. An international
development finance institution for the Asia-
Pacific region. Members are the governments of
47 countries in Asia and the Pacific, as well as in
Europe and North America. Environment Unit,
set up in 1987, works to "ensure the incorporation
of environmental and natural resources planning
and management concerns" in Bank activities. In
addition, ADB conducts in-house seminars on
environmental planning, and funds projects designed to promote environmentally-sound development (e.g., reforestation in the Philippines; lake
basin planning in Thailand; and strengthening the
national environmental protection agency in
China). Pub: Annual report (includes an environmental section); Environment Paper Series;
Environmental Planning and Management (symposium proceedings); *Economic Analysis of the
Environmental Impacts of Development Projects*;
guidebooks and guidelines.

Association of Southeast Asian Nations (ASEAN)
P.O. Box 2072, Jakarta, Indonesia. Established
1967. Fosters cooperation among 6 Southeast
Asian states. Two ASEAN committees are concerned with environmental and natural resource

matters. The Committee on Food, Agriculture, and Forestry (COFAF) has projects in afforestation, forest and watershed management, and timber technology. The Committee on Science and Technology (COST) includes an Environment Programme, the objective of which is "to promote the proper management of ASEAN environment so that it can sustain continued economic development while maintaining a high quality of life." Environmental projects, in an early stage of implementation in 1988, are (1) anti-pollution technologies for urban and rural areas; technology transfer on the treatment of effluents from palm oil and rubber industries; and a training program in environmental education for science teachers and supervisors. COST also has projects in marine science and climatology. The ASEAN Institute of Forest Management, located in Kuala Lumpur, Malaysia, provides expertise to member countries in forest resource inventory, forest management, and reforestation of natural tropical forests, as well as training. Members of ASEAN are the governments of Brunei Darussalam, Indonesia, Malaysia, Philippines, Singapore, and Thailand.
■ ASEAN Council for Higher Education in Environment (ACHEE), c/o School of Urban and Regional Planning, University of the Philippines, Diliman, Manila, Philippines. Established 1983 to strengthen activities of universities in the ASEAN countries in teaching, research, and extension in environmental matters.

Association of the Central Alps
(Association des Régions des Alpes Centrales) (ARGE ALP)
Amt der Tiroler Landesregierung, A-6010 Innsbruck, Austria. T: (53 5222) 28701, ext. 204. Tx: 53891. Founded 1972. Promotes transfrontier cooperation on common ecological, social, cultural, and economic problems of the Alpine regions of Austria, West Germany, Italy, and Switzerland. Members are regional authorities of the 4 countries.

Baltic Marine Environment Protection Committee
(Helsinki Commission) (HELCOM)
Mannerheimintie 12 A, SF-00100 Helsinki 10, Finland. T; (358 90) 602 366. Tx: 125105 hlcom sf. Fax: (358 90) 644 577. Established 1974. Works to protect the marine environment of the Baltic Sea area from all types of pollution. Members are the governments of Denmark, Finland, German Democratic Republic, Federal Republic of Germany, Poland, Sweden, and USSR.

Bonn Commission
New Court, 48 Carey St., London WC2A 2JE, England. Established 1969. Promotes cooperation among states to control pollution of the North Sea. Works closely with the Oslo and Paris Commissions.

CAB International (CABI)
Wallingford OX10 8DE, England. T: (44 491) 32111. Tx: 847964 comagg g. Fax: (44 491) 33508. Established 1928 as the Commonwealth Agricultural Bureaux. A major center for information and scientific services in agriculture and allied subjects, with over 400 employees. Members are the governments of 29 countries. CAB Abstracts, issued monthly or quarterly, are leading sources of information on scientific literature in agriculture and related fields; they include *Forestry Abstracts; Forest Products Abstracts; Irrigation and Drainage Abstracts; Leisure, Recreation & Tourism Abstracts; and Rural Development Abstracts.* CABI Abstracts have been designated by UNEP as a "special sectoral source" for information on agriculture and the environment. Other publications include *Soils and Fertilizers,* monthly, and *Biocontrol News and Information,* quarterly.
    CAB incorporates 4 institutes and 11 bureaus; among them is:
■ CAB International Institute of Biological Control (CIBC). Provides information and advice on biological control, undertakes research and implementation of biological control of major pests and weeds, and participates in integrated pest management programs in association with other agencies. CIBC has field stations in Switzerland, India, Pakistan, Kenya, and Trinidad and Tobago.

Caribbean Community (CARICOM)
P.O. Box 10827, Georgetown, Guyana. T: (592 2) 69281. Tx: 2263. C: CARIBSEC. A regional group of countries within the (British) Commonwealth. Includes:
■ Caribbean Environmental Health Institute (CEHI), P.O. Box 1111, the Morne, Castries, St. Lucia. T: (1 809) 45-22501. Established 1979. Provides technical and advisory services to member states of the Caribbean Community in all areas of environmental management. Major concerns are bacterial and pesticide pollution.

Caribbean Development Bank (CDB)
P.O. Box 408, Wildey, St. Michael, Barbados. T: (1 809) 42-61152. Tx: WB2287. C: CANIBANK. Established 1970. Regional development finance institution for the Caribbean; emphasis is on supporting infrastructure requirements such as roads, ports, and water supply. According to CIDIE, no environmental specialist has been appointed to the staff. Members are the governments of 20 states and territories.

Central American Bank for Economic Integration
(CABEI)
Apartado Postal 772, Tegucigalpa, Honduras. T: (504) 222230. Tx: 1103. C: BANCADIE. Established 1961. Regional development finance institution for Central America. The Bank has been implementing an Environmental Planning and Analysis System to introduce the environmental dimension in the financial planning process. Bank members are the governments of 5 countries.

Club of Friends of the Sahel
(Club des Amis du Sahel)
c/o CILSS, B.P. 7049, Ouagadougou, Burkina
Faso; or care of OECD Development Assistance
Committee, 2, rue André Pascal, F-75775 Paris,
France. T: (33 1) 45 24 90 22. Facilitates
coordination of development activities among
governments of Sahelian countries and donor
countries which are members of OECD. Control
of ecological deterioration is major concern. Also
known as Sahel Club (Club du Sahel).

Colombo Plan Bureau
This regional organization for cooperative economic development in Asia and the Pacific reports
that it does not deal with environmental matters.

**Commission for the Conservation of Antarctic
Marine Living Resources** (CCAMLR)
25 Old Wharf, Hobart, Tasmania 7000, Australia.
T: (61 02) 310366. Tx: AA57236. C: CCAMLR.
Fax: (61 02) 23 2714. Established 1980. Works
for the conservation and rational use of marine
living resources (including fish, mollusks, crusta-
ceans, and all other species of living organisms,
including birds) in the area south of 60° South
latitude and the area between that latitude and the
Antarctic Convergence. The Commission facilitates research; compiles data; disseminates information; identifies conservation needs; analyzes the
effectiveness of conservation measures; formulates, adopts, and revises conservation measures;
and implements a system of observation and
inspection. Maintains a Scientific Committee and
various technical working groups; sponsors occasional workshops on such topics as ocean variability, krill management, and the ecology of Southern
baleen whales. Members are the governments of
Argentina, Australia, Belgium, Brazil, Chile,
France, German Democratic Republic, Federal
Republic of Germany, India, Japan, Republic of
Korea, New Zealand, Norway, Poland, South
Africa, Spain, USSR, UK, and USA, and the
EEC. Pub: *Newsletter; Basic Documents;* reports
of meetings of the Commission and the Scientific
Committee.

**Commission for the Convention on Future
Multilateral Cooperation in North-East Atlantic
Fisheries**
Great Westminster House, Room 336, Horseferry
Road, London SW1P 2AE, England. T: (44 1) 216
6038. Tx: 21271. Established 1980 as successor to
the North-East Atlantic Fisheries Commission.
Works to manage fisheries in the North-East
Atlantic Ocean. Members are governments of 22
countries and the EEC.

**Committee of International Development
Institutions on the Environment** (CIDIE)
P.O. Box 30552, Nairobi, Kenya. T: (254 2)
333930. Tx: 22068 unep ke. Established 1980.
Encourages and facilitates the integration of the
environmental dimension into the development
assistance process. The principal mechanism for
doing so is an annual report by each member

institution. These are then discussed at an annual
meeting. Each year, meetings focus on different
priority subject areas, e.g., cooperative
arrangements with NGOs, incorporating natural
hazard assessment into project preparation, coun-
tering desertification in Africa, and use of pesticides. Bilateral donor governments and NGOs
attend meetings as observers. Other CIDIE activities include exchange of information and technical
cooperation. The CIDIE Secretariat is housed at
UNEP Headquarters. Members are: Arab Bank
for Economic Development in Africa, Asian
Development Bank, Caribbean Development Bank,
Inter-American Development Bank, World Bank,
Commission of the European Communities,
Organization of American States, UN Develop-
ment Programme, UNEP, African Development
Bank, European Investment Bank, International
Fund for Agricultural Development, Nordic In-
vestment Bank, and Central American Bank for
Economic Integration.

Commonwealth Secretariat
Marlborough House, Pall Mall, London SW1Y
5HX, England. Established 1965 as the focal
point for the Commonwealth, an association of
the UK and some 50 of its former colonies. Pub:
Commonwealth Currents, bimonthly magazine;
numerous reports, leaflets, and manuals (catalog
available). Under the Secretariat are:
■ The Commonwealth Fund for Technical Cooperation (CFTC) provides technical assistance to
developing Commonwealth countries. Mineral
exploitation, agriculture, forestry, and fisheries
have received major attention in the program.
■ The Commonwealth Science Council (CSC)
promotes cooperation among scientists in Commonwealth countries; it includes applied programs
in energy, renewable natural resources, and environmental planning. In each area, CSC brings
together specialists to define an area of work, sets
up a network, and raises funding.

**Cooperative Council for the Arab States of the
Gulf** (Gulf Cooperation Council) (GCC)
P.O. Box 7153, Riyadh 11462, Saudi Arabia. T:
(966 1) 4827777. Tx: 203635 tawini sj. Fax: (966
1) 4829089. The GCC works for cooperation
among the Arab countries of the Gulf region.
The GCC Supreme Council (heads of state) in
1985 approved "General Policies and Principles of
Environmental Protection for GCC States," which
led to adoption of an environmental action plan
which calls for six projects, each to be carried out
by a member state. The initial projects are
surveys of environmental problems, laws, research, education, training, and organizations in
the region. Technical meetings and studies have
focused on such topics as radiation protection,
environmental assessment, recycling, industrial air
pollution, and toxic substances. GCC members
are the governments of Saudi Arabia, Kuwait,
United Arab Emirates, Bahrain, Qatar, and Oman.
Pub: Surveys; brochures.

Council for Mutual Economic Assistance (CMEA)
Kalinin Prospect 56, 121205 Moscow G-205,
USSR. T: (7 095) 290 91 11. Tx: 411141. Established 1949. Promotes multilateral cooperation
among socialist countries. Members are the
governments of Bulgaria, Cuba, Czechoslovakia,
German Democratic Republic, Hungary, Mongolia, Poland, Romania, Viet-Nam, and USSR.
Includes (contact through Moscow office):
■ CMEA Coordinating Centre on Hygienic Aspects of Environmental Health
■ CMEA Coordinating Centre for Protection of
Ecosystems
■ CMEA Coordinating Centre for Atmospheric
Pollution
■ CMEA Coordinating Centre for Socioeconomic,
Organizational and Legal Aspects of Environmental Protection
■ CMEA Coordinating Centre for Study of World
Oceans, Development and Techniques for Exploration and Utilization of Resources.

Council of Europe
B.P. 431 R 6, F-67006 Strasbourg Cedex, France.
T: (44 88) 61 49 61. Tx: 870 943. Established
1949. An "organization of 21 parliamentary
democracies working together for the greater
unity of Europe," the Council is the oldest and
largest of the European political institutions.
One of the 15 permanent steering committees of
the Council is the European Committee for the
Conservation of Nature and Natural Resources,
which has Committees of Experts for the Planning
and Management of the Natural Environment; the
Conservation of Wildlife and Natural Habitats;
Protected Areas; and Environmental Education
and Training. Programs are carried out by the
Council's Environment and Natural Resources
Division, which includes the Documentation and
Information Centre for the Environment and
Nature. The Centre, working through national
agencies in member states, guides and coordinates
European action in this field. The Council also
administers the 1979 Convention on the Conservation of European Wildlife and Natural Habitats
(the Bern Convention), awards the European
Diploma "for natural areas, sites, or features of
international value," and has established the
European Network of Biogenetic Reserves. The
European Committee issues numerous recommendations (e.g., on pesticide use; on forestry policy;
and on soil protection). Members of the Council
of Europe are the governments of 21 Western
European countries. Pub: The Centre publishes a
newsletter and a journal, *Naturopa,* as well as
handbooks and reports.

Ecosystem Conservation Group.
See listing in Part 6

European Community (EC)
Rue de la Loi 200, B-1049 Brussels, Belgium.
T: (32 2) 235 11 11. Tx: 21877. C: COMEUR.
Consists of the European Coal and Steel Community (ECSC, established 1952), the European
Economic Community (EEC, established 1958),

and the European Atomic Energy Community
(EURATOM, established 1958). General purposes
are to achieve economic integration among
member countries through a common market,
common external tariff, and common policies and
institutions.

EC involvement in environmental matters
comes from (1) a commitment to improve living
standards in the Community; (2) preserving free
trade by harmonizing legislation; and (3) the
international nature of environmental problems.
Since 1973, the EC has enacted over 100 pieces of
environmental legislation and created programs
covering water, air, noise, and chemical pollution;
protection and rational management of land;
protection of fauna and flora; and waste
management. The EC also has its own program of
environmental research and development; has
established a common system of environmental
impact assessment for major public or private
development projects; and has organized a
network of pilot primary and secondary schools
teaching environmental studies as part of the
curriculum. The EC is a party to a number of
international conventions on environmental
problems, and participates in the environmental
activities of many other international organizations.

The EC nuclear energy research program
includes studies on nuclear safety and
management of nuclear waste. Environmental
considerations are integrated into other areas of
EC activity, e.g., agriculture, transportation, and
energy production.

Another concern is promoting the integration
of environmental requirements in Third-World
development activities of EC institutions such as
the European Investment Bank (listed below) and
European Development Fund, and also by
coordinating EC member states' individual
development policies. Members of the EC are the
governments of Belgium, Denmark, Federal
Republic of Germany, Greece, Spain, France,
Ireland, Italy, Luxembourg, Netherlands, Portugal,
and United Kingdom. Includes:
■ European Investment Bank (EIB), Boulevard
Konrad Adenauer 100, L-2950 Luxembourg-Ville
Luxembourg. T: (352) 43791. Tx: 3530. C:
BANKEUROP. Established 1957 under the EEC
Treaty. The EIB makes loans for, among other
purposes, economic development of the European
Community's less-privileged regions, primarily for
projects in industry, infrastructure, and energy.
Although the Bank has no separate environment
unit, some 35 technical advisors specializing in
individual economic sectors are responsible for
assessing the environmental impact of all projects
proposed for funding. In addition, many of the
projects funded relate to environmental
protection, including afforestation, sewerage,
water supply, erosion control, and energy
conservation.

Federation of Arab Scientific Research Councils (FASRC)
P.O. Box 13027, Baghdad, Iraq. T: (964 1) 5381090. C: BAHTHARAB. Tx: 212466 acars ik. Established 1976. Fosters collaboration among scientific bodies in all Arab states; plans joint research projects, emphasizing efforts related to Arab development plans. Maintains Committees on Health, Environment, and Housing Research, and on Natural Resources Research. Members are 16 Arab countries, represented by scientific research institutions.

Interafrican Committee for Hydraulic Studies (ICHS) (Comité Interafricain d'Etudes Hydrauliques) (CIEH)
B.P. 369, Ouagadougou, Burkina Faso. T: (226 3) 33 34 76. Tx: CIEH 5277 BF. Established 1960. Fosters cooperation among states and provides technical assistance in water sciences and technology, including climatology. Members are governments of 13 West and Central African countries.

Inter-American Development Bank (IDB)
1300 New York Avenue, NW, Washington, D.C. 20577, USA. T: (1 202) 623-1000. Established 1959. An international financial institution for social and economic development in Latin America. "In recent years, the IDB has taken systematic steps to increase its commitment to environmentally sound projects...In 1983, the Bank changed its own internal mechanism to ensure that policy and projects to be reviewed are subject to stringent environmental impact criteria at the earliest stage of the [funding] cycle." Maintains an Environmental Management Committee. Members of IDB are the governments of 44 countries in the region and elsewhere. Pub: Annual report; *Conference on the Environment* (proceedings of a 1987 meeting).

Inter-American Tropical Tuna Commission (IATTC)
c/o Scripps Institution of Oceanography, University of California, La Jolla, California 92093, USA. T: (1 619) 546-7100, ext. 301. Tx: 697 115. Established 1949. Conducts research on and works for conservation of the tuna fishery of the eastern Pacific Ocean; works to avoid needless and careless killing of porpoises in tuna fishing. Members are the governments of Nicaragua, Panama, USA, Japan, and France (Ecuador, Mexico, Costa Rica, and Canada have withdrawn).

International Association of Fish and Wildlife Agencies
444 North Capitol Street, NW., Suite 534, Washington, DC 20001, USA. T: (1 202) 624-7890. Promotes cooperation among governmental agencies at the national and sub-national (state and provincial) levels in the Western Hemisphere. Pub: Newsletter; proceedings of annual conference.

International Baltic Sea Fishery Commission (IBSFC)
ul. Hoza 20, PL-00 950 Warsaw, Poland. T: (48 22) 28 86 47. Tx: 817421 GOMO PL. Established 1973. Regulation of fisheries and conservation of living resources of the Baltic Sea. Members are the governments of Finland, German Democratic Republic, Poland, Sweden, and USSR, and the EEC.

International Centre for Integrated Mountain Development (ICIMOD)
P.O. Box 3226, Jawalakhel, Lalitpur, Kathmandu, Nepal. T: (977) 521575. Tx: 2439 icimod np. Established 1981, by agreement between Unesco and the Government of Nepal. Works to promote economically- and environmentally-sound development of the Hindu Kush Himalayas through regional cooperation. Activities focus on watershed management, rural energy planning, and engineering fragile environments, as well as creating off-farm employment. Members are the governments of Afghanistan, Bangladesh, Bhutan, Burma, China, India, Nepal, and Pakistan.

International Commission for Environmental Assessment (ICEA)
See Working Group on an International Commission for Environmental Assessment

International Commission for Scientific Exploration of the Mediterranean Sea (ICSEM)
16 boulevard de Suisse, MC-98030 Monte Carlo, Monaco. Established 1910. Promotes cooperation among institutions and individual researchers concerned with the Mediterranean environment. Main activity is a biennial assembly. Maintains a Committee on Combating Marine Pollution. Members are the governments of 17 countries. Pub: Proceedings of assemblies.

International Commission for the Conservation of Atlantic Tuna (ICCAT)
Príncipe de Vergara 17-7, E-28001 Madrid, Spain. T: (34 1) 431 03 29. Tx: 46330 iccat e. Established 1969. Works to maintain populations of tuna and tuna-like fish in the Atlantic Ocean in order to permit maximum sustainable catch. Members are governments of 23 countries.

International Commission for the Southeast Atlantic Fisheries (ICSEAF)
65 Paseo de la Habana, E-28036 Madrid, Spain. T: (34 1) 458 87 66. Tx: 45533. Established 1969. Works to ensure a "rational exploitation" of fisheries in the Southeast Atlantic Ocean. Members are governments of 17 countries.

International Council for the Exploration of the Sea (ICES)
Palægade 2-4, DK-1261 Copenhagen K, Denmark. T: (45 1) 15 42 25. Tx: 22498 ices dk. C: MEREXPLORATION. Founded 1902. The "oldest intergovernmental organization in the world concerned with marine and fishery science. Since its founding...ICES has been the scientific

forum for the exchange of information and ideas on the seas and their *living* resources and for the promotion and coordination of research undertaken by experts" within its member countries. The work of ICES is designed to meet the needs not only of its member countries but also of various regulatory commissions concerned with fish resources in the North Atlantic, including the North Sea and Baltic Sea, and with pollution. The Council is "concerned with all relevant aspects of oceanographic and marine biological research: the physical and chemical properties of the sea as the environment which supports marine life; the biology, ecology, and population dynamics of exploited fish and shellfish stocks; the contamination and quality of the marine environment; fish capture techniques; marine mammal studies; and mariculture." Holds annual meetings and symposia. Maintains a Marine Environmental Quality Committee, a Marine Mammals Committee, and Advisory Committee on Marine Pollution, and various technical committees on fish. Members of ICES are the governments of 18 countries in Europe and North America. Pub: Newsletter, semiannual; several scientific serials, including an annual statistical yearbook.

International Tropical Timber Organization (ITTO)
Sangyo Boeki Centre Building, 2 Yamashita-cho, Naka-ku, Yokohama 231, Japan. T: (81 45) 671 7045. Tx: 3822480 itto j. Fax: (81 45) 671 7007. Founded 1985. Provides a framework for cooperation and consultation between tropical timber producing and consuming countries; works to promote expansion and diversification of international trade in tropical timbers; promotes research and development to improve forest management and wood utilization; encourages processing in producing countries to promote industrialization and increase export earnings; encourages development of national policies aiming at sustainable utilization of tropical forests and their genetic resources, and at maintaining ecological balance. Maintains a Committee on Reforestation and Forest Management. Governed by the International Tropical Timber Council (ITTC), which meets annually. Pub: Annual report. Members are governments of 41 producing and consuming countries.

International Union for Conservation of Nature and Natural Resources (IUCN) (World Conservation Union)
See listing in Part 6

International Whaling Commission (IWC)
The Red House, Station Road, Histon, Cambridge CB4 4NP, England. T: (44 22023) 3971. Tx: 817960. Established 1946 under the International Convention for the Regulation of Whaling. "The main duty of the IWC is to keep under review and revise as necessary the measures laid down in the Schedule to the Convention governing the conduct of whaling. These measures provide for the complete protection of certain species of whales; designate specified ocean areas as whale sanctuaries; set the maximum catches on whales which may be taken in any one season; prescribe open and closed seasons and areas for whaling; fix size limits above and below which certain species of whales may not be killed; prohibit the capture of suckling calves and female whales accompanied by calves; and require the compilation of catch reports and other statistical and biological records. The Commission also encourages, coordinates, and funds research on whales and promotes studies into related matters such as the humaneness of the killing operations, and the management of aboriginal subsistence whaling."

Although there is currently a moratorium on commercial whaling, several countries conduct whaling for "scientific research purposes;" in addition, aboriginal subsistence whaling is permitted in Alaska, Siberia, Greenland, and St. Vincent and the Grenadines.

The IWC holds an annual meeting; maintains a Scientific Committee and a Technical Committee (which has standing subcommittees on Infractions and on Aboriginal Subsistence Whaling). Members of IWC are the governments of 38 countries. Pub: Annual report; Special Issues (e.g., bibliographies; scientific studies); statistics; regulations.

Inter-Parliamentary Union (IPU)
C.P. 438, CH-1211 Geneva 19, Switzerland. T: (41 22) 34 41 50. Tx: 289784. Established 1888. Promotes personal contacts among members of all parliaments. Publishes a newsletter on environmental affairs for parliamentarians in cooperation with UNEP and the IUCN Environmental Law Centre. Has an Ad Hoc Review Committee on Environment. Members of IPU are national groups in over 100 countries. Pub: *Inter-Parliamentary Bulletin*, quarterly; *Constitutional and Parliamentary Information*, quarterly; reports and conference proceedings.

Islamic Development Bank (IDB)
P.O. Box 5925, Jeddah 21432, Saudi Arabia. T: (966 2) 6361400. Tx: 601137. Fax: (966 2) 6366871. Established 1973. Fosters "economic development and social progress" in member countries and Muslim communities. No separate environment unit is indicated in IDB's annual report. Members are the governments of 44 countries in Asia and Africa. Pub: Annual report.

Latin American Housing and Human Settlements Development Organization
(Organización Latinoamericana de Vivienda y Desarollo de los Sentamientos Humanos) (OLAVI) Avenida 10 de Agosto y Cordero, Quito, Ecuador. T: (593 2) 459 291. A permanent organization of the Latin American Economic System, an intergovernmental body of 25 countries headquartered in Caracas, Venezuela.

League of Arab States. (LAS)
37 avenue Khereddine Pacha, Tunis, Tunisia. T: (216 1) 89 01 00. Tx: 13241 tn. Established 1945. Major regional intergovernmental organization, also known as the Arab League. Members are the governments of 22 countries. Includes:
■ Arab League Educational, Cultural and Scientific Organization (ALECSO), P.O. Box 24017, Safat, Kuwait. T: (965) 44 81 30. Tx: 3234. A specialized organization of LAS. Maintains a Department of Natural Sciences and Technology; administers the Red Sea and Gulf of Aden Environment Programme.
■ Arab Centre for the Studies of Arid Zones and Dry Lands (ACSAD), P.O. Box 2440, Damascus, Syria. T: (963 11) 755713. C: ACSAD. Tx: ACSAD 412697 sy. Established 1971 as a specialized organization of LAS. Promotes scientific and applied studies of problems related to aridity and dryness in the Arab countries, with emphasis on agriculture. Departments include Water Resources Studies, Soil Studies, Plant Studies, and Climatological Studies.
■ Arab Forestry Institute, Latakia, Syria.

Nordic Council (NC)
Box 19506, S-104 32 Stockholm, Sweden.
T: (46 8) 14 34 20. Tx: 12 867. Fax: (46 8) 11 75 36. Established 1952. Promotes cooperation among the Nordic countries. Issues recommendations and statements of opinion to the Nordic Council of Ministers (see below) and the respective governments. Maintains a Social and Environmental Committee as one of 6 major standing committees. Members of the NC are parliamentarians from Åland, Denmark, the Faroe Islands, Greenland, Finland, Iceland, Norway, and Sweden. Pub: *Nordic Cooperation,* quarterly; various yearbooks and reports.

Nordic Council of Ministers
Store Strandsstraede 18, DK-1255 Copenhagen K, Denmark. T: (45 1) 11 47 11. Tx: 155 44. Fax: (45 1) 11 47 11. Established 1971. Administers programs of cooperation among the five Nordic governments. Activities include harmonizing environmental regulations and conducting joint research on environmental and natural resource problems. The Council includes Nordic Senior Executives' Committees for Environmental Affairs, for Agricultural and Forestry Questions, and for Fishery Affairs. Members of the Council are the governments of Denmark, Finland, Iceland, Norway, and Sweden.

Nordic Investment Bank (NIB)
P.O. Box 249, Unionkatu 30, SS00171, Helsinki, Finland. T: (358) 018001. Established 1975. A regional development finance institution which provides loans for projects in both the Nordic countries and (since 1982) in developing countries.

North Atlantic Salmon Conservation Organization (NASCO)
11 Rutland Square, Edinburgh EH1 2AS, Scotland. T: (44 31) 228 2551. Tx: 265871. Established 1984. Works for conservation and rational management of salmon stocks in the North Atlantic. Has regional commissions for North America, Greenland, and the Northeast Atlantic. Members are governments of 8 countries and the EEC.

North Atlantic Treaty Organization (NATO)
B-1110 Brussels, Belgium. T: (32 2) 241 00 40. Tx: 23867. Established 1949. Organized primarily for mutual defense, NATO is also active in environmental matters. One of its 6 divisions is the Division of Scientific and Environmental Affairs, which includes the Committee on the Challenges of Modern Society (CCMS), established in 1969. A major purpose of CCMS is to promote international action to halt the degradation of the environment; work is carried out on a decentralized basis by NATO countries acting as pilot countries for individual projects, by stimulating national and international action, through open participation and results, and with concerted follow-up activity. Some 30 CCMS projects have been completed; they have ranged from investigations of solar energy and oil spill control to rural passenger transportation and hazardous materials. Some 15 studies are underway. Pub: *NATO Review*; various handbooks and reports.

North Pacific Fur Seal Commission (NPFSC)
c/o National Marine Fisheries Service, Washington, DC 20235, USA. Established 1958. Works to maintain the "maximum sustainable productivity" of the fur seal resources of the North Pacific Ocean. Members are the governments of Canada, USA, Japan, and USSR.

Northwest Atlantic Fisheries Organization (NAFO)
P.O. Box 638, Dartmouth, Nova Scotia B2Y 3Y9, Canada. T: (1 902) 469-9105. Promotes investigation, protection, and conservation of the fishery resources of the Northwest Atlantic. Members are governments of 22 countries. Supersedes the International Commission for the Northwest Atlantic Fisheries.

Organisation for Economic Co-operation and Development (OECD)
2 rue André Pascal, F-75775 Paris, France. T: (33 1) 45 24 82 00. Tx: 620160 ocde. Established 1961. Promotes economic and social welfare in member countries and harmonious development of the world economy. The OECD Environment Committee is responsible for economic and policy aspects of OECD's work in that field. Its work has led to adoption by member countries of agreements setting out guiding principles on the international trade aspects of environmental policies (e.g., the "polluter pays" principle); and of agreements on toxic chemicals, noise, waste, air pollution, water pollution, transfrontier pollution, energy production, and coastal management. The Committee also monitors changes in the state of the environment, studies the relationship between environmental and economic policies, and con-

ducts research on the impact of activities by industrialized countries on the environments of Third World countries. A special Chemicals Programme promotes cooperation among member governments in controlling some 80,000 hazardous products on the international market. Other OECD units concerned with environmental and natural resource problems include the Group on Urban Affairs (environmental aspects of the built environment) and the Committee for Fisheries. The OECD Development Assistance Committee (DAC) is an important forum for the main capital-exporting countries to consult on assistance to developing countries; its annual report is a basic source of information on flows of aid. Members of OECD are the governments of 24 industrialized countries: in North America and Western Europe, as well as Australia, Japan, and New Zealand (Yugoslavia has special status). Pub: *News from OECD*, monthly newsletter; *OECD Observer*, bimonthly magazine; numerous reports, including the annual *Development Co-operation Report*, a key source of data on aid flows.

Organization of American States (OAS)
17th St. and Constitution Ave., NW, Washington, DC 20006, USA. T: (1 202) 789-3000. Established 1890; "the oldest international regional organization in the world." Provides a forum for political, economic, social, and cultural cooperation among the 31 member states of the Western Hemisphere. Several OAS units are concerned with the environment and natural resources:
■ Inter-Secretarial Committee on the Human Environment, formed in 1972, coordinates OAS activities related to the environment.
■ General Secretariat. The permanent and central organ of the OAS in Washington. Carries out regional development projects that frequently include environmental and natural resource management components. The Department of Regional Development (DRD) is the "environmental focal point" for the General Secretariat of OAS and includes an Environmental Management Advisor. It is a significant source of technical assistance to member governments in pre-investment studies that result in fundable projects; such studies include environmental impact analysis. Examples of recent activities conducted by the Department: analysis of forestry management policy in Dominica; a soil conservation strategy for the Pastaza River Basin in Ecuador; and a plan to manage the natural resource base in the Eastern Caribbean. The OAS Department of Scientific Affairs (DSA) administers research projects related to environmental protection, and monitors the implementation of the 1940 Convention on Nature Protection and Wildlife Preservation in the Western Hemisphere, as well as the Convention on Protection of Flora, Fauna, and Scenic Beauty of the Western Hemisphere. OAS also sponsors the Inter-American Center for the Integral Development of Water and Land Resources (CIDIAT) and the Inter-American Center for Regional Development (CINDER). Secretariat

publications include such guidelines as *Minimal Conflict: Guidelines for Planning the Development of American Humid Tropical Environments* and *Environmental Quality and River Basin Development: A Model for Integrated Analysis and Planning*.
■ Pan American Health Organization (PAHO), 525 23rd Street, NW, Washington, DC 20037, USA. T: (1 202) 861-3200. This is both a specialized organization of the OAS and the regional agency of the World Health Organization.
■ Inter-American Indian Institute (IAII), Avenida Insurgentes Sur, Colonia Florida, Mexico DF 01030, Mexico. Established 1940. Conducts research, technical assistance, and training to help Indian groups in the Western Hemisphere with their health, educational, economic, and social problems. Recent projects have included workshops on bioenergy systems and rural development for Indian community workers.
■ Inter-American Institute for Cooperation on Agriculture) (IICA), Apartado 55-2200, Coronado, Costa Rica. T: (506) 29-0222. Tx: 2144. C: IICA. Fax: (506) 29-4741. Established 1942. The OAS specialized agency for agriculture.

Organization of Eastern Caribbean States (OECS)
Natural Resources Management Project, P.O. Box 1383, Castries, St. Lucia. T: (1 809) 45-21837. Tx: 6325 oecs nrmp lc. The Project, started in 1986, focuses at the regional level on improvement and harmonization of environmental legislation, strengthening of decision-making, and economic evaluation of natural resources. Country projects are concerned with land-use management, watershed and coastal zone management, and international exchange of professional staff. Local projects embrace self-help activities emphasizing community education. Members of OECS are the governments of 8 island countries. Pub: Newsletter; reports and working papers.

Oslo Commission (OSCOM)
New Court, 48 Carey St., London WC2A 2JE, England. T: (44 1) 242 9927. Established 1972. Controls disposal of waste at sea by regulating dumping and incinerating activities in the Northeast Atlantic. Works closely with the Bonn and Paris Commissions. Members are governments of 13 European countries; EEC is an observer.

Pan American Center for Sanitary Engineering and Environmental Sciences (Centro Panamericano de Ingeniería Sanitaria y Ciencias del Ambiente) (CEPIS)
Casilla Postal 4337, Lima 100, Peru. T: (51 14) 35 41 35. Tx: 21052. C: CEPIS. Established 1968 by the Pan American Health Organization, which is a joint agency of the Organization of American States and the World Health Organization. Provides technical assistance to PAHO member countries in planning, implementing, and evaluating environmental health programs.

Pan American Health Organization (PAHO)
See Organization of American States

Paris Commission (PARICOM)
New Court, 48 Carey St., London WC2A 2JE, England. T: (44 1) 242 9927. Established 1974. Works to prevent marine pollution in the Northeast Atlantic region from land-based sources. Works closely with the Bonn and Oslo Commissions. Members and observers are government representatives of 14 European countries and the EEC.

Permanent Interstate Committee for Drought Control in the Sahel
(Comité Permanent Inter-Etats de Lutte contre la Sécheresse dans le Sahel) (CILSS)
B.P. 7049, Ouagadougou, Burkina Faso.
T: (226 3) 30 67 59. Tx: 5263. Established 1973. Organizes joint efforts to control drought and its effects in the Sahel-Sudan zone of Africa. Maintains the Centre for Agrometeorology and Operational Hydrology (Niamey, Niger), for training; and the Institut du Sahel (Bamako, Mali), for coordination of research and training. The Club of Friends of the Sahel (separately listed) acts as the Committee's link to the broader international community. Members are the governments of Burkina, Cape Verde, Chad, Gambia, Guinea-Bissau, Mali, Mauritania, Niger, and Senegal. Includes:
■ Institute of the Sahel (Institut du Sahel), B.P. 1530, Bamako, Mali. T: 22 21 48. Tx: 432 insah. Conducts research, training, and dissemination of scientific and technical information in support of the objectives of CILSS. Includes a coordination cell for research in ecology and environment. Operates the computerized Sahelian Scientific and Technical Documentation and Information Network (RESADOC). Pub: Newsletter; bibliographies.

Permanent South Pacific Commission (Comisión Permanente del Pacífico Sur) (CPPS)
Calle 76, No. 9-88, P.O. Box 92292, Bogotá, Colombia. T: (57 1) 235-5145. Tx: 41299 cpps co. C: PACIFICO SUR. Established 1952. Coordinates maritime policies among member states, in cooperation with other international agencies; conducts scientific research and conservation projects to "protect, preserve, and exploit" the South East Pacific marine environment and its resources; training and information activities. Main current projects focus on studying the "El Niño" Phenomenon; fisheries development; marine pollution control; and nontraditional foodstuffs. Members are the governments of Colombia, Chile, Ecuador, and Peru. Pub: Newsletters (some in English and Spanish) and research reports (in Spanish). *See also* South Pacific Commission.

Ramsar Convention Bureau
Avenue du Mont-Blanc, CH-1196 Gland, Switzerland. T: (41 22) 64 71 81. Tx: 419624.
Fax: (41 22) 64 46 15. Administers the 1971 Convention on Wetlands of International Importance Especially as Waterfowl Habitat (the Ramsar Convention), under which signatory states designate protected wetlands for an "International List" (over 400 have been so designated to date) and agree to make "wise use" of wetlands, whether or not they are included on the List. Contracting parties are the governments of 51 countries. Pub: Newsletter, quarterly; *Directory of Wetlands of International Importance;* conference proceedings; regional inventories of wetlands; manuals.

Regional Organization for the Protection of the Marine Environment (ROPME)
P.O. Box 26388, 13124 Safat, Kuwait. T: (965) 5312140. Tx: 44591. C: ROPME, Kuwait. Fax: (965) 5312144. Established 1980. Works to protect the marine environment of the Gulf through collection of data, research and assessment, training, and legal and technical assistance to member states; operates a Marine Emergency Mutual Aid Centre (MEMAC). Major concern is pollution from the transport of oil. Members are the governments of Bahrain, Iran, Iraq, Kuwait, Oman, Qatar, Saudi Arabia, and the United Arab Emirates.

River, Lake, and Boundary Commissions.
Among the numerous bilateral and multilateral agencies organized to deal with the problems of managing resources that cross international boundaries are the following:
Africa: Gambia River Basin Development Organization (B.P. 2353, Dakar, Senegal), Lake Chad Basin Commission (B.P. 727, Njamena, Chad), Niger Basin Authority (B.P. 729, Niamey, Niger), Organization for the Management and Development of the Kagera River Basin (B.P. 297, Kigali, Rwanda), Permanent Joint Technical Commission for Nile Waters (P.O. Box 1542, Khartoum, Sudan), Senegal River Development Organization (46 rue Carnot, Dakar, Senegal).
Latin America: Intergovernmental Committee on the River Plate Basin (Paraguay 755, 2º Piso, 1057 Buenos Aires CF, Argentina).
North America: International Boundary and Water Commission, United States and Mexico, (c/o U.S. Section, 4171 N. Mesa Street, Building C, Suite 310, El Paso, Texas 79902, USA), International Joint Commission-United States and Canada (c/o Canadian Section, 100 Metcalfe Street, Ottawa, Ontario K1P 5M1, Canada).
East Asia: Committee for Coordination of Investigations of the Lower Mekong Basin (Bangkok, Thailand).
Europe: Central Commission for the Navigation of the Rhine (Palais du Rhin, F-67000 Strasbourg, France), Danube Commission (Benczur utca 25, H-1068 Budapest, Hungary), International Commission for the Protection of Lake Constance Water Against Pollution, (c/o Bundesamt für Umweltschutz, CH-303 Berne, Switzerland), International Commission for the Protection of the Moselle and the Sarre Against Pollution (c/o Ministère des Affaires Etrangères, Quai d'Orsay, Paris, France), International Commission for the

Protection of the Rhine Against Pollution (Postfach 309, D-5400 Koblentz 1, Federal Republic of Germany), International Commission for the Protection of the Saar Against Pollution (Postfach 120629, D-5300 Bonn 1, Federal Republic of Germany), International Commission for the Protection of the Waters of Leman Lake Against Pollution (C.P. 80, CH-1012 Lausanne, Switzerland), Joint Danube Fishery Commission (Safariková 20, CS-01180 Zilina, Czechoslovakia).

Secretariat for the Protection of the Mediterranean Sea
Plaça Lesseps 1, E-08023 Barcelona, Spain. T: (34 3) 217 16 95. Tx: 54 519. Established 1982. Promotes the protection of the Mediterranean Sea and region by facilitating information exchange and action among concerned municipalities. Organizes a periodic Intermunicipal Conference against the Contamination of the Mediterranean. Members are representatives of municipalities in 13 Mediterranean countries in Africa, Asia, and Europe.

South Asia Cooperative Environment Programme (SACEP)
P.O. Box 1070, Colombo 5, Sri Lanka. T: 589369. C: SACEP Colombo. Founded 1983. Promotes cooperation among countries of South Asia in environmental protection and management. Individual countries act as liaison centers for specific projects (e.g., India for training in wildlife management; Pakistan for mountain ecosystems). Members are governments of Afghanistan, Bangladesh, Bhutan, India, Maldives, Pakistan, and Sri Lanka.

South Asian Association for Regional Cooperation (SAARC)
GPO Box 4222, Kathmandu, Nepal. T: 221785. Tx: 2561. C: SAARC. Established 1985. Promotes collaboration and mutual assistance among the countries of South Asia in the economic, social, cultural, technical, and scientific fields. The 11 areas of cooperation include agriculture and forestry, meteorology, rural development, and transport. Members of SAARC are the governments of India, Pakistan, Bhutan, Bangladesh, Maldives, Nepal, and Sri Lanka.

South Pacific Commission (SPC)
B.P. D5, Noumea CEDEX, New Caledonia. T: (687) 26 20 00. Tx: 3139 nm sopacom. C: SOUTHPACOM. Fax: (687) 26 38 18. Established 1947. Serves as a consultative and advisory body to participating governments in matters affecting the economic, social, and health development of the South Pacific region. Includes the South Pacific Regional Environment Programme (SPREP), which had its origins in a SPC nature conservation project in 1974. SPREP, which held a Conference on the Human Environment in the South Pacific in the Cook Islands in 1982, has a coordinated regional approach to environmental problems, serving as an information referral center, and provider of technical assistance to participating countries. Work focuses on coastal water quality monitoring and control (including mangrove, seagrass, and coral reef ecosystems); protected areas and species conservation; environmental education; forestry and soil erosion control; waste management and toxics (including pesticide) control; and environmental planning and administration. Sponsors an Association of South Pacific Environmental Institutions (ASPEI), which includes several universities and research organizations. Members of SPC are 27 national governments and territorial administrations. Pub: Topic Review series; meeting reports; handbooks and educational materials. *See also* Permanent South Pacific Commission.

South Pacific Forum (SPF)
G.P.O. Box 856, Suva, Fiji. Established 1971. SPF is the gathering of heads of government of the independent and self-governing countries of the South Pacific (the South Pacific Commission, described above, includes the metropolitan states which have possessions in the region). The Forum facilitates cooperation and consultation among member countries on trade, economic development, transportation, tourism, and related matters. Among its programs is the South Pacific Forum Fisheries Agency.

Southern African Development Coordination Conference (SADCC)
Private Bag 0095, Gaborone, Botswana. T: (267 31) 51863. Established 1980. Promotes cooperation among majority-ruled states of Southern Africa. SADCC's program of action allots specific tasks to member governments; under it, Malawi is responsible for fisheries and wildlife. Secretariat has conducted or sponsored studies on a range of environmental and resource matters. Members are the governments of Angola, Botswana, Lesotho, Malawi, Mozambique, Swaziland, Tanzania, Zambia, and Zimbabwe.

Training Centre on Environmental Matters for Small Local Authorities in the EEC Mediterranean Countries
(Centre de Formation à l'Environnement pour les Elus et Techniciens Locaux des Pays Méditerranéens de la CEE)
Hôtel de Ville, Avenue de l'Europe Unie, F-13640 La Roque d'Anthéron, France. T: (33) 42 50 42 32. Tx: 430360. Founded 1985. Conducts training seminars in cooperation with the EC. Members are municipalities in France, Greece, Italy, Portugal, and Spain.

Tropical Agricultural Research and Training Center
(Centro Agronómico Tropical de Investigación y Enseñanza) (CATIE)
7170 Turrialba, Costa Rica. T: (506) 56-6431. Tx: 8005 catie cr. C: CATIE, turrialba. Fax: (506) 56-1533. Established 1973. Major center for research and training in agricultural and animals sciences and renewable natural resources in the American tropics, focusing particularly on

Central America and the Caribbean. The CATIE Department of Renewable Natural Resources concentrates its work on forests, watersheds, marginal areas for agriculture, and fauna and flora. Activities include research; designing methodologies for planning, management, and conservation; information collection and dissemination; and a seed bank. Members are the governments Costa Rica, Guatemala, Honduras, Nicaragua, Panama, and the Dominican Republic, and the Inter-American Institute for Cooperation on Agriculture (IICA).

University for Peace (UP)

Apartado 199, 1250 Escazú, Costa Rica. T: (506) 49-10-72. Tx: 2331 macaze cr. An international university created by the UN General Assembly in 1980 to promote peace through education. Constitution is intergovernmental. Program in Natural Resources and the Promotion of Peace, directed by former IUCN Director General Gerardo Budowski, offers short courses, workshops, and technical assistance in areas of natural resource management that are closely related to the promotion of peace and the understanding of conflict. A master's program is planned. UP held a major conference in June 1989 to prepare a "Universal Charter of Human Responsibilities for Peace and Sustainability."

Working Group on an International Commission for Environmental Assessment (ICEA)

P.O. Box 450, NL-2260 MB Leidschendam, Netherlands. T: (31 70) 20 93 67, ext. 3307. Tx: 32362. Fax: (31 70) 27 98 68. An international group set up in 1987 at the initiative of the Dutch Government to investigate the establishment of an international commission on environmental impact assessment which would advise on the application of impact assessment processes and techniques in developing countries and strengthen the capacity of countries to make their own appraisals. The Working Group has been carrying out a series of pilot assessments to demonstrate the potential demand for such services and to explore the best ways of doing so (the first such assessments are in Costa Rica, Egypt, Indonesia, Sri Lanka, and Zimbabwe). Members of the Working Group are senior officials from industrialized and developing countries.

World Tourism Organization (WTO)

Calle Capitán Haya 42, E-28020 Madrid, Spain. T: (34 1) 571 06 28. Tx: 42188. C: OMTOUR. Established 1975. The only intergovernmental organization whose activities cover all domains of tourism. Among those activities, WTO assists developing countries to promote tourism as a fundamental component of economic, social, and cultural development. WTO maintains an Environment Committee whose program (conducted in cooperation with UNEP) is concerned with such problems as planning and carrying capacity for tourism, national parks, protection of cultural heritage, and tourist environmental health. In a joint declaration on "Tourism and Environment" issued in 1982, WTO and UNEP affirmed that "The protection, enhancement, and improvement of the various components of man's environment are among the fundamental conditions for the harmonious development of tourism."

Part 6
International Non-Governmental Organizations

Advisory Committee on Pollution of the Sea
(ACOPS)
3 Endsleigh Street, London WC1H 0DD, England.
T: (41 1) 388 2117. Founded 1952 at the
initiative of Sir James Callaghan, former British
Prime Minister and now President of the
Committee. Promotes "the preservation of the
seas of the world from pollution by human
activities" through research, publicity, and
education, and in governmental forums. Provides
consultancy services to intergovernmental bodies
(such as the Commission of the European
Communities) and NGOs. Members of ACOPS
are individuals and representatives of British and
international organizations.

African NGOs Environment Network (ANEN)
(Réseau des ONG Africaines sur l'Environnement)
P.O. Box 53844, Nairobi, Kenya. T: (254 2)
26255. Tx: 25222 kengo ke. Founded 1982 by 21
representatives of indigenous NGOs from 9
African countries, to strengthen the capacity and
technical competence of African NGOs on
environment and development issues, facilitate
sharing of experiences and skills, and provide a
link between them and their governments, UN
agencies, and other international organizations.
"Since its formation, ANEN has played a critical
catalytic role in promoting the incorporation of
environmental dimensions in development work
and participation of local people, in particular
women and youth in ecodevelopment projects."
ANEN works to "collect, analyze, and disseminate
information and data on African environmental
NGOs, other African environmental institutions,
and on major environment-development issues;
provide advice and training for African NGOs on
the design and management of ecodevelopment
projects and research; and prepare and produce
development education and environment
awareness materials for use by policy-makers,
NGOs, and other community groups." Members
are over 350 NGOs in 37 African countries. Pub:
Ecoafrica, bimonthly; educational materials.

African Soil Science Association
Care of Department of Soil Science, Faculty of
Agriculture, Makerere University, P.O. Box 7062,
Kampala, Uganda. Founded 1986. Forum for
exchange of information on African soils and
their management; working to develop a suitable

soil policy so that African nations may protect
and properly use the environment. Members are
scientists working in or outside of Africa.

Air Pollution Action Network (AIRPLAN)
Postbus 5627, N-1007 AP Amsterdam,
Netherlands. Founded 1985.

Antarctica and Southern Ocean Coalition
201 D Street, NW, Washington, DC 20003, USA.
T: (1 202) 544-2600. Tx: 62949875. Founded
1978. Works to protect the Antarctic region in its
development; monitors governments and holds
them accountable for their actions; supports
maintaining the region as a global commons, a
science preserve, and a wildlife sanctuary.
Members are some 160 organizations in 36
countries.

**Anti-Slavery Society for the Protection of Human
Rights**
180 Brixton Road, London SW9 6AT, England.
T: (44 1) 582 40 40. Founded 1839. The world's
oldest human rights organization. Concerns
include the rights of indigenous peoples. Pub: *The
Anti-Slavery Reporter* (annual); Indigenous Peoples
Series; annual report; study reports.

Arctic Institute of North America
University Library Tower, 2500 University Drive,
NW, Calgary, Alberta T2N 1N4, Canada.
T: (1 403) 220-7515. Founded 1945. Research
organization devoted to acquiring, interpreting,
and disseminating knowledge of the polar regions,
including natural resource and environmental
problems. Members are some 2,500 individuals.
Pub: *Arctic Journal*; newsletter.

Arctic International Wildlife Range Society
c/o Nancy R. Leblond, 917 Leovista Avenue,
North Vancouver, British Columbia V1R 1R1,
Canada. T: (1 604) 986-0586. Works to promote
an international wildlife reserve along the border
between Alaska (USA) and Canada.

ASEAN Association for Planning and Housing
(AAPH)
Trans-Asia (Phils) Inc. Building, 111 Aguirre St.,
Legaspi Village, Makati, Manila 3117, Philippines.
T: (63 2) 816-3112. Tx: 22069 tap ph. Founded
1979. Promotes the study and practice of

regional, urban, and rural planning to improve human settlements and the environment. Affiliated with ASEAN. Members are individuals and institutions in ASEAN countries.

Asian Ecological Society
c/o Jun-Yi Lin, Tunghai University, P.O. Box 843, Taichung 40704, Taiwan. Founded 1977. Works to mobilize and encourage Asian scientists to study the ecosystems of their countries; collects baseline ecological data; promotes environmental impact analysis. Members are educational institutions in 6 countries.

Asian Environmental Society (AES)
8 Darya Ganj, New Delhi 110002, India. Founded 1972. A forum for discussion of environmental problems in Asia; formulates policy recommendations. Members are 60 organizations, as well as individuals, in 11 countries.

Asian Fisheries Society
c/o MCC, P.O. Box 1501, Makati, Manila, Philippines. Founded 1984. Promotes cooperation among fisheries scientists and technologists in Asia; fosters awareness of importance of aquatic resources. Holds a Triennial Asian Fisheries Forum.

Asian Institute of Technology (AIT)
P.O. Box 2754, Bangkok 10501, Thailand. T: (66 2) 529 0100. C: AIT, Bangkok. Tx: 84276 ait th. Fax: (66 2) 529 0374. Includes:
■ Interdisciplinary Natural Resources Development and Management Program, which conducts a range of educational and training activities in the region, emphasizing integrated management.
■ Regional Energy Resources Information Center (RERIC), which provides information services on renewable energy, energy conservation, and energy planning to the Asia-Pacific region. Members are over 500 institutions in over 90 countries. Pub: *RERIC International Energy Journal,* semiannual; newsletters; bibliographies; abstracts; research reports; conference proceedings.
■ Environmental Sanitation Information Center (ENSIC), which collects, repackages, and disseminates information on water supply and sanitation to developing countries; at the same time, it informs industrialized countries of the environmental sanitation problems of the Third World. Members are some 350 institutions in 80 countries. Pub: *Environmental Sanitation Review;* abstracts; newsletter; reports.

Asia-Pacific People's Environment Network (APPEN)
c/o Sahabat Alam Malaysia, 43 Salween Road, 10050 Penang, Malaysia. T: 376930. Founded 1983. Brings together diverse NGOs and individuals in the Asian-Pacific region to collect and disseminate information on environmental issues. Helps to organize local communities affected by environmental problems; educates trade union members on environmental occupational health problems; implements environmental education programs in schools. Tropical rainforests and indigenous people are particular concerns. Pub: *APPEN News Service* (every 2 weeks); newsletter; reports and papers.

Association for the Study of Man Environment Relations
Casilla Correo 13125, Montevideo, Uruguay. Promotes study of the biological, physiological, and social problems of humans in relation to their environments.

Association Internationale Futuribles
(International Futures Research Association) 55, rue de Varenne, F-75341 Cedex 07, France. T: (33 1) 42 22 63 10. Tx: 201220 fecpar f. An international network on future studies. Current major projects focus on new technologies, social policies, the impact of an aging population, lifestyle changes, and the emergence of an information society. Pub: *Futuribles,* monthly journal; bibliographies; research reports (all in French).

Association of Geoscientists for International Development (AGID)
c/o Asian Institute of Technology, P.O. Box 2754, Bangkok 10501, Thailand. T: (66 2) 529-011, ext. 2528. Tx: 84276. C: AIT. Founded 1974. Promotes activities in the geosciences related to the needs of developing countries; promotes among geoscientists an awareness of their responsible role in the management of natural resources. Concerns include groundwater resources and mineral exploration methods in tropical rainforests. Holds training courses and workshops; operates a geoscience information service. Members are institutions and individuals in some 100 countries. Pub: *AGID News,* quarterly; regional newsletters.

Athens Centre of Ekistics (ACE)
24 Stratiotikou Syndesmou St., P.O. Box 3471, 102-10 Athens, Greece. T: (30 1) 623 216. C: ATINST. Founded 1963 by the late Constantinos Doxiadis, a noted planner. Promotes research, education, documentation, and international cooperation in fields related to ekistics (the study of all aspects of human settlements). Corresponding members in 35 countries.

Atlantic Salmon Federation (ASF)
P.O. Box 429, St. Andrews, New Brunswick E0G 2X0, Canada. T: (1 506) 529-8889. Fax: (1 506) 529-4438. Founded 1982. Works for the preservation and wise management of the Atlantic salmon and its habitat through research, conservation projects, education, and promoting international cooperation. Pub: *The Atlantic Salmon Journal.*

Bank Information Center
731 Eighth St., SE, Washington, DC 20003. T: (1 202) 547-3800. Founded 1987. A

clearinghouse of information for NGOs concerned about the operations of the World Bank and other multilateral development banks and their impact on the environments of developing countries. Has issued a list of recommended reforms, as well as a critical report, *Financing Ecological Destruction.*

Bat Conservation International (BCI)
P.O. Box 162603, Austin, Texas 78716, USA. T: (1 512) 327-9721. Founded 1962. Works for conservation and protection of bats worldwide through education, advocacy, and promoting scientific research. Members are some 6,000 individuals in 35 countries.

Beauty Without Cruelty International (BWC)
11 Limehill Road, Tunbridge Wells, Kent YN1 1LJ, England. Founded 1958. An animal protection organization that campaigns for the use of "simulation fur garments, wearing apparel, accessories, beauty preparations, household goods, and food, the making and preparation of which have not involved cruelty or exploitation of any living creature." Works against fur farming, animal trapping, testing of cosmetics on animals, and use of certain animal fats and derivatives; works for use of synthetic substitutes. Members are individuals in a number of countries.

Better World Society International (BWS)
1140 Connecticut Avenue, NW, Washington, DC 20036, USA. T: (1 202) 331-3770. Founded 1985 by U.S. TV and sports figure Ted Turner. Produces and acquires "solution-oriented" TV programs for international distribution which help in "making people aware of global problems that threaten life on our planet," including "the worldwide depletion of natural resources and degradation of the environment." Supplements TV programs with ancillary educational materials. Members are individuals in a number of countries.

Buddhist Perception of Nature
5H Bowen Road, 1st Floor, Hong Kong. T: (852 5) 233464. Tx: 72149 sidan hx. Founded 1985. "Inspired by evidence that Buddhism has played a role in protection of species and habitats in Asia," this group conducts research on and assembles "traditional Buddhist teachings regarding man's interdependence with, and responsibilities to, the natural environment and all living things." It produces teaching materials, aims to serve "as a model or blueprint for similar projects involving other faiths and cultural traditions" and offers "support for the growing body of thought which finds that the importance of ethics in conservation work has been overlooked or under-employed." Offices in Dharamsala, India, and Bangkok, Thailand. Pub: *Tree of Life* (book in English, Tibetan, and Thai); *A Cry from the Forest* (book in Thai and English); calendars.

Canada-United States Environmental Council
1244 19th St., N.W., Washington, DC 20037, USA. T: (1 202) 659-9510. Founded 1971. A group of major Canadian and U.S. NGOs; facilitates exchange of information and cooperative action on issues affecting the two countries.

Caribbean Conservation Association
Savannah Lodge, The Garrison, St. Michael, Barbados. T: (1 809) 426-5373. Founded 1967. Works to coordinate conservation activities in the Caribbean region; carries on educational activities. Pub: *Caribbean Conservation.*

Caribbean Conservation Corporation (CCC)
P.O. Box 2866, Gainesville, Florida 32602, USA. T: (1 904) 373-6441. Founded 1959 by Archie Carr. Supports research on and conservation of marine turtles in the Caribbean and throughout the world. Operates a research station Tortuguero in Costa Rica and a semi-natural impoundment for turtles in the Bahamas. Pub: *Velador.*

Center for the Great Lakes
435 N. Michigan Avenue, Chicago, Illinois 60611, USA. T: (1 312) 645-0901. Concerned with the environments of the Great Lakes (U.S.-Canada).

Central American Federation of Non-Governmental Conservation Associations
(Federación Mesoamericana de Asociaciones Conservacionistas No-Gubernamentales) (FEMAC) Apartado 3089, 1000 San Jose, Costa Rica. T: (506) 25 88 04. Founded 1978. Contact group for conservation NGOs in Central America.

Central American Regional Water Resources Committee
(Comité Regional Centroamericano de Recursos Hidráulicos) c/o IRHE, Apartado Postal Zone 5-5285, Panama, Panama. T: (507) 62 7370. Tx: 2158 irhe pa.

Centre for Our Common Future
Palais Wilson, 52, rue des Pâquis, CH-1201 Geneva, Switzerland. T: (41 22) 32 71 17. Tx: 27910. Fax: (41 22) 34 07 97. Founded 1988. Works to follow up on the recommendations made in *Our Common Future,* the final report of the World Commission on Environment and Development *(which see).* "The participatory process of public hearings which helped frame the analysis and conclusions of *Our Common Future* and the presentation of the report throughout the world by its former chairman, Prime Minister Gro Harlem Brundtland, and by members of the Commission, have created an international constituency which stands ready and able to participate in a concerted global effort to achieve sustainable development. But to effect real change, the opportunity presented by the report must be seized. And that opportunity could be lost if the momentum created by the report is not maintained and its messages not continuously and broadly disseminated. Indeed, securing our common future may depend on no less than a

global movement to achieve sustainable development. The Centre has been established to help create such a movement."

The Centre, which is planned to have a 3-year existence, (1) acts as a central focal point for follow-up activities on the report; (2) encourages organizations and forums representing as many constituencies as possible to initiate their own work toward sustainable development in their own areas; (3) services these and existing follow-up activities; and (4) in doing the above, assists in laying the foundations for several proposed 1990 regional conferences on follow-up to the report and for the 1992 World Conference on Sustainable Development.

The Centre provides technical support for specific follow-up initiatives; is designing an industry guide to the report and encouraging industry-wide responses to it; is preparing language versions of an overview of the report, as well as interpretive and video materials; works to get *Our Common Future* onto the agendas of as many organizations as possible; prepares press materials; and maintains a central register of follow-up activities. Pub: *Brundtland Bulletin* (newsletter); materials on the Brundtland Report.

Clean World International
c/o Keep Britain Tidy Group, Bostel House, 37 West St., Brighton BN1 2RE, England.
T: (44 273) 23585. Founded 1975. Unites groups which work for litter prevention, beautification, tidiness, and recycling of resources; members are national groups in 22 countries. Pub: annual newsletter.

Club of Rome
c/o IBI, P.O. Box 10253, I-00144 Rome, Italy.
T: (39 6) 591 60 41. Founded 1968. Important futures study organization. The Club is a "group of individuals convinced of the urgent need to secure a deeper understanding of the rapidly-evolving world society so that it may be more wisely guided. It is an association of 100 members from some 40 countries of the 5 continents, from the East and from the West, from the North and from the South--scientists, economists, sociologists, business leaders, and senior officials--who offer a broad spectrum of competence and skills, but whose diversity of ideology and concepts seldom allow of easy consensus...Since its creation, the Club has based its thinking and action on 3 approaches: (1) the need to adopt a global approach to the vast and complex problems of a world in which interdependence is increasingly close between the nations within a single planetary system; (2) seeking a deeper understanding of the interactions within the tangle of contemporary problems--political, economic, social, cultural, psychological, technological, and environ-mental--for which the Club has coined the phrase, "the world problematique"; (3) focus on long-term perspectives and issues." Several of the influential reports sponsored by the Club, including *The Limits to Growth* (1972), *Mankind*

at *the Turning Point* (1974), and *Beyond the Age of Waste* (1978), have dealt with global environmental and resource issues in a broad context. Maintains an office in Paris. There are committees or national clubs in several countries. Pub: Reports (published commercially; list available).

Comité Arctique International (CAI)
(International Arctic Committee*)
16 boulevard de Suisse, MC-98000 Monte Carlo, Monaco. Founded 1979. Promotes multidisciplinary research and "objective discussions" concerning utilization of resources and protection of the environment in the Arctic; industrial developments and the concerns of native populations; and the significance of the Arctic in the perspective of global changes. Environmental pollution from polychlorinated hydrocarbons is a major concern. Conferences have focused on such topics as the fate of pollutants in the Arctic Ocean, Arctic energy resources, and marine living resources of the Far North. Members are Arctic scientists, supporting industries, and scientific institutions. Pub: Conference proceedings; newsletter. (*The French name of the organization is always used.)

Common Property Resource Network
Center for Natural Resource Policy and Management, University of Minnesota, 332e C.O.B., 1994 Buford Avenue, St. Paul, Minnesota 55108, USA. T: (1 612) 625-7019. Fax: (1 612) 625-0286. "Seeks to disseminate information dealing with common property resources, their management, and policies related to their use. It also seeks to foster communication between professionals who work with common property resources, whether as policy-makers, administrators, researchers, or educators. The ultimate goal of the network is to improve the conservation and wise use of these resources, and to improve the well-being of those people who depend on common property for their livelihood. Membership in the network is open to any individual or institution having an active professional interest in common property resources." Examples of common property resources are forests and fisheries, publicly-owned or otherwise, held in common. Main communication medium is the *Common Property Resource Digest*, quarterly.

Commonwealth Association of Architects (CAA)
66 Portland Place, London W1N 4AD, England.
T: (44 1) 636 8276. Tx: 22914 ref C001.
Fax: (44 1) 255 1541. Founded 1965. Promotes cooperation among professional societies of architects in Commonwealth countries. Main activities are a pan-Commonwealth conference every 2 or 3 years, participation in regional or specialized conferences, and collection and dissemination of information about architectural affairs in the Commonwealth. Interests include housing and city planning, particularly in developing countries. Pub: Audio-visual programs

and books.

Commonwealth Association of Planners (CAP)
Current address unknown. Founded 1971.
Fosters cooperation among Commonwealth
countries to promote city and regional planning
for improvement of the environment and well-
being of people. Holds a conference every 4
years. Members are professional planning
organizations in 18 countries. Pub: quarterly
newsletter; conference proceedings; reports.

Commonwealth Forestry Association (CFA)
c/o Oxford Forestry Institute, South Parks Road,
Oxford OX1 3RB, England. T: (44 865) 275072.
Founded 1921. "Brings together all who are
concerned with conservation, development, and
management of forests, especially of the tropical
and sub-tropical resources...although originally
constituted as a Commonwealth organization, the
Association now represents global concern about
forestry matters." Main activities are publishing a
journal and holding annual meetings, symposia,
and periodic Commonwealth Forestry
Conferences. Members are professional foresters,
forest and wood scientists, timber merchants,
ecologists, and resource managers and
conservationists from around the world, as well as
institutions and firms. Pub: *Commonwealth
Forestry Review,* quarterly; *Commonwealth
Forestry Handbook.*

Commonwealth Human Ecology Council (CHEC)
58 Stanhope Gardens, London SW7 5RF, England.
T: (44 1) 373 6761. Tx: 8951182 gecoms g. Fax:
(44 1) 318 1439. Founded 1952 as the Committee
on Nutrition in the Commonwealth; became
CHEC in 1969. Works to promote "understanding
and action in the development of resources for the
wholeness of human life and wellbeing, through
ecologically satisfactory policies and programs, in
the countries of the Commonwealth and
elsewhere." Holds conferences and seminars;
sponsors field projects in developing countries of
the Commonwealth; sponsors visits of
Commonwealth scholars to British universities;
provides education and training advice to
academic institutions; information referral
services. Members are individuals and organizations in some 25 countries. Pub: *CHEC Journal;
CHEC Points* (newsletter); *Human Ecology: A
Survey of Courses Offered at Institutions of
Higher Education in the Commonwealth* (2nd
edition 1988); books, conference reports,
bibliographies.

**Confederation of International Scientific and
Technological Organizations for Development
(CISTOD)**
51 boulevard de Montmorency, F-75016 Paris,
France. Concerns include energy resources in
developing countries.

**Consultative Group on International Agricultural
Research (CGIAR)**
1818 H Street, NW, Washington, DC 20433, USA.
Established 1971. An association of some 50
governments, international organizations, and
private foundations "dedicated to supporting a
system of agricultural research centers and
programs around the world...to improve the quan-
tity and quality of food production in developing
countries." The Group is co-sponsored by the
World Bank, FAO, and UNDP, and its secretariat
is located at World Bank Headquarters.

CGIAR works by supporting, "on a sustained
basis, a well-defined and closely-monitored
program of research...in agroecological zones" at
13 specialized centers. These are:
■ Centro Internacional de Agricultura Tropical
(CIAT) (International Center of Tropical
Agriculture), Apartado Aereo 6713, Cali,
Colombia
■ Centro Internacional de Mejoramiento de Maiz
y Trigo (CIMMYT) (International Center for
Improvement of Corn and Wheat), Apartado 6-
641, Mexico D.F. 06600, Mexico
■ Centro Internacional de la Papa (CIP)
(International Potato Center), Apartado 5969,
Lima, Peru
■ International Board for Plant Genetic Resources
(IBPGR), Food and Agriculture Organization of
the United Nations, Via delle Terme di Caracalla,
I-00100 Rome, Italy
■ International Center for Agricultural Research
in the Dry Areas (ICARDA), P.O. Box 5466,
Aleppo, Syria
■ International Crops Research Institute for the
Semi-Arid Tropics (ICRISAT), ICRISAT
Patancheru P.O., Andhra Pradesh 502 324, India
■ International Food Policy Research Institute
(IFPRI), 1776 Massachusetts Avenue, NW,
Washington, DC 20036, USA
■ International Institute of Tropical Agriculture
(IITA), PMB 5320, Ibadan, Nigeria
■ International Livestock Center for Africa
(ILCA), P.O. Box 5689, Addis Ababa, Ethiopia
■ International Laboratory for Research on
Animal Diseases (ILRAD), P.O. Box 30709,
Nairobi, Kenya
■ International Rice Research Institute (IRRI),
P.O. Box 933, Manila, Philippines
■ International Service for National Agricultural
Research (ISNAR), P.O. Box 93375, The Hague,
Netherlands
■ West Africa Rice Development Association
(WARDA), 01 B.P. 2551, Bouake 01, Côte d'Ivoire
According to CGIAR, sustainable agriculture
is receiving more emphasis at these centers.
Programs include research on genetic resource
conservation, biological control of pests, improved
soil and water management, and low-input
agriculture. Pub: Annual report; technical reports.
Each of the centers has its own publishing
program.

Coordination Group of Non Governmental Organizations in the Field of Man-Made Environment
(COG)
Winterthurerstrasse 52, CH-8006 Zurich, Switzerland. T: (41 1) 362 92 41. Founded 1977. An informal group of NGOs concerned with the "creation and the development of the environment in which man moves, lives, and works." Sponsors coordinated and joint actions, such as workshops, seminars, congresses, and publications. Meetings have been held on such topics as urban new towns, preservation of historic quarters of cities, and the use of wood. Members are 9 international NGOs concerned with the arts, urban planning, architecture, graphic design, monuments and sites, industrial design, interior design, landscape architecture, and crafts. Unesco is an observer. Pub: Conference proceedings.

Development Innovations and Alternatives
(Innovations et Réseaux pour le Développement) (IRED)
3 rue de Varembé, Case 116, CH-1211 Geneva 20, Switzerland. T: (41 22) 34 17 16. C: IRED, Geneva. Tx: 289 450 ired ch. Founded 1980. Promotes links to facilitate endogenous development in Third-World countries, particularly South-South exchanges and cooperation among national and local groups. Works through exchanges of individuals, groups, and tools; organizing local groups; and management training. Members in some 80 countries; regional offices in Africa, Asia, and Latin America.

East African Natural History Society
P.O. Box 44486, Nairobi, Kenya. T: (254 2) 742131. Concerns include nature conservation.

East African Wildlife Society
P.O. Box 20110, Nairobi, Kenya. Founded 1956. Works to safeguard wildlife and its habitats in Kenya, Tanzania, and Uganda, through research, supplying equipment for anti-poaching measures, and education and public awareness. Pub: *Swara*, bimonthly magazine.

Eastern Caribbean Institute for Agriculture and Forestry (ECIAF)
Centeno, Trinidad and Tobago

Eastern Regional Organization for Planning and Housing (EAROPH)
4-A Ring Road, Indraprastha Estate, New Delhi 110002, India. T: (91 11) 27 4809. C: Earoph. Founded 1958. Promotes the study and practice of town and country planning in the region. Offices in Japan, Indonesia, and Malaysia. Members are individuals and organizations in 15 countries.

Ecosystem Conservation Group (ECG)
Established 1975. A coordinating body whose members are FAO, UNEP, Unesco, and IUCN. A forum for coordination and cooperation on matters relating to nature conservation and natural resource management.

ELC International *See* Environment Liaison Centre International

Engineering Committee on Oceanic Resources (ECOR)
c/o Institute for Marine and Coastal Studies, University of Southern California, Los Angeles, California 90089, USA. Founded 1971. Provides an international focus for professional engineering interests in marine affairs, with emphasis on providing advice from an engineering viewpoint on policy, program, and organizational matters to international organizations and governmental agencies concerned with marine affairs. Members are national committees or academies in 14 countries. Pub: Quarterly newsletter.

Environment Liaison Centre International (ELC)
P.O. Box 72461, Nairobi, Kenya. T: (254 2) 24770. Tx: 23240. Founded 1974. Works to strengthen communication and cooperation among NGOs around the world that are concerned with environment and development issues, and serves as a link between NGOs and the UN Environment Programme, headquartered in Nairobi. Maintains a database on some 10,000 NGOs worldwide; administers a small grants program for Third-World NGOs; provides training and support services; has an internship program for staff members of grassroots NGOs; and provides a mechanism for NGO inputs to the UN, International Whaling Commission, FAO, and other international bodies. ELC is a founder of many issue-oriented and regional networks (e.g., Pesticide Action Network; African NGOs Environment Network). Current major themes in ELC's work are deforestation, water management, energy, and sustainable agriculture. Members are some 250 NGOs in over 60 countries; "in contact with over 7,000 other groups." Pub: *Ecoforum* (journal); *News Alert* (action-oriented bulletins); "how to" booklets; directories; monographs; annual report.

Environment and Development in the Third World
(Environnement et Développement du Tiers Monde) (ENDA)
B.P. 3370, Dakar, Senegal. T: (221) 22 42 29. Tx: 456 enda tm sg. C: ENDA. Founded 1972. Objectives are "to work with grassroots groups to help them determine and meet their needs and objectives; to participate in the quest for sustainable development activities at all levels as well as offering the various kinds of training programs needed to realize this type of development; and to stimulate intellectuals' and trained personnel's involvement in the setting up and implementation of development programs for the masses." Activities include formal courses in environmental management, counseling of young trainees and researchers, book publishing, preparing audio-visual materials, radio and TV broadcasts, study and promotion of peasant and

pastoral eco-cultures, and studies of ecosystems of Third-World towns. A major concern is to "save and rehabilitate the existing lore and spread the lessons that can be learned from it for a development model that roots rather than uproots the actors, who should be peasants and urban masses themselves instead of the international and national establishments." ENDA works primarily in Africa, but also in Latin America and Asia. Pub: *African Environment* (academic quarterly in English and French editions); *Vivre Autrement* (quarterly consumers' magazine that promotes indigenous products); booklets, comics, reports, and occasional papers (in French and English). ENDA publications are available from Faxon in the USA and from Blackwells Periodicals in the UK.

Europa Nostra: International Federation of Associations for the Protection of Europe's Cultural and Natural Heritage
9 Buckingham Gate, London SW1E 6JP, England. T: (44 1) 821 1171. Fax: (44 1) 828 6948. Founded 1963. Europa Nostra (which means "Our Europe" in Latin) is a "confederation of independent conservation associations which are working, throughout Europe, towards a general improvement in the quality of life, both in the natural and the built environment." It seeks "to awaken the pride of the European peoples in their common history and heritage of man-made and natural beauty; to draw attention to the dangers which threaten this heritage, and to call for the preservation and better management of such irreplaceable treasures"; to facilitate exchange of information; help develop environmental education; encourage high standards of planning and environmental management; and make recommendations to authorities. Holds conferences and workshops (e.g., on effects of air pollution on heritage sites; historic towns and tourism). Europa Nostra is especially noted for its awards to recognize projects which make outstanding contributions to preserving the European heritage. Members are several hundred NGOs in 22 countries. Pub: "Europa Nostra News," carried in the Council of Europe's publication *A Future for Our Past;* annual report; booklets; films.

European Association Against Aircraft Nuisance
c/o Dr. Manfred Lamers, Postfach 1780, D-4150 Krefeld, Federal Republic of Germany. T: (49 2151) 13 03. Founded 1968.

European Association for Aquatic Mammals (EAAM)
358 avenue Mozart, F-06600 Antibes, France. Founded 1972. Promotes scientific knowledge and conservation of aquatic mammals. Members are individuals (full members are zoologists, veterinarians, and other professional specialists in the field) and institutions in 19 countries in Europe and elsewhere.

European Association for Country Planning Institutions
(Association Européenne des Institutions d'Aménagement Rural) (AEIAR)
Care of Société Nationale Terrienne, Avenue de la Toison d'Or 72, B-1060 Brussels, Belgium. Founded 1965. Members are national and regional associations in 8 Western European countries.

European Association for the Science of Air Pollution (EURASAP)
c/o Dr. H.M. ApSimon, Environmental Safety Group, Mechanical Engineering Department, Imperial College, London SW7 2AZ, England. T: (44 1) 589 5111. Tx 261503. Founded 1986.

European Association of Development Research and Training Institutes (EADI)
10 rue Richemont, B.P. 272, CH-1211 Geneva 21, Switzerland. Founded 1975. EADI works to promote development research and training activities in economic, social, cultural, technological, institutional, and ecological areas. Members are about 170 institutions and 300 individuals in 23 European countries. Among its committees is:
■ EADI Working Group on Environment and Development (EWGED), care of Roberto Vanore, AISI, Via L. Lilio 19, I-00142 Rome, Italy. T: (39 6) 5923441. Tx: 612339 gbg i. Fax: (39 6) 5146089. EWGED carries out common research at the European level (West and East) on environment-development issues, primarily with reference to the Third World. Current themes include how international development institutions are facing environmental issues, and identification of research and training needs in both European and developing countries. Members are 15 individuals in several countries.

European Centre for Environmental Communication (ECEC)
55 rue de Varenne, F-75341 Paris Cedex 07, France. T: (33 1) 45 44 40 60. Tx: 201 220 fecpar f. Fax: (33 1) 42 22 65 54. Founded 1985 with initial support from the European Cultural Foundation. Promotes communication on the environment in Europe, particularly in the audio-visual media sector, and stimulates cooperation and exchanges in this field by developing a professional and specialized network. ECEC launches original projects, but also seeks to complement and multiply existing initiatives. Sponsors the biennial ECOVISION European environmental film festival. Pub: *ACE News*, (English and French editions), 5 times a year, on audiovisual programs; directories; research reports.

European Cetacean Society
c/o Zoology Department, South Parks Road, Oxford OX1 4PS, England.
Concerned with the study and protection of cetaceans (whales, porpoises, etc.).

European Committee for the Protection of Fur Animals
(Comité Européen pour la Protection des Animaux à Fourrure) (CEPAF)
Rue de Vrière 16, B-1020 Brussels, Belgium. Founded 1969. Works to protect seals and other fur-bearing animals from slaughter, exploitation, and human cruelty. Members are some 1,000 individuals in ten countries.

European Committee for the Protection of the Population Against the Hazards of Chronic Toxicity (EUROTOX)
c/o Prof. René Truhaut, Laboratoire de Toxicologie, Faculté des Sciences Pharmaceutiques, Université René Descartes, 4, avenue de l'Observatoire, F-75006 Paris, France. T: (33 1) 43 26 71 22. Founded 1957. Studies long-term effects of toxic agents and means of protection from them. Members are individuals in 22 countries.

European Committee of Landscape Architects
(Comité Européen des Architectes Paysagistes) (CEGAP)
Colmanstrasse 32, D-5300 Bonn 1, Federal Republic of Germany. T: (49 228) 65 54 88. Members are organizations in 9 countries.

European Council of Town Planners (ECTP)
c/o Royal Town Planning Institute, 26 Portland Place, London W1N 4BE, England. T: (44 1) 636 9107. Fax: (44 1) 323 1582. Founded 1985. Coordinates matters related to the town planning profession. Members are associations in 9 countries.

European Council of Environmental Law
(Conseil Européen du Droit de l'Environnement) (CEDE)
Université des Sciences Juridiques, Politiques et Sociales, Place d'Athènes, F-67084 Strasbourg CEDEX, France. Founded 1974. Promotes development and study of environmental law, with particular reference to Europe. Members are individuals in 8 countries.

European Environmental Bureau (EEB)
Luxemburgstraat 20, B-1040 Brussels, Belgium. T: (32 2) 647 01 99. Founded 1974. Information clearinghouse on environmental problems in Europe, primarily in EEC countries. Focus is on environmental policy, nature protection, pollution control, land use planning, transportation, energy, agriculture, and environmental education, as well as environmental aspects of European relations with developing countries. Members are some 100 NGOs in the 12 EEC countries. Pub: *RISED,* bimonthly; annual report.

European Federation for the Protection of Waters (EFPW)
c/o Gemeentelijk Centraal Milieulaboratorium, Amstelveenseweg 88, 1075-XJ Amsterdam, Netherlands. Founded 1956. Members are national associations in 13 Western European countries.

European Grassland Federation
c/o Institute for Soil Fertility, P.O. Box 30003, 9750 Haren, Netherlands. T: (31 50) 337315. Tx: 53990 ibhrn nl. Founded 1963.

European Group for the Ardennes and the Eifel
(Groupement Européen des Ardennes et de l'Eifel) (GEAE)
c/o UCL/CIRMAP, Boîte 3057, Clos Chapelle aux Champs 30, B-1200 Brussels, Belgium. Founded 1955. Promotes cooperation among the border areas of the Ardennes in Belgium, France, and Luxembourg, and the German Eifel. Maintains a Commission on Environment and Natural Resources. Members are individuals in 4 national sections.

European Herpetological Society
(Societas Europaea Herpetologica) (SEH)
Hessisches Landesmuseum Darmstadt, Zoologische Abteilung, Friendensplatz 1, D-6100 Darmstadt, Federal Republic of Germany. T: (49 6151) 125434. Founded 1979. Conducts and promotes scientific research and conservation related to reptiles and amphibians, especially in Europe. Maintains a Conservation Committee. Members are individuals and institutions in 39 countries.

European Institute for Water
2 rue Boussingault, F-67000 Strasbourg, France. T: (33 88) 61 16 31. Tx: 870 260 ulp f. Founded 1983. Brings together various European "socio-economic actors" concerned with water issues; promotes exchange of scientific, legislative, economic, and regulatory information; makes recommendations to the EC. Members are organizations in European countries.

European Institute of Ecology and Cancer
(Institut Européen d'Ecologies et de Cancérologie) (INEC) Avenue des Fripiers 24 bis, B-1000 Brussels, Belgium. T: (32 2) 219 08 30. C: Eurocancerinec. Founded 1962. Scientific and medical organization concerned with relationships between cancer and the environment, particularly pollution and ecological damage; studies prevention of cancer through harmonious adaptation and protection of nature. Members are individuals in 4 countries.

European Mediterranean Commission on Water Planning (EMCWP)
Via Cimarosa 10, I-45124 Catania, Italy. Founded 1970.

European Water Pollution Control Association (EWPCA)
Markt 71, D-5205 Sangkt Augustin 1, Federal Republic of Germany. T: (49 2241) 2320. Tx: 861183 atv d. Founded 1981. Professional organization; promotes the science and practice of water pollution control in Europe. Members are organizations in 15 countries.

European Youth Forest Action Foundation
P.O. Box 5627, 1007 AP Amsterdam, Netherlands.
T: (31 20) 851-049.

Federation of Hunting Associations of the EEC
(Fédération des Associations de Chasseurs de la
CEE) (FACE)
Rue de la Science 23-24, Boîte 16, B-1040
Brussels, Belgium. T: (32 2) 230 42 36. Tx: 25
816. Founded 1977. Promotes and defends in
Europe all forms of hunting as a sport based on
ecological principles; opposes harmful exploitation
of wildlife species; works to combat pollution and
destruction of habitat. Commissions study such
topics as acid rain and the impact of modern
farming practices on wildlife. Members are
national organizations in the 12 EEC countries.

**Federation of Nature and National Parks of
Europe**
Rathausgasse 1, D-8352 Grafenau, Federal
Republic of Germany. T: (49 8552) 28 39.
Founded 1973. Promotes practical work by
organizations and individuals in parks or
collaborating with them; contacts between parks
for the exchange of experience and information;
international collaboration both in the creation of
new parks and in the protection and enhancement
of existing parks; and knowledge of the protected
natural and cultural heritage of the parks by
means of training and education programs."
Members are individuals and groups from 16
countries in Eastern and Western Europe. Pub:
European Bulletin: Nature and National Parks,
quarterly; *FedNews,* newsletter (both in English,
French, and German).

Foundation for Environmental Conservation
7 Chemin Taverney, CH-1218 Grand-Saconnex,
Geneva, Switzerland. T: (41 22) 98 23 83.
Founded 1975. Sponsors the quarterly journal
Environmental Conservation (published by Elsevier
Sequoia), as well as two book series, the
Environmental Monographs and Symposia, and the
Cambridge Environmental Policy Series. Holds
the International Conferences on Environmental
Future and the Baer-Huxley Memorial Lectures.
Sponsors the World Council for the Biosphere, a
group of "eminent leaders in fields of endeavor
related to environmental concerns" which serves as
a "select international forum for the analysis and
appraisal of existing and foreseeable relationships
between human populations and economic
development on the one hand and, on the other,
the totality of living and life-support systems of
our planet." Objectives of the Council include
alerting decision-makers to threats to the
Biosphere, advising leaders on ways to improve
the sustainability of economic systems, and
fostering ecologically sensitive thinking.
Governing board consists of representatives of
IUCN and WWF and Dr. Nicholas Polunin.

**Foundation for Environmental Education in
Europe**
(Fondation pour l'Education à l'Environnement en
Europe) (FEEE)
Avenue Voltaire 154, B-1030 Brussels, Belgium

Friends of the Earth International (FOE
International)
3 Endsleigh Street, London WC1H 0DD, England.
T: (44 1) 278 9686. Founded 1971. Promotes
conservation, restoration, and rational use of the
environment and the Earth's natural resources
through public education and campaigning at the
local, national, and international levels. Activities
include organizing international networks for
action on environmental, consumer protection, and
peace issues. Holds an annual meeting and
conferences on specific topics. Members are FOE
organizations in some 30 countries (most of which
are listed in Part 7 of this book). Pub: *FOE Link,*
semi-annual.

Green Belt Movement
P.O. Box 67545, Nairobi, Kenya. T: (254 2)
34634. Founded 1977. Combats desertification
through projects to plant indigenous trees and
shrubs.

Greenpeace International
Temple House, 25-26 High Street, Lewes, East
Sussex BN7 2LU, England. T: (44 273) 478787.
Tx: 878182 gpint g. Fax: (44 273) 471631.
Founded 1971. "Greenpeace believes in using
direct action in its campaigns to protect wildlife
and the environment against destructive processes.
Our policy is one of complete non-violence, and
our actions cause neither injury to humans nor
damage to property. Our campaigns are based on
years of scientific study, with many highly-
regarded scientists and environmentalists both
supporting and endorsing Greenpeace actions.

"Greenpeace activities first began in Canada
with protests against atomic weapons testing. Our
current campaigns include: a moratorium on the
commercial slaughter of cetaceans and other
marine wildlife; a ban on the use of high seas
drift nets; an end to the testing of nuclear
weapons; prohibition of the dumping of nuclear
wastes in the oceans; reduction of the production,
dumping, and discharge of toxic chemical wastes
in the atmosphere, rivers, lakes, and oceans; and
the total protection of the Antarctic continent.

"Greenpeace currently has offices in 20
countries [listed in Part 6] and a worldwide
membership of over 3 million supporters. We are
in the process of establishing a network of new
offices throughout Latin America. All our work
is entirely funded by public donations."
Maintains an EEC-Unit at Avenue de Tervueren
36, B-1040 Brussels, Belgium.

Gulf and Caribbean Fisheries Institute
4600 Rickenbacker Causeway, Miami, Florida
33149, USA. T: (1 305) 361-4191. Founded
1948. Promotes fishery research in the Gulf of
Mexico and the Caribbean by means of an annual

meeting for scientists and industry and government representatives. Pub: Conference proceedings.

Habitat International Coalition (HIC)
c/o IULA, 41 Wassenaarseweg, NL-2596 CG The Hague, Netherlands. T: (31 70) 24 40 32. Tx: 32504. C: IULA. Founded 1978 as a result of Habitat: the UN Conference on Human Settlements (Vancouver, 1976). Acts as an international pressure group in defense of the homeless, the poor, and the inadequately housed; educates the public about human settlement problems; serves as an information clearinghouse and a forum for discussion of habitat issues. Holds an annual conference and sponsors seminars and workshops. Members are NGOs and research and educational institutions in some 50 countries.

Independent Commission of the South on Development Issues
(South-South Commission)
c/o Dr. Julius K. Nyerere, P.O. Box 9120, Dar es Salaam, Tanzania. T: (255 51) 23261. A group of 20 political and intellectual figures which acts independently of governments to develop and promote recommendations on development issues from a Third World perspective.

Independent Commission on International Development Issues (Brandt Commission)
A temporary organization chaired by former West German Chancellor Willy Brandt, which produced influential and widely-distributed reports, *North-South: A Programme for Survival* (1980), and *Common Crisis* (1983).

Institute for European Environmental Policy (IEEP)
Aloys-Schulte Strasse 6, D-5300 Bonn, Federal Republic of Germany. T: (49 228) 7290050. Tx: 886 885 fec d. "An independent body for the analysis of environmental policies in Europe. It seeks to increase the awareness of the European dimension of environmental protection and to advance European policy-making, thereby contributing to European unity...The Institute is characterized by a close involvement with parliaments, by a wide network of contacts, and by an ability to operate in several countries simultaneously." Program focuses on EC policy; chemicals and cross-media pollution control; agriculture and water; nature conservation; and East-West cooperation. IEEP is part of the European Cultural Foundation but has its own board. Field offices in Paris and London. Pub: *The Environment in Europe* (bimonthly newsletter; separate editions in English, French, and German); annual report; policy reports.

Inter-American Association of Sanitary and Environmental Engineering
(Asociación Interamericana de Ingeniería Sanitaria y Ambiental) (AIDIS). Carreta 7 A 69-53, Cundinamarca, Bogotá, Colombia. Tx: 45798 Jotro co. Founded 1948. Promotes knowledge and development of sanitary engineering and environmental sciences in the Americas. Members are national sections in 22 countries.

Inter-American Bar Association (IABA)
1889 F Street, NW, Suite 450, Washington, DC 20006, USA. T: (1 202) 789-2747. Tx: 64128. C: INTERBAR. Founded 1940. Works to advance the study of jurisprudence, acts as a forum for exchange of views on legal matters, and promotes uniformity of laws in the Americas. Maintains a Permanent Committee on Natural Resources and Environmental Protection. Pub: *IABA Newsletter*, quarterly; conference proceedings.

Inter-American Planning Society
(Sociedad Interamericana de Planificación) (SIAP)
Apartado Postal 27-716, Mexico City, D.F. 06760, Mexico. T: (52 5) 516 9756. C: SIAP, Mexico. Founded 1956. Promotes the principles and practice of comprehensive planning in the Americas. Members are institutions and individuals in 37 countries.

International Alliance for Sustainable Agriculture (IASA)
The Newman Center, University of Minnesota, 1701 University Avenue SE, Room 202, Minneapolis, Minnesota 55414, USA. T: (1 612) 331-1099. Founded 1983. Promotes sustainable agriculture worldwide, "an agriculture that is economically viable, ecologically sound, and socially just and humane." Major activities are research, documentation, network building, education, and public outreach. Members are individuals and groups in some 60 countries. Pub: *Manna*, quarterly newsletter; resource guides and reports.

International Arctic Committee
See Comité Arctique International

International Association Against Noise
(Association Internationale contre le Bruit) (AICB)
Hirschenplatz 7, CH-6004 Lucerne, Switzerland. T: (41 41) 51 30 13. Founded 1959. Research, documentation, public education, conferences, and development of internationally recognized standards and regulations. Members are national associations in 19 countries, mainly in Europe.

International Association for Ecology (INTECOL)
Care of Institute of Ecology, University of Georgia, Athens, Georgia 30602, USA. T: (1 404) 542-2968. Twx: 8107543908. Founded 1967. INTECOL is the international organization of professional ecological scientists. A separate association, it is also the Section of Ecology of the International Union of Biological Sciences. Its primary purpose is to foster international communication among ecologists and to represent professional scientific ecology concerns to intergovernmental bodies, particularly Unesco, UNEP, and the World Bank. The Association maintains working groups on Agroecology; Aquat-

ic Primary Productivity; Ecological Futures; Evolutionary Ecology of Mammals; Granivorous Birds; Physiological Ecology; Plankton Ecology; Tropical Ecology; Urban Ecology; and Wetlands. Conferences and workshops are held. INTECOL has individual members, but is mainly an umbrella organization consisting of 32 national and regional ecological societies and 7 international societies concerned with a subdiscipline of ecology, e.g., ecological modeling or tropical ecology. Pub: *INTECOL Newsletter*, bimonthly; *Intecol Bulletin Ecology International*, semiannual; books and reports.

International Association for Falconry and Conservation of Birds of Prey (IAF)
c/o Christian de Coune, Chaussée de Charleroi 24, B-1050 Brussels, Belgium. T: (32 2) 537 91 63. Founded 1968. Members are associations in 16 countries.

International Association for Impact Assessment (IAIA)
c/o Industrial and Systems Engineering, Georgia Institute of Technology, Atlanta, Georgia 30332, USA. Brings together researchers, practitioners, and users of technology assessment, environmental impact assessment, social impact assessment, risk assessment, and other forms of impact assessment. Holds world and regional meetings; sponsors research networks. Members are some 600 individuals in 34 countries. Pub: *Impact Assessment Bulletin*, quarterly journal; newsletter.

International Association for Medicine and Biology of Environment (IAMBE)
c/o Richard Abbou, AIMBE, 115 rue de la Pompe, F-75116 Paris, France. T: (33 1) 45 53 45 04. Tx: 614 584 ecomeb. C: ECOMEBIO. Founded 1971. Promotes study and research on medical and biological problems related to the environment. Organizes international and national courses and symposia. Maintains committees on such topics as the oceans; new technologies; habitat; and developing countries; and noise and health. Maintains a World Office of Information on Environmental Problems. Members are individuals in some 60 countries.

International Association for the Study of People and their Physical Surroundings (IAPS)
c/o Sue-Ann Lee, Architectural Psychology Unit, Kingston-upon-Thames Polytechnic, Knights Park, Surrey KT1 2QJ, England. Scholarly association. Holds a conference every two years.

International Association for Water Law (IAWL)
Via Montevideo 5, I-00198 Rome, Italy. T: (39 6) 844 12 47. Founded 1967. Promotes the science of water law. Members are individual experts in some 80 countries. Pub: Newsletter; journal; reports; conference proceedings.

International Association of Applied Psychology (IIAP)
c/o Psychological Laboratory, Catholic University of Nijmegen, Montessorilaan 3, NL-6500 HE Nijmegen, Netherlands. T: (31 80) 512639. Founded 1920. IIAP is a professional organization with individual members in over 80 countries. It includes a Division of Environmental Psychology (current Chairman: Dr. Arza Churchman, Faculty of Architecture and Town Planning, Technion-Israel Institute of Technology, Haifa 32000, Israel), which publishes a member newsletter and organizes sessions at IIAP international congresses.

International Association of Botanic Gardens (IABG)
c/o Botanic Garden, North Terrace, Adelaide, S.A. 5000, Australia. T: (61 8) 228 2320. Fax: (61 8) 223 1809. An autonomous organization which is affiliated with the International Union of Biological Societies. Promotes international cooperation between botanic gardens; promotes the "conservation and preservation of rare and/or endangered plants through their cultivation and by other means within botanic gardens, arboreta, and similar institutes." Reports that it "has no published document describing its activity."

International Association of Engineering Geology (IAEG)
c/o LCPC, 58 boulevard Lefebvre, F-75732 Paris CEDEX 15, France. T: (33 1) 48 56 52 43. Purposes include promoting the application of the earth sciences to protecting the environment.

International Association of Hydrological Sciences (IAHS)
c/o H.J. Colenbrander, TNO Committee on Hydrological Research, P.O. Box 297, 2501 BD The Hague, Netherlands. T: (31 70) 49 65 37. Tx: 31660 tnogv nl. Fax: (31 70) 85 57 00. Founded 1922. A semi-autonomous association under the International Union of Geodesy and Geophysics. "The oldest and foremost international non-governmental body dealing with hydrology and water resources." Promotes the study and discussion of scientific aspects of hydrology; publishing; initiates and coordinates research that requires international cooperation. IAHS includes the International Commission on Surface Water (ICSW); International Commission on Ground Water (ICGW); International Commission on Continental Erosion (ICCE); International Commission on Snow and Ice (ICSI); International Commission on Water Quality (ICWQ); International Commission on Water Resources Systems (ICWRS); and International Committee on Remote Sensing and Data Transmission (ICRSDT). Members of IAHS are some 2,000 individual hydrologists nominated by national committees for IAHS. Pub: Newsletter; *Hydrological Sciences Journal;* proceedings of conferences.

International Association of Meteorology and Atmospheric Physics (IAMAP)
c/o Prof. M. Kuhn, Institut für Meteorologie und Geophysik, Universität Innsbruck, Innrain 52, A-6020 Innsbruck, Austria. T: (43 5222) 724 218. Tx: (847) 52708. Founded 1919. Promotes meteorological research; provides a forum for discussion of research results and trends. A semi-autonomous association under the International Union of Geodesy and Geophysics. Maintains Commissions on Climate, and on Atmospheric Chemistry and Global Pollution. Pub: Newsletter; assembly proceedings.

International Association of Scientific Experts in Tourism
(Association Internationale d'Experts Scientifiques du Tourisme) (AIEST)
Varnbüelstrasse 19, CH-9000 St. Gallen, Switzerland. T: (41 71) 23 55 11. Tx: 77 425 tisg ch. Founded 1951. Professional society; promotes research on tourism. Environmental impacts of tourism have been the subject of several conferences. Pub: Conference proceedings.

International Association of Zoo Educators (IZE)
Care of National Zoological Park, 3001 Connecticut Avenue, NW, Washington, DC 20008, USA. T: (1 202) 673-4721. Works to expand the conservation educational potential of zoos and aquariums worldwide. Holds conferences. Members are individuals and institutions in some 25 countries. Pub: *Journal of the International Association of Zoo Educators.*

International Association on Water Pollution Research and Control (IAWPRC)
1 Queen Anne's Gate, London SW1H 9BT, England. Founded 1965. Works to encourage international communication, cooperative effort, and exchange of information on water pollution control research and control and water quality management. Sponsors regular international meetings and conferences. Maintains various Specialist Groups. Members of IAWPRC are national committees in 41 countries; there are also individual members. Pub: *Water Research,* monthly; *Water Science and Technology,* monthly (conference proceedings); *Water Quality International,* quarterly; yearbook; technical reports.

International Bar Association (IBA)
2 Harewood Place, Hanover Square, London W1R 9HB, England. T: (44 1) 629 1206. Tx: 8812664 inbar g. C: INBARASSOC. Fax: (44 1) 409 0456. The IBA, founded 1947, is "the leading international legal organization" with 91 member bar associations and law societies representing 800,000 members, as well as 8,000 individual members from 13 countries. It maintains a Section on Energy and Natural Resources Law (SERL), founded as a committee in 1970, which works "to advance the development and understanding of the law as it affects oil, gas, coal, uranium, and other mineral and energy sources." SERL holds seminars, has geographic area groups, and has committees on Oil and Gas Law, Mineral Law, Coal Law, Renewable Energy Law, and Nuclear Law. Pub: *Journal of Energy and Natural Resources Law,* quarterly; newsletter; conference proceedings.

International Biosciences Networks (IBN)
c/o ICSU, 51 boulevard de Montmorency, F-75016 Paris, France. T: (33 1) 45 25 03 29. Tx: 630 553. Founded 1980. A cooperative project of Unesco and the International Council of Scientific Unions (ICSU). Works to develop scientific infrastructures and human resources in the biological sciences in developing countries. Organizes regional networks and facilitates exchange of information among them. Holds training courses and symposia; sponsors fellowships and cooperative scientific research projects. Pub: Reports of symposia and workshops.

International Board for Soil Resources and Management (IBSRAM)
P.O. Box 9-109 Bangkhen, Bangkok 10900, Thailand. T: (66 2) 561-1230. Tx: 21505. C: IBSRAM. Founded 1983. Created to fill a need for an organization "whose primary concern is not a particular crop or group of crops, but the soil itself, and which would apply in local situations the fundamental research provided by international and national research organizations, in order to focus on soil management" in developing countries. IBSRAM "is not a center with its own land and research facilities, but a board designed to promote and test soil management technologies through networks of cooperating national organizations...It pays particular attention to problem soils...whose inherent difficulties have resulted in their productive potential having been largely underutilized so far by the small farmer, with whom IBSRAM is mainly concerned...The network approach involves nationally-based research teams working on a defined range of similar problems who collaborate with each other." Activities, which are mainly in Africa and Asia, and the Pacific, focus on Vertisols, acid tropical soils, and tropical land clearing for sustainable agriculture. Board members are leading scientists and resource managers from several developing and industrialized countries. Regional offices are planned in East and West Africa. Pub: Newsletter; annual report; seminar proceedings; scientific reviews.

International Center for Living Aquatic Resources Management (ICLARM)
P.O. Box 1501, Makati, Manila, Philippines. T: (63 2) 818-0466. C: ICLARM, Manila. Tx (ITT): 45658 ICLARM PM. Founded 1975. Conducts and fosters research and training on fisheries management and fish production, distribution, and use. Pub: Journal, bibliographies, educational materials, technical reports, conference proceedings.

International Centre of Comparative Environmental Law
(Centre International de Droit Compare de l'Environnement)
Place du Presidial, F-87031 Limoges, France

International Chamber of Commerce (ICC)
38 Cours Albert 1er, F-75008 Paris, France.
T: (33 1) 45 62 34 56. Tx: 650 770. C: INCOMERC. Fax: (33 1) 42 25 86 63. The ICC is "a non-governmental organization serving world business. ICC members in 110 countries comprise tens of thousands of business organizations and enterprises with international interests. ICC national committees or councils in 58 countries coordinate activities at national level." In 1978 ICC set up a Commission on the Environment "to promulgate sound environmental policies for industry and prepare business input into intergovernmental and other international projects." The Commission provides "a worldwide forum in which senior representatives of all business interests and sectors can meet to exchange views on environmental issues and developments; represents the business community at UNEP and other international agencies concerned with environmental questions; and formulates and projects specific environmental policies and positions on technical issues." Commission activities have included organizing (with UNEP) the World Industry Conference on Environmental Management (WICEM) in 1984; issuing ICC Environmental Guidelines for World Industry; calling for business cooperation with the recommendations of the 1987 report of the World Commission on Environment and Development (while issuing a number of specific reservations about it). Some specific concerns have been environmental auditing, chemical emergencies, potentially harmful chemicals, the ozone layer, and hazardous waste. The ICC Commission has about 60 members from 26 countries. ICC also includes the:
■ International Environmental Bureau (IEB), 61 route de Chêne, CH-1208 Geneva. IEB, established in 1986 by European and U.S. companies, is an international trans-industry clearinghouse for environmental management information. A specialized division of the ICC, it "complements the work of the Commission on Environment." The Bureau supplies information as responses to questions submitted by firms, governmental agencies, and others; in regular publications; in seminars; and in contacts with industry and trade associations in developing countries. Pub: Newsletter, bimonthly; reports.

International Coalition for Development Action (ICDA)
Rue des Bollandistes 22, B-1050 Brussels, Belgium. T: (32 2) 734 23 32. Founded 1875. Conducts joint international action and education campaigns on issues affecting developing countries, including such environmental issues as pesticide misuse and protection of plant genetic resources. Members are over 500 development groups in 21 industrialized countries. Pub: *ICDA News*, monthly; special reports.

International Coalition for Justice in Bhopal
Care of International Organization of Consumers Unions, P.O. Box 1045, Penang, Malaysia. Works for justice for the victims of the chemical plant explosion in Bhopal, India.

International Commission for the Protection of Alpine Regions
(Commission Internationale pour la Protection des Régions Alpines) (CIPRA)
Care of Dr. Ing. Mario F. Broggi, President, Heiligkreuz 52, FL-9490 Vaduz, Liechtenstein. An NGO whose members are individuals in 7 European countries.

International Commission of Agricultural Engineering (Commission Internationale du Génie Rural) (CIGR)
17, rue de Javel, F-75015 Paris, France. T: (33 1) 45 77 60 66. Founded 1930. Professional association. "1st Technical Section" is concerned with soil and water science applied to agricultural engineering for soil conservation, irrigation, and land improvement and reclamation. An intersection working group deals with applying agricultural engineering techniques in developing countries. CIGR holds conferences and workshops. Pub: Conference proceedings.

International Commission on Irrigation and Drainage (ICID)
48 Nyaya Marg, Chanakyapuri, New Delhi 110021, India. T: (91 11) 3016837. Tx: 031-65920 icid in. C: INTCOIR. Founded 1950. ICID is "the leading non-governmental, scientific and technical international organization in the fields of irrigation, drainage, flood control, and river training. The objects of ICID are to stimulate and promote the development and application of the arts, sciences, and techniques of engineering, agriculture, economics, ecology, and social science in managing water and land resources" in these fields, with special attention to the needs of developing countries. Activities include collection, analysis, and interchange of information; organizing conferences and meetings; and promoting consultations and cooperation among participating countries and with international organizations. Maintains technical committees and working groups on such topics as irrigation efficiency and drainage construction. ICID members are representative national committees in over 80 countries. Pub: *ICID Bulletin*, semiannual; reports; state-of-the-art compilations; manuals; reference books.

International Commission on Large Dams (ICOLD)
151 boulevard Haussmann, F-75008 Paris, France. T: (33 1) 47 64 68 24. Tx: 641320. Founded 1928. Encourages improvements in the design, construction, maintenance, and operation of large dams through research and exchange of

information. Main activity is a triennial congress. Members are national committees in 77 countries. Pub: *ICOLD Technical Bulletin*, 3 or 4 times a year; congress proceedings; reference books.

International Commission on Occupational Health (ICOH)
10 avenue Jules-Crosnier, CH-1206 Geneva, Switzerland. T: (41 22) 47 61 84. A scientific organization whose members are individual specialists in occupational health, including physicians and industrial hygienists. Includes Scientific Committees on Pesticides, and on Health Effects of Physical Environmental Factors.

International Commission on Radiological Protection (ICRP)
P.O. Box 35, Didcot OX11 ORJ, England. T: (44 235) 83 39 29. Tx: 838897 icrp g. Founded 1928. Produces and continually reviews recommendations for protection against radiation, which are adopted by many intergovernmental organizations. Members of the commission and its committees are individual specialists from 20 countries.

International Committee on Coral Reefs
(Comité International dés Recifs Coralliens) Care of Dr. Bernard Salvat, Ecole Pratique des Hautes Etudes, Laboratoire de Biologie Marine, 55 rue de Buffon, F-75005 Paris, France. Scientific group concerned with coral reefs and related problems.

International Council for Bird Preservation (ICBP)
32 Cambridge Road, Girton, Cambridge CB3 0PJ, England. T: (44 223) 277318. Founded 1922. Assesses the status and compiless data on bird species throughout the world; identifies conservation problems and priorities; and initiates, promotes, and coordinates conservation projects and international conventions. ICBP maintains World Working Groups on families of birds having special conservation problems; it has national sections and representatives in over 100 countries. Pub: *ICBP Bulletin; Newsletter; Endangered Birds of the World: The ICBP Red Data Book;* study reports; symposia; regional surveys.

International Council for Environmental Education in French-Speaking Countries
(Conseil International d'Education Mésologique des Pays de Langue Française) (CIEM) C.P. 39, Sillery, Quebec G1T 2P7, Canada. Founded 1977. Promotes environmental education and conservation in French-speaking countries, primarily in the Third World. Emphasis is on personal contact through maintaining a network "to break the intellectual isolation affecting so many countries and to keep them up-to-date on activities of concern to them throughout the world." An outgrowth of a project sponsored by IUCN. Has conducted projects in cooperation with UNEP and Unesco. Members are individuals in 32 countries.

International Council for Game and Wildlife Conservation
(Conseil International de la Chasse et de la Conservation du Gibier) (CIC) 15 rue de Teheran, F-75008 Paris, France. T: (33 1) 45 63 51 33. Founded 1930. Promotes hunting "in harmony with nature conservancy and wildlife protection." Members are individuals and groups in 57 countries. Pub: Annual report.

International Council for Research in Agroforestry (ICRAF)
P.O. Box 30677, Nairobi, Kenya. T: (254 2) 332304. Tx: 22048. C: ICRAF. Founded 1977. Initiates, stimulates, and supports research leading to more sustainable and productive land use in developing countries through the integration or better management of trees in land-use systems. Projects in various countries of Africa, Malaysia, and Peru. Collaborates with national and international institutions in implementing research programs. Pub: Newsletter; bibliographies; research reports.

International Council of Environmental Law (ICEL)
Adenauerallee 214, D-5300 Bonn 1, Federal Republic of Germany. T: (49 228) 269240. Founded 1969. Fosters exchange and dissemination of information about environmental law, policy, and administration; encourages advice and assistance among its membership. Maintains an extensive library and computerized information base. ICEL works closely with the IUCN Commission on Environmental Policy, Law, and Administration, and is located on the same premises as the IUCN Environmental Law Centre. Members are some 250 individual lawyers, professors, and policy-makers, as well as organizations in this field. Pub: *Environmental Policy and Law* (semiannual journal published for ICEL by North Holland); *References* (bibliographic bulletin); directory of members.

International Council of Scientific Unions (ICSU)
51 boulevard de Montmorency, F-75016, France. T: (33 1) 45-25-03. Established 1919; present name adopted 1931. ICSU is the keystone of organized world science. It is an association of international scientific unions and national scientific organizations in many countries (see "Note on ICSU Members," below). ICSU works to encourage and coordinate international scientific activity through the international and national bodies. It has done this in part by organizing major interdisciplinary scientific programs such as the International Geophysical Year (1956-57); the International Biological Programme (1964-74); the International Lithosphere Programme (1981-); and the current International Geosphere-Biosphere Programme: A Study of Global Change. ICSU also organizes scientific and educational symposia, conferences, and other major meetings (in one recent year 600 such meetings were held);

appoints committees, commissions, and working groups, which hold their own smaller meetings; works to safeguard the pursuit of science; provides a wide range of fellowships and grants; sponsors lectures and courses in Third-World countries; and represents the scientific community in certain negotiations with intergovernmental and some international non-governmental bodies.

Note on ICSU members: *National Members* of ICSU (including associates and observers) include 71 national scientific academies or other national groups of scientists (these are listed in Part 6 of this book with the notation "ICSU national member"). Twenty *International Scientific Unions* belong to ICSU. Those concerned directly with the management of the environment and natural resources, and which are listed separately in this directory, are: International Union of Geodesy and Geophysics; International Union of Biological Sciences; and International Geographical Union. Among the *scientific associates* of ICSU that are listed in this directory are: Pacific Science Association; International Society of Soil Science; International Association on Water Pollution Research and Control; International Union of Forestry Research Organizations; and Third World Academy of Sciences.

Pub: *Science International* (ICSU newsletter). The ICSU Press publishes books, conference proceedings, and other monographs, as well as 3 scholarly journals.

Major ICSU units concerned with the environment and resources are:
■ Scientific Committee on Problems of the Environment (SCOPE). Created in 1970, SCOPE works to "advance knowledge of the influence of humans on their environment, as well as the effects of these environmental changes upon people, their health, and their welfare--with particular attention to those influences and effects which are either global or shared by several nations; to serve as a non-governmental, interdisciplinary, and international council of scientists; and as a source of advice for the benefit of governments and intergovernmental and non-governmental bodies with respect to environmental problems. The effectiveness of SCOPE's role as a source of advice can be illustrated by a number of examples: (1) in 1971, SCOPE submitted to the Secretariat of the UN Conference on the Human Environment a study entitled 'Global Environmental Modelling.' This was later updated into an Action Plan...(2) also in 1971 SCOPE put forward a proposal and began work on an International Registry of Potentially Toxic Chemicals..." The main emphasis of the SCOPE program is currently on biogeochemical cycles; ecotoxicology; genetically-designed organisms in the environment (biotechnology), subsiding coastal areas, global change, groundwater contamination, and the use of scientific information towards sustainable development. SCOPE has Scientific Advisory Committees on these and other subjects. (A booklet is available describing the SCOPE program in detail.)

■ Special Committee for the International Geosphere-Biosphere Programme (SC-IGBP). Created 1986. Concerned with the environment as a whole, this program is concentrating its initial activities on: terrestrial biosphere (atmospheric chemistry interactions); marine biosphere (atmosphere interactions); biospheric aspects of the hydrological cycle; effects of climate change on terrestrial ecosystems; global geosphere-biosphere modeling; data and information systems; techniques for extracting environmental data of the past; and geo-biosphere observatories.
■ Committee on Water Research (COWAR). Created 1964. Promotes "necessary contacts between international non-governmental water-oriented organizations" regarding water research. A joint committee with the Union of International Technical Associations.
■ Committee on Science and Technology in Developing Countries (COSTED). Created 1966. Works to coordinate and encourage efforts by ICSU and the international scientific unions to facilitate the "greatest possible participation in their programs by scientists in the developing countries."
■ Scientific Committee on Antarctic Research (SCAR). Created 1958. Provides a forum for scientists of all countries with research activities in the Antarctic to discuss their field activities and plans and to promote collaboration.
■ Scientific Committee on Biotechnology (COBIOTECH). Created 1986. Works "to promote biotechnology for the benefit of humankind and to provide information and advice on biotechnology for the international community as a whole."
■ Scientific Committee on Oceanic Research (SCOR). Created 1957. Works to further scientific activity in all branches of oceanic research. "To do so, SCOR examines problems and identifies elements that would benefit from enhanced international action; fosters recognition of individual marine scientists and laboratories; presents the views of marine scientists to the appropriate international community;" and cooperates with other groups concerned with marine affairs.
■ Inter-Union Commission on the Application of Science and Technology to Agriculture, Forestry, and Aquaculture (CASAFA). Created 1978. Promotes cooperation in research between institutions in developed and developing countries toward the resolution of problems of food production and processing in developing countries.
■ Inter-Union Commission on the Lithosphere (ICL). Created 1980. Concerned with "interdisciplinary research for an improved understanding of the earth, especially those aspects on which human society depends for its well-being...One special goal is to strengthen the earth sciences and to make their application in the developing countries more effective."
■ International Biosciences Networks (IBN). *See* separate entry.
■ Committee on Climatic Changes and the Ocean (CCCO). Created 1979. This is a joint

ICSU/SCOR-Unesco/IOC effort charged with formulating the research programs required to meet the oceanographic objectives of the World Climate Research Programme (WCRP). Main function is to "improve our understanding of the ocean's role in climate change and variability and to identify the most climatologically-significant processes and the means for their incorporation into mathematical models." CCCO cooperates closely with the ICSU-WMO Joint Scientific Committee for the World Climate Research Programme.

■ ICSU-WMO Joint World Climate Research Programme (WCRP). Created 1980. A joint program of ICSU and the World Meteorological Organization (WMO), which is described in Part 4 of this book. WCRP, which is recognized in international circles to be the "only" world program of its kind, has as its "long-term objectives a better understanding of climate change and variability and their causes, whether from natural or human influences."

International Council of Voluntary Agencies (ICVA)

13 rue Gautier, CH-1201 Geneva, Switzerland. T: (41 22) 31 66 01. Tx: 22891 icva ch. C: VOLAG. Founded 1962. ICVA is an "independent, international association of non-governmental, non-profit-making organizations active in the fields of humanitarian assistance and development cooperation." It "provides a permanent international liaison structure for voluntary agency consultation and cooperation...ICVA does not implement relief or development projects itself, but provides services and support to its member agencies to enable them to cooperate and perform more effectively." Maintains a Sub-Group on Environment and Sustainable Development. Adopted in 1988 "A Policy Statement and Action Plan for International Development, Environment and Population NGOs endorsed by the International Council of Voluntary Agencies," which calls for greater cooperation among organizations in the three fields. Pub: *ICVA News,* bimonthly; *NGO Management* (newsletter); annual report; member agency profiles; policy and program reports.

International Council of Women (ICW)

13 rue Caumartin, F-75009 Paris, France. T: (33 1) 47 42 19 40. Founded 1888. An umbrella association for voluntary women's organizations worldwide; works to promote the welfare of mankind, the family, and the individual. Maintains a Standing Committee on Environment and Habitat. Pub: *ICW Newsletter.*

International Council on Monuments and Sites (ICOMOS)

Hôtel Saint Aignan, 75 rue du Temple, F-75003 Paris, France. T: (33 1) 42 77 35 76. C: ICOMOS. Founded 1965. ICOMOS is "the only international non-governmental organization that works to promote the application of theory, methodology, and scientific techniques to the conservation of architectural heritage." Adopts guidelines and defines management techniques for cultural properties; develops training programs; organizes expert missions on particular conservation questions; advises Unesco on cultural properties to be included on the World Heritage List; sponsors the International Day for Monuments and Sites (April 18); maintains a documentation center. Maintains specialized international committees on such topics as Rock Art; Vernacular Architecture; Archaeological Management; Historic Gardens and Sites; Cultural Tourism; and Historic Towns. ICOMOS has national committees in some 60 countries. Members are qualified individuals and institutions. Pub: *Icomos Information,* quarterly.

International Development Ethics Association (IDEA)

c/o David A. Crocker, Department of Philosophy, Colorado State University, Fort Collins, Colorado 80523, USA. T: (1 303) 491-6315. Founded 1987. Members are philosophers and development theorists, policy-makers, and practitioners who apply ethical reflection to development goals and strategies and to the relations between rich and poor countries. Holds conferences.

International Esperanto Society for Nature Conservation

c/o Rezso Baross, Balzac u. 11, H-1136 Budapest, Hungary. Founded 1978. Promotes international exchange of information about nature conservation using the language Esperanto.

International Federation for Housing and Planning (IFHP)

43 Wasenaarseweg, NL-2596 CG The Hague, Netherlands. T: (31 70) 244557. Tx: 31578. C: IFHP. Founded 1913 by Ebenezer Howard under the name "International Garden Cities and Town Planning Association." IFHP's objectives are to "improve general knowledge in housing, planning, and related fields, and thereby to improve housing and planning practice throughout the world." Activities include organizing study tours, seminars, conferences, and an annual congress. Standing committees include Energy and Environment; Education in Planning; Urban Land Policy; New Towns; and Managing the Metropolis. Members are governmental and private organizations and individuals in 65 countries. Pub: *Prospect* (journal); reports; conference proceedings.

International Federation of Chemical, Energy and General Workers' Unions (ICEF)

109 avenue Emil de Béco, B-1050 Brussels, Belgium. T: (32 2) 647 02 35. Founded 1907. Members are 200 affiliated trade unions with 6.5 million members in 72 countries. Concerns include health and safety issues related to workplace environments in chemical, energy, and other industries. Pub: *Quarterly Bulletin;* occasional reports (e.g., *The Trade Union Report on Bhopal*).

International Federation of Institutes for Advanced Study (IFIAS)
39 Spadina Road, Toronto, Ontario M5R 2S9, Canada. T: (1 416) 926-7570. Fax: (1 416) 926-9481. Founded 1972. An "international association of 37 leading independent research institutions from 24 countries, which have agreed to collaborate in addressing major world problems of long-term importance...IFIAS both develops and facilitates international scientific research programs...During the first fifteen years of its existence, IFIAS has organized some 70 project workshops and seminars all over the world, generated more than 100 books, reports, and articles in learned journals, and carried out some 15 programs and research projects. The direction of IFIAS research has been largely determined by the need to anticipate and respond more effectively to long-term problems in the face of inevitable and accelerating global change. Such problems, by their very nature, require an interdisciplinary approach, and it is here that IFIAS possesses unique advantages." Much of the Federation's work has focused on global resource and environmental problems. Currently, IFIAS programs include: Human Response to Global Change (a major program initiated in 1987, which seeks over a decade to obtain greater understanding of the human causes of global change and develop strategies for appropriate responses); Coastal Resources Management; Understanding Complex Systems (focusing on ecosystems); Urban Risk Assessment; and Greening the Desert (combating desertification). The 37 member institutes include, for example, El Colegio de Mexico (Mexico City); Food Research Institute (Stanford, California); Institute for Future Studies (Copenhagen, Denmark); Japan Economic Research Center (Tokyo); Marga Institute (Colombo, Sri Lanka); and Institute of World Economics (Budapest, Hungary). There is a field office in Maastricht, Netherlands. Pub: *The IFIAS Global Commentary* (annual report designed to make findings of member institutes more available); reports and working papers.

International Federation of Landscape Architects (IFLA)
4 rue Hardy, F-78009 Versailles, France. T: (33 1) 30 21 13 15. Founded 1948. Promotes the profession of landscape architecture. Activities include active participation in international activities related to environmental protection, including studies and projects on structure of the urban and rural landscape, roads, protection of green areas, preservation of coastlines, and the impact of tourism on the environment. Maintains International Committees on Coastlines, Endangered Landscapes, Historical Landscapes, Landscape Planning in Rural Areas, and Landscape Planning in Urban Areas. Members are professional societies in 40 countries. Pub: *IFLA News*, semi-annual; yearbook; congress proceedings and reports.

International Federation of Organic Agriculture Movements (IFOAM)
c/o Ökozentrum Imsbach, D-6695 Tholey-Theley, Federal Republic of Germany. Founded 1972. Promotes cooperation among groups concerned with developing ecological or "organic" approaches to agriculture. Members are 125 associations and 300 individuals in some 50 countries.

International Foundation for Development Alternatives (IFDA)
4 place du Marché, CH-1260 Nyon, Switzerland. T: (41 22) 61 82 81. Tx: 419 953. Founded 1976. President is Marc Nerfin. Acts as a forum for information exchange and mutually-educating dialogues both between citizens' movements and governmental actors and among citizens' movements themselves toward development alternatives that focus on satisfying human needs, self-reliance, and harmony with the environment. Promotes the "third system" (voluntary associations apart from government and business). Council members are from over 40 countries. Pub: *IFDA Dossier* (a widely-circulated bimonthly bulletin of ideas, opinion, and news of new publications and projects); *Special United Nations Service* (a daily news service on UN activities related to Third World development).

International Foundation for the Conservation of Game (IGF)
15, rue de Téhéran, F-75008 Paris, France. T: (33 1) 45 63 51 33. Tx: IGF 640 430 F. Founded 1977. Works to conserve wildlife and nature; promotes "rational and reasonable" harvesting of game populations. Governed by a board of individuals from 9 countries.

International Foundation for the Survival and Development of Humanity (IF)
c/o Evgeny Velikhov, Vice President, Academy of Sciences of the USSR, Leninsky Prospect 14, 117901 Moscow, USSR. T: (7 95) 232 2910. Founded 1988 as a private international foundation to pursue an agenda related to "urgent problems of international security, development, and environment." According to *Science* (25 November 1988), board members include Velikhov, Robert McNamara, Theodore Hesburgh, Armand Hammer, and Jerome Wiesner. Offices are planned for Stockholm and Washington. Initial work on the environment will focus on African development and protection of the Baltic Sea.

International Friends of Nature (IFN)
(Naturfreunde-Internationale (NFI)
Diefenbachgasse 36, A-1150 Vienna, Austria. T: (43 222) 85 97 51. Founded as part of a working people's movement in Vienna in 1895; revived in 1945. A cultural and leisure-time organization "committed to the goals of democratic socialism." Activities include hiking, mountaineering, and environmental protection. Maintains over 1,000 Nature Friend Houses as meeting places and hostels. Holds occasional

conferences on environmental protection issues. Members are some 350,000 individuals in 15 countries (in Europe, as well as Israel, USA, and Mexico). International Young Nature Friends (IYFN) is an independent part of IFN. Pub: *Naturfreunde International* (magazine in German).

International Fund for Animal Welfare
P.O. Box 193, Yarmouth Port, Massachusetts 02675, USA. T: (1 508) 362-4944. Founded 1969. Works for protection of wild and domestic animals. Current focus is on seals in Canada and Alaska, vicuña in Peru, monarch butterflies in the U.S., and dog and cat abuse in Asia. Offices in England, Netherlands, Canada, and West Germany. Members are some 500,000 individuals in various countries.

International Geographical Union (IGU)
c/o Department of Geography, University of Alberta, Edmonton, Alberta T6G 2H4, Canada. T: (1 403) 432-3287. Tx: 037-2979 geography. Fax: (1 403) 432-7219. Founded 1922. Promotes the study of geographical problems. Among its various units are Commissions on Mountain Geoecology and Coastal Environment, and a Study Group on Historical Geography of Global Environmental Change. Members are 90 country committees for the IGU. Pub: *IGU Bulletin; Circular Letter;* conference proceedings.

International Institute for Applied Systems Analysis (IIASA)
A-2361 Laxenburg, Austria. T: (43 2236) 715210. Tx: 079137. Fax: (43 2236) 71313. A "nongovernmental, multidisciplinary research institution supported by scientific organizations in 16 countries. IIASA's objectives are to promote international cooperation in addressing problems arising from social, economic, technological, and environmental change; to develop and formalize systems analysis and the sciences contributing to it, and to promote the use of the analytical techniques needed to address complex problems; to create a network of institutions in the countries with national member organizations and elsewhere for joint scientific research; and to inform policy advisors and decision-makers about the application of IIASA's work to current problems." IIASA's Environment Program currently focuses on biosphere dynamics (global vegetation, ecological sustainability in Europe, European forest decline, and boreal forest dynamics); transboundary air pollution; water resources (including decision support systems for managing large international rivers, and water resources in a changing environment); and environmental monitoring. Pub: *Options* (newsletter); *Research Plan, Environment Program* (annual); working papers and research reports.

International Institute for Environment and Development (IIED)
3 Endsleigh Street, London WC1H 0DD, England. T: (44 1) 388 2117. Tx: 261681. Fax: (44 1) 388 2826.
■ IIED Latin America, Corrientes 2835, 6ª piso, 1193 Buenos Aires, Argentina. T: (54 1) 961-3050.
Founded 1971. Conducts policy research and advocacy to promote sustainable development. "Until recently the Institute worked largely behind the scenes with governments, international aid agencies and, most importantly, at the local level with small community groups in the South." Programs: Energy and Development (currently concentrating on the "firewood crisis" of developing countries); Forestry and Land Use (concentrating on the tropics); Human Settlements (including housing and health, basic services, population and urban change, and housing and human rights); Drylands Agriculture (in Africa); Economics (defining and applying concepts of sustainable development); Marine Resources (Antarctica, fisheries management); and Sustainable Agriculture (advice and training in the Third World). The Latin American office, opened in 1988 as an autonomous organization, focuses on urban environment-development problems, natural disasters and building a Latin American coalition for research and action on environment-development issues. IIED cosponsors the London Environmental Economics Centre at University College, University of London. Earthscan Publications Ltd., a wholly-owned subsidary, is the book publishing arm of IIED. The North American office of IIED has become part of the World Resources Institute (listed under in Part 6 under USA). IIED, a non-membership organization, is governed by an international board. Pub: *Perspectives* (newsletter); annual report; *Haramata* (newsletter of the Drylands Agriculture Program); books (catalog available).

International Institute for Environment and Urban Planning
c/o Dr. Jorge E. Hardoy, Avenida Corrientes 2835, 6ª piso, Cuerpo A, 1193 Buenos Aires, Argentina

International Institute for Land Reclamation and Improvement (ILRI)
P.O. Box 45, NL-6700 AA Wageningen, Netherlands. Research, training, and advisory work in irrigation, drainage, and other water resources problems, particularly in developing countries. Pub: Bulletins and bibliographies.

International Institute for Water
(Centre International de l'Eau)
149, rue Gabriel Péri, F-54500 Vandoeuvre-lès-Nancy, France. T: (33 8) 356 64 33. Founded 1984. Fosters exchanges, information dissemination, and international cooperation in the field of water and sanitation.

International Institute of Fisheries Economics and Trade
Office of International Research and Development, Snell Hall 400, Oregon State University, Corvallis, Oregon 97331, USA. T: (1 503) 754-2228. Tx: 5105960686 ossu cid covs. Promotes discussion and research on international fishery policy and seafood trade matters. Members are representatives of governments, industry, and universities from a number of countries.

International Irrigation Management Institute (IIMI)
Digana Villaga, Kandy, Sri Lanka. T: (94 8) 74274. Tx: 22318 iimi hq ce. Founded 1983. Works to strengthen national efforts to improve and sustain the performance of irrigation systems in developing countries. Conducts research, training and information exchange. Maintains field units in various countries. Not a membership organization.

International Law Association (ILA)
3 Paper Buildings, The Temple, London EC4Y 7EU, England. T: (44 1) 353 2804. C: PAXUNA. Founded 1873. Promotes the study, elucidation, and advancement of international law. Among its units are Committees on International Water Resources Law, the Exclusive Economic Zone, and Legal Aspects of Long-Distance Air Pollution. Members of ILA are national branches in 41 countries. Pub: Conference reports; research reports.

International League for the Protection of Cetaceans
Podere II Falco (Loc. Acquaioli), Città della Pieve, I-06062 Perugia, Italy

International Mountain Society (IMS)
P.O. Box 3128, Boulder, Colorado 80307, USA. T: (1 303) 494-9228. Founded 1981. Works to further international collaboration for protection of mountain lands and peoples and for the rational development of mountain resources. Assists in creating research centers and national institutions; organizes conferences. Members are individual scientists, planners, developers, and concerned citizens in some 100 countries. Pub: *Mountain Research and Development*, quarterly; reports.

International Network of Resource Information Centers (INRIC)
c/o Dennis Meadows, Executive Secretary, H Box 8000, Dartmouth College, Hanover, New Hampshire 03755, USA. Also known as the Balaton Group. Links resource managers and global modelers to exchange information on creating "conditions in which people in all parts of the globe can and will manage the earth's resources to meet human needs." Members are centers in 22 countries.

International Network on Soil Fertility and Sustainable Rice Farming
Care of IRRI, P.O. Box 933, Manila, Philippines. T: (63 2) 742 0717. Fax: (63 2) 817 8470. Coordinated by the International Rice Research Institute (IRRI).

International Nuclear Law Association (INLA)
Square de Meeûs 29, B-1040 Brussels, Belgium. T: (32 2) 513 68 45. Founded 1970. Promotes research and knowledge about legal problems relating to peaceful use of nuclear energy, keeping in mind the protection of people and the environment. Members are legal experts.

International Ocean Institute (IOI)
P.O. Box 524, Valetta, Malta. T: 226596. Tx: 1946. C: INTEROCEAN. Founded 1972. Promotes research on peaceful uses of ocean space and resources through research, fellowships, information dissemination, courses, and seminars, and "Pacem in Maribus" convocations. Main activity is a training program on management and conservation of ocean resources. Members are trustees and planning council members from 23 countries. Pub: *Across the Oceans*, semi-annual; *Ocean Yearbook*; proceedings of convocations; reports.

International Oceanographic Foundation
3979 Rickenbacker Causeway, Virginia Key, Miami, Florida 33149, USA. T: (1 305) 361-5786. Founded 1953. Promotes scientific study and exploration of the oceans; conducts public education about the vital role of the oceans. Members: 25,000 individuals. Pub: *Sea Frontiers*.

International Organization for Biological Control of Noxious Animals and Plants (IOBC)
c/o CSIRO Biological Control Unit, 335 avenue Parguel, F-34100 Montpelier, France. A independent organization, IOBC is also a commission of the International Union of Biological Sciences. It works "to stimulate scientific activities around the world in order to develop effective and harmless methods of controlling pest species. The research operations concentrate on the use of biological control agents, whether alone or in combination with other control measures in the general frame of integrated pest management." Organizes scientific meetings and symposia; sponsors working groups on problems of particular importance (e.g., fruit flies); maintains regional groups. Members are individuals and institutions throughout the world. Pub: *Entomophaga* (quarterly journal); newsletter.

International Organization for Standardization (ISO)
C.P. 56, CH-1121 Geneva 20, Switzerland. T: (41 22) 34 12 40. Tx: 23 887. C: ISORGANIZ. Fax: (41 22) 33 34 30. Founded 1947. Promotes the development of standardization to facilitate international exchange of goods and services and to develop cooperation in intellectual, scientific, technological, and economic activity. ISO works

through an extensive network of technical committees, many of which relate directly or indirectly to the environment, e.g., on air and water quality standards, and toxicity limits in ceramic ware). Pub: *ISO Bulletin*, monthly; ISO International Standards (catalog available)

International Organization of Consumers Unions (IOCU)
Emmastraat 9, NL-2595 EG The Hague, Netherlands. T: (31 70) 47 63 31. Tx: 33561. C: INTEROCU. Fax: (31 70) 83 49 76.
■ Regional Office for Asia and the Pacific, P.O. Box 1045, 10830 Penang, Malaysia. T: (604) 20391. Tx: 40164 apiocu ma.
■ Regional Office for Latin America and the Caribbean, Casilla 10993, Suc. 2, Montevideo, Uruguay. T: (598 2) 901901. Tx: 23135 iocu uy. Founded 1960. "Links the activities of consumer organizations in some 50 countries...promotes the expansion of the consumer movement worldwide [particularly in developing countries], and functions as an international consumer advocate." Concerns include hazardous products, technologies, and wastes. Generates campaigns on such issues as "Bhopal, Chernobyl, food irradiation, and biotechnology." Pesticide safety has been an important focus; IOCU helped set up the Pesticide Action Network (PAN) in 1982, and it works with PAN to monitor the effectiveness of FAO's pesticide code. Pub: *IOCU, The Hague*, 10 issues per year; *IOCU Newsletter*. From Penang office: *Consumer Currents*, 10 times per year. Policy and educational reports.

International Planned Parenthood Federation (IPPF)
Regent's College, Regent's Park, London NW1 4NS, England. T: (44 1) 486 0741. Tx: 919573. C: IPEPEE. Fax: (44 1) 487 7950. Founded 1952. The leading international NGO in the family planing field. Works "to promote the education of peoples of the world in family planning and responsible parenthood; to preserve and protect the good health, both mental and physical, of parents, children, and young people through promoting and supporting effective family planning services; to educate people in the demographic problems of their own communities and of the world; and to stimulate appropriate research." IPPF has given increasing attention to the interrelationships between population and environment, and publishes "Earthwatch" as a regular supplement to its monthly magazine. It has led in bringing together representatives of population and conservation groups, particularly through a British group called Common Ground, and through IUCN, which set up a Task Force on Population and Sustainable Development. Members are family planning associations in 125 countries. Pub: *People*, quarterly magazine; annual report; numerous studies and educational materials.

International Primate Protection League (IPPL)
P.O. Box 766, Summerville, South Carolina 29484, USA. Founded 1973. Works for the protection of primates (apes, lemurs, monkeys, etc.) through public education, raising funds for anti-poaching efforts and sanctuaries, monitoring conditions in zoos and laboratories, as well as trade in primates, and action research. Has field representatives in some 20 countries. Maintains a gibbon sanctuary in South Carolina. Members are interested individuals in many countries. Pub: Newsletter.

International Primatological Society (IPS)
3500 Market Street, Philadelphia, Pennsylvania 19104, USA. Founded 1964. Promotes research on, and protection of, primates, with special attention to intensification of international cooperation. Members are 750 individuals and 4 institutions in some 40 countries. Pub: *IPS News*.

International Professional Association for Environmental Affairs (IPRE)
25, rue de la Science, Boîte 18, B-1040 Brussels, Belgium. T: Luxembourg (352) 34 82 77. Founded 1976. Members are some 165 individuals who work professionally in environmental affairs. Organizes "gatherings during which environmental problems can be discussed in the broadest possible way," and publishes results. Meetings, which usually last two days, are held about twice a year in various European cities and focus on such topics as waste disposal, hazardous substance control, and effective communication of environmental information.

International Radiation Protection Association (IRPA)
10 rue Poussin, F-75016 Paris, France. T: (33 1) 42 88 08 24. Founded 1966. An international forum for interaction and exchange of information among those involved in radiation protection activities. Seeks to protect humans and the environment from the hazards of ionizing radiation, and works to facilitate the use of radiation and atomic energy for the good of humankind. Publishes guidelines for limits to exposure to various types of radiation.

International Reference Centre for Community Water Supply and Sanitation (IRC)
P.O. Box 93190, 2509 AD Den Haag, Netherlands. T: (31 70) 814911. C: Worldwater, The Hague. Tx: 33296. Founded 1968 by an agreement between WHO and the Dutch Government. Promotes safe drinking water supplies and adequate sanitation facilities in developing countries through providing information, education and training, advice, and demonstrations. Members are national organizations in some 30 countries.

International Research Centre on the Environment 'Pio Manzù'
I-47040 Verucchio, Italy. T: (39 541) 678 139. Tx: 550423. C: PIO MANZU. Fax: (39 541) 668 249. Founded 1969. Promotes research into

the effects of technology and industry on the human and cultural environment. Holds an annual international conference in Italy. Members are individuals in 19 countries. Pub: *Environmental Structures*, 3 times a year; conference proceedings.

International Society for Ecological Economics (ISEE)
Care of Coastal and Estuarine Policy Program, Chesapeake Bay Laboratory, University of Maryland, P.O. Box 38, Solomons, Maryland 20688, USA. T: (1 301) 326-4281. "Concerned with extending and integrating the study and management of 'nature's household' (ecology) and 'mankind's household' (economics). This integration is implied in the common Greek root 'oikos' shared by the two disciplines. Unfortunately, at present they share little else. Conceptual and professional isolation have led to economic and environmental policies which are mutually destructive rather than reinforcing over the long run. Because the two fields are too narrowly defined, there is a tendency for economists to ignore nature while ecologists tend to ignore humans. No discipline studies what we might call the ecology of man or the economy of nature, the web of interconnections uniting the economic subsystem to the overall ecosystem of which it is a part. ISEE aims to remedy this situation by publication of the journal *Ecological Economics* [quarterly, first issue January 1989], sponsorship of regional and international scientific meetings, and in general fostering and encouraging research in the area." Scope of interest includes, e.g., valuation of natural resources, sustainable development, integrated ecological-economic modeling, and energy accounting. Members are individual professionals.

International Society for Ecological Modelling (ISEM)
International Secretariat, Langkær Vænge 9, DK-3500 Væerlose, Copenhagen, Denmark. Founded 1975. A professional society in the field of ecological and environmental modeling (British spelling "modelling") through computer technology. Holds a biennial international conference. Facilitates exchange of new software among members. Some examples of interests (from a recent issue of *EM*): "Model Complexity and Data Worth: An Assessment of Changes in the Global Carbon Budget"; "Population Dynamics of the Forest Tent Caterpillar." Members are some 500 individuals. Has an active branch in North America. *Pub: Ecological Modelling*, (journal); newsletter (3 issues per year).

International Society for Environmental Education
c/o Prof. Craig B. Davis, School of Natural Resources, Ohio State University, 2021 Coffey Road, Columbus, Ohio 43210, USA

International Society for Tropical Ecology (ISTE)
Care of Department of Botany, Banaras Hindu University, Varanasi 221005, India. T: 54291, ext. 352. Founded 1960. Promotes "the cause of ecology" in the tropics and subtropics. Organizes international symposia. Members are interested individuals in many countries, although membership is concentrated in India. Pub: *Tropical Ecology*, semiannual; *Directory and Handbook*.

International Society of Biometeorology (ISB)
Witikonerstrasse 446, CH-8053 Zurich, Switzerland. Founded 1956. Members are some 400 biometeorologists (specialists in the relation between climate and life) working in over 50 countries in the fields of agriculture, botany, forestry, entomology, human, veterinary, and zoological biometeorology. Holds a triennial congress. Pub: *International Journal of Biometeorology*, quarterly; *Progress in Biometeorology*; congress proceedings.

International Society of City and Regional Planners (ISoCaRP)
Mauritsgade 23, N-2514 HD The Hague, Netherlands. T: (31 70) 46 26 54. Founded 1965. Promotes the profession of city and regional planning; fosters education and research in the field. Holds workshops and an annual congress. Members are some 375 individuals in 50 countries. Pub: *ISoCaRP News Bulletin*, semi-annual.

International Society of Soil Science (ISSS).
P.O. Box 353, 6700 AJ Wageningen, Netherlands. T: (31 8370) 19063. Tx: 45888 intas nl. Founded 1924. Promotes the scientific study of soils. Members are some 7,000 individual soil scientists and 60 affiliated national societies. Includes a Subcommission on Soil Conservation and Environment, as well as a Working Group on Desertification Control. Pub: *Bulletin*.

International Society of Tropical Foresters (ISTF)
5400 Grosvenor Lane, Bethesda, Maryland 20814, USA. T: (1 301) 897-8720. Founded 1950; reactivated 1979. Committed to the "protection, wise management, and rational use of the world's tropical forests." Sponsors workshops and symposia. Members are 1,700 individuals in over 100 countries. Pub: *ISTF News*, quarterly newsletter; membership directory.

International Soil Reference and Information Centre
9 Duivendaal, P.O. Box 353, 6700 AJ Wageningen, Netherlands. T: (31 8370) 19063. C: ISOMUS. Tx: 45888 (via IAC). Founded 1966. Reference center on all major soils of the world for the benefit of sustained land use and sound agriculture, particularly for developing countries, to which it provides technical assistance in soil mapping and classification.

International Solid Wastes and Public Cleansing Association (ISWA)

Vester Farimagsgade 29, DK-1606 Copenhagen V, Denmark. T: (45 1) 15 65 65. Fax: (45 1) 93 71 71. Works "to promote the adoption of acceptable systems of solid wastes management and of public cleansing, through technological development and improvement of practices, for the protection of the environment and conservation of materials and energy resources." Maintains a Working Group on Hazardous Wastes. Holds international symposia. Members are national committees in some 20 countries, as well as organizations, individuals, and firms working in the field. Pub: *Waste Management and Research*, quarterly; *ISWA Times*, newsletter; book series; reference materials.

International Training Centre for Water Resources Management (ITCWRM)

B.P. 13, Sophia Antipolis, F-06561 Valbonne CEDEX, France. T: (33 1) 93 74 31 00. Tx: 461311. Founded 1978. Initiated by the French Government and UNEP. Serves the political, administrative, economic, and technical leaders of developing countries by providing information, training, meetings, and exchanges. Activities take place at the Centre and in developing countries. Members are representatives of government ministries or national water organizations in 24 countries.

International Union for Conservation of Nature and Natural Resources (IUCN)

See IUCN-The World Conservation Union

International Union for the Scientific Study of Population (IUSSP)

Rue des Augustins 34, B-4000 Liege, Belgium. T: (32 41) 22 40 80. Tx: 42648. Founded 1926. Promotes demography as a science through international cooperation. Members are some 1,800 individual experts in 115 countries. Pub: Newsletter; conference proceedings; papers, reports, and reference books.

International Union of Air Pollution Prevention Associations

136 North Street, Brighton BN1 1RG, England. T: (44 273) 26313. C: POLLUTION. Founded 1964. Promotes public education worldwide in matters related to the value of clean air and methods of air pollution control. Convenes a triennial Clean Air Congress; fosters exchange of information on legislation and techniques. Members are national associations in 20 countries. Pub: Newsletter; reference books; congress proceedings.

International Union of Alpinist Associations

(Union Internationale des Associations d'Alpinisme) (UIAA)
c/o SAC-Geschäftsstelle, Helvetiaplatz 4, CH-3005 Berne, Switzerland. T: (41 31) 44 46 24. Tx: 912 388. Founded 1932. A federation of mountaineering associations in 43 countries with a total membership of 2.5 million. Purposes of UIAA include protection of mountain environments. Maintains a Commission on Mountain Protection. Pub: *Bulletin UIAA*, quarterly.

International Union of Anthropological and Ethnological Sciences (IUAES),

University College of North Wales, Bangor, Gwynedd, Wales LL57 2DG. T: (44 248) 351151, ext. 482. Tx: 61100 ucnwsl g. IUAES is composed of national scientific societies in the fields of anthropology and ethnology. Among its commissions is:
■ Commission on Human Ecology, c/o Prof. Napoleon Wolanski, Department of Human Ecology, Polish Academy of Sciences, Nowy Swiat 72, 00-330 Warsaw, Poland. Coordinates academic work in human ecology, by which is meant "transdisciplinary, synthetic knowledge about man and his culture as a dynamic part of ecosystems." Interests include biological status of human populations as a monitor of environmental impact; modeling of human settlements according to energy and information flows; and in general the impact of human activities on the environment and vice versa. Holds conferences and other meetings. Members are some 35 anthropologists from a number of countries. Pub: Newsletter.

International Union of Architects

(Union Internationale des Architectes) (UIA)
51 rue Raynouard, F-75016 Paris, France. T: (33 1) 45 24 36 88. C: UNIARCH. Founded 1948. A union of national architectural organizations with some 900,000 architects. One of UIA's 6 work programs is "Development of Man and Society, the aim of which is the participation of the UIA and that of architects in seeking solutions to urgent problems of humanity in contemporary society." Maintains Work Groups on Urban and Regional Planning; Habitat; and Heritage (protection of architectural heritage). Major congresses are held every 3 years. Represents architects with international organizations, particularly the UN, UNIDO, ILO, Unesco, WHO, and UNCHS. Pub: *UIA Newsletter*, monthly; congress reports; directories, etc.

International Union of Biological Sciences (IUBS)

51 boulevard de Montmorency, F-75016 Paris, France. T: (33 1) 45 25 00 09. Tx: 630553. Founded 1919. Promotes the biological sciences; facilitates and coordinates research and other scientific activities that require international cooperation. IUBS scientific programs are interdisciplinary in nature and undertaken in collaboration with other international organizations. These programs include the Decade of the Tropics, biological monitoring of the state of the environment (bioindicators), biotechnology, biological education, and biological oceanography. Members of IUBS are 44 national organizations and 69 international scientific societies. Pub: *Biology International* (news magazine).

International Union of Directors of Zoological Gardens (IUDZG)
c/o Scottish National Zoological Garden, Murrayfield, Edinburgh EH12 6TS, Scotland. T: (44 31) 334 9171. Founded 1946. Holds an annual conference.

International Union of Forestry Research Organizations (IUFRO)
A-1131 Vienna-Schönbrunn, Austria. T: (43 222) 82 01 51. Tx: 132981 (attn. iufro). Fax: (43 222) 82 93 55. Founded 1890. Works to rationalize research techniques, standardize systems of measurement, and promote international cooperation in scientific studies in forestry, including forestry operations, forest products, and related environmental questions. IUFRO is organized in 6 divisions: Forest Environment and Silviculture; Forest Plants and Forest Protection; Forest Operations and Techniques; Planning, Economics, Growth and Yield, Management and Policy; Forest Products; and General Subjects. Maintains a Task Force on Air Pollution and Forest Decline. Holds conferences and workshops and a periodic world congress. Members are national forestry research organizations in various countries. Pub: *IUFRO News;* annual report.

International Union of Geodesy and Geophysics (IUGG)
c/o Observatoire Royal de Belgique, 3 avenue Circulaire, B-1180 Brussels, Belgium. T: (32 2) 375 24 84. Tx: 21565. Founded 1919. Dedicated to the scientific study of the Earth and the applications of the knowledge gained by such studies to the needs of society, including environmental preservation. IUGG is composed of 7 semi-autonomous international associations. The two most concerned with environmental problems, the International Association of Meteorology and Atmospheric Physics (IAMAP) and the International Association of Hydrological Sciences (IAHS) are listed separately in this directory. IUGG maintains Commissions on Mountain Geoecology and Coastal Environment.

International Union of Pure and Applied Chemistry (IUPAC)
Bank Court Chambers, 2-3 Pound Way, Cowley Centre, Oxford OX4 3Y5, England. T: (44 865) 71 77 44. Founded 1919. Scientific body composed of 42 national committees. Maintains Subcommissions on Water Chemistry, Atmospheric Chemistry, and Pesticide Chemistry, and a Standing Committee on Chemical Research Applied to World Needs.

International Union of Societies of Foresters (IUSF)
c/o Canadian Institute of Forestry, 51 Slater St., Suite 815, Ottawa, Ontario K1P 5H3, Canada. T: (1 613) 977-1107. Founded 1969. Promotes cooperation for advancement of forestry and foresters. Holds congress every 5 years. Members are national societies in 28 countries.

International Union of Speleology (Union Internationale de Spéléologie) (UIS)
Draschestrasse 77, A-1232 Vienna, Austria. Founded 1964. A federation of national groups of speleologists (cave explorers) in 50 countries. Maintains a Department of Protection and Management. Pub: *International Journal of Speleology;* reports; conference proceedings.

International Water Resources Association (IWRA)
205 N. Mathews, University of Illinois, Urbana, Ilinois 61801, USA. T: (1 217) 333-6275. Founded 1972. "An interdisciplinary worldwide organization for water managers, scientists, planers, manufacturers, administrators, educators, lawyers, physicians, and others concerned with the future o our water resources." Holds a triennial world congress, as well as other meetings. Sponsors regional committees. Members are 1,400 individuals in over 100 countries. Pub: *Water International,* quarterly journal; *IWRA Update,* quarterly newsletter; conference proceedings; reports.

International Water Supply Association (IWSA)
1 Queen Anne's Gate, London SW1H 9BT, England. T: (44 1) 222 8111. Tx: 918518. Founded 1949. Concerned with improving knowledge and practice of public supply of water. Maintains a Special Commission on Pollution and Protection of Water Supplies, and Commissions on Water Quality and Treatment, and Cooperation in Developing Countries.

International Waterfowl and Wetlands Research Bureau (IWRB)
Slimbridge, Glos. GL2 7BX, England. T: (44 45) 389 333. Tx: 437145 wwf g. Fax: (44 45) 389 827. Founded 1954. Collaborates with other international and national organizations to "implement an effective program for the worldwide conservation of wetlands and their waterfowl." Provides technical support to the Ramsar Convention Bureau *(which see),* a section of which is located at the IWRB headquarters. IWRB's Waterfowl Division conducts studies of the status and trends of waterfowl populations worldwide and promotes research into their ecological requirements and population dynamics, with the aim of formulating management plans for waterfowl populations and recovery plans for endangered species. Examples of current projects: investigation of lead poisoning in Mediterranean waterfowl; a symposium on hunting harvest in the USSR; an analysis of Asian waterfowl counts. Wetlands Division monitors the status of wetlands worldwide, holds on-site workshops and training courses, and urges governments to safeguard wetlands. IWRB is an NGO governed by a board with delegates from some 40 countries and coordinators of 17 research groups. Pub: Newsletter; directories; research reports; educational materials.

International Wilderness Leadership Foundation (IWLF)
211 W. Magnolia, Fort Collins, Colorado 80521, USA. T: (1 303) 498-0303. Tx: 9103506369. Fax: (1 303) 498-0403. Founded 1974. Major activity is holding a major World Wilderness Congress every 3 years; works to follow up on congress recommendations. Pub: *The Leaf* (newsletter); congress proceedings.

International Wildlife Coalition (IWC)
See listing in Part 7 under USA.

International Work Group for Indigenous Affairs (IWGIA)
Fiolstræde 10, DK-1171 Copenhagen K, Denmark. T: (45 1) 12 47 24. An "independent, international organization which supports indigenous peoples in their struggle against oppression." Development and environmental questions are frequently involved in the issues with which IWGIA is concerned ("grass-roots development should be under the control of the peoples affected"; "the right to development is inextricably bound with the right to self-determination"). Proposed projects and activities which would harm the environment often have negative impacts on indigenous peoples as well. Pub: Newsletter; reports.

International Youth Conference on the Human Environment (IYCHE)
28 avenue Habib Bourguiba, Tunis, Tunisia. T: (216 1) 24 50 88. Tx: 13606. C; ENERGY. A periodic conference first held in 1977.

International Youth Federation for Environmental Studies and Conservation (IYF)
Klostermolle, Klostermollevej 48, DK-8660 Skanderborg, Denmark. Founded 1956 under the auspices of IUCN. IYF, a federation of regional, national, and local self-governing youth organizations concerned with the study and conservation of the environment, has 130 member organizations in 54 countries. It supports the work and coordinates the activities of the member organizations; promotes the development of a voluntary youth movement for conservation throughout the world; and acts as a world forum of young environmentalists. Activities include exchange of information; facilitating direct cooperation, youth exchanges, and joint action campaigns; organizing groups where they do not exist; representing young environmentalists in international organizations; and offering training courses. Main issues of concern are environment-development problems, tropical forests, agriculture, pesticides exported to developing countries, marine pollution, and acid rain. IYF has 2 semi-autonomous regional groups, the Federación Latinoamericana de Jóvenes Ambientalistas (FLAJA) (Latin American Federation of Young Environmentalists), in Panama, and Youth and Environment Europe (YEE), in Denmark, as well as representatives in India and Ghana. Pub: *Taraxacum* (member

magazine); booklets on issues; *Youth in Environmental Action: An International Survey* (1987).

Inuit Circumpolar Conference (ICC)
P.O. Box 280, Kuujjuaq, Quebec J0M 1C0, Canada. T: (1 819) 964-2431. Founded 1977. An "international organization representing all Inuit from Alaska, Greenland, and Canada. The ICC continues to encourage the active participation of the Siberian Inuit within ICC." Objectives include working to "promote long-term management and protection of arctic and sub-arctic wildlife, environment, and biological productivity." IC is preparing an Inuit Regional Conservation Strategy. Members are delegates from areas within the region. ICC has offices in Ottawa, Canada; Anchorage, Alaska; and Nuuk, Greenland.

Islamic Network of Water Resources Management
P.O. Box 12412-5012, Amman, Jordan. T: (962 6) 669955. Tx: 22439 WAJ JO. Founded 1987.

Islamic Academy of Sciences (IAS)
P.O. Box 830036, Amman, Jordan. T: (962 6) 822104. Tx: 21276 JO. Founded 1987. Promotes interaction among Muslim intellectuals in science and technology; includes a Standing Committee on Natural Resources Development.

IUCN-The World Conservation Union
Avenue du Mont-Blanc, CH-1196 Gland, Switzerland. T: (41 22) 64 91 14. Tx: 419 605. C: IUCNATURE. Fax: (41 22) 642926. Founded 1949. Legal name: International Union for Conservation of Nature and Natural Resources. An independent international organization which is a union of sovereign states, governmental agencies, and non-governmental organizations concerned with the initiation and promotion of scientifically-based action that will ensure the perpetuation of man's natural environment. Its objectives are: (a) to ensure that development is sustainable so that the potential of renewable natural resources is maintained for the present and future benefit of people; (b) to ensure that areas of land or sea which do not have special protection (the vast majority) are managed so that natural resources are conserved and the many species and varieties of plants and animals can persist in adequate numbers; (c) to protect areas of the land, and of fresh and sea waters, which contain representative or exceptional communities of plants and animals; (d) to devise special measures to ensure that species of fauna and fauna do not become endangered or extinct.

IUCN undertakes four basic activities: (a) monitoring what is happening in conservation and drawing conservation requirements to the attention of the organizations that can undertake action on the ground; (b) planning conservation action at the strategic, program, and project levels--action which is scientifically sound and realistic in socio-economic terms, using the information obtained through monitoring; (c) promoting conservation action by governments, intergovernmental bodies, and NGOs through the effective dissemination of information; (d) providing assistance and advice necessary for the achievement of conservation action. IUCN's program of monitoring, planning, promoting, and offering assistance is based upon authoritative information and advice provided by its members and commissions, and the many other scientists and professionals with whom they and the IUCN Secretariat are in touch.

IUCN's work is undertaken at a strategic level: for example, through the publication and promotion of the World Conservation Strategy, through a 3-year program of activities, and at the project level. IUCN designs and undertakes projects of its own, many in collaboration with UNEP and WWF. These projects are funded by development assistance agencies and foundations and managed by a field operations division. In addition, IUCN has formal working relations with a wide range of intergovernmental and international non-governmental organizations.

Programs: IUCN currently has 12 programs, with Secretariat staff attached to each: Conservation and Development; Population and Resources; Conservation Science; Species Conservation; Plants Conservation; Protected Area Management; Coastal and Marine Conservation; Wetlands Conservation; Tropical Forest Conservation; Arid Lands; Education, Training, and Awareness; and Conservation Law.

Commissions: Much of IUCN's work is accomplished through 6 commissions composed of volunteer experts. These are the Commissions on Ecology; Education and Training; Environmental Policy, Law, and Administration; National Parks and Protected Areas; Species Survival (which is divided into numerous specialist groups on types of animals and plants, ranging from ants to orchids); and Sustainable Development.

Conservation strategies: The first edition of the World Conservation Strategy, a global plan for conservation of living resources, was issued by IUCN, WWF, and UNEP in 1980. A second edition is in progress. Inspired by the world document, some 60 national or subnational conservation strategies have been prepared or are in process. IUCN is helping to write conservation strategies for a number of developing countries.

Members of IUCN are some 600 sovereign states, governmental agencies, and national and international NGOs in 117 countries; there are also some 700 non-voting "supporters" in 70 countries. IUCN has regional offices in Africa, Latin America, and Asia. Pub: *IUCN Bulletin,* bimonthly; commission and program newsletters; Red Data Books (describing threatened species of animals and plants); *United Nations List of National Parks and Protected Areas;* books and reports (catalog available).
■ World Conservation Monitoring Centre (WCMC), 219c Huntingdon Road, Cambridge CB3 0DL, England. T: (44 223) 277314. Tx: 817036. C: REDBOOK. Fax: (44 223) 277136. WCMC, a joint activity of IUNC, WWF, and UNEP,

collects, analyzes, interprets, and disseminates data as a basis for conservation. It is concerned primarily with the status of animal and plant species, wildlife trade, and protected areas. Publications include the Red Data Books, as well as special reports tailored to the needs of clients.
■ IUCN Environmental Law Centre (ELC), Adenauerallee 214, D-5300 Bonn 1, Federal Republic of Germany. T: (49 228) 26 92 231. The ELC, the "legal arm" of the IUCN Secretariat, monitors and maintains data bases on legal trends and developments in the environmental field, including international agreements, binding instruments of international organizations, national legislation, and legal literature. It also develops specific data bases (e.g., on species protection); contributes to the work of other organizations working in this field; supports activities of other IUCN components (e.g., organizing an international symposium on legal aspects of wetlands protection); and develops and carries out specifically legal activities (e.g., drafting international treaties).

Joint Committee on Global Ecology
A joint committee of the National Academy of Sciences of the USA and the Academy of Sciences of the USSR, created in December 1988 to address pressing global environmental problems, including the greenhouse effect, deterioration of the ozone layer, and loss of plant and animal species. The Committee's "special mission" will be to provide an early warning system for identifying long-range environmental problems and bringing them to the attention of the U.S. and Soviet governments. For information, contact either academy.

Latin American Association for the Promotion of Habitat, Architecture, and Urbanism
(Asociación Latinoamericana para la Promoción del Habitat, del Urbanismo de la Arquitectura) (ALAHUA)
Casilla Postal 9179, Sucursal 7, Quito, Ecuador. T: (593 2) 52 47 95. Founded 1980. Conducts research and integrated development projects in technical and social aspects of human settlements, including promotion of alternative technologies. Members are institutions and individuals in 7 countries.

Latin American Committee on National Parks
(Comité Latinoamericano de Parques Nacionales) (CLAPN)
c/o Instituto Nacional de Parques, Avenidas FCO, de Mirandec/av FCO, Fajardo, Edificio Sur, Parque del Transporte, Caracas 107, Venezuela. Founded 1964. Organizes courses, seminars, and technical meetings for personnel of national parks in the region; makes recommendations to governments. Members are representatives from 15 countries.

Latin American Federation of Young Environmentalists
(Federación Latinoamericana de Jóvenes Ambientalistas) (FLAJA)
Apartado Aéreo 413, Medellin, Colombia. Founded 1981, under the sponsorship of the International Youth Federation for Environmental Studies and Conservation (IYF). Promotes youth involvement in conservation; holds training courses. Members are NGOs in 10 countries.

Latin American Network of Environmental NGOs
(Red Latinoamericana de ONGs Ambientalistas)
c/o Grupo Investigación y Conservación, CIPFE, Casillo Correo 13125, Montevideo, Uruguay. Founded 1985. Exchange of information and joint activities among Latin American non-governmental organizations concerned with the environment. Members are 28 organizations in 12 countries.

Latin American Plant Sciences Network
(Red Latinoamericana de Botánica) (RLB)
c/o Mary T. Kalin Arroyo, Facultad de Ciencias, Universidad de Chile, Casilla 653, Santiago, Chile. T: (56 2) 271-2865. Founded 1988. Works to stimulate graduate studies annd research in the plant sciences in the region, particularly as they bear on biodiversity, conservation, and sustainable agriculture. Relies on 6 regional graduate training centers in Argentina, Brazil, Chile, Costa Rica, Mexico, and Venezuela.

Latin American Society of Soil Science
(Sociedad Latinoamericana de la Ciencia del Suelo)
c/o Prof. I. Pla-Sentis, Las Acacias, Apartado 1131, Maracay, Venezuela.

Law Association for Asia and the Pacific
(LAWASIA)
170 Phillip St., Sydney, NSW 2000, Australia. T: (61 2) 221 2970. Founded 1966. Promotes the rule of law through developing the law, legal education, and public information. Members are organizations and individuals in 20 countries. Maintains a Committee on Environmental Law.

Men of the Trees (MotT)
Turners Hill Road, Crawley Down, Crawley RH10 4HL, England. T: (44 342) 712536. P.O. Box 29045, Nairobi, Kenya. T: (254 2) 592241. Founded 1922. Works for large-scale tree planting throughout the world and for conservation of existing forests. Has some 30 branches in various countries.

Mesoamerican Center for the Study of Appropriate Technology
(Centro Mesoamericano de Estudios sobre Tecnología Apropiada) (CEMAT)
4a Avenida 2-28, Zona 1, Apartado Postal 1160, Guatemala, Guatemala. T: (502 2) 21 153. Founded 1977. Activities include working for environmental improvement and conservation of natural resources in Middle America (Central America and Mexico). Conducts action projects; exchange of information; training. Members are individuals and organizations in 22 countries.

Minority Rights Group (MRG)
29 Craven Street, London WC2N 5NT, England. T: (44 1) 930 6659. Founded 1970. Publicizes the violations of the rights of minority and majority groups. Concerns include indigenous peoples. Members are contacts and groups in 16 countries. Pub: Newsletter; research reports.

No More Bhopals Network
c/o Mr. Simitu Kothari, Lokayan, 13 Alipur Road, New Delhi 11054, India. Network of NGOs working for continued relief and rehabilitation of victims of the Bhopal chemical plant accident; documents the location of industries using and producing hazardous chemicals around the world and campaigns for closure of unsafe plants; related studies and public education.

Nordic Council for Ecology
c/o Dr. Pehr H. Enckell, Ecology Building, University of Lund, S-223 62 Lund, Sweden. T: (46 46) 14 81 88. Founded 1965. Promotes education and research in the science of ecology in the region. Members are individuals in the 5 Nordic countries.

Nordic Council for Wildlife Research
c/o Helmuth Strandgaard, NKV, Vildbiologisk Station, Kalo, DK-8410 Ronde, Denmark. T: (45 6) 37 25 00. Founded 1971. Promotes cooperation among wildlife researchers in the region. Members are individuals in the Nordic countries.

Nordic Forestry Federation
c/o Sveriges Skogsvardsforbund, P.O. Box 273, S-182 52 Djursholm, Sweden. T: (46 8) 753 03 90. Founded 1946. Promotes cooperation among Nordic countries in the field of forestry. Members are organizations in Denmark, Finland, Iceland, Norway, and Sweden.

Nordic Society for Radiation Protection
c/o Bente Lewinsky, Statens Institut for Stralehygiejne, Frederikssundsvej 378, DK-2700 Bronshoj, Denmark. T: 94 37 73. Founded 1964. Exchange of information and experience.

Organization for Flora Neotropica (OFN)
c/o Scott Mori, New York Botanic Garden, Bronx, New York 10458, USA. Founded in 1962 under Unesco auspices to prepare and publish a complete flora of the tropical American region through cooperation among botanists and institutions throughout the world. Annual meeting. Pub: Monographs of *Flora Neotropica*.

Organization for the Phyto-Taxonomic Investigation of the Mediterranean Area (OPTIMA)
c/o Botanischer Garten und Museum, Königen-Luise-Strasse 6-8, D-1000 Berlin 33, Federal

Republic of Germany. T: (49 30) 83006132. Founded 1974. Fosters research, exploration, resource studies, and conservation related to the plant life of the Mediterranean area. Members are institutions and individuals in 44 countries.

Oxfam
274 Banbury Road, Oxford OX2 7D2, England. T: (44 865) 56777. C: Oxfam, Oxford. Tx: 83610. Founded 1942. A major private supplier of aid to Third-World countries; two-thirds of its funds are spent for long-term development projects, the remainder for emergency and relief work. Clean water supplies are a major emphasis. Sister organizations in Australia, Belgium, Canada, and USA. Field offices in Africa, Asia, and Latin America.

Pacific Science Association (PSA)
P.O. Box 17801, Honolulu, Hawaii 96817, USA. T: (1 808) 847-3511. Founded 1920. Provides a multidisciplinary forum for discussing common scientific concerns in the Pacific Basin. Holds congresses and other meetings. Committees include Coral Reefs; Ecology, Conservation, and Environmental Protection; and Forestry.

Pan-African Council for Protection of the Environment and for Development
(Conseil panafricain pour la Protection de l'Environnement et le Développement)
c/o Dr. Wa Nsanga, B.P. 994, Nouakchott, Mauritania. T: 530 77. C: CPPED, Nouakchott. Tx: NOSOM-LIPAM 656/mtn. Founded 1982. Works to combat desertification with a multi-disciplinary approach that incorporates the objectives and needs of local communities.

Panos Institute
8 Alfred Place, London WC1E 7EB, England. T: (44 1) 631 1590. Tx: 9419293. Founded 1986. "An international information and policy studies institute dedicated to working in partnership with others towards greater public understanding of sustainable development." Recent projects have focused on AIDS and the Third World; promoting sustainable development in the international aid community; and environment and development in the Arctic and the Sahel. Pub: *Panoscope* (magazine about NGO activity in the Third World); books, dossiers, and audio-visual materials. Offices in Washington and Paris.

People and Physical Environment Research (PAPER)
c/o Ross Thorne, I.B. Fell Research Centre, University of Sydney, Sydney, NSW 2006, Australia. Members are individual scholars in the Southwest Pacific region. Concerned with systematic study of the relationship between people and their physical environment and the application of such knowledge to design and planning. Holds a conference every two years.

Pesticide Action Network (PAN)
P.O. Box 610, San Francisco, California 94101. T: (1 415) 541-9140. Founded 1982. An "international coalition of citizens' groups and individuals opposed to the overuse and misuse of pesticides. PAN aims to raise public awareness of pesticide-related problems and to promote safe and sustainable alternative pest control practices around the world. PAN was actively involved in developing the [FAO's] International Code of Conduct on the Distribution and Use of Pesticides." PASN focuses primarily on developing countries, "where, unfortunately, information is very scarce." A "Dirty Dozen" campaign targets 12 especially dangerous pesticides that are used primarily in the Third World. Members of PAN are some 400 NGOs in over 50 countries. San Francisco office is the PAN regional center for North America; there are also regional centers in Asia and the Pacific (International Organization of Consumer Unions Regional Office, Penang, Malaysia); Europe (Oxfam, Oxford, UK); and Latin America (Fundacion Natura, Quito, Ecuador). Pub: Newsletter; educational and policy materials.

Rainforest Action Network (RAN)
300 Broadway, Suite 28, San Francisco 94133. T: (1 415) 398-4404. Fax: (1 415) 788-7324. Founded 1985. Sponsored by Earth Island Institute. Works to save the world's rainforests through "direct action, such as letter-writing campaigns, boycotts, consumer campaigns, and demonstrations; grassroots organizing in the U.S ...conducting research; facilitating communication between U.S. and Third World organizers; and spearheading public education and media outreach projects." Main concerns are tropical timber imports, logging, cattle ranching, the programs of multilateral development banks, and rights of indigenous peoples. Pub: *World Rainforest Report*, quarterly; action alerts; educational materials.

Regional Mangrove Information Network
c/o National Mangrove Committee, Natural Resources Management Center, Triumph Building, 1610 Quezon Ave., P.O. Box AC-493, Quezon City, Philippines

Regional Network of Non-Governmental Conservation Organizations for Sustainable Development in Central America (Redes-Centroamerica)
c/o Lic. Juan José Montiel R., Apartado Postal 2431, Managua, Nicaragua. T: (505 2) 3765 or 4448. Founded 1987. Regional network of environmental NGOs. Board of directors is composed of an NGO representative from each member country. Members are NGOs from Belize, Costa Rica, El Salvador, Guatemala, Honduras, Nicaragua, and Panama.

Renewable Energy and Environmental Conservation Association in Developing Countries (RRECA)
c/o KENGO, P.O. Box 48197, Nairobi, Kenya.
T: (254 2) 749747.

Sea Shepherd Conservation Society
P.O. Box 7000-S, Redondo Beach, California 90277. T: (1 213) 373-6979. Founded 1977. An activist and educational group that works for conservation and protection of wildlife. Current focus is on illegal whaling, grey seals off Ireland and Scotland, and the hunting of harp seals, wolves, and caribou in Canada. Owns 2 ships named *Sea Shepherd*. Members are 15,000 individuals in various countries. Pub: *Sea Shepherd Log*.

Seed Action Network
Apartado 23398, E-08080 Barcelona, Spain. T: (34 3) 215 8949. Founded 1985. Works to preserve genetic resources through village-level conservation and breeding of endangered plants and animals in the Third World, and to increase public control over and promote free exchange of such resources.

SOS Sahel International
B.P. 5220, Dakar, Senegal. T: (221) 22 29 02. Tx: 261 Anthel sg. Founded 1976. Disseminates information to non-governmental organizations worldwide about the drought in the Sahel region of Africa and what is being done about it; sponsors training and research for development, as well as aid to affected populations. Members are associations in 10 Sahelian and Western European countries.

Society for Ecological Restoration and Management (SERM)
University of Wisconsin Arboretum, 1207 Seminole Highway, Madison, Wisconsin 53711, USA

Society for Ecology
c/o Prof. Dr. W. Kuttler, FB9, Landschaftsökologie Universität-GH-Essen, Postfach 103 764, D-4300 Essen 1, Federal Republic of Germany. T: (49 201) 183 2734. Founded 1970. An international German-language scholarly association concerned with ecology and related disciplines. Holds an annual meeting which focuses on a particular area or problem (e.g., forest ecosystems; the Alps). Pub: Proceedings of the annual meeting.

Society for International Development (SID)
Palazzo Civiltà del Lavoro, I-00144 Rome, Italy. T: (39 6) 591 7897. Tx: 612339 gbg for sid. C: SOCINTDEV. Founded 1957. Brings together individuals and organizations committed to social and economic development. Sponsors the North South Round Table, an independent forum for a constructive dialogue between rich and poor countries on a new world order. Members of SID are some 9,000 individuals and organizations.

There are 87 SID chapters in 56 countries. Pub: *Compass*, quarterly; *Development: Seeds of Change*, quarterly; conference proceedings.

Speleological Federation of Latin America and the Caribbean
(Federación Espeliológica de América Latina y el Caribe) (FEALC)
c/o Sociedad Venezolana de Espeliología, Apartado 47334, Caracas 1041-A, Venezuela. Founded 1981. Promotes exchange of information about, and conservation of, caves and karst regions in the region. Members are associations and individuals in 28 countries.

Third World Academy of Sciences (TWAS)
c/o International Centre for Theoretical Physics, P.O. Box 586, Trieste, Italy. T: (39 40) 224 0328. Tx: 460392. C: CENTRATOM. Fax: (39 40) 224163. Founded 1983. Works to develop and support high-level scientists in developing countries. Holds a biennial general conference.

Third World Forum (TWF)
P.O. Box 43, Orman, Cairo, Egypt. C: TRIFORUM. Founded 1975. A network of social and other scientists and intellectuals from developing countries which works for a "self-reliant, needs-oriented, endogenous development" through exchange of views, devising policy options, stimulating research, and seeking to influence policy-making. Regional offices in Senegal, Sri Lanka, Mexico, and Egypt.

Union of European Foresters (UEF)
Bergweg 6, D-7835 Teningen-Heimbach, Federal Republic of Germany. T: (49 7641) 2203. Founded 1965. Professional organization; facilitates exchange of information at a European level. Sponsors a reforestation program in Greece. Members are individuals and associations in 13 countries.

Union of International Associations (UIA)
Rue Washington 40, B-1050 Brussels, Belgium. T: (32 2) 640 41 09. Tx: 65080 INAC B. Fax: (32 2) 649 32 69. Founded 1907. Activities include editing and publishing the *Yearbook of International Associations*, *Global Action Networks*, the *Encyclopedia of World Problems and Human Potential*, and other reference books which include much detailed information about international organizations' activities related to the environment.

University of the South Pacific-Institute of Natural Resources (INR)
P.O. Box 1168, Suva, Fiji. T: (679) 302403. Tx: 2712. C: INR. Fax: (679) 300373. The University is a regional international institution serving the Cook Islands, Fiji, Kiribati, Nauru, Vanuatu, Niue, Solomon Islands, Tokelau, Tonga, Tuvalu, and Western Samoa. The Institute was established in 1977 to conduct short training courses, undertake research and consulting, and organize workshops and seminars. Fields of

interest are energy, environmental protection, remote sensing, food science, soil resources, water resources, analytical chemical services, and plant resources. Pub: Research reports.

Wildlife Preservation Trust International
34th Street and Girard Avenue, Philadelphia, Pennsylvania 19104, USA. T: (1 215) 222-3636. Founded 1971. Works to preserve endangered animal species through captive propagation, education, and field work. Affiliated with the Jersey Wildlife Preservation Trust, Jersey, Channel Islands. Members are some 7,000 individuals.

World Association of Girl Guides and Girl Scouts (WAGGGS)
12c Lyndhurst Road, London NW3 5PQ, England. T: (44 1) 794 1181. C: WORLDBURO. Founded 1928. Program includes environmental action projects and public awareness campaigns. Members are 112 national girl scout/guide organizations with a total membership of some 8 million.

World Association of Soil and Water Conservation (WASWC)
317 Marvin Avenue, Volga, South Dakota 57071, USA. T: (1 605) 627-9309; May-October: (1 218) 864-8506. Founded 1982 by the Soil and Water Conservation Society of the U.S. An international forum for scientists, conservation professionals, and policy-makers to assess soil and water conservation needs worldwide. Cooperates with International Soil Conservation Organization in organizing biennial conferences and editing proceedings; is sponsoring an international workshop on conservation farming on hillslopes (Taiwan, 1989). Pub: Newsletter; *Conservation Farming on Steep Lands*.

World Blue Chain: for the Protection of Animals and Nature
Avenue de Visé 39, B-1170 Brussels, Belgium. T: (32 2) 673 52 30. Founded 1962. Promotes worldwide education to protect animals against bad treatment and cruelty and protect nature and the environment. Emphasis is on halting cruelty to domestic and farm animals. Members are some 30,000 individuals in 21 countries. Pub: *La Chaine*, quarterly; films.

World Commission on Environment and Development (Brundtland Commission) (WCED)
Created in 1983 as a consequence of a UN General Assembly resolution. WCED completed its work in early 1988. Chaired by Norwegian Prime Minister Gro Harlem Brundtland, the Commission was composed of 21 distinguished leaders evenly divided between industrialized and developing countries. WCED was charged with proposing long-term environmental strategies for achieving sustainable development; recommending ways in which concern for the environment may be translated into greater international cooperation; considering ways by which the international community can deal more effectively with environmental concerns; and helping to define shared perceptions of long-term environmental issues. WCED's final report, *Our Common Future* (1987), has been published in many countries. Follow-up activities are being carried out by the Centre for Our Common Future, *which see.*

World Underwater Federation
(Confédération Mondiale des Activités Subaquatiques) (CMAS)
34 rue de Colisée, F-75008 Paris, France. T: (33 1) 42 25 85 85. Tx: 641 078. Founded 1959. An organization of international competitors in underwater spearfishing and diving. Has an active concern with protection of aquatic environments. Members are national federations and clubs in 70 countries. Pub: *Information Bulletin*, quarterly.

World Council for the Biosphere
See Foundation for Environmental Conservation.

World Council of Churches (WCC)
P.O. Box 66, CH-1211 Geneva 20, Switzerland. T: (41 22) 91 61 11. Tx: 23 423 oik ch. Founded 1948. Organization of churches in over 90 countries representing the major Protestant and Orthodox denominations. Promotes cooperation and facilitates common action by the churches. The WCC Commission on the Churches' Participation in Development (CCPD) was set up in 1970 to stimulate reflection and experimental action aimed at justice, self-reliance, growth, and participatory development. CCPD's Ecumenical Development Fund (EDF) provides financial assistance to development projects.

World Council of Indigenous Peoples (WCIP)
555 King Edward Ave., Ottawa, Ontario K1N 6N5, Canada. T: 1 613) 230-9030. Tx: 0533338. Founded 1975. Works to protect the rights and further the interests of indigenous people in accordance with their own cultures. Maintains regional councils in the Pacific-Asia region, the Nordic region, and South, Central, and North America. Members are organizations and individuals in 29 countries and territories.

World Federation of Engineering Organizations
Current address unknown. Maintains a Committee on Engineering and the Environment.

World Future Studies Federation (WFSF)
c/o Social Science Research Institute, University of Hawaii, Honolulu, Hawaii 96822, USA. T: (1 808) 948-6601. Tx: 7238962. Founded 1973. Serves as a forum for the exchange of information and opinions to stimulate cooperative research activities in all fields of futures research. Holds regional and global futures studies conferences. Programs focus on education, cultural aspects of peace, political institutions, communication and information, social support, development, and social forecasting and design. Members are professional futurists in more than

70 countries. Pub: Newsletter; conference proceedings; reports.

World Industry Conference on Environmental Management (WICEM).
A single event held in Versailles in 1983 by the International Chamber of Commerce *(which see)* and the United Nations Environment Programme.

World Institute of Ecology and Cancer (WIEC)
Rue des Fripiers 24 bis, B-1000 Brussels, Belgium. T: (32 2) 219 08 30. Links European associations concerned with environmental causes of cancer.

World Leisure and Recreation Association (WLRA)
P.O. Box 309, Sharbot Lake, Ontario K0H 2PO, Canada, T: (1 613) 2798-3173. Fax: (1 613) 279-3130. Founded 1956. Provides a worldwide forum for discussion of issues related to leisure and recreation. Environmental impacts of tourism and development of tourist facilities have been the subject of discussions at WLRA conferences.

World Organization of the Scout Movement (WOSM)
5, rue de Pré-Jérôme, CH-1205 Geneva, Switzerland. T: (41 22) 20 42 33. C: Worldscout, Geneva. Tx: 428 139 wbs ch. Founded 1920. Promotes and advises national Scout organizations in over 150 countries and territories. At its 31st world conference in 1988, the Organization recognized the fundamental importance of the environment and environmental education in scouting, and recommended that national Scout organizations increase their environmental activities and their efforts to provide environmental education for their members.

World Pheasant Association (WPA)
P.O. Box 5, Lower Basildon, Reading RG8 9PFT, England. T: (44 7357) 5140. Founded 1975. Conservation of all species of the Order *Galliformes*; regional programs in Australia, Latin America, and Asia. Members are individuals in some 30 countries.

World Society for Ekistics (WSE)
P.O. Box 3471, 102 10 Athens, Greece. T: (30 1) 3623 216. Tx: 215227. Founded 1965. Promotes the development of knowledge and ideas about human settlements. Holds conferences, produces publications, and encourages education in ekistics; works to foster an interdisciplinary approach to the needs of human settlements. Members are individuals in some 50 countries.

World Society for the Protection of Animals
P.O. Box 190, Boston, Massachusetts 02130, USA. T: (1 617) 522-7000. Founded 1981 by merger of the International Society for the Protection of Animals and the World Federation for the Protection of Animals. Works for protection and conservation of animals worldwide. Examples of current concerns: cruelty to horses in Europe and Latin America; killing of baby seals in Canada; alternatives to using living animals in scientific experiments. Members are individuals and over 300 animal protection organizations in some 60 countries. Field offices in Colombia, Costa Rica, England, Canada, and Switzerland. Pub: *Animals International* (newsletter).

WorldWIDE
P.O. Box 40885, Washington, D.C. 20016, USA. T: (1 202) 331-9863. Founded 1982. An international organization that "exists to mobilize women to maintain and improve environmental quality and natural resource management in economic development." Goals are "to establish a worldwide network; educate the public and policy-makers about the vital linkages between women, natural resources, and sustainable development; ensure that women and their environmental perceptions are incorporated in the design and implementation of development policies; and support and enhance the capacities of women, individually and in organizations, to engage in environmental and natural resource projects and programs." WorldWIDE Forums, modeled on the idea of the village well, are locally-organized and operated affiliates of WorldWIDE. Members are individuals in various countries. Pub: *WorldWIDE News*, bimonthly newsletter; *Directory of Women in Environment*.

World Wide Fund for Nature (WWF)
Avenue du Mont-Blanc, CH-1196 Gland, Switzerland. T: (41 22) 64 71 81. Tx: 419624. Fax: (41 22) 64 46 15. Founded 1961. President is Prince Philip, Duke of Edinburgh. Formerly known as the World Wildlife Fund, and still known by that name in Australia, Canada, and the USA. "The largest private international nature conservation organization, with more than 3 million supporters and 26 national and associate organizations on all continents. WWF promotes public awareness of conservation problems and raises funds for the protection of threatened species and environments." Since its founding, WWF has channeled more than US$130 million into 5,000 projects in over 130 countries. Grants support work undertaken by educators, scientists, other NGOs, and government bodies. Priority is given to conservation of forests and woodlands, and wetlands and coasts. Transboundary air pollution is also a major concern. TRAFFIC, WWF's international network of wildlife trade monitoring centers, now in 10 countries, works to prevent illegal exports and imports of wildlife. WWF has played a leading role in promoting debt-for-nature swaps, which involve the acquisition of a developing country's debt by a conservation organization, at a discount, and its redemption in money or bonds to be used locally for conservation purposes; the first such swaps were in Ecuador, Costa Rica, and the Philippines. In 1986, WWF initiated a "new alliance" with the world's leading religions, each of which produced a Declaration on Nature; a WWF Network on Conservation and Religion continues this

partnership. In 1989, an International Sacred Literature Trust was established to produce accurate new translations of the sacred texts of major religions to enable more people to undertand what they teach about conservation. WWF national and associate organizations are listed by country in Part 6 of this directory. Direct contributors to the world organization become members of Friends of WWF-International. Pub: Annual report; *WWF News* (newspaper); *WWF Special Report* (focused on single topics); *WWF Reports* (capsule project descriptions); *The New Road: The Bulletin of the WWF Network on Conservation and Religion;* position papers.

World Wildlife Fund. *See* World Wide Fund for Nature

Xerces Society
10 S.W. Ash Street, Portland, Oregon 97204, USA. T: (1 503) 222-2788. Founded 1971. An international organization working for habitat protection for rare or endangered invertebrates, especially butterflies; and "enhancing the public's positive feelings for insects by emphasizing their beneficial roles in natural ecosystems." Members are 1,100 individuals. Pub: *Wings* (magazine for members).

Part 7
Country and Area Listings

AFGHANISTAN

Government:

Ministry of Agriculture and Land Reform, Kabul. T: 41151. Includes a Forestry and Range Department and a Department of Environmental Protection.

Ministry of Public Health, Kabul. T: 62583.

Ministry of Water Resources Development and Irrigation, Kabul. T: 40743.

ALBANIA

Government:

Central Committee for the Protection of the Environment, Tiranë. Responsible to the Council of Ministers.

Ministry of Agriculture, Tiranë

Ministry of Hygiene, State Sanitary Inspectorate, Tiranë. Responsibilities include environmental health, pollution monitoring, and research on control measures.

Hydrometeorology Institute, Tiranë. Monitors air and water pollution.

Akademia Shkencave R.P. Shqiperise (Academy of Science of the People's Republic of Albania), Tiranë

Other organizations:

Universiteti Shteterur i Tiranë, Fakulteti Shkencave te Natyres (State University of Tiranë, Faculty of Natural Science), Boulevard Stalin, Tiranë

Instituti i Kerkimeve Shkencore Bujqesore (Agricultural Research Institute), Lushnje. Studies include agricultural pollution control.

Instituti i Larte i Bujqesar (Agricultural Institute), Kamez, Tiranë. Program includes research on water, land-use, and forestry problems.

ALGERIA

Government:

Agence National pour la Protection de l'Environnement (National Agency for the Protection of the Environment), B.P. 154, El-Annaser. T: (213) 771414. Tx: 65439 enl dz. Broad responsibilities.

Ministère de la Santé (Ministry of Health), 25 boulevard Laala Abd ar-Rahmane, El-Madania, Algiers. T: (213) 663315. Tx: 51263.

Ministry of Water Resources, Forestry, and Fishing, Le Grand Seminaire, Kouba, Algiers. T: (213) 589500. Tx: 62560.

Other organizations:

Institut National de Recherche Forestière (National Institute of Forestry Research), B.P. 37, Cheraga. T: (213) 849790. Tx: 61407 cnref dz. Founded 1984. Focus includes desertification.

AMERICAN SAMOA

Government:

Office of the Governor, Pago Pago. T: (684) 633-4116. Tx: 782501.

ANDORRA

Government:

Conselleria d'Agricultura (Agricultural Council), Edifici CASS, 5e Pis, Carrer J. Maragall S/N, Andorra la Vella. T: (33 628) 2 12 34.

ANGOLA

Government:

Ministerio da Agricultura, C.P. 74, Luanda. T: 32 39 34. Tx: 3322 minagrian. Responsibilities include natural resource management.

Ministry of Health, Rua Diego Cao, Luanda

ANGUILLA
British territory.

Government:

Ministry of Lands, Agriculture, Fisheries, and Health, The Secretariat, The Valley. Tx: 9313.

ANTARCTICA

Seven countries have claims to territory in Antarctica: Argentina, Australia, Chile, France, New Zealand, Norway, and the United Kingdom. The USSR and the USA have adopted policies of nonrecognition of any territorial claims on the continent.

The Antarctic Treaty, which went into effect in 1959, ensures the permanent use of the continent for peaceful purposes, prohibits military operations (including nuclear testing) there, calls for exchange of scientific data, and permits each signatory to carry out inspections in any part of Antarctica. There are now 22 full members of the Treaty: Argentina, Australia, Belgium, Brazil, Chile, China, France, German Democratic Republic, Federal Republic of Germany, India, Italy, Japan, New Zealand, Norway, Poland, South Africa, Spain, Sweden, USSR, United Kingdom, USA, and Uruguay.

Intergovernmental organizations: Two intergovernmental organizations are directly concerned with Antarctica's environment and natural resources: the Commission for the Conservation of Antarctic Living Marine Resources (CCAMLR), listed in Part 5; and the Commission for the Convention on the Regulation of Antarctic Mineral Resource Activities (CRAMRA), which was opened for signature in 1988 and will eventually have a permanent secretariat.

International NGOs (see Part 6): Among those most concerned are the Antarctic and Southern Ocean Coalition; Friends of the Earth International; Greenpeace International; Scientific Committee on Antarctic Research (ICSU).

National organizations (see Part 7): *Argentina:* Antarctic Project. *Australia:* Australian Conservation Foundation. *Chile:* Chilean Antarctic Institute. *Federal Republic of Germany:* Alfred Wegener Institute for Polar and Marine Research. *United Kingdom:* Scott Polar Research Institute. *United States:* National Science Foundation; Antarctica Project.

ANTIGUA AND BARBUDA

Government:

Ministry of Agriculture, Lands, and Fisheries, High Street, St. John's, Antigua. T: (1 809) 462-1007. Broad responsibilities for resource management; responsible for two marine parks.

National Parks Authority, P.O. Box 1283, Antigua

Other organizations:

Historical and Archaeological Society of Antigua and Barbuda, P.O. Box 103, St. John's, Antigua. T: (1 809) 462-3946. Concerns include natural history and environmental problems.

ARCTIC OCEAN

The following organizations are directly concerned with the Arctic Ocean. *See also* "Oceans, Coastal Zones, and Islands" in Part 2.

International NGOs (see Part 6): Arctic Institute of North America; Comité Arctique International; Inuit Circumpolar Conference.

ARGENTINA

Directories: A computerized *Directory of Argentine and Uruguayan Environmental Scientists* is maintained by the Sistema para el Apoyo a la Investigación y Desarrollo de la Ecología en la República Argentina (SPAIDERA), Uruguay 263, Oficina 64, 1015 Buenos Aires. T: (54 1) 45-6649.

Government:

Secretaría General de la Presidencia, Subsecretaría de Política Ambiental (General Secretariat of the Presidency, Subsecretariat of Environmental Policy), Corrientes 1302, 1er Piso, 1043 Buenos Aires. T: (54 1) 40-6721. Advises the President on environmental policy; coordinates government activities.

Instituto Forestal Nacional (IFONA) (National Forestry Institute), Pueyrredón 2446, 1119 Buenos Aires. T: (54 1) 803-3913.

Secretaría de Agricultura y Ganadería (Secretariat of Agriculture and Livestock). Includes:
■ Dirección Nacional de Fauna (National Wildlife Directorate), Paseo Colón 982, Oficina 201, 1305 Buenos Aires. T: (54 1) 362-1207. Tx: 21535 daagar.

■ Administración de Parques Nacionales (National Parks Administration), Avenida Santa Fé 690, 1059 Buenos Aires. T: (54 1) 311-6633.

Secretaría de Energía, Programa de Control Ambiental (Secretariat of Energy, Program of Environmental Control), Buenos Aires

Consejo Nacional de Investigaciones Científicas y Técnicas (National Council of Scientific and Technical Research), Rivadavia 1917, 1033 Buenos Aires. ICSU national member. Has an International Relations office.

Other organizations:

Amigos de la Tierra (Friends of the Earth), Anchorena 633, 1170 Buenos Aires. T: (54 1) 88-3815. Affiliated with Friends of the Earth

International (see listing in Part 6 of this book).
Asociación Amigos de los Parques Nacionales (AAPN) (Friends of National Parks Association), Rivadavia 830, Sede Cultural del Touring Club Argentino, 1002 Buenos Aires. T: (54 1) 665-5986. Defends national parks and natural monuments; works to create new protected areas.

Asociación Argentina de Ecología (Argentine Ecology Association), Casilla de Correo 1025, Correo Central, 5000 Córdoba. Brings together scientific professions and the general public to promote a social-ecological consciousness.

Asociación Ornitólogia del Plata (AOP) (Ornithological Association of the Plate), 25 de Mayo 749, 2 piso, Dpto. 6, 1002 Buenos Aires. T: (54 1) 312-8958. Protection and study of bird life.

Asociación para la Protección del Ambiente (APA) (Association for the Protection of the Environment), Uruguay 1053, 1er Piso, 1016 Buenos Aires. T: (54 1) 42-9611. Plans, develops, and implements projects and provides technical assistance and training in natural resource conservation.

Centro de Estudios y Proyectación del Ambiente (CEPA) (Center for Studies and Planning of the Environment), Calle 53, No. 506, La Plata, 1900 Buenos Aires. T: (54 1) 32-601. Research; environmental mediation; conferences; postgraduate courses for architects and urban planners.

Centro de Protección de la Naturaleza (Center for Protection of Nature), San Jerónimo 6843, 3000 Santa Fé. T: (54 42) 6-0922. Protection of the country's natural resources and environment; groups in various cities.

Federación Argentina de Protectores de Animales (FADEPA) (Argentine Federation of Animal Protectors), Moreno 1270, 4to Piso, Oficina 401, 1437 Buenos Aires. T: (54 1) 37-9328. Preservation of wild animals, as well as protection of domestic animals. Member groups throughout the country.

Fundación Ambiente y Recursos Naturales (Fundación ARN) (Environment and Natural Resources Foundation), Monroe 2142, 1er piso, 1428 Buenos Aires. T: (54 1) 49-5481. Tx: 22088 carte ar. Focuses on environmental legislation. Consulting; symposia.

Fundación Bariloche (Bariloche Foundation), Casilla Postal 138, 8400 San Carlos de Bariloche, Rio Negro. T: 2-5755. Tx: 80702. Major research and postgraduate educational institution, located in the foothills of the Andes; maintains a Department of Natural Resources and Energy.

Fundación Biología Integral Organizada para Sobrevivir (Fundación BIOS) (Integral Biology Foundation for Survival), Paraguay 1255, 1057 Buenos Aires. T: (54 1) 393-2474. Promotes biological sciences and preservation of the natural environment.

Fundación Vida Silvestre Argentina (FVSA) (Argentine Wildlife Foundation), Defensa 245-P.6, 1065 Buenos Aires. T: (54 1) 331-4864. Maintains specialist groups on raptors, cetaceans, etc.; local chapters. An associate organization of the World Wide Fund for Nature (WWF International).

Greenpeace Argentina, Junín 45, 3er piso, 1026 Buenos Aires. National office of Greenpeace International, listed in Part 6.

Instituto Argentino de Investigaciones de las Zonas Aridas (Argentine Institute of Arid Zone Research), Casilla de Correo 507, 5500 Mendoza. T: (54 61) 24-1995. Tx: 55438 cytme ar. Founded 1972.

Red Informática Ecologísta (RIE) (Ecologists' Information Network), Avenida Córdoba 1522, 1er piso, 1055 Buenos Aires. T: (54 1) 44-1834. Connects private and governmental scientists and naturalists with information to promote ecological equilibrium.

ARUBA
A dependency of the Netherlands.

Government:

Ministry of Utilities and Public Works, Oranjestad

ATLANTIC OCEAN

The following organizations are directly concerned with the Atlantic Ocean. *See also* "Oceans, Coastal Zones, and Islands" in Part 2.

UN system (see Part 4): The UN Environmental Program has regional seas programs for the Mediterranean, West and Central Africa, and the Caribbean.

Other intergovernmental organizations (see Part 5): Baltic Marine Environment Protection Committee; Bonn Commission; Commission for the Convention on Future Multilateral Cooperation in North-East Atlantic Fisheries; International Baltic Sea Fishery Commission; International Commission for the Scientific Exploration of the Mediterranean Sea; International Commission for the Conservation of Atlantic Tuna; International Commission for the Southeast Atlantic Fisheries; International Council for the Exploration of the Sea (North Atlantic); North Atlantic Salmon Conservation Organization; Northwest Atlantic Fisheries Organization; Oslo Commission; Paris Commission; Secretariat for the Protection of the Mediterranean Sea.

International NGOs (see Part 6): Atlantic Salmon Federation; Caribbean Conservation Association; Caribbean Conservation Corporation; Gulf and Caribbean Fisheries Institute.

AUSTRALIA
Including adjacent island territories.

Commonwealth (federal) government:

Department of the Arts, Sport, the Environment, Tourism, and Territories, G.P.O. Box 1252, Canberra, ACT 2601. T: (61 62) 46-7211. Tx: 62960 home aa. Fax: (61 62) 48-0334. Department of Foreign Affairs, Australian International Development Assistance Bureau (AIDAB), P.O. Box 887, Canberra City 2601. T: (61 62) 48-0865. C: AUSTDEVAID. Tx: 62012.

Australian Heritage Commission, P.O. Box 1567, Canberra, ACT 2601

Australian National Parks and Wildlife Service, G.P.O. Box 636, Canberra, ACT 2601. T: (61 62) 46-6008. Tx: AA62971.

Commonwealth Scientific and Industrial Research Organisation (CSIRO), P.O. Box 225, Dickson, ACT 2602. T: (61 62) 48-4211. Tx: 62003. Includes various units concerned with resources and the environment, including Divisions of Water and Land Resources; Atmospheric Research; Fisheries Research; Forest Research; Ground Water Research; Oceanography; Soils; Wildlife and Range Research; and Environmental Mechanics.

State governments:

The 6 state governments and the government of the Northern Territory have important responsibilities for natural resources and the environment.

Other organizations:

Australian Academy of Science, P.O. Box 783, Canberra City, A.C.T. 2601. T: (61 62) 47 53 30. Tx: 62406 aa. ICSU national member. Maintains a National Committee for the Environment to advise the Academy on environmental questions and foster scientific study of the environment.

Australian Conservation Foundation, 672-B Glenferrie Road, Hawthorn, Victoria 3122. T: (61 3) 819 2888. Founded 1967. Research, information, and advocacy; broad interests.

Australian Council of National Trusts, P.O. Box 1002, Civic Square, Canberra, ACT 2608

Australian National Parks Council, G.P.O. 2227, Canberra ACT 2601. Founded 1971. Promotes national park systems throughout Australia.

Australian National University, Center for Forestry in Rural Development, P.O. Box 4, Canberra, ACT 2601. T: (61 62) 49-2579. Tx: AA61670. Fax: (61 62) 49-0746. Founded 1986. Conducts research, consulting, and courses related to forestry in developing countries and areas.

Australian Rangeland Society, P.O. Box 2134, Alice Springs, NT 5750. Founded 1975. Professional society affiliated with the Society for Range Management, USA.

Friends of the Earth, P.O. Box 530-E, Melbourne, Victoria 3001. Founded 1974. Affiliated with Friends of the Earth International, listed in Part 6.

Greenpeace Australia, Private Bag 6, 134 Broadway, Sydney, NSW 2007. National office of Greenpeace International, listed in Part 6.

Institute of Foresters of Australia, P.O. Box E73, Queen Victoria Terrace, Canberra, ACT 2600. Professional society.

Wild Life Preservation Society of Australia, G.P.O. 3428, Sydney, NSW 2001. T: (61 2) 89-3705. Founded 1909. Watchdog and advisory group concerned with protection of fauna and flora.

Wilderness Society, 130 Davey Street, Hobart, Tasmania 7000

World Wildlife Fund-Australia, St. Martins Tower, Level 17, 31 Market Street, GPO Box 528, Sydney, NSW 2001. T: (61 2) 261 5572. Affiliate of the World Wide Fund for Nature (WWF International), listed in Part 6.

AUSTRIA

Federal government:

Ministry of Environment, Youth, and Family. Includes:
■ Umweltbundesamt (Federal Environmental Agency), Biberstrasse 11, A-1010 Vienna. T: (43 222) 52 35 21. Broad responsibilities.

Ministry of Agriculture and Forestry, Stubenring 1, A-1010 Vienna

Ministry of Foreign Affairs, Department for Development Cooperation, A-1014 Vienna. T: (43 222) 6615. Tx: 137091.

State governments:

The governments of the 9 federal states have primary responsibility for nature protection.

Other organizations:

Die Österreichische Akademie der Wissenschaften (The Austrian Academy of Sciences), Ignaz Seipel

Platz 2, A-1010 Vienna. T: (43 222) 51581. Tx: 0112628. ICSU national member.

Friends of the Earth, Rembrandtstrasse 14, A-1020 Vienna. Affiliated with Friends of the Earth International, listed in Part 6.

Greenpeace Austria, Mariahilfer Gürtel 32, A-1060 Vienna. National office of Greenpeace International, listed in Part 6.

Österreichische Gessellschaft für Natur- und Umweltschutz (Austrian Society for Nature and Environmental Protection), Holzgasse 2a, A-6020 Innsbruck. T: (43 5222) 33134. Major association.

Östereichischer Naturschutzbund (Austrian Nature Protection Union), Arenbergstrasse 10, A-5020 Salzburg

Verband Alpiner Vereine Österreichs (Federation of Austrian Alpine Clubs), Bäckerstrasse 16/2, A-1010 Vienna. Interests include conservation of mountain areas.

Welt Natur Fonds-Österreich (World Wide Fund for Nature-Austria), Ottakringerstrasse 114-116/9, Postfach 1, A-1162 Vienna. T: (43 222) 46 14 63. Affiliate of the World Wide Fund for Nature (WWF International), listed in Part 6.

BAHAMAS, THE

Government:

Ministry of Agriculture, Trade, and Industry, P.O. Box N-3028, Nassau. T: (1 809) 323-1777.

Ministry of Health, Office of Environmental Health Services, P.O. Box N-3730, Nassau. Tx: 20264.

Other organizations:

Bahamas National Trust, P.O. Box N-4105, Nassau. Works to preserve natural and historic areas.

BAHRAIN

Government:

Environmental Protection Committee (EPC), P.O. Box 26090, Manama. T: (973) 27 57 92. Tx: 8511 health bn.

Environmental Protection Technical Secretariat (EPTS), Manama. Develops and implements environmental legislation. Includes Marine Studies and Pollution Control Sections.

Ministry of Commerce and Agriculture, P.O. Box 5479, Manama. T: (973) 53 15 31. Tx: 9171. Includes a Directorate of Fisheries.

Other organizations:

Arabian Gulf University, Desert and Arid Zones Sciences Programme. P.O. Box 26671, Manama. T: (973) 27 72 09. Tx: 7319. Programme founded 1986. Includes research and training in environmental problems.

Bahrain Centre for Studies and Research, P.O. Box 496, Manama

BANGLADESH

Government:

Department of Environment Pollution Control, 6/11/F Lalmatia Housing Estate, Satmasjid Road, Dhaka-7. T: 31 57 77.

Ministry of Agriculture, Forest Department, Banabhaven, Gulshan Road, Mohaklahi, Dhaka

Ministry of Irrigation, Water Development, and Flood Control, Dhaka

Other organizations:

Bangladesh Academy of Sciences, 3/8 Asad Avenue, Muhammadpur, Dhaka-7. T: (880 2) 310425. C: SCIENCE. ICSU national member.

Friends of the Earth Bangladesh, 15/1 Farashgonj, Dhaka-1. Affiliated with Friends of the Earth International, listed in Part 6.

Monsoon Region Environment Society (MONRES), G.P.O. 2676, Dhaka. T: (880 2) 409445. Broad interests; research, education, and policy recommendations. [85]

Society for the Conservation of Nature and Environment (SCONE), 146 Shantinagat, Dhaka-17. T:(880 2) 403760. C: ENVIRON. Founded 1979. Youth organization. [85]

Wildlife Society of Bangladesh, c/o Department of Zoology, University of Dhaka, Dhaka-2

BARBADOS

Government:

Ministry of Agriculture, Food, and Fisheries, Graeme Hall, P.O. Box 505, Christ Church. T: (1 809) 428-4150.

Ministry of Employment, Labour Relations, and Community Development, Marine House, Hastings, Christ Church. T: (1 809) 427-5420. Responsible for management of parks, beaches, and caves. Includes the National Conservation Commission.

Ministry of Housing and Lands, Marine House, Hastings, Christ Church. T: (1 809) 427-5420. Tx: 386222.

Ministry of Health, Jemmotts Lane, St. Michael. T: (1 809) 426-5080. Environmental health.

Ministry of Transport, Works, and Telecommunications, The Pine, St. Michael. T: (1 809) 429-2191. Includes responsibility for water quality and water resources.

Other organizations:

Barbados National Trust, Ronald Tree House, 2 Tenth Avenue, Belleville, St. Michael. T: (1 809) 426-2421. Preservation of natural and cultural resources.

University of the West Indies, Center for Resource Management and Environmental Studies, P.O. Box 64, Bridgetown. T: (1 809) 425-1310.

BELGIUM

Government:

Walloon Region: Ministère de la Région Wallonne, Direction Générale des Ressources Naturelles et de l'Environnement (Ministry of the Walloon Region, General Directorate of Natural Resources and the Environment), Namur

Flemish Region: Ministerie van de Vlaamse Gemeenschap, Administratie voor Ruimtelijke Ordening en Leefmilieu (Ministry of the Flemish Region), Administration for Planning and the Environment), Brussels

Brussels Region: Ministère de la Région Bruxelloise, Service des Eaux et Forêts (Ministry of the Brussels Region, Water and Forest Service), Brussels

Ministère de l'Agriculture, Administration de la Recherche Agronomique (Ministry of Agriculture, Agronomic Research Administration), Manhattan Centre, 7e étage, avenue du Boulevard 21, B-1210 Brussels. Responsible for the country's international relations concerning nature protection.

Secretary of State for Development Cooperation, rue des Quatre-Bras 2, B-1000 Brussels. T: (32 02) 516 81 11.

Belgian Development Assistance Organization (AGCD), A.G. Building, place de Champs de Mars 5, B.P. 57, B-1050 Brussels. T: (32 02) 513 90 60.

Other organizations:

Académie Royale de Belgique (Royal Academy of Belgium), Palais des Académies, rue Ducale 1, B-1000 Brussels. ICSU national member.

Bond Beter Leefmilieu-Vlaanderen (Union for Environmental Quality-Flanders), Aaerlenstraat 25, B-1040 Brussels. T: (32 02) 230 94 10. Federation of some 50 environmental

organizations in the Flanders (Flemish-speaking) region.

Centre Permanent d'Education à la Conservation de la Nature (CPECN) (Permanent Center for Nature Conservation Education), Centre Nature de Mariemont, rue du Parc 29, B-6518 La Hestre. Founded 1986.

Entente Nationale pour la Protection de la Nature (National Alliance for Protection of Nature), rue de la Paix 83, B-6168 Chappelle-lez-Herlaimont. T: (32 64) 44 33 03.

Fonds Mondial pour la Nature-Belgique (World Wide Fund for Nature-Belgium), chausée de Waterloo 608, B-1060 Brussels. T: (32 02) 347 3030. Affiliate of the World Wide Fund for Nature (WWF International), listed in Part 6.

Greenpeace Belgium, Waversesteenweg 335, B-1040 Brussels. National office of Greenpeace International, listed in Part 6.

Inter-Environnement-Wallonie, rue d'Arlon 25, B-1040 Brussels. T: (32 02) 512 30 10. Federation of 70 environmental groups in the Walloon (French-speaking) region.

Les Amis de la Terre (Friends of the Earth), rue de l'Esplanade 1, B-1050 Brussels. Affiliated with Friends of the Earth International, listed in Part 6.

BELIZE

Government:

Ministry of Agriculture, Belmopan. T: (501 08) 2112.

Ministry of Health, Belmopan

Ministry of Natural Resources, Belmopan. T: (501 08) 2333.

Other organizations:

Belize Audubon Society, P.O. Box 1001, Belize City. T: (501 02) 7369. Nature protection; public education.

Belize Center for Environmental Studies, P.O. Box 666, Belize City. Public education; information base; forum for discussion of conservation and development issues.
Programme for Belize. *See* listing under USA.

BENIN

Government:

Direction Nationale des Eaux et Forêts (National Directorate of Water and Forests), B.P. 393, Cotonou. T: (229) 33 06 62.

Direction de l'Agriculture (Agriculture
Directorate), B.P. 58, Porto-Novo. T: (229) 21 32
90.

Direction Générale de l'Aménagement du
Territoire et de l'Urbanisme (General Directorate
of Planning), B.P. 239, Cotonou. Tx: 5200 mi-
naff.

Ministère de la Santé Publique (Ministry of Public
Health), B.P. 882, Cotonou. T: (229) 31 26 70.
Environmental health.

BERMUDA
British colony.

Government:

Ministry of the Environment, Government
Administration Building, 30 Parliament Street,
Hamilton HM 12. T: (1 809) 55151.

BHUTAN

Government:

Planning Commission, Royal Government of
Bhutan, Thimphu. T: 2503 C: BHUTANPLAN.

BOLIVIA

Government:

Comisión del Medio Ambiente y Recursos
Naturales (Commission of Environment and
Natural Resources), La Paz. Policy and
coordination.

Ministerio de Asuntos Campesinos y
Agropecuarios (MACA) (Ministry of Rural and
Farming Affairs), Avenida Camacho 1471, 4 piso,
Oficina 404, La Paz. T: (591 2) 37-4265. Tx:
2697 maca bv. Management of lands, forests, and
wildlife.

Other organizations:

Academia Nacional de Ciencias de Bolivia
(National Academy of Sciences of Bolivia),
Avenida 16 de Julio No. 1232, Casilla 5829, La
Paz. T: (591 2) 36 39 90. ICSU national member.

Asociación Pro Defensa de la Naturaleza
(PRODENA) (Association for Defense of Nature),
c/o of LIDEMA, Casilla 7000, La Paz. Founded
1979. Wildlife is main concern; plans to work in
agroforestry and environmental education.

Centro de Datos para la Conservación (Data
Center for Conservation), Casilla 11250, La Paz.
T: (591 2) 35-2071. Identifies conservation
priorities; maintains computerized data base on
the natural resources of the country.

Liga para la Defensa del Medio Ambiente
(LIDEMA) (League for the Defense of the

Environment), Casilla 7000, La Paz. T: (591 2)
35-6249. Tx: 2488 comitiw bv. Founded 1985.
Umbrella group for 10 Bolivian environmental
organizations. Research; advocacy; services to
member groups.

Sociedad Boliviana de Ecología (SOBE) (Bolivian
Society of Ecology), c/o LIDEMA, Casilla 7000,
La Paz. Research; conferences; public education;
reforestation projects.

BOTSWANA

Government:

Ministry of Agriculture, Private Bag 003,
Gaborone. T: 51171. Responsibilities include
management of natural resources.

Ministry of Commerce and Industry, Department
of Wildlife and National Parks, P.O. Box 131,
Gaborone. T: 51461. Tx: 2414 bd. C: GAME.

Ministry of Local Government and Lands, Private
Bag 006, Gaborone. T: 51380. Responsibilities
include environmental health and town and regional planning C: MERAFE.

Ministry of Mineral Resources and Water Affairs,
Private Bag 0049, Gaborone. T: 52641.
Responsibilities include water, air pollution
control, and energy.

Other organizations:

Forestry Association of Botswana (FAB), P.O. Box
2088, Gaborone. T: 51660. Tx: 2435 bd.
Founded 1983. Promotes reforestation, protection
of trees and shrubs, and scientific research.

Kalahari Conservation Society, P.O. Box 859,
Gaborone

Kweneng Rural Development Association
(KRDA), Private Bag 7, Molepolole. T: 385.
Program includes forestry and other conservation
projects.

University of Botswana, Department of
Environmental Science, P.O. Box 0022, Gaborone.
T: 351151. Tx: 2429 bd. Research and extension.

BRAZIL

Directories: The Special Secretariat of the
Environment publishes the *Cadastro Nacional das
Instituicoes que Atuam na Area do Meio Ambiente*
(Registry of Institutions Working in
Environmental Studies) (3rd edition, 1987), which
lists federal, state, and local government bodies
and NGOs.

Federal Government:

Ministerio de Habitacao, Urbanismo e Meio Ambiente--Secretaria Especial do Meio Ambiente (SEMA) (Ministry of Housing, Urbanism, and Environment--Special Secretariat of the Environment), SEPN, Av. W3 Norte - Q. 510, Ed. Cidade de Cabo Frio, Brasilia DF 70.750. T: (55 61) 274-6515. Tx: 061-1429 sema br. Broad responsibilities for policy and coordination of environmental protection and natural resource conservation.

Ministerio de Agricultura, Instituto Brasileiro de Desenvolvimento Florestal (Ministry of Agriculture, Brazilian Institute for Forestry Development), Setor das Areas Isoladas Norte, Av. L-4 Norte, Brasilia DF. T: (55 61) 226-7665. Tx: 061-1711. Major responsibilities for the country's forests. Includes:
■ Departamento Nacional de Parques e Reservas Equivalentes (National Department of Parks and Equivalent Reserves), SBN 13o Andar, Brasilia DF 70.000. T: (55 61) 225-8125. Tx: (061) 1711.

Ministerio da Ciencia e Tecnologia (Ministry of Science and Technology). Includes two units which carry out applied environmental research and outreach activities in the Amazon region:
■ Instituto Nacional de Pesquisas da Amazonia (INPA), (National Institute for Investigations of the Amazon), Caixa Postal 478, Manaus AM 69.000. T: 236-9050. Tx: 92-2269.
■ Museu Paraense Emilio Goeldi (Emilio Goeldi Pará Museum), Caixa Postal 399, Belem, PN 66.040. T: (55 91) 229-1332. Tx: 91-1419.

State governments:

The governments of the states have important responsibilities for environmenal protection. For information about state agencies and state NGOs, see the directory noted above or contact the national organizations listed here.

Other organizations:

Note: In Brazil, state and regional NGOs have an important role; they can be contacted through the key organizations described below.

Amigos da Terra (Friends of the Earth), Rua Miguel Tostes 694, Porto Alegre 90.000. Affiliated with Friends of the Earth International, listed in Part 6.

Associacao Brasiliera de Ecologia (Brazilian Ecology Association), Av. Atlantica 734, Apto. 1201, Rio de Janeiro, RJ

Associacao de Defesa do Meio Ambiente (Association for Defense of the Environment), C.P. 832, Sao Paulo, SP 04.531

Centro de Estudios e Atividades de Conservacao da Natureza (CEACON), C.P. 20684, Sao Paulo,

SP 01.498. T: (55 11) 284-8342. Wildlife protection and environmental education activities.

Conselho Nacional de Desenvolvimento Cientifico e Technologico-CNPQ (National Council of Scientific and Technological Development), Av. W-3 Norte, Quadra 507-B, C.P. 11.1142, Brasilia DF 70.740. T: (55 61) 274-1155. Tx: 0611089. ICSU national member.

Fundacao Brasileira para a Conservacao da Natureza (FBCN) (Brazilian Foundation for the Conservation of Nature), Rue Miranda Valverde 103, Rio de Janeiro, RJ 22.281. T: (55 21) 226-2654. Tx: 21-37984 fbcn. Research; habitat protection; environmental education.

Fundacao Pro Natureza (FUNATURA), C.P. 02-0186, Brasilia, DF 70.001. T: (55 61) 274-5449. President is Maria Tereza Jorge Pádua; seeks to strengthen the role of the private sector in protecting Brazil's natural environment and to reach out to all sectors of Brazilian society. Works through education, training, research, and land preservation projects.

Instituto de Estudios Amazonicos (IAE) (Institute of Amazonian Studies), Rua Itupava 1220, Curitiba, PR 80.040. T: (55 41) 262-9494. Promotes sustainable development alternatives for the Amazon region.

BRITISH INDIAN OCEAN TERRITORY
No separate information available.

BRUNEI

Government:

Ministry of Education and Health, Lapangan Terbang Lama Berakas. T: (673 2) 44233. Tx: 2577.

Other organizations:

Brunei Museum, Kota Batu, Bandar Seri Begawan

BULGARIA

Government:

State Committee for Environmental Protection, ul. Triaditza 2, Sofia. Tx: 22145.

Komitet za Opazvane na Prirodnata Sreda (Committee for Conservation of the Natural Environment), ul. Vladimar Pontonov, 67 100 Sofia

Ministry of Forests and Protection of the Natural Environment, ul. Antim I 17, 1000 Sofia

Other organizations:

Bulgarian Academy of Sciences, 1 7th of November St., Sofia. ICSU national member.

Includes:
■ Nautchnokoordinarionniyat Center Popazvane i Voproysvodstvo na Okruzshavazshchta Sreda (NKCOVOS) (Research and Coordination Center for Conservation of the Environment), ul. Gagarin 2, 1113 Sofia. Coordinates environmental and nature protection research in various organizations; undertakes studies on protected areas and their management.

Center for Scientific, Technical, and Economic Information, bulv. Lenin 125, Block 1, 1113 Sofia. Evaluates, coordinates, and processes information on agriculture, forestry, and environmental protection.

Ecological and Environmental Center, c/o Academy of Sciences, ul. Gagarin 2, 1113 Sofia

Obshchenarodniya Komitet za Zashchita na Prirodata (All-National Committee for Nature Conservation of the National Council of the Patriotic Front), bulv. Vitosha 18, 1000 Sofia. Coordinates voluntary environmental conservation groups.

Scientific Center for Protection of Natural Environment and Water Resources, Industrialna 7, Sofia 1202

Society of Natural Sciences, Ruski 1, Sofia. Undertakes studies in natural science.

BURKINA FASO

Government:

Ministère de l'Environnement et du Tourisme (Ministry of the Environment and Tourism), B.P. 7044, Ouagadougou. T: (226) 33 32 13. Tx: 5283 minitour uv.

Ministère de l'Agriculture et d'Élevage (Ministry of Agriculture and Livestock), B.P. 7005, Ouagadougou

Other organizations:

Centre National de la Recherche Scientifique et Technologique (National Center of Scientific and Techological Research), B.P. 7192, Ouagadougou. ICSU national member.

Centre Technique Forestier Tropical (Tropical Forestry Technical Center), B.P. 1759, Ouagadougou. T: 333903. Founded 1963. Sponsored by French Government.

BURMA

Government:

Ministry of Agriculture and Forests, Rangoon

Ministry of Livestock and Fisheries, Mogul Street, Rangoon

Ministry of Health, 36 Theinbyu Road, Rangoon. Includes a Environmental Sanitation Division.

Ministry of Home and Religious Affairs, Rangoon. Includes responsibility for pollution control in harbors and the Irrawaddy River, as well as for urban waste management.

BURUNDI

Government:

Institut National pour la Conservation de la Nature (National Institute for the Conservation of Nature), B.P. 2757, Bujumbura

Ministère de la Santé Publique (Ministry of Public Health), Bujumbura. T: 6020. Environmental health.

CAMBODIA

Government:

Ministère de l'Economie et des Finances, Département de l'Environnement (Ministry of the Economy and Finance, Department of the Environment), c/o Permanent Mission of Democratic Kampuchea to ESCAP, United Nations Building, Rajadamnern Avenue, Bangkok 2, Thailand

CAMEROON

Government:

Service de la Faune et des Parcs Nationaux (Wildlife and National Park Service), Yaounde

Ministère de l'Enseignement Superieur et de la Recherche Scientifique (Ministry of Higher Education and Scientific Research). Includes:
■ Centre de Recherches Forestières (Center of Forestry Research), B.P. 2102, Yaounde

Ministère de la Santé Publique (Ministry of Public Health), Yaounde. T: (237) 22 29 01. Tx: 8565. Environmental health.

Other organizations:

Association des Clubs des Amis de la Nature du Cameroun (ACAN) (Association of Friends of Nature Clubs of Cameroon), B.P. 271, Garoua. T: (237) 27 11 25. Founded 1975; 51 clubs. Public awareness; environmental education in schools.

CANADA

Directories: *Conservation Directory*, published annually by the National Wildlife Federation in the USA, includes a brief section on Canadian governmental and non-governmental organizations. The Canadian Nature Federation publishes the *Canadian Conservation Directory*

(most recent edition 1981; out of print), with much more detail on Canadian organizations. The Ontario Environment Network (P.O. Box 125, Station P, Toronto, Ontario M5S 2Z7) publishes an *Environmental Resource Book* listing many groups in the Province of Ontario.

Federal government:

Department of the Environment (Environment Canada), Ottawa, Ontario K1A 1G2. T: (1 819) 997-2800. Includes the Canadian Forestry Service, Canadian Wildlife Service, Parks Canada (national parks), and units concerned with air and water pollution control, water resources, atmospheric science, land use policy, and impact assessment.

Department of Agriculture (Agriculture Canada), 930 Carling Avenue, Ottawa, Ontario K1A 0C5. Concerns include soil conservation and pesticides.

Department of Energy, Mines, and Resources (EMR), Ottawa, Ontario K1A 0E4. T: (1 613) 995-3065. Earth and mineral science and policy.

Department of Fisheries and Oceans, Ottawa, Ontario K1A 0E6. T: (1 613) 923-0600.

Department of Health and Welfare, Ottawa, Ontario K1A 0K9. T: (1 613) 996-4950. Environmental health.

Department of Indian and Northern Affairs, Ottawa, Ontario K1A 0H4. T: (1 613) 997-0011. Northern Affairs Program is broadly concerned with the environment and resources of the Canadian North.

Atomic Energy Control Board, P.O. Box 1046, Ottawa, Ontario K1P 5S9. T: (1 613) 995-6941.

Canadian International Development Agency (CIDA), 200 Promenade du Portage, Hull, Quebec K1A 0G4. T: (1 819) 997-6100. Tx: 053-4140. Includes a Resources Branch and Office of Environmental Advisor.

International Development Research Centre (IDRC), P.O. Box 8500, Ottawa, Ontario K1G 3H9. T: (1 613) 236-6163. C: RECENTRE. Established 1970 to "stimulate and support scientific and technical research by developing countries for their own benefit." Areas of focus include forestry, fisheries, energy, water supplies, and population studies. Regional offices in Asia, Africa, and Latin America. Pub: Numerous public-interest and scientific publications and audio-visuals (catalog available).

Provincial governments:

The 10 provincial governments have major responsibilities for environmental protection and natural resource management. Provincial agencies are listed in the directories described above.

Other organizations:

Arctic Institute of North America. *See* listing in Part 6.

Atlantic Center for the Environment. *See* listing under USA.

Canada-U.S. Environmental Council. *See* listing in Part 6.

Canadian Arctic Resources Committee, 111 Sparks Street, 4th Floor, Ottawa, Ontario K1P 5B5. T: (1 613) 236-7379. Founded 1971. Concerned with environmental impacts of northern development.

Canadian Climate Centre, 4905 Dufferin Street, Downsview, Ontario M3H 5T. Concerns include the nature and impacts of global climate change.

Canadian Environmental Law Association, 243 Queen Street West, 4th Floor, Toronto, Ontario M5V 1Z4. T: (1 416) 977-2410. Founded 1971. Uses laws to protect the environment; promotes environmental legislation.

Canadian Institute of Forestry, 151 Slater Street, Suite 1005, Ottawa, Ontario K1P 5H3. T: (1 613) 234-2242. Founded 1908. Professional society.

Canadian Nature Federation, 453 Sussex Drive, Ottawa, Ontario K1N 6Z4. T: (1 613) 238-6154. Naturalists' organization with 120 affiliated groups; promotes conservation.

Canadian Parks and Wilderness Society, 69 Sherbourne Street, Suite 313, Toronto, Ontario M5A 3X7. T: (1 416) 366-3494. Founded 1963.

Canadian Society of Environmental Biologists, P.O. Box 962, Station F, Toronto, Ontario M4Y 2N9. Founded 1959. Program includes conservation work.

Canadian Wildlife Federation, 1673 Carling Avenue, Ottawa, Ontario K2A 3Z1. T: (1 613) 725-2191. Founded 1961; over 500,000 members.

Conservation Council of Ontario, 74 Victoria Street, Toronto, Ontario M5C 2A5. T: (1 416) 362-2218. Founded 1952. Coordinates work of 33 NGOs in Ontario Province.

Friends of the Earth, 701-251 Laurier Avenue West, Ottawa, Ontario K1P 5J6. Affiliated with Friends of the Earth International, listed in Part 6.

Greenpeace Canada, 578 Bloor Street West, Toronto M6G 1K1. National office of Greenpeace International, listed in Part 6.

Institute for Research on Public Policy, 275 Slater Street, Ottawa, Ontario. T: (1 613) 238-2296. Includes an Environment and Sustainable

Development Programme, directed by Jim MacNeill, former Secretary-General of the World Commission on Environment and Development.

International Centre for Ocean Development (ICOD), 5670 Spring Garden Road, 9th Floor, Halifax, Nova Scotia B3J 1H6. T: (1 902) 426-1512. Tx: 019-21670 icod hfx. Founded 1985. Fosters cooperation between Canada and developing countries on "environmentally sound ocean development."

Inuit Tapirisat of Canada (ITC), 176 Gloucester Street, Ottawa, Ontario. Native association interested in conservation.

National Research Council of Canada, Building M-58, Montreal Road, Ottawa, Ontario K1A 0R6. T: (1 613) 996-6810. ICSU national member. Has an Environmental Secretariat and a Bureau of International Relations.

The Nature Conservancy of Canada, 794A Broadview Avenue, Toronto, Ontario M4K 2P7. T: (1 416) 469-1701. Founded 1963. Acquires and preserves ecologically-significant areas.

North-South Institute, 185 Rideau Street, Ottawa, Ontario K1N 5X8. T: (1 613) 236-3535. Founded 1976. Conducts policy research on issues of relations between industrialized and developing countries. Concerns include resources and environment.

Pollution Probe Foundation, 12 Madison Avenue, Toronto, Ontario M5R 2S1. T: (1 416) 926-1907. Founded 1969. Policy research and public education, with major focus on hazardous materials and pollution control.

Sierra Club. See description under USA. Chapters in Canada are:
■ Sierra Club of Ontario, 229 College Street, Room 303, Toronto, Ontario M5T 1R4. T: (1 416) 596-7778.
■ Sierra Club of Western Canada, 620 View Street, Room 314, Victoria, British Columbia V8W 1J6. T: (604) 386-5255.

Union Québécoise pour la Conservation de la Nature (Quebec Union for Nature Conservation), 2728 rue de l'Anse, Sainte-Foy, Quebec G1W 2G5

University of Alberta, Boreal Institute for Northern Studies, Edmonton, Alberta T6G 2E9. T: (1 403) 432-4512. Tx: 037-2979. Founded 1960. Research and education on development of Canada's North, including environmental problems.

World Wildlife Fund-Canada, 20 St. Clair Avenue East, Suite 201, Toronto, Ontario M4T 1N5. T: (1 416) 923-8173. Affiliate of the World Wide Fund for Nature (WWF International), listed in Part 6.

CAPE VERDE

Government:

Ministerio do Desenvolvimento Rural (Ministry of Rural Development), Rua António Pussich, Praia. T: 335. Tx: 6072. Includes:
■ Instituto Nacional de Investigacao Agraria (National Institute of Agrarian Research), P.O. Box 84, Praia. Program includes research and teaching in natural resource management.

Ministry of Health and Social Affairs, C.P. 47, Praia. T: 422. Tx: 6059. Environmental health.

CAYMAN ISLANDS
A British territory.

Government:

Department of Development and Natural Resources, George Town, Grand Cayman

CENTRAL AFRICAN REPUBLIC

Government:

Ministère de l'Agriculture (Ministry of Agriculture), Bangui. Includes a Directorate General of Water and Forests.

Ministère des Travaux Publics et de l'Urbanisme (Ministry of Public Works and Town Planning), Bangui. T: 61 28 00.

CHAD

Government:

Ministère du Tourisme et de l'Environnement (Ministry of Tourism and the Environment), B.P. 447, N'Djamena. T: 2121.

CHILE

Government:

Ministerio de Agricultura (Ministry of Agriculture). Includes:
■ Corporación Nacional Forestal y de Protección de Recursos Naturales Renovables (CONAF) (National Corporation for Forestry and Protection of Renewable Natural Resources), Avenida Bulnes 285, Oficina 501, Santiago. T: (56 2) 696-0783. Tx: 240001 conaf cl. Responsibilities include forestry, watershed management, and a system of national parks and reserves.

Instituto Antártico Chileno (INACH) (Chilean Antarctic Institute), Avenida Luis Thayer Ojeda 814, Santiago. T: (56 2) 231-0105. Responsible for Chilean policies and research activities in the Antarctic.

Instituto de Fomento Pesquero (IFOP) (Institute of Fisheries Development), Avenida Pedro de

Valdivia 2633, Santiago. T: (56 2) 225-2331. Research and development in fisheries and oceanography.

Servicio Nacional de Pesca (SERNAP) (National Fishery Service), Teatinos 120, 8º piso, Santiago. T: (56 2) 698-0543. Tx: 230481 pesca cl.

Other organizations:

Centro de Investigación y Planificación del Medio Ambiente (CIPMA) (Center for Research and Planning of the Environment), Juan Jacques 2268, Santiago. T: (56 2) 223-9216. Research projects; holds major conference every 3 years, Encuentro Cientifico sobre el Medio Ambiente Chileno (Scientific Encounter on the Chilean Environment).

Comisión Nacional de Investigaciones Científicas y Tecnológicas (National Commission of Scientific and Technological Research) (CONICYT), Casilla 297-V, Santiago. T: (56 2) 74-4537. Tx: 340191 cnct cl. ICSU national member. Has a National ICSU Committee.

Comité Nacional Pro-Defensa de la Fauna y Flora (National Committee for Defense of the Fauna and Flora), Casilla 3675, Santiago 9. T: (56 2) 37-4280. Broad interests.

Instituto de Ecología de Chile (Institute of Ecology of Chile), Calle Agustinas 641, Oficina 11, Santiago. T: (56 2) 30-963. Education and information.

Instituto de la Patagónia (Institute of Patagonia), Casilla 596, Punta Arenas. T: 23039. Research on natural resources of Patagonia, the southernmost region of Chile which includes the Strait of Magellan and Cape Horn. Affiliated with the University of Magallanes.

Instituto Nacional de Recursos Naturales (IREN) (National Institute of Natural Resources), Casilla 14995, Santiago. T: (56 2) 223-6641. Tx: 242017 ciren cl.

Sociedad de Vida Silvestre de Chile (Wildlife Society of Chile), Casilla 805, Santiago

CHINA
See also Taiwan

Government:

Ministry of Urban and Rural Construction and Environmental Protection, Baiwanzhuang, Beijing. T: (86 1) 8992211. Tx: 22477. C: MURCEP. Includes an Environmental Protection Bureau. Responsibilities include air and water pollution control, wildlife management, and environment-development issues.

Ministry of Animal Husbandry and Fisheries, Hepingli, Dongcheng District, Beijing. T: (86 1) 463061.

Ministry of Forestry, Hepingli, Dongcheng District, Beijing. T: (86 1) 22237.

Ministry of Public Health, 44 Houbaibeiyan, Beijing. T: (86 1) 440531. Tx: 22193.

Ministry of Water Resources and Electric Power, 1 Lane, Baiguang Street, Guanganman, Beijing. T: (86 1) 365563. Tx: 22466.

Other organizations:

China Association for Science and Technology, Beijing. T: (86 1) 898116. Tx: 20035 cast. ICSU national member.

Chinese Academy of Preventative Medicine, Institute of Environmental Health Monitoring, 10 Tian Tan Xi Li, Beijing

Chinese Academy of Sciences (Academia Sinica). Includes:
- Institute of Botany, 141 Hsi Chih Men Wai Ta Chie, Beijing
- Commission for Integrated Survey of Natural Resources (CISNAR), P.O. Box 767, Beijing. T: (86 1) 446551.
- Institute of Desert Research (IDRAS), 14 Donggang West Road, Lanzhou, Gansu Province. T: 26726. Tx: 3097. Major research and extension center with a professional staff of over 200. Includes an International Desertification Control Research and Training Center.
- Research Center for Eco-Environmental Sciences, P.O. Box 934, Beijing. T: (86 1) 28-5176.
- International Research and Training Center on Erosion and Sedimentation, 10 West Chegongyhuang Road, P.O. Box 366, Beijing

Institute of Labor Protection, Tao Ran Ting Road, Beijing. T: (86 1) 3320. Program includes occupational environmental health.

China Wildlife Conservation Association, He Pingli, Beijing

Chinese Society for Environmental Sciences, Division of Nature Protection, c/o Environment Protection Bureau, Ministry of Urban and Rural Construction and Environmental Protection, Baiwanzhuang, Beijing

Wuhan University, International and Environmental Law Programs, Wuhan

CHRISTMAS ISLAND
Australian possession.

Government:

Administrator, Christmas Island 6798, Indian
Ocean

COCOS (KEELING) ISLANDS
Australian possession.

Government:

Administrator, Cocos (Keeling) Islands 6799,
Indian Ocean

COLOMBIA

Government:

Departamento Nacional de Planeación (DNP)
(National Department of Planning), Calle 25, no.
13-19, Bogotá. T: (57 1) 282-4055. Responsible
for economic and social development.
Agricultural Development Unit includes a
Division of Renewable Natural Resources,
Regional Development Unit includes a Division of
Environmental Policy.

Ministerio de Agricultura (Ministry of
Agriculture). Includes:
■ Instituto Nacional de los Recursos Naturales
Renovables y del Ambiente (INDERENA)
(National Institute of Renewable Natural
Resources and the Environment), Apartado Aéreo
13458, Bogotá. T: (57 1) 285-4417. Broad
responsibilities for natural resource and
environmental management.

Corporación Nacional de Investigación y Fomento
Forestal (CONIF) (National Corporation of
Forestry Research and Development), Parque La
Florida, Apartado Aéreo 095153, Bogotá. T: (57 1)
267-6844. C: CONIF. Public-private organization;
research, agroforestry, and information services.

Other organizations:

Academia Colombiana de Ciencias Exactas, Físicas
y Naturales (Colombian Academy of Exact,
Physical, and Natural Sciences), Apartado 44,763,
Bogotá. ICSU national member.

Fundación Natura (Nature Foundation), Apartado
Aéreo 55402, Bogotá. Founded 1984. Protection
of nature and natural resources; cooperates with
government agencies; manages Conservation Data
Center.

Fundación para un Mejor Ambiente (FMA)
(Foundation for a Better Environment), Apartado
Aéreo 1565, Cali. Founded 1985. Public
education, research, and support of legislation.

Fundación Merenberg para la Protección de la
Flora y la Fauna (Merenberg Foundation for the
Protection of Flora and Fauna), Apartado Aéreo
889, Popayán (Cauca)

Fundación para la Investigación y Protección del
Medio Ambiente (FIPMA) (Foundation for
Research and Protection of the Environment),
Apartado Aéreo 2741, Cali. T: (57 3) 80-3761.

Sociedad Colombiana de Ecología (Colombian
Society of Ecology), Carrera 3a, No. 17-23,
Edificio Academia de la Lengua, Costado
Oriental, Bogotá

COMOROS

Government:

Ministère de l'Équipement et de l'Environnement
(Ministry of Industry and Environment), B.P. 12,
Moroni

Other organizations:

Mouvement des Jeunes pour le Developement et la
Paix (Youth Movement for Development and
Peace), B.P. 328, Mutsamudu-Anjouan. T: 456.
Founded 1982; 180 groups. Program includes
reforestation.

CONGO

Government:

Ministère du Tourisme, Loisirs et de
l'Environnement (Ministry of Tourism,
Recreation, and the Environment), B.P. 958,
Brazzaville. T: 81-30-46. Direction de
l'Environnement (Environmental Directorate) has
broad responsibilities for natural resources,
environmental health, and environmental
protection.

COOK ISLANDS
Internally governing state in free association with
New Zealand.

Government:

Ministry of Marine Resources, Avarua, Rarotonga

Ministry of Education, Agriculture, Health, and
Conservation, Avarua, Rarotonga

COSTA RICA

Government:

Ministerio de Agricultura y Ganadería, Servicio
de Parques Nacionales (Ministry of Agriculture
and Livestock, National Parks Service), Apartado
10094, 1000 San José. T: (506) 23-5267.

Ministerio de Recursos Naturales, Energía y
Minas (Ministry of Natural Resources, Energy,
and Mines), Apartado 10104, 1000 San José

Ministerio de Salud (Ministry of Health), Apartado 10123, San José. T: (506) 23-0333. Environmental health.

Other organizations:

Amigos de la Naturaleza (Friends of Nature), Apartado 162, Guadalupe. Tx: 2845 procex cr. Broad interests; uses media.

Asociación Costarricense para la Conservación de la Naturaleza (ASCONA) (Costa Rican Association for Conservation of Nature), Apartado 8-3790, San José. T: (506) 36-5011. Promotes development without destruction of ecosystems; works through public education and political action.

Centro Científico Tropical (Tropical Science Center), Apartado 83870, San José. T: (506) 22-6241. Applies scientific research to conservation problems; Joseph A. Tosi, Jr. is the longtime administrator.

Consejo Nacional de Investigaciones Científicas y Tecnológicas (CONICIT) (National Council of Scientific and Technological Research), Apartado 10318, San José. T: (506) 24 41 72. Tx: 3338 coni'cr.

Fundacíon de Parques Nacionales (National Parks Foundation), Apartado 236, 1002 San José. T: (506) 33-0003. Founded 1981.

Fundacíon Neotropica (Neotropic Foundation), Apartado 236-1002, San José. T: (506) 33-0003. Founded 1985. Matches conservation projects with organizations interested in assisting them. Examples of projects: A national park management plan; a national environmental awareness program; state of the environment report for the country.

Greenpeace Costa Rica, Apartado 230, Centro Colon, San José. National office of Greenpeace International, listed in Part 6.

Monteverde Conservation League, Apartado 10165, 1000 San José. Group of Quakers of U.S. origin and others who maintain an important ecological reserve in the Monteverde cloud forest and work on behalf of other conservation efforts.

Organización para Estudios Tropicales (Organization for Tropical Studies) (OTS), Ciudad Universitaria, San Pedro de Montes de Oca. A major training center in tropical ecology; sponsors include U.S. and Latin American universities.

Voluntarios en Recuperación y Defensa Ecológia (Volunteers for Ecological Restoration and Protection), Apartado 790-2050, San Pedro de Montes de Oca

COTE D'IVOIRE (IVORY COAST)

Government:

Commission Nationale de l'Environnement (National Environment Commission), B.P. V-67, Abidjan. T: (225) 22 53 54.

Ministère de l'Agriculture, des Eaux et Forêts (Ministry of Agriculture, Water, and Forests), B.P. V82, Abidjan. Tx: 23612.

CUBA

Government:

Academia de Ciencias de la República de Cuba (Academy of Sciences of the Republic of Cuba), Capitolio Nacional, Havana 2. T: 68914. Tx: 511290 cubacad. ICSU national member. Includes the Comisión Nacional para la Protección del Medio Ambiente y Conservación de los Recursos Naturales (COMARNA) (National Commission for Protection of the Environment and Conservation of Natural Resources), which has investigative and enforcement powers.

Other organizations:

Sociedad Cubana para la Conservación de la Naturaleza y los Recursos Naturales (Cuban Society for Conservation of Nature and Natural Resources), Apartado 7097, Havana. [85]

CYPRUS

Government:

Ministry of Agriculture and Natural Resources, Nicosia. T: (357 2) 40 25 86. Tx: 4660 minagri. Broad responsibilities for resource management and environmental protection.

Other organizations:

Cyprus Association for the Protection of the Environment, P.O. Box 3810, Nicosia. T: (357 2) 45 20 60.

Cyprus Forestry Association, Department of Forests, Nicosia. T (357 2) 45 01 68.

Cyprus Ornithological Society (COS), 4 Kanari Street, Strovolos 154. T: (357 2) 42 07 03. Program includes nature conservation.

Cyprus Wildlife Society, c/o Mr. A. Demetropoulous, Department of Fisheries, Nicosia. T: (357 2) 40 32 79.

Friends of the Earth, Lanarca District, Maroni. Affiliated with Friends of the Earth International, listed in Part 6.

CZECHOSLOVAKIA

Federal government:

Federal Ministry of Technological Development and Investments, Department of the Environment, Slezska 9, CS-120 29 Prague. T: (42 2) 25 55 51. Tx: 121107.

Federal Ministry of Agriculture and Food, Prague

Republic governments:

Environmental protection and resource management is largely the responsibility of the governments of the two constituent republics, which have corresponding ministries:

Czech Republic:

Czech Ministry of Interior and Environment, Prague. Includes:
■ Statni Ustav Pamatkove Pece a Ochrany Prirody (SUPPOP) (State Institute for Protection of Monuments and Nature Conservation), Mala Strana, Waldstejnske Namesti 1, CS-118 01 Prague

Slovak Republic:

Slovak Ministry of Interior and Environment, Bratislava. Includes:
■ Statni Ustav Pamatkove Pece a Ochrany Prirody (USPPOP) (State Institute for Protection of Monuments and Nature Conservation), Mostova 6, CS-811 02 Bratislava

Slovak Ministry of Culture, Bratislava. Includes:
■ Ustredie Statnej Ochrany Prirody (USOP) (State Center for Nature Conservation), Heyrovsteho 1, CS-841 03 Bratislava

Other organizations:

Ceskoslovenska Akademie Ved (Czechoslovak Academy of Science), Narodni Trida 3, CS-111 42 Prague 1. T: (42 2) 26 66 84. Tx: 121040 acad c. ICSU national member. Includes the Institute of Landscape Ecology and the Institute of the Physics of the Atmosphere.

Cesky Svaz Ochrancu Prirody (CSOP) (Czech Union of Nature Conservationists), Na Skalce 5, CS-150 00 Prague. Union of conservation groups in the Czech Republic.

Czechoslovak Research and Development Center for Environmental Pollution Control, Laca, Movomestskeho 2, CS-Bratislava 816 43

Slovensky Zvaz Ochrancov Prirody a Krajiny (SZOPK) (Slovak Union of Nature and Landscape Conservationists), Leningradska 1, CS-811 01 Bratislava. Union of conservation groups in the Slovak Republic.

Ustav Krajinne Ekologie (CSAV) (Landscape Ecology Institute), Na Sadkach 7, CS-370 05 Budejovice. Promotes the application of ecology to land-use planning.

Vyskumny Ustav Lesneho Hespodarstva (VULH) (Forest Research Institute), Markova 2175/22, CS-960 92 Zvolen

DENMARK
See also Faroe Islands.

Government:

Miljoestyrelsen (Agency of Environmental Protection), Strandgade 29, DK-1401 Copenhagen K. T: (45 1) 57 83 10. Tx: 31209 miljoe dk. Includes the National Forest and Nature Agency.

Landbrugsministeriets Vildtforvaltning (Ministry of Agriculture, Wildlife Administration), Kalo, DK-8410 Ronde

Ministry of Foreign Affairs, Department of International Development (DANIDA), Asiatic Place 2, DK-1448 Copenhagen K

Naturfredningsraadet (Nature Conservation Council), Amaliegade 13, DK-1256 Copenhagen K

Other organizations:

Danmarks Naturfredningsforening (Society for the Protection of Nature in Denmark), Norregade 2, DK-1165 Copenhagen K. T: (45 1) 87 11 01. Broad interest in environmental protection. Over 200,000 members; some 175 local committees.

Greenpeace Denmark, Thomas Laubsgade 11-13, DK-2100 Copenhagen 0. National office of Greenpeace International, listed in Part 6.

Kongelige Danske Videnskabernes Selskab (Royal Danish Science Society), 35 H.C. Andersons Blvd., DK-1553 Copenhagen V. T: (45 1) 11 32 40. ICSU national member.

NOAH (Union of Working Groups Against Pollution), Bronlund Alle 25, DK-2900 Hellerup. Affiliated with Friends of the Earth International, listed in Part 6.

World Wide Fund for Nature-Denmark, Osterbrogade 94, DK-2100 Copenhagen 0. T: (45 1) 38 20 20. Affiliate of the World Wide Fund for Nature (WWF International), listed in Part 6.

DJIBOUTI

Government:

Service de l'Agriculture et des Forêts (Agriculture and Forest Service), B.P. 224, Djibouti

Ministère de la Santé (Ministry of Health), B.P. 296, Djibouti. T: 351491. Tx: 5871. Environmental health.

Other organizations:

Institut Superieur d'Études et de Recherches Scientifiques et Techniques (ISERST) (Higher Scientific and Technical Study and Research Institute), B.P. 486, Djibouti. T: 352795. Tx: 5811 obsi dj. Program includes research and extension in natural resource management, particularly in anti-desertification and forestry.

DOMINICA

Government:

Ministry of Agriculture and Lands. Includes:
■ Forestry and National Parks Service, P.O. Box 71, Roseau. T: (1 809) 448-2732.

Other organizations:

Dominica Conservation Association, P.O. Box 71, Roseau

DOMINICAN REPUBLIC

Government:

Comisión Ambiental (Environmental Commission), Dr. Delgado 58, Apartado 1351, Santo Domingo. T: (1 809) 689-3808. Tx: 346-0461.

Secretaría de Agricultura (Secretariat of Agriculture), Centro de los Héroes de Constanza, Santo Domingo. T: (1 809) 533-7171. Responsibilities include fisheries and wildlife.

Dirección Nacional de Parques (National Parks Directorate), Apartado 2487, Santo Domingo. T: (1 809) 685-1316.

Other organizations:

Floresta, Apartado 22368, Santo Domingo. T: (1 809) 682-5472. Tx: 326 4399 4124 (RCA). Agroforestry and tree planting.

Fundación Natura Dominicana (Dominican Nature Foundation), Apartado 30155, Santo Domingo

Fundación para el Mejoramiento Humano (PROGRESSIO), Apartado 22036, Santo Domingo. T: (1 809) 685-9562. Tx: 3460669 (ITT). Founded in 1983 by a savings and loan association. Focus on reforestation and water.

Sociedad Dominicana para la Conservación de Recursos Naturales (Dominican Society for Conservation of Natural Resources), Apartado 174-2, Santo Domingo. T: (1 809) 567-6211.

ECUADOR

Government:

Consejo Nacional de Desarrollo (CONADE), Programa de Recursos Naturales y Medio Ambiente (National Council of Development, Program of Natural Resources and Environment), Quito

Instituto Ecuatoriano de Obras Sanitarias (IEOS), Departamento de Saneamiento Medio Ambiental (Ecuadorian Institute of Sanitary Works, Department of Environmental Sanitation), Toledo 684 y Lerida, Quito. T: (593 2) 562-810. Pollution control.

Instituto Ecuatoriano de Recursos Hidráulicos (INERHI), (Ecuadorian Institute of Water Resources), Juan Larrea 534 y Riofrio, Quito. T: (593 2) 545-566. C: INERHI. Tx: 21136 inerhi ed. Responsibilities include watershed protection and water pollution control.

Ministerio de Agricultura y Ganadería (Ministry of Agriculture and Livestock), Quito. T: (593 2) 541-955. Tx: 2291 mag ed. Includes National Parks Department and National Forestry Directorate, as well as the Instituto Nacional de Colonización de la Región Amazónica (INCRAE) (National Institute for Colonization of the Amazon Region), which is responsible for environmental management in that region.

Ministerio de Energía y Minas, Dirección General de Medio Ambiente (Ministry of Energy and Mines, General Directorate of Environment), Santa Prisca y 10 de Agosto, Quito. T: (593 2) 570-767. Environmental management and rehabilitation of mining areas.

Other organizations:

Acción Ecológica (Ecological Action), Pasaje San Luis 104, Santa Prisca, Edificio Recalde, Oficina 401, Quito. T: (593 2) 570-443. Information and public education.

Fundación Charles Darwin para las Islas Galápagos (Charles Darwin Foundation for the Galapagos Islands), Casilla 3991, Quito. T: (593 2) 527-912. Carries out scientific, conservation, and educational activities in the islands. Mantains the Estación Cientifica Charles Darwin (Charles Darwin Scientific Station), Santa Cruz, Islas Galápagos, Ecuador.

Fundación Fauna y Flora (Flora and Fauna Foundation), Depto. de Forestación, Ministerio de Agricultura, Casilla 15149, Guayaquil. T: (593 4) 330-950. Nature preservation.

Fundación Natura, Casilla 243, Quito. T: (593 2) 249-780. Tx: 21211 natura ed. Broad interests in environmental protection; Executive Director is Yolanda Kakabadse. An associate organization of the World Wide Fund for Nature (WWF International).

Fundación Ornitológica del Ecuador (Ornithological Foundation of Ecuador), Casilla 9068 S-7, Quito. T: (593 2) 244-314. Tx: 2849 idima ed. Bird conservation and research.

Fundación Pedro Vicente Maldonado para las Ciencias del Hombre y la Tierra (Pedro Vicente Maldonado Foundation for the Sciences of Man and the Earth), Casilla 10904, Guayaquil. T: (593 4) 303-938. Tx: 4-3509 espolg ed. Program includes research on coastal and other resources.

Sociedad de Defensa de la Naturaleza (SODENA) (Society for Defense of Nature), Pasaje San Luis 104, Edificio Recalde, Oficina 401, Quito. T: (593 2) 570-443.

Tierra Viva, (Living Earth), Casilla 1891, Cuenca. Affiliated with Friends of the Earth International, listed in Part 6.

EGYPT

Government:

Environmental Affairs Agency, Cabinet of Ministers, Kasr Al-Aini Street, Cairo. A policy and coordination unit.

Ministry of Agriculture and Land Reclamation, Cairo

General Organization for Desert Rehabilitation, Dokki, Cairo

Suez Canal Authority, Ismailia. T: 2201. Tx: 2153.

Other organizations:

Academy of Scientific Research and Technology, Department of Scientific Societies and International Unions, 101 Kasr El-Eini Street, Cairo. T: (20 2) 31985. Tx: 93069. ICSU national member. Includes a Council for Environmental Research.

Agricultural Research Centre, Cairo. Includes:
■ Desert Research Institute, Al-Matariyah, Cairo. Program includes research in natural resource management.
■ Soil and Water Research Institute, 9 Gamma Street, Giza, Cairo

Egyptian Association for the Conservation of Natural Resources, Zoological Gardens, Giza, Cairo. [85]

National Institute of Occupational Safety and Health, 166 El-Hegaz Stret, Heliopolis, Cairo. T: (20 2) 872794. Tx: 208.

EL SALVADOR

Government:

Comité Nacional de Protección del Medio Ambiente (National Committee of Environmental Protection), c/o Ministerio de Planificación, San Salvador. Tx: 30309 miplan.
Ministerio de Agricultura y Ganadería, Centro de Recursos Naturales Renovables (Ministry of Agriculture and Livestock, Center of Renewable Natural Resources), Blvd. de los Héroes y 21 Calle Poniente, San Salvador

Ministerio de Salud Pública y Asistencia Social (Ministry of Public Health and Social Assistance), 9a Avenida Norte 120, San Salvador. Reponsibilities include environmental health.

Other organizations:

Amigos de la Tierra de El Salvador (Friends of the Earth of El Salvador), Segunda Avenida Norte 1-2, Santa Tecla, San Salvador. T: (503) 25-2603.

Asociación Salvadoreña de Conservación del Medio Ambiente (ASACMA) (Salvadoran Environmental Protection Association), Urbanización Buenos Aires, Calle Masquilishuat 208, San Salvador. T: (503) 26-5514. Broad interests.

Grupo Ecologista de Montecristo (Montecristo Ecologist Group), Colonia Las Mercedes, Calle Los Eucaliptos 23, San Salvador. T: (503) 23-0534. Founded 1984. Environmental education.

La Unidad Ecológica Salvadoreña (UNES) (Salvadoran Ecological Unity), c/o CESTA, 33 Calle Poniente, no. 316, San Salvador. T: (503) 25-6746.

EQUATORIAL GUINEA

Government:

Ministerio de Aguas, Bosques y Repoblación Forestal (Ministry of Water Resources and Forestry), Malabo

Ministry of Agriculture, Malabo

Ministry of Health, Malabo

ETHIOPIA

Government:

Ministry of Mining, Energy, and Water Resources, P.O. Box 486, Addis Ababa. T: (251 1) 448250.

Ministry of Urban Development and Housing, P.O. Box 386, Addis Ababa. T: (251 1) 447743.

Environment Health Division, P.O. Box 5504, Addis Ababa. T: (251 1) 441944.

State Forest Development and Conservation Department, P.O. Box 1034, Addis Ababa. T: (251 1) 155490.

Other organizations:

Agri-Service Ethiopia (ASE), P.O. Box 2460, Addis Ababa. T: (251 1) 164811. Tx: 21542 ase et. Founded 1969. Program includes soil, water, and forestry conservation projects.

Ethiopian Wildlife Conservation Organization, P.O. Box 386, Addis Ababa

FALKLAND ISLANDS (ISLAS MALVINAS)
British possession.

Government:

Falkland Islands Government, Stanley

Other organizations:

Falkland Islands Foundation. Listed under United Kingdom

FAROE ISLANDS
A self-governing overseas administrative division of Denmark.

Government:

Government Offices, P.O. Box 64, Tórshavn. T: (45 42) 11080. Includes:
■ Ministry of Fisheries
■ Ministry of Agriculture
■ Ministry of Social Services

FIJI

Government:

Ministry of Lands, Local Government, and Housing--Lands Department, P.O. Box 2222, Government Buildings, Suva. T: (679) 211515.

Ministry of Agriculture and Fisheries, P.O. Box 358, Suva. T: (679) 22993. Tx: 2290. Includes a Fisheries Department.

Ministry of Health and Social Welfare, P.O. Box 2223, Government Buildings, Suva. T: (679) 211305. Includes a Department of Health, concerned with environmental health.

Other organizations:

Fiji National Youth Council, P.O. Box 961, Suva. T: (679) 312197. Founded 1967. Council of some 27 youth groups; program includes environmental education.

The National Trust for Fiji, 208 Waimanu Road, P.O. Box 2089, Government Buildings, Suva. Works to preserve natural and historic areas.

FINLAND

Government:

Ministry of the Environment, Ratakatu 3, P.O. Box 399, SF-00531 Helsinki. T: (358 0) 19911. Tx: 123717. Fax: (358 0) 1991 499. Broad responsibilities for environmental and natural resource protection. Has an International Affairs Division.

Ministry of Agriculture and Forestry, P.O. Box 232, SF-00171 Helsinki 17. Includes a Bureau of Nature Reserves.

Finnish International Development Agency (FINNIDA), Ministry of Foreign Affairs, Ritarikatu 2 B, SF-00170 Helsinki 17

National Board of Health, Office of Environmental Hygiene, P.O. Box 221, SF-00531 Helsinki. T: (358 0) 77231.

Other organizations:

Delegation of Finnish Academies of Science and Letters, Snallmaninkatu 9-11, SF-00170 Helsinki. ICSU national member.

Suomen Luonnonsuojeluliitto (Finnish Association for the Protection of Nature), Perämiehenkatu 11 A 8, SF-00150 Helsinki. T: (358 0) 642881. Major organization with some 40 regional branches.

Natur och Miljö (Nature and Environment), P.O. Box 240, SF-00150 Helsinki. Central organization of Swedish-speaking conservationists in Finland. World Wide Fund for Nature-Finland, Uudenmaankatu 40, SF-00120 Helsinki 12. T: (358 080) 644 511. Affiliate of the World Wide Fund for Nature (WWF International), listed in Part 6.

FRANCE
See also French Guiana, French Polynesia, Guadeloupe, Martinique, Mayotte, New Caledonia, Reunion, and Wallis and Futuna.

Government:

Ministère de l'Environnement et du Cadre de Vie (Ministry of the Environment), 14 boulevard du General-Leclerc, F-92524 Neuilly-sur-Seine. Tx: 620602.

Ministère de l'Agriculture (Ministry of Agriculture). Includes:
■ Service des Forêts (Forest Service), 1-ter Avenue de Lowendal, F-75700 Paris
■ Service de l'Hydraulique (Water Resources Service), 19 avenue de Maine, F-75732 Paris

Ministère de la Cooperation (Ministry of Cooperation), 20 rue Monsieur, F-75007 Paris. T: (33 1) 567 55 90. Administers France's program of assistance to developing countries.

Institut Français de Recherche Scientifique pour le Développement en Cooperation (ORSTOM) (French Institute of Scientific Research for Development Cooperation), 213 rue La Fayette, F-75010 Paris. T: (33 1) 48 03 77 77. Tx: 214627. Founded 1943 as the Office de la Recherche Scientifique et Technique Outre-Mer; name changed 1983. Major programs of action-oriented research in some 45 developing countries, emphasizing former French possessions. Natural resource management and environmental protection are central themes.

Other organizations:

Académie des Sciences, (Academy of Sciences), Institut de France, 23 Quai Conti, F-75006 Paris. ICSU national member.

Centre International de Recherche sur l'Environnement et le Développement (CIRED) (International Research Center on Environment and Development), 54 boulevard Raspail, no. 311, F-75270 Paris Cedex 06. T: (33 1) 45 44 38 49, ext. 219. Directed by Ignacy Sachs. Research and conferences on ecodevelopment. Pub: NEED (newsletter; separate French and English editions); working papers; research reports.

Centre Technique Forestier Tropical (Tropical Forestry Technical Center), 45 bis, avenue de la Belle Gabrielle, F-94130 Nogent-sur-Marne. Program includes research and education in nature protection and other areas of tropical resource management, as well as forestry.

Fédération Française des Sociétés de Protection de la Nature (FFSPN) (French Federation of Nature Protection Societies), 57 rue Cuvier, F-75231 Paris. Tx: 260921. Founded 1968. Umbrella organization of some 150 national, regional, departmental, and local groups active in nature conservation and environmental protection. Concerns include French overseas territories.

Fonds Français pour la Nature et l'Environnement (French Foundation for Nature and the Environment), 45 rue de Lisbonne, F-75009 Paris

Fonds Mondial pour la Nature-France (World Wide Fund for Nature-France), 151 Boulevard de la Reine, F-78000 Versailles. T: (33 1) 39 50 75 14. Affiliate of the World Wide Fund for Nature (WWF International), listed in Part 6.

Les Amis de la Terre (Friends of the Earth), 15 rue Gambay, F-75011 Paris. Affiliated with Friends of the Earth International, listed in Part 6.

Mouvement National de Lutte pour l'Environnement (MNLE) (National Movement of the Struggle for the Environment), B.P. 79, F-93505 Pantin Cédex

Société Française pour le Droit de l'Environnement (French Society for Environmental Law), Université III, place d'Athènes, F-67084 Strasbourg

Société Nationale de Protection de la Nature (National Society for Nature Protection), 57 rue Cuvier, F-75231 Paris

FRENCH GUIANA
An overseas department of France.

Government:

Ministère des Départements et Territoires d'Outre-Mer (Ministry of Overseas Departments and Territories), 27 rue Oudinot, F-75700 Paris, France. T: (1 33) 47 83 01 23.

FRENCH POLYNESIA
An overseas territory of France. *See also* France.

Government:

Ministry for Health, the Environment, and Scientific Research, Papeete

Ministry for Agriculture, Traditional Crafts, and the Cultural Heritage, Papeete

Ministry for the Sea, Equipment, Energy, Ports, and Telecommunications, Papeete

Other organizations:

Union Polynesienne pour la Sauvegarde de la Nature - Te Rauatiati a tau a Hiti Noa Tu (Polynesian Union for Protection of Nature - May Nature be Conserved Forever), B.P. 1602, Papeete, Tahiti. Founded 1987. Broad interests.

FRENCH SOUTHERN AND ANTARCTIC LANDS
An overseas territory of France.

Government:

Central Administration of the French Southern and Antarctic Lands, 34 rue des Renaudes, F-75017 Paris, France. Tx: 640980.

GABON

Government:

Ministère de l'Environnement et de la Protection de la Nature (Ministry of the Environment and Nature Protection), B.P. 3241, Libreville. T: (241) 73 17 07.

GAMBIA, THE

Government:

Ministry of Water Resources and Environment, 5 Marine Parade, Banjul. T: (220) 27307. Tx: 2204 presof gv. Broad responsibilities for natural resources and environmental protection.

GERMAN DEMOCRATIC REPUBLIC (EAST GERMANY)

Government:

Ministerium für Umweltschutz und Wasserwirtschaft (Ministry of Environmental Protection and Water Management), DDR-1020 Berlin. T: (37 2) 233 6714. Tx: 11 52 347.

Ministerium für Land, Forst und Nahrungsgüterwirtschaft (Ministry of Agriculture, Forest Management, and Food), Kopenickerallee 39-57, DDR-1157 Berlin. Responsibilities include nature protection.

Other organizations:

Akademie der Wissenschaften der D.D.R. (Academy of Sciences of the G.D.R.), Otto-Nuschke Strasse 22-23, DDR-1086 Berlin. T: (37 2) 20700. Tx: 0112456. ICSU national member.

Arche (Arche Ecological Network), Rigärstrasse 25, DDR-1035 Berlin. Has project groups investigating air pollution, forestry, waste, energy, and urban environmental problems.

Forschungsstelle Umweltgestaltung (FUG) (Environmental Formation Research Institute), 29 Karl-Liebknecht Strasse, DDR-102 Berlin. Conducts studies on environmental quality.

Institut für Landschaftsforschung und Naturschutz Halle (Landscape Research and Nature Protection Institute), Neuwerk 4, DDR-4020 Halle

Kulturbund der Deutschen Demokratischen Republik (Culture League of the G.D.R.), Johannisstrasse 5, DDR-1040 Berlin. Includes a Nature Conservation Section.

GERMANY, FEDERAL REPUBLIC OF (WEST GERMANY)

Federal government:

Bundesministerium für Umwelt, Naturschutz und Reaktorsicherheit (Federal Ministry for the Environment, Nature Conservation, and Reactor Safety), Abteilung N, Postfach 120629, D-5300 Bonn 1. T: (49 228) 681 4164. Broad responsibilities.

Bundesministerium für Wirtschaftliche Zusammenarbeit (BMZ) (Federal Ministry for Economic Cooperation), 185 Kaiserstrasse, D-5300 Bonn. Rresponsible for international development assistance. Includes an Environmental Section.

Bundesforschungsanstalt für Naturschütz und Landschaftsökologie (Federal Institute for Nature Consrervation and Landscape Management), Konstantinstrasse 110, D-5300 Bonn 2

Federal Institute for Geosciences and Natural Resources, Stilleweg 2, D-3000 Hanover 51. Includes an Environmental Protection Division.

State (land) governments:

The governments of the 10 Länder or federal states and West Berlin have important responsibilities for the environment and resource management.

Other organizations:

Alred-Wegener-Institut für Polar- und Meeresforschung (Alfred Wegener Institute for Polar and Marine Research), Bremerhaven

Bund für Umwelt- und Naturschutz-Deutchland (Union for Environmental and Nature Protection-Germany), Postfach 12 05 36, D-5300 Bonn. Broad interests.

Deutsche Forschungsgemeinschaft (German Research Association), Kennedyallee 40, Postfach 205004, D-5300 Bonn 2. T: (49 228) 885 2346. Tx: 17228312. ICSU national member.

Deutscher Bund für Vogelschutz (German Union for Bird Protection), Achalmstrasse 33, D-7014 Kornwestheim

Deutscher Naturschutzring (DNR) (German Federation of Nature Conservation Societies), Kalkuhlstrasse 24, D-5300 Bonn 3. T: (49 228) 44 15 05. Members are some 90 organizations with over 3 million members.

Greenpeace Germany, Vorsetzen 53, D-2000 Hamburg 11. National office of Greenpeace International, listed in Part 6.

Institute for Water Resources Research, Callinstrasse 32, D-3000 Hanover. T: (49 511) 762 22 37.

Schutzgemeinschaft Deutches Wild (SDW) (German Association for the Protection of Forests and Woodlands), Meckheimerallee 79, D-5300 Bonn 1. T: (49 228) 658 462. Focuses on forest protection and reforestation; has some 300 local groups and 500 youth groups.

Vereinigung Deutscher Gewässerschutz (VDG), (German Union for Water Protection), Matthias-Grünewald-Strasse 1-3, D-5300 Bonn 2

Welt Natur Fonds (World Wide Fund for Nature-Germany), P.O. Box 70 11 27, D-6000 Frankfurt a/M 70. T: (49 69) 60 50 030. Affiliate of the World Wide Fund for Nature (WWF International), listed in Part 6.

Wissenschaftszentrum Berlin für Sozialforschung (WZB) (Social Science Research Center, Berlin), Reichpietschufer 50, D-1000 Berlin 30. T: (49 30) 25 49 1-0. Founded 1969. WZB's Research Unit on Standard Setting and Environment continues the work done by two earlier WBZ programs, the International Institute for Environment and Society and the Research Unit on Environmental Policy, which conducted studies on environmental monitoring and assessment, environmental behavior, and evaluation of environmental policies. Examples of subjects of recent projects: approaches to the analysis of international environmental policy; clean air policy in Europe; Japanese environmental policy.

W.W. Brehm-Fonds für Internationalen Vogelschutz (W.W. Brehm Fund for International Bird Conservation), Vogelpark Walsrode, D-3030 Walsrode. T: (49 5161) 2015. Tx: 924 333 wowa d.

GHANA

Government:

Environmental Protection Council, P.O. Box M326, Ministries' Post Office, Accra. T: (233) 66 46 97. Tx: 65421 (via Ministry of Foreign Affairs). C: ENVIRON.

Ministry of Lands and Natural Resources, P.O. Box M212, Accra

Forestry Commission, P.O. Box M239, Accra

Other organizations:

Council for Scientific and Industrial Research (CSIR), P.O. Box M.32, Accra. T: 77561. C: SCIENCES. Program includes research on resources and environmental problems.

Friends of the Earth, P.O. Box 3794, Accra. Affiliated with Friends of the Earth International, listed in Part 6.

Ghana Academy of Arts and Sciences, P.O. Box M-32, Accra. T: 77651. C: SCIENCES. ICSU national member.

Ghana Wildlife Society, P.O. Box 460, Kumasi. [85]

GIBRALTAR
British possession.

Government:

Ministry of Public Works, Electricity, and Telecommunication, Gibraltar

GREECE

Government:

Ministry of Physical Planning, Housing, and the Environment--Environment Directorate, Pouliou 8, GR-115 23 Athens. T: (30 1) 64 61 189. Tx: 222088.

Ministry of Energy and Natural Resources, Zalokosta 1, GR-106 71 Athens. T: (30 1) 36 09 320. Includes the Department of Water and Natural Resources.

Ministry of Agriculture, Department of Forest Research and Education, Terma Alkmanos Ilisia, GR-115 28 Athens. T: (30 1) 77 84 850.

Other organizations:

Akadimia Athinon (Greek Academy of Sciences), 28 Panepistimiou Street, GR-106 79 Athens. ICSU national member.

Elliniki Etairia (Greek Society), 36 Voukourestiou, GR-106 73 Athens. Tx: 215244. Founded 1972. Works for protection of the country's cultural and natural heritage.

Friends of the Forest Association, 3 place Mitropoleos, Athens. T: (30 1) 322 13 37.

Hellenic Society for the Protection of Nature, 24 Nikis Stret, GR-105 57 Athens. T: (30 1) 322 49 44. Founded 1951. Focuses on establishing national parks and protected areas and on wildlife conservation.

Panellhnio Kentro Oikologikon Ereynon (PAKOE) (Panhellenic Center of Environmental Studies), 7 Sufliou Street, Ampelokopi, GR-115 27 Athens. Founded 1979. Broad interests. Conducts research; promotes policies to ensure ecological balance; environmental education projects.

GREENLAND
A self-governing overseas administrative division of Denmark.

Government:

Greenland Home Rule Government. P.O. Box 1015, 3900 Nuuk, Greenland. T: 009-299-2-30-00. Tx: 90613. Includes:
- Secretariat for Fisheries and Industry
- Secretariat for Social Affairs
- Office in Denmark: Sjæleboderne 2, DK-1122 Copenhagen K, Denmark. T: (45 1) 13 42 24.

GRENADA

Government:

Ministry of Agriculture, Forestry Division, Archibald Avenue, St. George's. T: (1 809) 440-3083. Includes a National Parks and Protected

Areas program.

Ministry of Health and Housing, St. George's.
T: (1 809) 440-2649.

National Science and Technology Council,
Tanteen, St. George's. T: (1 809) 440-3118.
Program includes environmental research.

Other organizations:

Grenada National Trust, c/o Grenada National
Museum, Young Street, St. George's. Activities
include environmental education and documentation of "old technologies."

GUADELOUPE
An overseas department of France.

Government:

Ministère des Départements et Territoires
d'Outre-Mer (Ministry of Overseas Departments
and Territories), 27 rue Oudinot, F-75700 Paris,
France. T: (1 33) 47 83 01 23.

GUAM
A U.S. territory.

Government:

Office of the Governor, Agana, Guam 96910

GUATEMALA

Government:

Comisión Nacional del Medio Ambiente (National
Environment Commission), Presidencia de la
República, 9a Avenida entre 14 y 15, Zona 1,
Oficina no. 10, Edificio Antigua Corte Suprema,
Guatemala. T: (502 2) 2-1816. Environmental
policy; coordination of government activities.

Instituto Guatamalteco de Turismo (INGUAT)
(Guatemalan Institute of Tourism), Centro Cívico,
Zona 4, Guatemala. Responsible for protected
areas; environmental education; promotes eco-
tourism.

Ministerio de Agricultura, Ganadería y
Alimentación--Instituto Nacional Forestal
(Ministry of Agriculture, Livestock, and
Food--National Forestry Institute), 7a Avenida
11-63, 6º nivel, Edificio Galerias España, Zona 9,
Guatemala. T: (502 2) 31-9147.

Other organizations:

Academia de Ciencias Médicas, Físicas y
Naturales de Guatemala (Academy of Medical,
Physical, and Natural Sciences of Guatemala),
Apartado Postal 569, Guatemala. ICSU national
member.

Asociación de Amigos del Bosque (Friends of the
Forest Association), 9a Calle 2-23, Zona 1,
Guatemala. T: (502 2) 8-3486. Protection of
nature and natural resources; reforestation
projects; public education.

Asociación Guatemalteca de Historia Natural
(Guatemalan Natural History Association), Parque
Zoológico La Aurora, Zona 13, Guatemala.
T: (502 2) 72-0507. Research, public education,
and legislative action.

Asociación Guatamalteca de Orquideología
(Guatemalan Orchid Asociation), 13 Calle 6-20,
Zona 9, Guatemala. T: (502 2) 31-6586. Works
to preserve Guatemalan species of orchids.

Asociación Guatamalteca pro-Defensa del Medio
Ambiente, (Guatemalan Association for
Environmental Protection), 20 Calle 19-44, Zona
10, Apartado 1352, Guatemala. T: (502 2) 68-
1327. General interests.

Centro de Estudios Conservacionistas (CECON)
(Center of Conservation Studies), Avenida La
Reforma 0-63, Zone 10, Guatemala. T: (502 2)
31-0904. Affiliated with the National University
of San Carlos. Working on a conservation
database to support research and activists.

Defensores de la Naturaleza (Defenders of
Nature), 7a Avenida 13-01, 2do nivel, Edificio La
Cúpula, Zona 9, Guatemala. T: (502 2) 32-5064.
Founded 1983. Members are scientists,
professionals, students, and workers; public
information and creation of private nature
reserves.

GUINEA

Government:

Direction de l'Environnement (Environment
Directorate), B.P. 3118, Conakry. T: 46 10 12.

GUINEA-BISSAU

Government:

Ministerio do Desenvolvimento e Pescas (Ministry
of Rural Development and Fisheries), C.P. No. 71,
Bissau. T: 212617. Responsibilities include
fisheries, wildlife, forests, and environmental
protection.

GUYANA

Government:

Ministry of Forestry, 1 Water Street and Battery
Road, Kingstown, Georgetown

Ministry of Agriculture, Regent and Vlissingen
Roads, Georgetown. T: (592 2) 69154.

Ministry of Health and Public Welfare, Homestretch Avenue, D'Urban Park, Georgetown. T: (592 2) 65861.

Other organizations:

Guyana Ecological Society, c/o Ivan Welch, Secretary, 5 Bel Air Promenade, Georgetown

HAITI

Government:

Ministère de l'Agriculture, Direction des Ressources Naturelles et de l'Environnement (Ministry of Agriculture, Directorate of Natural Resources and the Environment), B.P. 1441, Port-au-Prince. T: (509 1) 2-1862. Includes the Environmental Protection Service.

Institut de Sauvegarde du Patrimoine National (ISPAN) (Institute for Protection of the National Heritage), B.P. 2484, Port-au-Prince. T: (509 1) 2-5286. Responsibilities include protection of wildlands and wildlife.

Other organizations:

Fédération des Amis de la Nature--Haïti Verte (FAN), (Friends of Nature Federation--Green Haiti), c/o Institut Pédagogique National, rue du Docteur Audain, Port-au-Prince. T: (509 1) 2-1337. Founded 1986.

Société Audubon d'Haïti pour la Protection de l'Environnement (SAHPE) (Audubon Society of Haiti for Environmental Protecton), c/c Robert Cassgnol, 25 rue Garoute, Pacot, Port-au-Prince. T: (509 1) 5-4604. Founded 1985. Public education and international contacts.

HOLY SEE

Pontifical Council *Cor Unum*, I-00120 Vatican City. T: (39 6) 698-7226. The Vatican office charged with international humanitarian and development aid. An encyclical issued by Pope John Paul II in February 1988, "Sollicitudo Rei Socialis" ("The Social Concern of the Church") refers to "ecological concern" and the "need to respect the integrity and cycles of nature and to take them into account when planning for development rather than sacrificing them to certian demagogic ideas about the latter."

Pontificia Academia Scientiarum (Pontifical Academy of Science), Casina Pio IV, I-00120 Vatican City. T: (39 6) 698-3195. Tx: 2024 dirgentel va. ICSU national member.

HONDURAS

Government:

Ministerio de Recursos Naturales (Ministry of Natural Resources), Edificio Camara de Comercio, Boulevard Centroamérica, Tegucigalpa. T: (504) 32-7704.

Ministerio de Planificación, Departamento Forestal y Pesca (Ministry of Planning, Forestry and Fisheries Department), Tegucigalpa

Other organizations:

Asociación de Jóvenes Ambientalistas de Honduras (Association of Young Environmentalists of Honduras), Departamento de Biología, Universidad Autónoma de Honduras, Tegucigalpa. T: (504) 32-2208. Focus is on environmental education.

Asociación Hondureña de Ecología (AHE) (Honduran Ecology Association), Apartado T-250, Toncontín, Tegucigalpa. T: (504) 32-9018. Founded 1981. Stresses nature protection and conservation; public education ("A Green Honduras by 2000").

Comité de Mejoramiento y Conservación del Ambiente (Committee for Environmental Improvement and Conservation), Apartado T-250, Tegucigalpa

HONG KONG
British possession. *See also* United Kingdom.

Government:

Environmental Protection Department, Sincere Building, 17th Floor, 173 Des Voeux Road, Central Hong Kong

Agriculture and Fisheries Department, Canton Road Government Offices, 393 Canton Road, 12th Floor, Kowloon

Other organizations:

Friends of the Earth, One Earth Centre, 61 Wyndham Street 1/F, Mezzanine Floor, Central Hong Kong. Affiliated with Friends of the Earth International, listed in Part 6.

World Wide Fund for Nature-Hong Kong, The French Mission, 1 Battery Path, Central Hong Kong. T: (852 5) 264 473. Affiliate of the World Wide Fund for Nature (WWF International), listed in Part 6.

HUNGARY

Government:

Ministry for Environment and Water Management, Fö-u. 46-50, Pf 351, H-1011 Budapest. T: (36 1) 166-245. Tx: 22-6115. Includes an Institute for Environmental Protection.

Ministry of Building and Planning, National Committee for the Protection of Clean Air, P.O. Box 613, H-1370 Budapest

Other organizations:

Danube Circle (no address available). Activities related to the protests concerning the planned Nagymaros Dam on the Danube River (presently under suspension).

Elte Conservation Club (ETK), Villanyi ut 28/b IV em, H-1113 Budapest. Activist group; has working groups on pollution issues and disseminates information to the public.

Erdeszeti Tudomaryos Intezet (ERTI) (Forest Research Institute), Frankel Leo Utca 42-44, H-1023 Budapest. Broad research interests in environmental management.

Magyar Termeszetvedä Szevelses (Hungarian Nature Conservation Federation), c/o XII, Kóltö u 21, H-1121 Budapest. Founded 1989. Association of 9 major environmental groups. Includes study groups on birds, forests, and the Danube River.

Magyar Tudomanyos Akademia (Hungarian Academy of Sciences), Roosevelt Tér 9, P.O. Box 6, H-1361 Budapest V. T: (36 1) 172-575. Tx: 224139. ICSU national member.

Patriotic People's Front, Budapest. Includes the Voluntary Guard of Environmental Protection, which involves the general public in environmental conservation activities.

ICELAND

Government:

Nature Conservation Council, Hverfisgötu 26, ISL-101 Reykjavik. T: (354 1) 22520.

Ministry of Health and Social Security, Laugavegi 116, Reykjavik. Responsibilities include pollution control and environmental health.

Other organizations:

Association of Icelandic Nature Conservation Societies, Sundsstraeti 24, ISL-400 Isafjördur

Landvernd (Icelandic Environment Union), Skolavördustigur 25, ISL-101 Reykjavik. T: (354 1) 25242.

National Research Council, Laugavegur 13, ISL-101 Reykjavik. ICSU national member.

INDIA

Directories: *Environmental NGOs in India: A Directory* (1984), published by World Wildlife Fund-India (now World Wide Fund for Nature-India).

Government:

Ministry of Environment and Forests, B Block, Paryavaran Bhavan, CGO Complex, Lodi Road, New Delhi 110003. T: (91 11) 30 61 56. Tx: 66185.

Ministry of Agriculture and Rural Development, Krishi Bhavan, Dr. Rajendra Prasad Road, New Delhi 110001. T: (91 11) 382651. Tx: 3165423.

Ministry of Health and Family Welfare, Nirman Bhavan, New Delhi 110011. T: (91 11) 3018863.

Ministry of Ocean Development, Block 12, CGO Complex, Lodi Road, New Delhi 110003. T: (91 11) 360874.

Ministry of Science and Technology, Technology Bhavan, New Mehrauli Road, New Delhi 110016. T: (91 11) 661439.

Ministry of Urban Development, Nirman Bhavan, New Delhi 110011. T: (91 11) 3019377.

Ministry of Water Resources, Shram Shakti Bhavan, Rafi Marg, New Delhi 110001. T: (91 11) 383098.

Other organizations:

Bombay Natural History Society, Hornbill House, Opposite Shahid Bhagat Singh Road, Bombay 400023. T: (91 22) 243869. C: HORNBILL. Purposes include conservation of wildlife and habitat through research and education.

Centre for Science and Environment, 807 Vishal Bhawan, 95 Nehru Place, New Delhi 110019. T: (91 11) 683394. Publishes *Green File*, an information pack of clippings and feature articles from Indian newspapers and magazines.

Dasholi Gram Swarajya Mamdal (Chipko Movement), P.O. Gopeshwar District, Chamoli, Uttar Pradesh 246401. T: 83. An indigenous movement, widely publicized around the world, that works to prevent the felling of trees, promote community forestry projects, and create environmental awareness among rural people in the hill regions of India. [85]

Development Alternatives, B-32 Institutional Area, New Mehrauli Road, Hauz khas, New Delhi 110016. T: (91 11) 665370. Tx: 031-61735 vc in. President is Ashok Khosla. A countrywide network of groups and individuals "dedicated to devising and promoting better approaches for the development of India...functions as an agent of change, particularly on the problems of the poor of our country and acts as a bridge between what is within their reach and what could be in their grasp." Works in appropriate technology, environmental management, and systems design. Branch offices elsewhere in the Third World and in Europe and North America.

Forest Research Institute and Colleges, P.O. New Forest, Dehra Dun, Uttar Pradesh 248006. T: 23452. Tx: 595258. C: FORESEARCH. Founded 1878. A prominent center for research and education in forestry; 5 sub-centers throughout the country.

Indian Institute of Science, Centre for Ecological Research, Bangalore 560012

Indian National Science Academy, 1 Bahadur Shah Zafr Marg, New Delhi 110 002. T: (91 11) 331-2450. Tx: 3161835 insa in. ICSU national member.

International Society for Tropical Ecology. See listing in Part 6. Membership is largely in India.

University of Rajasthan, Indira Gandhi Centre for Human Ecology, Environmental, and Population Studies, Jaipur, Rajasthan 302004. T: (91 141) 75765. Centre founded 1985. Small unit for research and teaching.

Wildlife Preservation Society of India, G-28 Nizamuddin West, New Delhi 110013. T: (91 11) 619758. Conservation of wildlife and habitats. [85]

World Wide Fund for Nature-India, c/o Godrej & Boyce Ltd., Lalbaug, Parel, Bombay 400 012. T: (91 22) 413 2927. Affiliate of the World Wide Fund for Nature (WWF International) listed in Part 6.

INDIAN OCEAN

The following organizations have a direct interest in the Indian Ocean. See also "Oceans, Coastal Zones, and Islands" in Part 2.

   UN system (see Part 4): The UN Environment Programme has regional seas program for the (Arabian or Persian) Gulf, the Red Sea, and the Eastern African region. The Food and Agriculture Organization of the UN has an Indian Ocean Fisheries Commission.

   Other intergovernmental organizations (see Part 5): Cooperative Council for the Arab States of the Gulf (Arabian or Persian Gulf); Regional Organization for the Protection of the Marine Environment (Arabian or Persian Gulf).

INDONESIA

Government:

Ministry of State for Population and Environment, Jalan Merdeka Barat no. 15, 3rd Floor, Jakarta. T: (62 21) 371-295. Tx: 46143. Includes an Environmental Management and Development Institute.

National Committee on the Environment, Jalan Raden Saleh 43, Jakarta Pusat

Ministry of Forestry, Directorate General of Forest Protection and Nature Conservation, Jalan Ir. H. Juanda 9, Bogor. T: 24013. C: BADAK. Responsibilities include national parks and other protected areas, forests, wildlife, marine protection, and environmental education.

Other organizations:

Borneo Institute of Technology (BIT), Jalan R.E. Martadinata RT 29/46, Balikpapan 76122, East Kalimantan. Conducts education and research in conservation, emphasizing the problems of tropical forest development.

Institute for Social and Economic Research, Education, and Information (LP3ES), Jalan S. Parman no. 81, Slipi, P.O. Box 493 JKT, Jakarta Barat. Includes projects on pollution control.

Lembaga Ilmu Pengetahuan Indonesia (IIPI) (Indonesian Institute of Sciences), Widya Graha LIPI, Jalan Gatot Subroto 10, Jakarta. T: (62 22) 511542. ICSU national member.

Sekretariat Kerjasama Pelestarian Hutan Indonesia (SKEPHI) (NGO Network for Forest Conservation in Indonesia), Jalan Suryopranoto No. 8, Lantai IV, Jakarta 10130. T: (62 21) 371374. Founded 1982. Serves as coordinator and mediator in forest conservation activities launched by concerned NGOs. Public information, training, and outings.

Wahana Lingkungan Hidup Indonesia (WALHI) (Indonesian Environmental Forum) (IEF), Jalan Penjernihan I Kompleks Keuangan No. 15, Pejompongan, Jakarta 10210. T: (62 2) 371-374. Founded 1980. Network of some 400 community-based and other environmental NGOs in Indonesia. Broad interests, including environment-development questions, population, forestry, wildlife, and the marine environment. Training and education; information exchange; technical assistance to NGOs.

IRAN

Government:

Department of the Environment, Ostad Nejat-Ollahi, Avenue no. 187, P.O. Box 4565-15875, Teheran. T: (98 21) 891261. C: ENVIRONMENT. Attached to the Office of the Prime Minister; operates under the Environmental High Council. Broad responsibilities.

Ministry of Agriculture. Includes:
■ Research Organization of Agriculture and Natural Resources, P.O. Box 13185-116, Teheran. T: (98 21) 944199.

Other organizations:

Center for Co-ordination of Environmental Studies, Ghods Avenue no. 43, Teheran

Iranian Academy of Sciences, P.O. Box 11/1213, Teheran. ICSU national member.

IRAQ

Government:

Higher Council for Environmental Protection and Improvement, c/o Ministry of Health, P.O. Box 423, Baghdad. The Council, chaired by the Minister of Health, is composed of the heads of ministries concerned with environmental problems, scientific institutions, and regional environmental councils.

Other organizations:

Scientific Research Council, P.O. Box 2441, Jadiryia, Baghdad. Tx: 2187. ICSU national member.

University of Basrah, Marine Science Centre, Basrah

IRELAND

Directories: *See* "Directories" under United Kingdom.

Government:

Department of the Environment, Custom House, Dublin 1. T: (353 1) 74 2961. Tx: 31014. Broad responsibilities.

Department of Fisheries and Forestry, Leeson Lane, Dublin 2. Includes responsibility for wildlife.

Department of Energy, Clare Street, Dublin 2. T: (353 1) 71 5233.

Inter-Departmental Environment Committee, c/o Department of the Environment. Coordinates environmental protection activities of various government departments; concerned with international environmental affairs.

Department of Foreign Affairs, Dublin. Development Cooperation Division is responsible for Ireland's program of aid to developing countries.

Other organizations:

An Taisce-The National Trust for Ireland, Tailors Hall, Back Lane, Dublin 8. T: (353 1) 78 3940. Protection of areas of natural and historical significance; environmental quality.

Earthwatch, Harbour View, Bantry, County Cork. Affiliated with Friends of the Earth International, listed in Part 6.

Greenpeace Ireland, 29 Lower Baggot Street, Dublin 2. National office of Greenpeace International, listed in Part 6.

Irish Futures Society, Shelbourne House, Shelbourne Road, Ballsbridge, Dublin 4. T: (353 1) 68 3311. Information center for futures studies in Ireland.

Irish Wildbird Conservancy (IWC), Southview, Church Road, Greystones, County Wicklow. T: (353 1) 87 5759. Research, education, and promotion of conservation of wild birds and their environment; maintains reserves. Local branches.

Irish Wildlife Federation, Ferry House, 4th Floor, Lower Mount Street, Dublin 2. T: (353 1) 60 83 46.

The Royal Irish Academy, 19 Dawson Street, Dublin 2. T: (353 1) 76 4222. The national academy of sciences. ICSU national member.

Society of Irish Foresters, c/o Royal Dublin Society, Ballsbridge, Dublin 4. T: (353 1) 86 7751. Professional society; also works to educate the public about forestry through meetings and outings.

ISRAEL

Government:

Ministry of the Interior, Environmental Protection Service, P.O. Box 6158, Jerusalem 91061. T: (972 2) 660151. Tx: 26162 ieps il. Broad responsibilities.

Ministry of Agriculture, Hakirya, Tel Aviv 61070. T: (972 3) 211550. Responsibilities include soil consevation and regulation of pesticides.

Ministry of Health, Public Health Services, P.O. Box 39264, Tel Aviv 61392. T: (972 3) 420868. Responsibilities include environmental health.

Nature Reserves Authority, 78 Yirmeyahu Street, Jerusalem 94467

Jewish Agency, Settlement Department, P.O. Box 7011, Tel Aviv 61070. T: (972 3) 211561. Major responsibilities for land and resource management in certain areas.

Other organizations:

Ben Gurion University of the Negev, Jacob Blaustein Institute for Desert Research, Sede Boqer 84993. T: (972 57) 36086. Tx: 5280. Institute founded 1973. Focus is on natural resources.

"Hai-Bar" Society for the Establishment of Biblical National Wildlife Reserves in Israel, c/o Nature Reserves Authority, 78 Yirmeyahu Street, Jerusalem 94467. Works to establish reserves for animals referred to in the Bible.

Hebrew University of Jerusalem, Center for Agricultural Research in Arid and Semi-Arid Lands, Faculty of Agriculture, P.O. Box 12, Rehovot. T: (972 8) 481105. Tx: 381331. Fax: (972 8) 462181. Program includes studies in natural resource management.

Institute for Applied Research, P.O. Box 1025, Beer-Sheva 84110. T: (972 57) 58382. Program includes research on utilization of natural resources.

Israel Academy of Sciences and Humanities, P.O. Box 4040, Jerusalem 91040. T: (972 2) 636211. ICSU national member.

Israel Society for Ecology and Environmental Quality Scinces, c/o Prof. Menachem Luria, Department of Environmental Sciences, Hebrew University, Givat Ram, Jerusalem 91904. T: (972 2) 224218.

Society for the Protection of Nature in Israel (SPNI), 4 Hashfela Street, Tel Aviv 66183. T: (972 3) 375063. Founded 1953. Israel's largest independent membership organization. Outings, action research, lobbying, and environmental education. Network of 25 field study centers. Conducts international seminars on informal environmental education for both developed and developing countries. Has support groups in the UK and USA.

Tel-Aviv University, Institute of Nature Conservation Research, Tel Aviv. T: (972 3) 420813.

ITALY

Government:

Ministry of the Environment, Piazza Venezia 11, I-00187 Rome. T: (39 6) 67 97 124.

Ministero dell'Agricoltura e delle Foreste (Ministry of Agriculture and Forests), 18 via XX Settembre, I-00187 Rome. T: (39 6) 47 50 567. Tx: 610251. Responsibilities include forests, wildlife, fisheries, and nature protection.

Ministry of Foreign Affairs, Development Cooperation Department, Piazzale delle Farnesina, I-00100 Rome

Ministry of Cultural Heritage, Via del Collegio Romano 27, I-00186 Rome. T: (39 6) 67 97 124.

Other organizations:

Amici della Terra (Friends of the Earth), Piazza Sforza Cesarini 28, I-00186 Rome. Affiliated with Friends of the Earth International, listed in Part 6.

Associazione per la Conservazione del Suolo, delle Acque e per il Riequilibrio degli Ecosistemi (Gruppo CSARE-SILVA) (Association for Soil and Water Conservation and Re-Equilibrium of Ecosystems), Via L. Lillo, 19 (Pal. A), I-00143 Rome, Italy. T: (39 6) 5923442. Tx: 612339 gbg. Fax: (39 6) 5146089. Founded 1978; formerly a branch of the Italian Society for International Development. Professional association of agronomists, agricultural economists, and rural sociologists concerned with development in the South of Italy and the Third World.

Consiglio Nazionale delle Ricerche (National Research Council), Piazzale Aldo Moro 7, Rome. ICSU national member. Has an International Relations Service.

Federnatura, via Farini 24, I-40124 Bologna. T: (39 51) 26 88 09.

Fondo Mondiale per la Natura-Italia (World Wide Fund for Nature-Italy), Via Salaria 290, I-00199 Rome. T: (39 6) 85 24 92. Affiliate of the World Wide Fund for Nature (WWF International), listed in Part 6.

Italia Nostra (Our Italy), Corso Vittorio Emanuele II 287, I-00186 Rome. T: (39 6) 65 65 75. A "national association for the protection of the historic, artistic, and natural heritage of Italy." Nonpartisan political action.

Greenpeace Italy, 28 Viale Manlio Gelsomini, I-00153 Rome. National office of Greenpeace International, listed in Part 6.

IVORY COAST
See Côte d'Ivoire

JAMAICA

Government:

Ministry of Agriculture, Science, and Technology. Includes:
■ Natural Resources Conservation Department, P.O. Box 305, 53½ Molynes Road, Kingston 10. T: (1 809) 923-5155. Broad resource management responsibilities.
■ Department of Forestry and Soil Conservation, 4 Hillman Road, Kingston 8. T: (1 809) 924-2667.

Ministry of Health, Environmental Control Division, Life of Jamaica Building, 61 Half Way Tree Road, Kingston 10. T: (1 809) 929-6463. Environmental health and pollution control.

Other organizations:

Entity, 17 Linstone Crescent, Kingston 10.
T: (1 809) 927-9122. Environmental education.

Jamaica Conservation and Development Trust,
P.O. Box 1225, Kingston 8

Jamaica Conservation Trust, 2 Starlight Avenue,
Kingston 6. Founded 1986. Works to establish
protected areas and national parks; cooperates
closely with the government.

Natural History Society of Jamaica, c/o Natural
History Division, Institute of Jamaica, 12 East
Street, Kingston. Founded 1940. Study and
preservation of Jamaica's natural environment.

Scientific Research Council, Hope Gardens, P.O.
Box 350, Kingston 6. T: (1 809) 927-1912.
Tx: 3631. ICSU national member.

JAPAN

Government:

Environment Agency of Japan, 1-2-2
Kasumigaseki, Chiyoda-ku, Tokyo 100. T:
(International Affairs Division): (81 3) 580-4982.
Includes Nature Conservation Bureau; Air Quality
Bureau; Water Quality Bureau. Also coordinates
activities of various ministries related to the
environment.

Ministry of Health and Welfare, Environmental
Health Bureau, 1-2-2 Kasumigaseki, Chiyoda-ku,
Tokyo 100. T: (81 3) 501-4867.

Ministry of Labor, National Institute of Industrial
Health, 21-1 6-chome, Nagao, Tama-ku,
Kawasaki-shi, Kanagawa 214. T: (81 44)
865-6111. Concerns include occupational
environmental health.

National Committee on Nature Conservation, c/o
Prof. Yoichi Fukushima, Chairman, Science
Council of Japan, 22-34 Roppongi 7-chome,
Minato-ku, Tokyo 105

Japan Meteorological Agency, 1-3-4 Ote-Machi,
Chiyoda-ku, Tokyo 100. T: (81 3) 211-7084.

Japan International Cooperation Agency, P.O. Box
216, 2-1, Nishi-Shinjuku, Shinjuku-ku, Tokyo
160. T: (81 03) 346-5311.

Other organizations:

Aircraft Nuisance Prevention Asociation, 2-8-1
Hanedakuko, Ohta-ku, Tokyo 144. T: (81 03)
747-0175.

Asian Community Trust (ACT), c/o Japan Center
for International Exchange, 4-9-17 Minami-
Azabu, Minato-ku, Tokyo, Japan. T: (81 3)
446-7781. Tx: J23230. C: JAPACENEX.

General purpose is to promote mutual
understanding between people in Japan and
neighboring Asian countries by assisting activities
that contribute to development. Environmental
protection is a major theme.

Chikyu no Tomo (Friends of the Earth), 501
Shinwa Building, 9-17 Sakuragaoka, Shibuya-ku,
Tokyo 150. Founded 1980. Affiliated with
Friends of the Earth International, listed in Part
6.

Clean Japan Center, No. 2 Akiyama Building, 6-2
Toranomon 3-chome, Minato-ku, Tokyo 105.
T: (81 03) 432-6301.

Environmental Research Center, Shinmaru
Building 8F, Marunuchi 1-5-1, Chiyoda-ku,
Tokyo 100. T: (81 03) 212-2747. Technical and
policy research on pollution control.

Japan Air Cleaning Association, Tomoeya
Building, 2-14 Uchikanda 1-chome, Chiyoda-ku,
Tokyo 101. T: (81 03) 233-1486. Professional
society of air pollution control specialists.

Japan Center for Human Environmental Problems,
c/o Faculty of Law, Tokyo Metropolitan
University, 1 Yakumo, Meguro-ku, Tokyo 152

Japan Environment Association, Office
Toranoman - 1 Building, 5-8 Toranoman - 1,
Minato-ku, Tokyo 105

Japan Environmental Sanitation Center, 10-6
Yotsukami-cho, Kawasaki-ku, Kawasaki-shi,
Kanagawa 210. T: (81 44) 288-4896.

Japan Fisheries Resource Conservation
Association, Zenkoku-Choson-Kaikan 11-35,
Nagatacho 1-chome, Chiyoda-ku, Tokyo 100.
T: (81 3) 593-2481.

Japan Forest Technical Association, 7 Rokuban-
cho, Chiyoda-ku, Tokyo. T: (81 3) 261-5281.
Founded 1921. Professional society of foresters;
carries out technical assistance and research
projects in developing countries.

Japan Wildlife Research Centre, Hongo 3-39-12,
Bunkyo-ku, Tokyo 113

Man-Environment Research Association (MERA),
c/o Masaaki Asai, Department of Psychology,
College of Humanities and Sciences, Nihon
University, 3-25-40 Sakurajyosui, Setagaya-ku,
Tokyo 156

Marine Ecology Research Institute, 300 Iwamada,
Onjuku-Machi, Isumi-Gun, Chiba 299-51

National Institute for Environmental Studies, 16-2
Onogawa, Yatabe, Tsukuba-Gun, Ibaraki 305. T:
(81 298) 51-6111. Major research program.

National Parks Association of Japan, Toranomon Denki Building, 2-8-1 Toranomon, Minato-ku, Tokyo 105

Nature Conservation Society of Japan, Toranomon Denki Building, 2-8-1 Toranomon, Minato-ku, Tokyo 105. T: (81 3) 503-4896.

Science Council of Japan, 22-34 Roppongi, 7-chome, Minato-ku, Tokyo 106. ICSU national member.

World Wide Fund for Nature-Japan, Nihonseimei Akabanebashi Building 7F, 3-1-14 Shiba, Minato-ku, Tokyo 105. T: (81 3) 769 1711. Affiliate of the World Wide Fund for Nature (WWF Intenational), listed in Part 6.

Wild Bird Society of Japan, Aoyama Flower Building, 1-1-4 Shibuya, Shibuya-ku, Tokyo 150

JOHNSTON ATOLL
U.S. possession

Government:

Administered by the Nuclear Defense Agency, U.S. Department of Defense, Washington, DC 20305, USA. T: (1 202) 325-7047.

JORDAN

Government:

Ministry of Municipal and Rural Affairs and the Environment, Department of the Environment, P.O. Box 35206, Amman

Ministry of Agriculture, Department of Forests and Soil Conservation, P.O. Box 2179, Amman. T: (962 6) 84 27 51.

Water Authority, P.O. Box 2412, Amman. T: (962 6) 66 61 11.

Other organizations:

Royal Scientific Society, P.O. Box 925819, Amman. T: (962 6) 84 47 01. Tx: 21276 ramah jo. ICSU national member.

Royal Society for the Conservation of Nature (RSCN), P.O. Box 1387, Amman. T: (962 6) 81 16 89.

KENYA

Government:

Ministry of Environment and Natural Resources, P.O. Box 67839, Nairobi. T: (254 2) 332383.

Ministry of Tourism and Wildlife, P.O. Box 30027, Nairobi. T: (254 2) 891601.

Permanent Presidential Commission on Soil Conservation and Afforestation, Office of the President, P.O. Box 30510, Nairobi. T: (254 2) 21034. C: RAIS. Established 1981. Extension work and instruction.

Other organizations:

Green Belt Movement, National Council of Women of Kenya, P.O. Box 43741, Nairobi. T: (254 2) 24634. Founded 1977. Promotes tree planting and agroforestry among small-scale farmers (target is 15 million trees). Led by Ms. Wangari Maathai.

Kenya Energy and Environment Organisations (KENGO), P.O. Box 48197, Nairobi. T: (254 2) 749747. Tx: 25222. Umbrella organization representing over 200 local-level community groups and mid-level NGOs. Plans, initiates, and coordinates projects on renewable energy and community development; training and technical assistance. Main focus is on wood energy, public information, agroforestry, and protection of indigenous trees and genetic resources.

Kenya National Academy of Sciences, P.O. Box 39450, Nairobi. ICSU national member.

Mazingira Institute, P.O. Box 14550, Nairobi. T: (254 2) 47066. Founded 1978. Action research in resource and environmental management. ("Mazingira" is Kiswahili for environment.)

Teachers Environmental Asociation (TEA), P.O. Box 119, Kisii, Homa Bay. T: Rangwe 1. Founded 1983; 2,000 members. Conservation education and action.

Wildlife Clubs of Kenya (WCK), P.O. Box 40658, Nairobi. T: (254 2) 742564. Founded 1968; 1,300 clubs with 80,000 members. Resource conservation; environmental education and action.

KIRIBATI

Government:

Ministry of Natural Resource Development, P.O.B. 64, Bikenibeu. T: 21099. Tx: 77039.

Ministry of Health and Family Planning, P.O.B. 268, Bikenibeu, Tarawa. T: 28081.

KOREA, DEMOCRATIC PEOPLE'S REPUBLIC OF (NORTH KOREA)

Government:

Ministry of Forestry, Pyongyang

Ministry of Natural Resources Development, Pyongyang

Ministry of Public Health, Pyongyang

Fisheries Commission, Pyongyang

Other organizations:

Academy of Sciences of the Democratic People's Republic of Korea, Sosong District, Changsan Street, Ryonmot-Dong, Pyongyang. C: Academy of Sciences. ICSU national member.

Natural Conservation Union of the Democratic People's Republic of Korea, No. 220-93-7-24 Dongsong Street, Central District, Pyongyang

KOREA, REPUBLIC OF (SOUTH KOREA)

Government:

Environment Administration, 17-16 Sincheon-dong, Songpa-gu, Seoul 134-240. Concerned with air, water, and land pollution, and solid waste. Includes a Publicity and International Relations Division.

Ministry of Agriculture and Fisheries, Seoul. Responsibilities include farmland protection, water, fisheries, agricultural chemicals, soil conservation, and marine pollution.

Ministry of Construction, Land Planning Bureau, 1 Jooang-Dong, Gwacheon-Myeon Siheung-Gun, Gyeonggi-Do, Seoul. T: (82 2) 593-1393.

Ministry of Health and Social Affairs, Seoul. Responsibilities include environmental health.

Ministry of Home Affairs, Division of Nature Preservation, Government United Building, 77 Sejong-ro, Chongro-go, Seoul 110

National Parks Authority, Gun-Sol-Kwi-Kwan 71-2, Non Hyung-dong Kangnam-gu, Seoul 135-010

Other organizations:

Korean Association for the Conservation of Nature, c/o Forest Research Institute, San-1, 207 Cheongryangri-Dong, Dongdaemun-ku, Seoul 131-012

Korean Central Council for Nature Preservation, 36-3, 5-ka Chungmu-ro, Jung-ku, Seoul 100

Korean Environmental Preservation Association, 111 Sogong-Dong Choong-gu, Seoul 100. T: (82 2) 753-4940.

Korean Society for the Protection of Wild Animals, Dongdaemun, P.O. Box 177, Seoul

National Academy of Sciences of the Republic of Korea, 1 Sejongro, Jongro-gu, Seoul. ICSU national member.

National Environmental Protection Institute, 280-17 Bulkwang-Dong Eunpyung-ku, Seoul 122.

T: (82 2) 385-5711. Tx: 25783. C: ENVIROK. Fax: (82 2) 384-6177. Research in pollution control.

National Parks Association of Korea, Sahak Building, Room 706, 19 Neja-Dong, Chong-Ro-ku, Seoul 110

KUWAIT

Government:

Environment Protection Council, P.O. Box 24885, 13104 Safat. T: (965) 45 6833. Tx: 46408. Responsible for policy recommendations, coordination of government environmental protection programs, research, and public awareness.

Ministry of Public Health, Environmental Protection Department, P.O. Box 35035, Al Shaab

Agricultural Affairs and Fish Resources Authority, P.O. Box 21422, 10375 Safat. T: (965) 47 11155. Tx: 30072 agrfish kt. Responsibilities include fisheries and forestry.

Kuwait Fund for Arab Economic Development, P.O. Box 2921, Kuwait. T: (965) 43 9075. Tx: 2025 alsunduk kt.

Other organizations:

Kuwait Institute for Scientific Research, P.O. Box 24885, 13109 Safat. T: (965) 81 6988. Tx: 22299. C: SCIENCE. Concerns include natural resources.

Kuwait Environment Protection Society, P.O. Box 1869, 13019 Safat

LAOS

Government:

Ministry of Agriculture, Forestry, Irrigation, and Agricultural Cooperatives, Vientiane

Ministry of Public Health, Vientiane

LEBANON

Government:

Council for Development and Reconstruction, Présidence, Baabda. Tx: 21000 pr l.

Other organizations:

Conseil National de la Recherche Scientifique (National Council of Scientific Research), B.P. 8281, Beirut. ICSU national member.

LESOTHO

Government:

National Environment Secretariat, Prime Minister's Office, P.O. Box 527, Maseru. T: (266) 23861.

Ministry of Water, Energy, and Mining, P.O. Box 772, Maseru

LIBERIA

Government:

Ministry of Local Government, Monrovia. Tx: 4374 miniplan. Includes environmental responsibilities.

Ministry of Agriculture and Marketing, P.O. Box 24, Monrovia

Ministry of Health and Social Welfare, P.O. Box 9000, Monrovia. T: (231) 261-398. Includes a Division of Environmental Health.

Forestry Development Authority, P.O. Box 3010, Monrovia

LIBYA

Government:

National Committee for the Protection of the Environment, Tripoli. T: (218 21) 30838.

Other organizations:

Alfateh University, Faculty of Agriculture, P.O. Box 2547, Tripoli. T: (218 21) 36010. Tx: 20629. Program includes research in desert resource management.

LIECHTENSTEIN

Government:

Ministry of Agriculture, Forestry, and Environment, FL-9490 Vaduz

Other organizations:

Liechtensteinische Gesellschaft für Umweltschutz (Liechtenstein Association for Environmental Protection), Postfach 254, FL-9490 Vaduz. T: (41 75) 2 48 19.

LUXEMBOURG

Government:

Ministère de l'Environnement et des Eaux et Forêts (Ministry of the Environment, Water, and Forests), 5a rue de Prague, Luxembourg-Ville. T: (352) 44 15 08. Tx: 2536. Fax: (352) 40 04 10. Broad responsibilities.

Other organizations:

Greenpeace Luxembourg, B.P. 229, L-4003 Esch/Alzette. National office of Greenpeace International, listed in Part 6.

Ligue Luxembourgeoise pour l'Etude et la Protection des Oiseaux et de la Nature (Luxembourg League for Study and Protection of Birds and Nature), B.P. 709, Luxembourg-Ville. T: (352) 48 61 37.

Mouvement Ecologique (Ecological Movement), B.P. 927, Luxembourg-Ville. T: (352) 287 27.

Natura, 18 place d'Armes, Luxembourg-Ville. T: (352) 255 88.

MACAU
Portuguese territory.

Government:

Secretariat for Public Works and Housing, Macau

Secretariat for Education, Social Affairs, and Health, Macau

MADAGASCAR

Government:

Direction des Eaux et Forêts (Directorate of Water and Forests), B.P. 243, Antananarivo 101

Other organizations:

Association pour la Sauvegarde de l'Environnement (Association for Environmental Protection), B.P. 412, Antisiranana. [86]

Centre National de la Recherche Appliquée au Développement Rural (National Center for Research Applied to Rural Development), B.P. 1690, Antananarivo. T: 25676. Program includes applied studies in fisheries, forestry, and other natural resource problems.

Conseil National de la Recherche Scientifique et Technique (National Council of Scientific and Technical Research), Antananarivo. ICSU national member.

Fonds Mondial pour la Nature (World Wide Fund for Nature), B.P. 4373, Antananarivo. T: 25541. Founded 1979. Broad interests. Affiliated with the World Wide Fund for Nature (WWF International).

MALAWI

Government:

Office of the President, Environmental Department, Private Bag 388, Lilongwe 3. T: (265) 722780.

Ministry of Forestry and Natural Resources, P.O. Box 30131, Lilongwe 3. T: (265) 731322. Tx: 4113.

Other organizations:

Forestry Research Institute of Malawi (FRIM), P.O. Box 270, Zomba. T: (265 50) 522866.

National Fauna Preservation Society of Malawi, P.O. Box 30293, Lilongwe 3

MALAYSIA

Federal government:

Ministry of Science, Technology, and the Environment, 14th Floor, Wisma Sime Darby, Jalan Raja Laut, 50662 Kuala Lumpur. T: (60 3) 293 8955. Tx: 28154 mostec ma. C: KEMSAINS. Includes:
- Department of the Environment, with Air Pollution Control, Water Pollution Control, Marine Pollution Control, and Environmental Impact Assessment Units.
- National Council of Scientific Research and Development, which is the ICSU national member.
- Department of Wildlife and National Parks, Peninsular Malaysia, K20 Government Offices Complex, Duta Road, Kuala Lumpur.

State governments:

The state governments have important responsibilities for forests, wildlife, and parks.

Other organizations:

Environmental Protection Society Malaysia, 17 Jalan SS 2/53, Petaling Jaya. T: (60 3) 757767. Founded 1974. Activist group with broad interests. [85]

Persatuan Pencinta Alam (Malayan Nature Society), 17 SS 2/53, Petaling Jaya. T: (60 3) 753330. Founded 1940. Promotes interest in the natural history of Malaysia and Southeast Asia. Program includes conservation advocacy and education.

Sahabat Alam Malaysia (SAM) (Friends of the Earth Malaysia), 43 Salween Road, 10050 Penang. T: 376930. Founded 1977. Important activist and educational group affiliated with Friends of the Earth International, which is listed in Part 6. Also acts as coordinator for Asian-Pacific Peoples Environment Network. Since 1980 has produced a series of annual reports on the state of the Malaysian environment, said to be the first of their kind in the world. Broad interests.

Forest Research Institute Malaysia, Kepong, Selangor
University of Malaya, Institute of Advanced Studies (IPT), IPT Asian Wetland Bureau for Conservation, Research, and Management (AWB),

Lembah Pantai, 59100 Kuala Lumpur. T: 7572176. Tx: 37453 unimal ma. Successor to INTERWADER, founded 1983. Inventories, research, training, education, and information services throughout Asia.

World Wide Fund for Nature-Malaysia, 8th Floor, Wisma Damansara, Jalan Semantan, P.O. Box 10769, 50724 Kuala Lumpur. T: (60 3) 255 44 95. Founded 1972. Affiliate of the World Wide Fund for Nature (WWF International), listed in Part 6.

MALDIVES

Government:

Ministry of Home Affairs and Social Services, Male. Includes the Maldives Environment Programme.

Ministry of Health, Male

MALI

Government:

Ministère des Ressources Naturelles et de l'Elevage (Ministry of Natural Resources and Livestock), B.P. 275, Bamako. T: 225850.

Other organizations:

Groupe de Recherche et d'Applications Techniques (GRAT), B.P. 2502, Bamako. Tx: 2502. C: 2428. Founded 1981. Appropriate technology research and development; reforestation; watershed management.

Institut National de la Recherche Zootechnique, Forestière et Hydrobiologique (INRZFH) (National Institute for Zoological, Forestry, and Hydrobiological Research), B.P. 1704, Bamako. T: 226428. Founded 1927.

MALTA

Government:

Department of Health, Environment Division, Valletta. T: (356) 22 40 71. Tx: 1114 ise mt. The country's main environmental agency.

Other organizations:

National Trust of Malta, 133 Brittania Street, Valletta. [85]

Ornithological Society, P.O. Box 498, Valletta. T: (356) 44 02 78.

Society for the Study and Conservation of Nature, P.O. Box 459, Valletta. T: (356) 33 29 84.

University of Malta, International Environment Institute, Old University Building, St. Paul's Street, Valletta

MARSHALL ISLANDS

A republic in free association with the United States.

Government:

Ministry of Resources and Development, Majuro

Ministry of Health Services, Majuro

MARTINIQUE

An overseas department of France.

Government:

Ministère des Départements et Territoires d'Outre-Mer (Ministry of Overseas Departments and Territories), 27 rue Oudinot, F-75700 Paris, France. T: (33 1) 47 83 01 23.

Other organizations:

Comité de Résistance à la Destruction de l'Environnement Martiniquais (CORDEM) (Committee of Resistance against Nature Destruction in Martinique), Voie No. 5, rue du Professeur Garcia, 97200 Fort-de-France. Founded 1982. Activist group with broad concerns.

MAURITANIA

Government:

Ministère du Développement Rural--Direction Protection Nature, Reboisement et Faune (Ministry of Rural Development--Directorate of Nature Protection, Reforestation, and Wildlife), B.P. 170, Nouakchott. T: 51836. Tx: 585 mtn.

Ministère de l'Hydraulique et de Habitat (Ministry of Water Resources and Housing), Nouakchott

Other organizations:

Conseil Pan-Africain pour la Protection de l'Environnement et le Développement (CCPED) (Pan-African Council for Protection of the Environment and Development), B.P. 994, Nouakchott. T: 53-77. Tx: NOSOM-LIPAM, 565 mtn. C: CCPED. Founded 1982. Desertification control, pollution control, and water conservation.

MAURITIUS

Government:

Ministry of Housing, Lands, and the Environment, Edith Cavell Street, Port-Louis. Tx: 2275 seytob sz.

Ministry of Agriculture, Fisheries, and Natural Resources, Reduit. T: 4-1091.

Other organizations:

Action for Development (AFORD), P.O. Box 1042, Port-Louis. T: 6-4970. Founded 1964. Program includes conservation and agroforestry projects.

Mauritius Council for Development, Environmental Studies, and Conservation (MAUDESVO), P.O. Box 1124, Port-Louis. T: 2-1886. Research, training, public education, lobbying.

Mauritius Institute, Port-Louis. Program includes research on native species and ecosystems.

Mauritius Young Environmentalists, 24 Sir Charles Lees Street, Curepipe. [85]

MAYOTTE

French possession.

Government:

Prefecture, Dzaoudzi

Ministère des Départements et Territoires d'Outre-Mer (Ministry of Overseas Departments and Territories), 27 rue Oudinot, F-75700 Paris, France. T: (33 1) 47 83 01 23.

MEXICO

Government:

Secretaria de Desarrollo Urbano y Ecología (SEDUE) (Secretariat of Urban Development and Ecology), Avenida Constituyentes 947, Edificio B, PB, Mexico, D.F. T: (52 5) 271-0355 or 271-3000.

Secretaria de Agricultura y Recursos Hídraulicos (Secretariat of Agriculture and Water Resources) (SARH), Mexico City

Comisión Nacional Forestal (National Forestry Commission), Avenida México 190, Coyoacán, 04100 Mexico, D.F. T: (52 5) 534-9707 or 524-7862. An intersecretarial agency which coordinates federal government forestry policies and activities.

Other organizations:

Amigos de Sian Ka'an (Friends of Sian Ka'an), Apartado 770, 77500 Cancun, Quintana Roo. Founded 1986. Provides financial and logistical support for the 1.2-million-acre Sian Ka'an Man and the Biosphere Reserve in the state of Quintana Roo.

Academia Mexicana de Derecho Ecológico (Mexican Academy of Environmental Law), Liverpool 39, Colonia Juarez, Del. Cuauhtemoc, 06600 Mexico, D.F. T: (52 5) 533-2560. Provides information; advises other groups on legal aspects of environmental protection.

Arizona-Sonora Desert Museum. *See* listing under USA.

Asociación Mexicana de Proconservación de la Naturaleza (PRONATURA) (Mexican Association for Conservation of Nature), Apartado 14, 53160 Naucalpan, State of Mexico. T: (52 5) 545-1776. Founded 1981. Conservation of species and habitats; has several regional chapters and aims to establish programs in every state.

Biocenosis, Cerrada de Banderillas 25-13, San Jerónimo, 10200 Mexico D.F. T: (52 5) 595-6761. Wildlife conservation; projects in several parts of the country.

Chihuahuan Desert Research Institute. *See* listing under USA.

Consejo Nacional de Ciencia y Tecnología (CONACYT), (National Council of Science and Technology) Circuito Cultural, Centro Cultural Universitario, Ciudad X Universitaria, 04515 Mexico, D.F. T: (52 5) 652-3744. ICSU national member.

Ducks Unlimited de México, A.C. (DUMAC), Apartado 776, 64000 Monterrey, Nuevo León. T: (52 83) 335-4032. Part of a major North American duckhunters' organization which works for protection of habitat for aquatic birds and other wildlife.

Federación Conservacionista Mexicana (FECOMEX) (Mexican Conservation Federation), Apartado 10-974, 11000 Mexico, D.F. T: (52 5) 540-6144. Founded 1985. Federation of 28 organizations devoted to conservation of nature and natioonal use of natural resources.

Fundación Mexicana para la Restauración Ambiental (RA) (Mexican Foundation for Environmental Restoration), Campos Eliseos 400, Piso 19, Colonia Lomas de Chapultepec, 11000 Mexico, D.F. T: (52 5) 520-4428. Tx: 017 71390 atmme. Projects throughout the country; active publishing program.

Fundación Universo Veintiuno (21st Century Foundation), Campos Eliseos 400, Piso 19, Colonia Lomas de Chapultepec, 11000 Mexico, D.F. Promotes public-private collaboration in conservation and environmental improvement.

Instituto Mexicano de Recursos Naturales Renovables (IMERNAR) (Mexican Institute of Renewable Natural Resources), Avenida Dr. Vertiz 724, Colonia Narvarte, 03020 Mexico, D.F. T: (52 5) 519-1633. Major research center directed for many years by Dr. Enrique Beltrán.

Instituto Nacional de Investigaciones sobre Recursos Bióticos (INIREB) (National Institute of Research on Biotic Resources), Apartado Postal

63, 91000 Xalapa, Veracruz. T: (52 29) 75090. Tx: 015532 inrbme. Academic studies on a wide area of resource questions.

Mariposa Monarca (Monarch Butterfly), Avenida Constituyentes 345-806, Colonia Danile Garza, 11830 Mexico, D.F. T: (52 5) 515-9910. Protection of the magnificent Monarch butterfly, which migrates between small areas of central Mexico and the central coast of California.

Pacto de Grupos Ecologistas (Pact of Environmental Groups), Amores 1814, Colonia del Valle, 03100 Mexico, D.F. T: (52 5) 534-1023. A federation of some 50 environmental organizations; maintains committees on such topics as rainforests and energy.

Wildlife Society of Mexico, Apartado 13-432, 03500 Mexico, D.F. Founded 1983. Professional society with an active interest in environmental policy. Affiliated with the Wildlife Societies of the U.S. and Canada.

MICRONESIA, FEDERATED STATES OF
A republic in free association with the United States.

Government:

Department of Resources and Development, Kolonia, Pohnpei, Eastern Caroline Islands 96941

Department of Social Services, Kolonia, Pohnpei, Eastern Caroline Islands 96941

MIDWAY ISLANDS
U.S. possession

Government:

Under jurisdiction of the U.S. Department of the Navy, Washington, DC 20350, USA. T: (1 202) 695-0965.

MONACO

Government:

Departement des Travaux Publics (Public Works Department), MC-98015 Monaco-Ville. T: (33 93) 30 19 21. Responsibilities include environmental management in the Principality.

Other organizations:

Centre Scientifique de Monaco (Scientific Center of Monaco), 16 boulevard de Suisse, MC-98000 Monte Carlo. T: (33 93) 25 89 54. ICSU national member.

MONGOLIA

Government:

State Committee on Science and Technology, Ulan

Bator. T: 29957. Coordinates environmental protection measures to be included in the country's annual and 5-year plans.

Ministry of Forestry and Wood Processing Industry, Ulan Bator

Ministry of Water Economy, Ulan Bator

Other organizations:

Academy of Sciences of the Mongolian People's Republic, Ulan Bator. ICSU national member.

Mongolian Association for Nature Conservation, Ulan Bator. [85]

MONTSERRAT
British possession.

Government:

Ministry of Trade, Lands, and Housing, Plymouth. T: 2546.

Ministry of Education, Health, and Community Services, Plymouth. T: 3321.

Other organizations:

Montserrat National Trust, P.O. Box 86, Plymouth. Founded 1970. Works for nature reserves and a national park system; public education.

MOROCCO

Government:

Ministère de l'Agriculture (Ministry of Agriculture). Includes:
■ Direction des Eaux et Forêts et de la Conservation des Sols (Directorate of Water and Forests and Soil Conservation), B.P. Rabat Chellah, Rabat. T: (212 7) 625-65. Tx: 31696 m. Includes the Service de la Protection de la Nature (Nature Protection Service).

Ministère de l'Habitat et de l'Aménagement du Territoire (Ministry of Housing and Land Management), Rabat. T: (212 7) 602-62.

Other organizations:

Centre National de Coordination et de Planification de la Recherche Scientifique et Technique (National Council of Coordination and Planning of Scientific and Technical Research), Chari Omar-Ibn-Khattab, Agdal, B.P. 1346, Rabat. T: (212 7) 728 03. Tx: 32072 bahitilm m. ICSU national member.

Institut National de la Recherche Agronomique (INRA) (National Institute of Agronomy Research), B.P. 415, Rabat. T: (212 7) 74003. Tx: 31702. Major institution; program includes

some work in natural resource management. Library has the "most important collection in Africa" in its fields.

MOZAMBIQUE

Government:

Ministerio da Agricultura, Direccao Nacional de Florestas e Fauna Bravia (Ministry of Agriculture, National Directorate of Forestry and Wildlife), Caixa Postal 3652, Maputo

Ministry of Health, Maputo.

NAMIBIA (SOUTH WEST AFRICA)

Government:

Department of Agriculture and Nature Conservation, Private Bag 13306, Windhoek 9000

Other organizations:

Desert Ecological Research Unit, P.O. Box 953, Walvis Bay 9190. T: SRR 226, via Walvis Bay Radio. Founded 1963.

Namibia Wildlife Trust, P.O. Box 6173, Ausspannplatz, Windhoek 9000

NAURU

Government:

Ministry for Island Development, Nauru

Ministry for Health and Education, Nauru

NEPAL

Government:

National Commission for Conservation of Natural Resources, Babarmahal, Kathmandu

Ministry of Forestry, P.O. Box 860, Kathmandu. T: 215912. Includes the Department of National Parks and Wildlife Conservation.

Ministry of Agriculture, Khumaltar, Patan. T: 521149. Includes responsibility for soil conservation.

Ministry of Health, Kathmandu

Ministry of Housing and Physical Planning, Kathmandu

Ministry of Land Reform and Management, Kathmandu

Ministry of Water Resources, Kathmandu. Tx: 2312.

Other organizations:

Royal Nepal Academy of Science and Technology, P.O. Box 3323, New Baneswar, Kathmandu. T: 213060. Tx: 2369 np. C: RONAST. ICSU national member.

NETHERLANDS, THE

Government:

Ministerie van Landbouw en Visserij (Ministry of Agriculture and Fisheries), Department for Nature Conservation, Environmental Protection, and Wildlife Management, Postbus 20401, NL-200 EK The Hague. T: (31 70) 793266. Tx: 32040. Includes a Bureau of International Affairs.

Ministerie van Volkshuisvesting, Ruimtelijke Ordening en Milieubeheer (Ministry of Housing, Planning, and the Environment), Postbus 20951, NL-2500 EZ The Hague. T: (31 70) 264201. Responsible for environmental protection.

Ministry of Foreign Affairs, Department of Development Cooperation, Lange Houtstraat 11, The Hague. T: (31 70) 614941.

TROPENBOS, State Forest Service of the Netherlands, Postbus 20020, NL-3502 LA Utrecht. T: (31 30) 852446. Tx: 47542 lvutr nl. Established 1986. Global research program on conservation and development of tropical rainforest.

Other organizations:

Centrum voor Milieukunde (Center for Environmental Studies), Postbus 9518, NL-2300 RA Leiden. T: (31 71) 148333, ext. 2221. Tx: 39427. Includes a Division of Environment and Development and an international information service on wetlands conservation and management.

Greenpeace Netherlands, Damrak 83, NL-1012 LN Amsterdam. National office of Greenpeace International, listed in Part 6.

Information Centre for Low External Input and Sustainable Agriculture (ILEIA), Postbus 64, NL-3830 AB Leusden. T: (31 33) 943086. Tx: 79380 etc nl. Fax: (31 33) 940791. Focus is global. Holds workshops; maintains a database. Pub: Newsletter; conference proceedings.

Koninklijke Nederlandse Akademie van Wetenschapen (Royal Netherlands Academy of Sciences), Kloveniersburgwal 29, Postbus 19121, NL-1000 GC Amsterdam. T: (31 20) 222 29 02. Tx: 16064 nrz. ICSU national member.

Landbouwhogeschool (Agricultural University), Postbus 9100, NL-6700 HA Wageningen. T: (31 8370) 83063. Major programs of research in agriculture and conservation problems, especially of developing countries.

Nederlandse Raad voor Zeeonderzoek (Netherlands Council of Oceanic Research), Postbus 19121, NL-1000 GC Amsterdam. T: (31 20) 222902.

Socially Appropriate Technology Information Services (SATIS), Mauritskade 63, NL-1092 AD Amsterdam. T: (31 20) 926892. Tx: 15080. Disseminates information on viable technology alternatives through networks in the Third World and northern industrialized countries. Subject areas include water and sanitation; energy and power; and agriculture, forestry, and fisheries. Annual *Publications Catalogue* lists over 1,500 publications and audio-visual materials; bibliography of AT and development journals.

Stichting IUCN-Ledencontact (Netherlands National Committee for IUCN), Damrak 28-30, NL-1012 LJ Amsterdam. T: (31 20) 261732. Tx: 70890. Coordinates work of IUCN members in the country. Also sponsors BothENDS (ENvironment and Development Service for NGOs), which provides technical and scientific information to environmental and related NGOs in the Third World, as well as help in identifying possible donors to them.

Stichting Milieu-Educatie (SME) (Institute for Environmental Education), Postbus 13030, NL-3507 LA Utrecht. Founded 1975. Specializes in formal and informal environmental education.

Stichting Natuur en Milieu (Nature and Environment Foundation), Donkerstraat 17, NL-3511 KB Utrecht. T: (31 30) 331328. A major umbrella organization for local and provincial NGOs. Lobbying, research, and public education.

Stichting tot Internationale Natuurbescherming (Foundation for International Nature Protection), c/o Institute of Taxonomic Zoology, Zoological Museum, University of Amsterdam, Mauritskade 61, NL-1092 AD Amsterdam

Study and Information Center on Environmental Research (TNO), TNO Complex Zuidpolder, Postbus 186, NL-2600 Delft. T: (31 15) 569330. Tx: 38071 zptno.

TRAFFIC (Netherlands), Postbus 7, NL-3700 AA Zeist. T: (31 3404) 19438. Monitors trade in endangered species; part of TRAFFIC International (see World Wide Fund for Nature in Part 6).

Vereniging Milieudefensie (Environment Defense Organization), Damrak 26, 1012 LJ Amsterdam. Affiliated with Friends of the Earth International, listed in Part 6.

Vereniging tot Behoud van Natuurmonumenten in Nederland (Society for Protection of Nature Reserves in the Netherlands), Noordereinde 60, NL-1243 JJ The Hague. T: (31 35) 62004. Major nature protection organization with a large membership.

World Wide Fund for Nature-Netherlands, Postbus 7, NL-3700 AA Zeist. T: (31 3404) 22 164. Affiliate of the World Wide Fund for Nature (WWF International), listed in Part 6.

NETHERLANDS ANTILLES
An autonomous part of the Netherlands.

Government:

Ministry of Health, Heelsumstraat, Willemstad, Curaçao. T: (599) 614555.

Other organizations:

Stichting Nationale Parken Nederlandse Antillen (Netherlands Antilles National Parks Foundation), P.O. Box 2090, Curaçao

NEW CALEDONIA
An overseas territory of France.

Government:

Ministère des Départements et Territoires d'Outre-Mer (Ministry of Overseas Departments and Territories), 27 rue Oudinot, F-75700 Paris, France. T: (33 1) 47 83 01 23.

Other organizations:

Association pour le Sauvegarde de la Nature Néo-Caledonienne (Association for the Protection of New Caledonian Nature), 50 rue Anatole-France, Noumea. Founded 1971. Activist and educational organization interested in pollution as well as nature protection.

NEW ZEALAND
See also Cook Islands.

Directories: *An Environmental Directory* (Ministry for the Environment, 1988) lists governmental and private organizations, national and private, without descriptions.

Government:

Department of Conservation, P.O. Box 10-420, Wellington. T: (64 4) 710-726. Responsible for natural resource management, including a system of national parks and reserves.

Department of Scientific and Industrial Research, Private Bag, Lower Hutt. T: (64 4) 694-859. Includes an Ecology Division.

Ministry for the Environment, P.O. Box 10362, Wellington. T: (64 4) 734-090. Fax: (64 4) 710-195. Broad responsibilities for environmental protection.

Ministry of Agriculture and Fisheries, P.O. Box 297, Wellington. T: (64 4) 861-029. Tx: 31532.

Ministry of Foreign Affairs, Office of External Aid, Private Bag, Wellington. T: (64 4) 328-4800.

Ministry of Works and Development, Water Conservation Division, Wellington North. T: (64 4) 729-929. Tx: 3844.

Other organizations:

Antarctic and Southern Ocean Coalition, P.O. Box 11-057, Wellington. T: (64 4) 846-971.

Environment and Conservation Organisations of New Zealand (ECO), P.O. Box 11-057, Wellington 1. T: (64 4) 846-971.

Friends of the Earth (NZ), Ltd., P.O. Box 39-065, Auckland West. T: (64 9) 34-319. Affiliated with Friends of the Earth International, listed in Part 6.

Greenpeace New Zealand, Private Bag, Wellesley Street, Auckland. T: (64 9) 776-128. National office of Greenpeace International, listed in Part 6.

Royal Forest and Bird Protection Society of New Zealand, P.O. Box 631, Wellington. T: (64 4) 728-154. Fax: (64 4) 742-952. Major conservation organization.

Royal Society of New Zealand, Private Bag, Wellington. T: (62 4) 727-421. C: ROYALSOC. Scientific society with broad interests. ICSU national member. Has a National Committee on Scientific Problems if the Environment.

Tussock Grasslands and Mountain Lands Institute, Lincoln College, P.O. Box 56, Canterbury. T: (64 3) 252-811.

World Wide Fund for Nature-New Zealand, 35 Taranaki Street, 2nd Floor, P.O. Box 6237, Wellington. T: (62 4) 854 524. Affiliate of the World Wide Fund for Nature (WWF International), listed in Part 6.

NICARAGUA

Government:

Instituto Nicaragüense de Recursos Naturales y del Ambiente (IRENA) (Nicaraguan Institute of Natural Resources and Environment), Apartado 5123, Managua. T: (505 2) 3-1110. Tx: 1328. Broad responsibilities for environmental and resource management.

Other organizations:

Asociación de Biólogos y Ecólogos de Nicaragua (ABEN) (Association of Biologists and Ecologists of Nicaragua), Apartado 3257, Managua. T: (505 2) 2-3765. Founded 1981. Professional society. Developing a national environmental education campaign; hosted 4th international

Biennial Conference on the Fate of the Earth in 1989. Affiliated with Friends of the Earth International, listed in Part 6.

Colectivo Habitat (Habitat Collective), Apartado 69, Managua. T: (505) 7-0352, ext. 215. General conservation interests; environmental education.

NIGER

Government:

Ministère de l'Hydraulique et de l'Environnement (Ministry of Water Resources and the Environment), B.P. 578, Niamey. T: 73 33 329. Includes responsibility for environmental protection and natural resource management.

Direction de l'Hygiène et de l'Assainissement (Directorate of Hygiene and Sanitation), B.P. 371, Niamey. T: 72 37 83. Environmental health protection.

Other organizations:

Institut National de Recherches Agronomiques du Niger (INRAN), B.P. 429, Niamey. T: 722714. Tx: 5201. Founded 1975. Program includes studies in ecology and agroforestry.

Projet Tapis Vert (PTV) (Project Greenbelt), B.P. 2605, Niamey. Indigenous organization which works to combat desertification by planting trees, village education, and other means.

NIGERIA

Federal government:

Federal Ministry of Works and Housing, Environmental Planning and Protection Division, P.M.B. 12698, Lagos. T: (234 1) 682625.

Federal Department of Forestry, Ije Village, Obalende, P.M.B. 12613, Lagos. T: (234 1) 684178.

Federal Ministry of Health, Ikoyi, Lagos. Responsibilities include pollution control.

Other organizations:

Forestry Association of Nigeria, University P.O. Box 4185, Ibadan. Founded 1970. Tree-planting, academic research, information, and planning.

Forestry Research Institute, P.M.B. 5054, Ibadan. [85]

Nigerian Academy of Science, c/o Department of Computer Sciences, Faculty of Science, University of Lagos, P.M.B. 1004, University of Lagos Post Office, Lagos. ICSU national member.

Nigerian Conservation Foundation, Mainland Hotel, First Floor, P.O. Box 467, Lagos

NIUE
A New Zealand possession.

Government:

Ministry of Finance, Agriculture, and Fisheries, Alofi

Ministry of Education, Community Affairs, and Health, Alofi

NORFOLK ISLAND
An Australian possession.

Government:

Ministry for Commerce and Health, Kingston 2899

Ministry for Planning, Kingston 2899

NORTHERN MARIANA ISLANDS
A U.S. commonwealth.

Government:

Government of the Northern Mariana Islands, Saipan, CM 96950

NORWAY

Government:

Royal Ministry of Environment, Myngtgaten 2, Postboks 8013-Dep., N-0030 Oslo 1. T: (47 2) 34 57 15. Tx: 21480. Fax: (47 2) 11 60 08. Includes an International Division.

Ministry of Development Corporation, Postboks 8114-Dep., 7 Juni Plass 1, Oslo 1. T: (47 2) 20 4170.

Other organizations:

Agricultural University of Norway, Norwegian Center for International Agricultural Development, Postboks 2, N-1432 Ås-NLH. Active interest in environmental problems of developing countries.

Det Norske Videnskaps-Akademi (The Norwegian Science Academy), Drammensveien 78, N-0271 Oslo 2. ICSU national member.

Greenpeace Norway, St. Olavsgt. 11, Postboks 6803, St. Olavs Plass, N-0130 Oslo 1. National office of Greenpeace International, listed in Part 5.

Norges Naturvernforbund (Norwegian Society for the Conservation of Nature), Postboks 6804, N-0130 Oslo 1. T: (47 2) 42 95 00.

World Wide Fund for Nature-Norway, Hegdebaugsveien 22, N-0167 Oslo 1. T: (47 2) 69 61 97. Affiliate of the World Wide Fund for

Nature (WWF International), listed in Part 6.

OMAN

Government:

Council for Conservation of Environment and Water Resources, P.O. Box 5575, Ruwi. T: (968) 704006. Tx: 3590. Broad responsibilities; coordinates government activities.

Ministry of Health, Environmental Health Section, P.O. Box 393, Muscat.

Ministry of Agriculture and Fisheries, P.O. Box 467, Muscat. T: (968) 702066. Tx: 3503 agrifish.

Ministry of Environment and Water Resources, P.O. Box 323, Muscat. T: (968) 696444. Fax: (968) 697048.

PACIFIC OCEAN

The following organizations have a direct interest in the Pacific Ocean. *See also* "Oceans, Coastal Zones, and Islands" in Part 2.

UN system (see Part 4): The UN Environment Programme has regional sea programs for the Southeast Pacific, South Pacific, East Asia, and South Asia regions.

Other intergovernmental organizations (see Part 5): North Pacific Fur Seal Commission; Permanent South Pacific Commission (Southeast Pacific); South Pacific Commission; South Pacific Forum.

International NGOs (see Part 6): Pacific Science Association; University of the South Pacific, Institute of Natural Resources.

PAKISTAN

Government:

Ministry of Food, Agriculture, and Cooperatives. Includes:
■ National Council for Conservation of Wildlife in Pakistan, 485 Street 84, G-6/4, Islamabad
■ Pakistan Agricultural Research Council, Arid Zone Research Institute (AZRI), Brewery Road, Quetta, Baluchistan. T: 75006. Tx: 7836 icarda pk. Institute founded 1977. Emphasizes agricultural uses of natural resources.
■ Pakistan Forest Institute, P.O. Forest Institute Campus, Peshawar. T: 8320. Tx: 40580 pakfi. Research and teaching.

Ministry of Housing and Works, Block B, Pakistan Secretariat, Islamabad. Includes:
■ Environment and Urban Affairs Division. T: (92 51) 27812. C: ENVIRONMENT.

Ministry of Health, Special Education, and Social Welfare, Block C, Pakistan Secretariat, Islamabad.

T: (92 51) 824960.

Ministry of Petroleum and Natural Resources, Block A, Pakistan Secretariat, Islamabad. T: (92 51) 821220. Tx: 5851.

Other organizations:

Pakistan Association for the Advancement of Science, 6-B Gulberg II, Lahore 11. T: (92 42) 876182. ICSU national member.

Scientific and Cultural Society of Pakistan, B-7 Street No. 25, Model Colony, Karachi 75100. Program includes disseminating information and promoting education and research on conservation.

World Wide Fund for Nature-Pakistan, P.O. Box 1312, Lahore. T: (92 42) 85 11 74. An affiliate of the World Wide Fund for Nature (WWF International), listed in Part 6.

PALAU
UN Trust Territory under U.S. administration.

Government:

Ministry of Natural Resources, Koror, Palau, Western Caroline Islands 96960

Ministry of Social Services, Koror, Palau, Western Caroline Islands 96960

PANAMA

Government:

Ministerio de Planificación y Política Económica, Comisión Nacional del Medio Ambiente (Ministry of Planning and Economic Policy, National Environment Commission), Apartado 2694, Zona 3, Panama. T: (507) 32-6055. Commission has broad responsibilities for environmental management.

Instituto de Recursos Naturales Renovables (INRENARE) (Institute of Renewable Natural Resources), Apartado 2016, Paraíso. T: (507) 32-4209). Administers the renewable natural resources of the country.

Other organizations:

Asociación Estudiantil para la Conservación Ambiental de Panamá (AECAP) (Panamanian Student Association for Environmental Conservation), Apartado 2797, Balboa. T: (507) 67-0002. Environmental education at the secondary level.

Asociación Nacional para la Conservación de la Naturaleza (ANCON) (National Association for Conservation of Nature), Apartado 1387, Panamá 1. T: (507) 63-7950. Founded 1985. Protection of forests and other natural lands; efforts concentrated in the field. Maintains a Conservation Data Center for Panama.

Asociación para la Investigación y Propagación de Especies Panameñas (AIPEP) (Association for Investigation and Propagation of Panamanian Species), Apartado 2320, Balboa. T: (507) 32-6055. Research, education, and action to preserve Panamanian plant and animal species.

Fundación de Parques Nacionales y Medio Ambiente (PaNaMA) (Foundation for National Parks and the Environment), Apartado 6-6623, El Dorado, Panama. T: (507) 25-3676. Umbrella group for 25 Panamanian conservation groups; environmental action and public education.

Proyecto de Estudio para el Manejo de Areas Silvestres de Kuna Yala (PEMASKY) (Study Project for Management of Wild Areas of the Kuna Yala), Apartado 2012, Paraíso. Works for integration of environmental protection and development in the area of the Kuna Yala, an indigenous community.

Smithsonian Tropical Research Institute (STRI) (mailing address: APO Miami, Florida 34002, USA), located on Barro Colorado Island. An important center for advanced studies in tropical biology. Also administers a tropical forest reserve "which is less disturbed and has a more complete animal community than any other equally accessible tract of tropical forest." Part of the Smithsonian Institution, USA.

Sociedad Audubon de Panamá (Panama Audubon Society), Apartado 2026, Balboa. Broad wildlife and environmental interests; a chapter of the National Audubon Society of the USA.

Universidad de Panamá, Centro de Estudios de Recursos Bióticos (University of Panama, Center for Studies on Biotic Resources), Apartado 6403, Zona 5, Panamá. T: (507) 63-6133, ext. 319. Active role in national conservation planning and environmental education.

PAPUA NEW GUINEA

Government:

Department of Environment and Conservation, Central Government Buildings, Waigani, P.O. Box 6601, Boroko. T: (675) 271788. Tx: 22327.

Other organizations:

Friends of the Earth, P.O. Box 4028, Boroko. Affiliated with Friends of the Earth International, listed in Part 6.

University of Papua New Guinea, Department of Environment Sciences, Box 320, University P.O. T: (675) 245228.

Wau Ecology Institute, P.O. Box 77, Wau. T: (675) 446341. C: ECOLOGY. Founded 1971. Research and education in natural history and conservation.

PARAGUAY

Government:

Ministerio de Agricultura y Ganadería (Ministry of Agriculture and Livestock), Asunción. Responsibilities include forests, water, soil and pesticides.
Ministerio de Salud Pública y Bienestar Social (Ministry of Public Health and Social Welfare). Includes:
■ Servicio Nacional de Saneamiento Ambiental (SENASA) (National Service for Environmental Sanitation, Mariscal Estigarribia y Tacuary 796, Asunción. T: (595 21) 94399. Tx: 5279.

Other organizations:

Alter Vida: Centro de Estudios y Formación para el Ecodesarrollo (Alter Vida: Center for Studies and Education for Ecodevelopment), Casilla 2334, Asunción. T: (595 21) 200-605.

Fundación Physis, Yegros 471, Asunción. T: (595 21) 43484. Study and conservation of Paraguay's environmental resources.

Sociedad Paraguaya para la Protección de la Naturaleza (PRONATURA) (Paraguayan Society for the Protection of Nature), Casilla 2497, Asunción. T: (595 21) 46369. Protection of natural resources and cultural values.

Sociedad Protectora de Animales y Planteas del Paraguay (Animal and Plant Protective Society of Paraguay), Casilla 3209, Asunción. Activities include wildlife research and protection and environmental education.

PERU

Government:

Ministerio de Agricultura, Dirección General Forestal y de Fauna (DGFF) (Ministry of Agriculture, General Directorate of Forestry and Wildlife), Natalio Sanchez 220, 3er piso, Lima 11. T: (51 14) 23-3978. Tx: 323150.

Oficina Nacional de Evaluación de los Recursos Naturales (ONERN) (National Office of Natural Resource Evaluation), Apartado 4992, Calle 17, No. 355, Urbanización El Palomar, San Isidro, Lima 27. T: (51 14) 41-0245. C: ONERN. Investigates and inventories soil, water, and forest resources.

Other organizations:

Asociación de Defensa del Medio Ambiente (ADMA) (Association for Defense of the Environment), Avenida Universitaria 318, Correo UV3, Lima 1. T: (51 14) 27-7366. C: ADMA. Provides legal and scientific counsel to environmental organizations.

Asociación de Ecología y Conservación (Association of Ecology and Conservation), Vanderghen 560-2A, San Isidro, Lima 27.

Asociación Peruana para la Conservación de la Naturaleza (APECO), Parque José de Acosta 187, Lima 17. T: (51 14) 61-6316. A leading conservation education organization.
Centro de Datos para la Conservación (Data Center for Conservation), Departamento de Manejo Forestal, Universidad Nacional Agraria, Apartado 456, Lima. T: (51 14) 35-2035.

Centro de Investigación y Promoción Amazónica (CIPA) (Center for Amazonian Research and Promotion), Avenida Ricardo Palma 666-D, Lima 18. T: (51 14) 46-4823.

Fundación Peruana para la Conservación de la Naturaleza (FPCN) (Peruvian Foundation for Conservation of Nature), Apartado 18-1393, Lima 1. T: (51 14) 42-2796. Tx: 25129 noving pe. Founded 1984. Works to improve management of national parks, coordinate Peruvian conservation groups, and develop policy recommendations.

Pro Defensa de la Naturaleza (For Defense of Nature), Avenida Nicolás de Piérola 742, Oficina 703, Edificio Internacional, Lima.

PHILIPPINES

Government:

National Environmental Protection Council, PHCA Building, 6th Floor, Dilima, Quezon City. T: (63 2) 980-421.

Department of the Environment and Natural Resources, Quezon Avenue, Diliman, Quezon City 1100. T: (63 2) 976-626.

Department of Agriculture, Elliptical Road, Diliman, Quezon City. T: (63 2) 998-741. Tx: 27726.

Department of Health, San Lazaro Hospital Compound, Rizal Avenue, Santz Cruz, Metro Manila. T: (63 2) 266-806.
National Water Resources Council, NIA Building EDSA, 8th Floor, Quezon City. T: (63 2) 952-603.

Other organizations:

Ecological Society of the Philippines, 53 Tamarind Road, Forbes Park, Makati, Metro Manila

National Research Council of the Philippines, Bicutan, Tagig, Metro Manila. T: (63 2) 845-0409. ICSU national member.

Philippine Council for Agriculture and Resources Research and Development (PCARRD), Los Baños, Laguna 3732. T: 50015. Program includes work in forestry, fisheries, and water resources

and quality.

Philippine Federation for Environmental Concern, 13 Kapilagan Street, P.O. Box 772, Quezon City. T: (63 2) 602-508. Founded 1979. Research and public education. [85]

World Ecologists Foundation (WE), Gold Building, 15 Annapolis St., Greenhills, Metro Manila. T: (63 2) 722-4016. Activist group. Project Fruitopia plants fruit-bearing trees.

PITCAIRN ISLANDS
British possession under the jurisdiction of the British High Commissioner in Wellington, New Zealand.

POLAND

Government:

Ministerstwo Ochrony Srodowiska i Zasobow Naturalnych (Ministry of Environmental Protection and Natural Resources), ul. Wawelska 52-54, PL-02-067 Warsaw. Includes:
■ Panstwowa Rada Ochrony Przyrody (National Council for Protection of Nature)

Ministerstwo Rolnictwa, Lesnictwa i Gospodarki Zywnosciowej (Ministry of Agriculture, Forests, and Food), ul. Wspola 30, PL-00-522 Warsaw

Other organizations:

Ecological Library, ul. Ryboki 6/A, Poznan. Stocks environmental literature; linked to the Green Library (listed under USA).

Liga Ochrony Przyrody (LOP) (Nature Conservation League), Zarzad Glowny, ul. Wawelska 52/54, PL-02-067 Warsaw. Founded 1928. The official nature conservation association; active in environmental education and awareness.

Polish Green Party, P.O. Box 783, PL-30-960 Krakow. Founded 1988. Focuses on environmental issues.

Polska Akademia Nauk (Polish Academy of Sciences), Palac Kultury i Nauki, Pok 2603, PL-00-901 Warsaw. Includes:
■ Zaklad Ochrony Przyrody i Zasobow Naturalnych (Research Center for the Protection of Natural Resources), ul. Arianska I, PL-31-505 Krakow
■ Instytut Badawczy Lesnictwa (Forest Research Institute), ul. Wery Kostrzewy 3, PL-00973 Warsaw
■ Instytut Podstaw Inzynierii Srodowiska (Environmental Engineering Institute), ul. M. Curie-Sklodowskiej 34, PL-41-800 Zabrze. Program includes studies into air pollution control.
■ Instytut Ksztaltowania Srodowiska (Environmental Development Research Institute), ul. Krzywickiego 9, PL-02-078 Warsaw.

Conducts studies on problems related to the planned development of the human environment.
■ Instytut Ochrony Srodowiska (IOS) (Institute of Environmental Protection), ul. Krucza 5/11, PL-00-548 Warsaw. T: (48 22) 29 92 54. Tx: 813493 iks pl. The main research body in Poland for complex environmental issues; focus is on pollution, environmental economics, and natural resource management.
■ Komitet Ochrony Przyrody (Nature Protection Committee), ul. Lubicz 46, PL-31-512 Krakow
■ Instytut Panstwa i Prawa, Zespol Prawnych Problemow Ochrony i Ksztaltowania Srodowiska (Institute of State and Law, Research Group on Environmental Law), ul. Kuznicza 46/47, PL-50-138 Wroclaw. T: 44-47-47.

Polski Kluby Ekologiczne (PKE) (Polish Ecological Clubs), Rynek Glowny 27, PL-31-010 Krakow. The major independent body which assesses government policies and offers alternative actions. Works through a regional structure to disseminate information, identify sources of industrial pollution, and campaign for closing polluting factories. Affiliated with Friends of the Earth International, listed in Part 6.

Polskie Towarzystwo Turystyczno-Krajoznawcze (Polish Tourist-Patriotic Society), ul. Senatorska II, PL-00-075 Warsaw. Includes a Commission for Nature Conservation which works to improve public awareness of the role of nature conservation in outdoor recreation and tourism.

Wolalem Byc (I'd Rather Be), ul. Buczka 4110, PL-70-420 Szczecin. An information movement associated with a youth weekly; concerns include nuclear energy and air pollution.

Wolnosc i Pokoj (WIP) (Freedom and Peace) (no address available). A militant organization concentrating on major promotional campaigns such as calling for closing the Siechnice steel works and an end to nuclear power development.

PORTUGAL
See also Macau.

Government:
Ministerio do Plano e da Administracao do Territorio (Ministry of Planning and Land Management). Includes:
■ Secretaria de Estado do Ambiente e dos Recursos Naturais (Secretariat of State for Environment and Natural Resources), Rua do Seculo, 51-20, P-1200 Lisbon

Other organizations:

Academia das Ciencias de Lisboa (Academy of Sciences of Lisbon), Rua da Academia das Ciencias 19, P-1200 Lisbon. T: (351 1) 36 38 66. ICSU national member.

Amigos da Terra (Friends of the Earth), Rue Pinheiro Chaves 28, 2 Dto., P-1000 Lisbon

Centro Ecologico (Ecological Center), Apartado 4045, P-1501 Lisbon Codex

Liga para a Proteccao da Natureza (League for the Protection of Nature), Estrada do Calhariz de Benfica no. 187, P-1500 Lisbon. T: (351 1) 780097. Fax: (351 1) 780097.

Nucleo Portugues de Estudo e Proteccao da Vida Selvagem (Portuguese Core Group for Wildlife Studies and Protection), Bairro Fundo de Fomento de Habitacao, Bloco D R/C, P-5300 Braganca

PUERTO RICO
A commonwealth associated with the United States.

Commonwealth government:

Department of Agriculture, P.O. Box 10163, San Juan, PR 00908, USA. T: (1 809) 722-2120. Includes a Land Use and Preservation Office.

Department of Health, P.O. Box 10427, Hato Rey, PR 00922, USA. T: (1 809) 767-9264. Responsibilities include environmental health.

Department of Natural Resources, P.O. Box 5887, Puerta de Tierra Station, San Juan, PR 00906, USA. T: (1 809) 724-8774.

Other organizations:

Natural History Society of Puerto Rico, G.P.O. Box 1036, San Juan, PR 00936, USA. Conservation group affiliated with the National Wildlife Federation (USA).

Conservation Trust of Puerto Rico, P.O. Box 4747, San Juan, PR 00905, USA. T: (1 809) 722-5834. Founded 1970. Broad interests.

QATAR

Government:

Environmental Protection Committee, c/o Ministry of Public Health, P.O. Box 42, Doha. Chaired by the Minister of Public Health; responsible for recommending and implementing environmental policies, as well as environmental monitoring and coordination of government activities.

Ministry of Industry and Agriculture, P.O. Box 1966, Doha. T: (974) 433400. Tx: 4751. Responsibilities include wildlife and water matters.

REUNION
An overseas department of France.

Government:

Ministère des Départements et Territoires d'Outre-Mer (Ministry of Overseas Departments and Territories), 27 rue Oudinot, F-75700 Paris, France. T: (33 1) 47 83 01 23.

Other organizations:

Société Réunionnaise pour l'Etude et la Protection de l'Environnement (Reunion Society for the Study and Protection of the Environment), B.P. 1109, 97481 Saint-Denis CEDEX

ROMANIA

Government:

National Council for Environmental Protection, Piata Victoriei 1, Bucharest. T: (40 0) 14 34 00. Includes Commissions for: Air Protection and the Struggle Against Noise; Water Protection; Soil and Subsoil Protection; Protection of Flora, Fauna, and the Monuments of Nature; and Protection of Human Settlements.

Other organizations:

Academia de Stiinte Agricole si Silvice (Academy of Agriculture and Forestry), Bul. Marasti 61, Bucharest
Academia Republicii Socialiste Romania (Academy of the Socialist Republic of Romania), Calea Victoriei 125, Bucharest. T: (40 0) 50 76 80. Tx: 11907 C 742 acadr b. ICSU national member.

Institutul de Cercetari si Amenajari Silvice (Forest Research and Design Institute), 128 Soseaua Stefanesti, Sector 2, Bucharest. Founded 1933.

Institutul de Cercetari si Proiectari "Delta Denarii." (Danube Delta Research and Design Institute), Strada Alexandru Sahia 2, 8800 Tulcea

Institutul de Cercetari si Proiectari si Amenajasi Silvice (ICAS) (Silvicultural Research Institute), Bucharest. Forestry research.

Institutul Roman de Cercetari Marine (Marine Research Institute of Romania), Bul. Lenin 300, 8700 Constanta. Conducts studies on Black Sea ecosystems and water pollution.

RWANDA

Government:

Ministère de l'Agriculture et de l'Élevage (Ministry of Agriculture and Livestock), B.P. 621, Kigali

Ministère de la Santé Publique et des Affaires Sociales (Ministry of Public Health and Social Affairs), B.P. 84, Kigali

Office Rwandais du Tourisme et des Parcs Nationaux (Rwandan Office of Tourism and National Parks), Présidence de la République, B.P. 905, Kigali

Other organizations:

Association Rwandaise pour la Promotion du Developpement Integré (ARDI) (Rwandan Association for Promotion of Integrated Development), B.P. 1295, Kigali. T: 3967. Tx: 566 cepd. C: ARDI. Founded 1981.

Institut National des Recherches Scientifiques (National Institute of Scientific Research), B.P. 218, Butare. T: 395. Program includes research in natural resources.

ST. CHRISTOPHER AND NEVIS (ST. KITTS)

Government:

Ministry of Agriculture, P.O. Box 186, Basseterre. T: (1 809) 465-2521. Responsibilities include forests, parks, beaches, and water supply.

Nevis Historical and Conservation Society, Alexander Hamilton Museum, Charlestown. Founded 1980. Interests include natural resource conservation.

Society for the Restoration of Brimstone Hill, P.O. Box 229, Basseterre. T: (1 809) 465-2166. Founded 1965. Oldest environmental group in country.

ST. HELENA AND DEPENDENCIES
British possession.

Government:

Council Committee on Agriculture and Natural Resources, Jamestown, St. Helena

Council Committee on Public Health, Jamestown, St. Helena

ST. LUCIA

Government:

Ministry of Agriculture, Lands, Fisheries, and Cooperatives, Manoel Street, Castries. T: (1 809) 452-2526. Includes an Environmental Commission, which has a general advisory role; and a Forestry Division, whose responsibilities include water resources management and soil conservation.

Other organizations:

National Research and Development Foundation of St. Lucia, P.O. Box 1097, Barnards Hill, Castries. T: (1 809) 452-4253. A development group that works with international organizations on environmental projects.

St. Lucia National Trust, P.O. Box 525, Castries. T: (1 809) 425-5005. Founded 1975. Protects natural and historic areas.

St. Lucia Naturalists Society, P.O. Box 783, Castries. Educational and conservation activities.

ST. PIERRE ET MIQUELON
French territory.

Government:

Prefecture, F-97500 St. Pierre. T: (1 508) 412801.

Ministère des Départements et Territoires d'Outre Mer (Ministry of Overseas Departments and Territories), 27 rue Oudinot, F-75700 Paris, France. T: (33 1) 47 83 01 23.

ST. VINCENT AND THE GRENADINES

Government:

Ministry of Trade and Agriculture, Kingstown, St. Vincent. Concerns include conservation.

Other organizations:

St. Vincent and the Grenadines National Trust, P.O. Box 198, Kingstown, St. Vincent. Works to protect natural and historic areas.

SAN MARINO

Government:

Ministry of State for the Environment, San Marino

SAO TOME AND PRINCIPE

Government:

Ministry of Planning, C.P. 67, Sao Tome. T: (239 12) 22308. Tx: 225 miplano st. Concerns include environmental management.

SAUDI ARABIA

Government:

Ministry of Defense and Aviation. Includes:
■ Meteorology and Environmental Protection Administration (MEPA), P.O. Box 1358, Jeddah 21431. T: (966 2) 665-0084. Tx: 40236. Broad responsibilities, including pollution control.

National Commission for Wildlife Conservation and Development (NCWCD), P.O. Box 61681, Riyadh 11575

Saudi Fund for Development, P.O. Box 5711, Riyadh. T: (966 1) 464 0292. Tx: 201145.

Other organizations:

King Abdulaziz City for Science and Technology, P.O. Box 6086, Riyadh 11442. T: (966 1) 4788000. Tx: 201590 kacst sj. C: MAWSOAH. ICSU national member.

King Faisal University, Water Studies Center, P.O. Box 380, Al-Ahsa 31982

King Saud University, Center for Desert Studies, P.O. Box 2454 Riyadh 11451. T: (966 1) 4675571. Tx: 401019. Program includes studies of conservation and management of natural resources in the Saudi desert.

SENEGAL

Government:

Direction de l'Environnement (Environment Directorate), Dakar

Direction des Eaux et Forêts et Chasses (Water, Forests and Wildlife Directorate), Dakar

Centre National de Recherche Forestière (National Center of Forestry Research), B.P. 2312, Dakar. T: (221) 213219.

Other organizations:

Association Sénégalaise des Amis de la Nature (Senegalese Association of Friends of Nature), B.P. 1801, Dakar. T: (221) 222573. Founded 1983. Conservation action and education in forestry and watershed management.

Conseil des Organisations Non Gouvernementales d'Appui au Developpement du Sénégal (CONGAD) (Council of Non-Governmental Organizations in Support of the Development of Senegal), B.P. 4109, Dakar. T: (221) 214720. Tx: 671 sg, attn. CONGAD. Founded 1982; 38 member groups. Coordinated action program integrates environmental, agricultural, and socio-economic elements.

Institut Sénégelais de Recherches Agricoles (ISRA) (Senegalese Institute of Agricultural Research), B.P. 3120, Dakar. T: (221) 212425. Tx: 3117 sg. Founded 1975. Program includes studies and action projects related to natural resource management. Includes:
■ Direction des Recherches sur les Productions Forestières (DRPF) (Directorate of Research on Forestry), B.P. 2312, Hann, Dakar

SEYCHELLES

Government:

Ministry of National Development, Independence House, P.O. Box 199, Victoria, Mahe. T: (248) 22881. Tx: 2312. Includes the National Environment Commission (which is the ICSU national member) and the Division of Land Use and Environment.

SIERRA LEONE

Government:

Ministry of Agriculture and Forestry, Tower Hill, Freetown. T: 24821.

Ministry of Natural Resources and Fisheries, State Avenue, Freetown

Ministry of Health, New England, Freetown

Other organizations:

Sierra Leone Environment and Nature Conservation Association (SLENCA), P.M.B. 376, Freetown. T: 41353. C: NATURE. Broad interests: research, education, information, policy development, tree-planting.

SINGAPORE

Government:

Ministry of the Environment, Princess House, Alexandra Road, Singapore 0315. T: (65) 635111. Tx: 34365. Broad responsibilities.

SOLOMON ISLANDS

Government:

Ministry of Natural Resources, P.O.B. G24, Honiara. T: 22944. Tx: 66306.

Ministry of Health and Medical Services, P.O.B. 349, Honiara. T: 23600.

SOMALIA

Government:

National Range Agency, P.O. Box, Mogadishu. Tx: 736. Responsibilities include anti-desertification, water and soil conservation, forestry, and range management.

Other organizations:

National University of Somalia, Faculty of Agriculture, P.O. Box 801, Modadishu. T: 25035. Includes faculties in botany and range management; conducts anti-desertification studies.

SOUTH AFRICA

National government:

Department of Environment Affairs, Private Bag X447, Pretoria 0001

Department of Agriculture and Water Supply, Pretoria 0001

National Parks Board, P.O. Box 787, Pretoria 0001

Provincial governments:

The four provincial governments have important responsibilities for resource conservation. Information is available from the South African IUCN Secretariat.

Other organizations:

Africa Tree Center, P.O. Box 90, Plessislaer, Natal. T: (27 331) 20693. Founded 1978. A group led by black South Africans that works to combat soil erosion by tree-planting and public education.

Endangered Wildlife Trust, Private Bag X11, Parkview 2122

Foundation for Research Development (FRD), P.O. Box 395, Pretoria 0001. T: (27 12) 841-2879. Tx: 321312 sa. Fax: (27 12) 862856. C: NAVORS. Includes the South African ICSU Secretariat.

South African IUCN Secretariat, Ecosystem Programmes, Foundation for Research Development, P.O. Box 395, Pretoria 0001. Secretariat for some 17 IUCN member organizations in South Africa.

Southern African Nature Foundation, P.O. Box 456, Stellenbosch 7600. T: (27 2231) 72892.

Wildlife Society of Southern Africa, 100 Brand Road, Durban 4001

Worldwide Fund for Nature-South Africa, P.O. Box 456, Stellenbosch 7600. T: (27 2231) 72892. Affiliate of the World Wide Fund for Nature (WWF International), listed in Part 6.

SOUTH GEORGIA AND THE SOUTH SANDWICH ISLANDS

A British territory under jurisdisction of the Governor of the Falkland Islands, *which see.*

SPAIN

Government:

Ministerio de Obras Publicas y Urbanismo--Dirección General de Medio Ambiente (DGMA) (Ministry of Public Works and Urban Planning--General Directorate for the Environment), Paseo de la Castellana 67, E-28071 Madrid. T: (34 1) 233 49 00. Tx: 22325. Includes the Instituto Nacional para la Conservación de la Naturaleza (ICONA) (National Institute for Conservation of Nature).

Other organizations:

Asociación para el Estudio, Defensa y Protección de la Naturaleza (Association for the Study, Defense, and Protection of Nature) c/ Campomanes 13, Madrid 13

Consejo Superior de Investigaciones Científicas (Higher Council of Scientific Research), Serrano 117, E-28006 Madrid. T: (34 1) 261 98 00. Tx: 42182. Fax: (34 1) 411 30 77. ICSU national member.

Federación de Amigos de la Tierra (FAT) (Friends of the Earth Federation), Avenida Betanzos 55, 11.1, E-28025 Madrid. Affiliated with Friends of the Earth International, listed in Part 6.

Greenpeace Spain, Rodriquez San Pedro 58, 4 piso, E-28015 Madrid. National office of Greenpeace International, listed in Part 6.

Real Sociedad Española de Historia Natural (Royal Spanish Society of Natural History), Facultad de Ciencias Biológicas, Ciudad Universitaria, Madrid

Fondo Mundial para la Naturaleza-España (World Wide Fund for Nature-Spain), 6 Santa Engracia, E-Madrid 10. T: (34 1) 410 24 01. Affiliate of the World Wide Fund for Nature (WWF International), listed in Part 6.

SRI LANKA

Government:

Central Environmental Authority, Maligawatte New Town, Colombo 10. T: (94 1) 549455. Broad responsibilities, including policy recommendations, research, public education, long-range planning, and enforcement.

Natural Resources, Energy, and Science Authority of Sri Lanka, 47/5 Maitland Place, Colombo 7. T: (94 1) 596771. ICSU national member.

Ministry of Lands and Land Development, P.O. Box 512, Colombo 10

Ministry of State, Department of Wildlife Conservation, Transworks House, Lower Chatham Street, Colombo 1

Other organizations:

Ceylon Bird Club, P.O. Box 11, Colombo. T: (94 1) 20551. Tx: 21204. C: LANKABAUR. Founded 1935. Interested in natural history and environmental problems. [85]

Environmental Foundation Ltd. (EFL), 6 Boyd Place, Colombo 3. Founded 1981. Public interest law firm working on environmental issues.

Marga Institute, P.O. Box 601, Colombo. T: (94 1) 85186. Tx: 21642. Founded 1972. Multidisciplinary research and educational organization focused on improving socio-economic conditions in Sri Lanka and throughout the Third World. Interests include environmental and natural resource management.

Sri Lanka Environmental Congress, 335 Galle Road, Colombo 6. Founded 1986. Coordinates activities of some 120 NGOs.

Sri Lanka Parisara Ekabaddha Sangamaya (Sri Lanka Environmental Federation), 215 G-2/5 Park Road, Colombo 5. T: (94 1) 81519. Founded 1978. Coordinates work of environmental NGOs in Sri Lanka; advocacy and education. [85]

Wildlife and Nature Protection Society of Sri Lanka, Chaitiya Road, Marine Drive, Fort, Colombo 1. Founded 1894. T: (94 1) 25248.

SUDAN

Government:

Ministry of Agriculture. Includes:
■ Range and Pasture Administration, P.O. Box 2513, Khartoum. T: 75231. C: MWARID. Concerns include controlling desertification.
■ Soil Conservation, Land Use, and Water Programming Administration, P.O. Box 1942, Khartoum. T: 70059.
■ Wildlife Conservation and National Parks, P.O. Box 336, Khartoum. T: 76486. C: SAYADIN.

Ministry of Health, Occupational Health Department, P.O. Box 303, Khartoum. T: 80628. Concerns include pollution control.

National Council for Research, P.O. Box 2404, Khartoum. T: 70717. Tx: 22342. ICSU national member. Includes the National Committee for Environment, which coordinates the environment-related activities of governmental agencies.

Other organizations:

Agricultural Research Corporation, Forest Research Centre, P.O. Box 658, Soba. T: 221918.

Desertification and Drought Control Association, P.O. Box 2718, Khartoum. Founded 1986. Promotes tree-planting, agroforestry, soil conservation.

Environmentalists Society, Institute of Environmental Studies, University of Khartoum, Khartoum. T: 80993. Founded 1985. Academic and action research, public education, and tree-planting.

Renewable Energy Research Institute, Sudan Renewable Energy Project, P.O. Box 4032, Khartoum. Research and public education on renewable energy technology and agroforestry.

Sudan Environmental Conservation Society (SECS), Khartoum Zoological Gardens, P.O. Box 336, Khartoum. T: 76925. Broad interests; action research, lobbying, information, public education, reforestation.

University of Khartoum, Institute of Environmental Studies, P.O. Box 321, Khartoum. T: 80993.

Wildlife Research Centre, P.O. Box 16, El Mourada, Omdurman. T: 76925. Broad interest in resource and environmental management.

SURINAME

Government:

Foundation for Nature Protection in Surinam (STINASU), P.O. Box 436, Paramaribo. T: (597) 758-45, ext. 343541. Responsible for nature reserves. [85]

Other organizations:

Stichting voor een Schoon Suriname (SVSS) (Foundation for a Pure Suriname), P.O. Box 9166, Paramaribo

SVALBARD
Norwegian territory. No separate information available.

SWAZILAND

Government:

Ministry of Natural Resources, P.O. Box 57, Mbabane. T: (268) 23442.
Ministry of Health, P.O. Box 5, Mbabane. T: (268) 42431.

SWEDEN

Government:

National Swedish Environment Protection Board, P.O. Box 1302, S-171 25 Solna. T: (46 8) 799 10 00. Tx: 11131. Fax: (46 8) 29 23 82. Broad responsibilities for pollution control, waste management, nature protection, forests, and wildlife. Publishes English-language materials on Sweden's critical acid rain problem, including *Acid Magazine* and *Acidification Research in Sweden* (both irregular).

Swedish International Development Authority (SIDA), Box 342, S-11121 Stockholm. T: (46 8) 15 01 00. C: SIDA. Tx: 11450. Responsible for Sweden's bilateral development assistance program, which concentrates on certain countries in Africa, Central America, and South and Southeast Asia.

Swedish Agency for Research Cooperation with Developing Countries (SAREC), Birger Jarlsgatan 61, S-105 25 Stockholm. T: (46 8) 15 01 00. An independent agency that promotes research "which can support the developing countries in their efforts to achieve self-reliance and economic and social justice."

Commission for Research on Natural Resources, P.O. Box 6710, S-113 85 Stockholm. T: (46 8) 151580. Broad interests.

National Board of Fisheries, P.O. Box 2565, S-403 17 Gothenburg. T: (46 31) 63 03 00. Concerns include fisheries, water quality, and fresh- and saltwater ecosystems.

National Board of Forestry, S-551 83 Jönköping. T: (46 36) 16 94 00. Tx: 70358 sjn s.

National Board of Health and Welfare, S-106 30 Stockholm. T: (46 8) 783 30 00. Tx: 16773 nbhw s. Responsibilities include environmental health.

National Board of Occupational Safety and Health, S-171 84 Solna. T: (46 8) 730 90 00. Tx: 15816 arbsky s. Concerns include occupational environmental health.

National Board of Physical Planning and Building, P.O. Box 12513, S-102 29 Stockholm. T: (46 8) 737 55 00. Tx: 12841 havkom s. City and regional planning and land use.

National Chemicals Inspectorate, P.O. Box 1384, S-171 27 Solna. T: (46 8) 730 57 00. Control of toxic substances.

National Marine Resources Commission, P.O. Box 295, S-401 24 Gothenburg. T: (46 31) 15 60 70. Broad concerns with ocean and coastal affairs.

Other organizations:

Beijer Institute (International Institute for Energy, Related Resources, and the Human Environment), P.O. Box 50005, S-104 05S Stockholm. T: (46 8) 16 04 90. Tx: 17073. Conducts research in environmental policy, agroforestry, energy, environmental assessment, and resource management. Policy studies on the impacts of global climate change are a major focus.

Dag Hammarskjöld Foundation (DHF), Övre Slottsgatan 2, S-752 20 Uppsala. T: (46 18) 10 54 72. Tx: 76234. C: DHCENTRE. Founded 1962. Organizes invitational seminars and conferences on issues facing the Third World; publishes results in a journal, *Development Dialogue*. Has had a strong interest in environmental and natural resource problems, most recently in the impact of biotechnology on developing countries.

Greenpeace Sweden, Box 7183, S-402 34 Gothenburg. National office of Greenpeace International, listed in Part 6.

Institute for Environmentally Sound Technologies (IET), c/o Ambassador G. Svenson, Ministry of Foreign Affairs, Malmtorgsgatan 3, S-104 16 Stockholm. Tx: 10590. Founded 1988. Works to bring the concept of "ecotechnology" into the mainstream of industry and development.

Kungliga Vetenskapsakademien (Royal Academy of Sciences), P.O. Box 50005, S-104 05 Stockholm. T: (46 8) 15 04 30. Tx: 17073 royacad s. Fax: (46 8) 15 24 64. ICSU national member. Maintains an Environment Protection Committee.

Jordens Vänner (Friends of the Earth), Regeringsgatan 70C, S-111 39 Stockholm. Affiliated with Friends of the Earth International, listed in Part 6.

Miljöförbundet (Swedish Association of Environmental Groups), P.O. Box 64, S-150 13 Trosa. T: (46 31) 12 18 08.

Riksförbundet för Hembygdsvård (National Association for the Preservatio of Culture and Nature), P.O. Box 20031, S-104 60 Stockholm. T: (46 8) 23 31 50. Citizen advocacy group.

Svenska Naturskyddsföreningen (Swedish Society for the Conservation of Nature), P.O. Box 6400, S-113 82 Stockholm. T: (46 8) 15 15 50. Major citizens' association; broad interests.

Swedish NGO Secretariat on Acid Rain, c/o Miljövård, Vallgatan 22, S-411 16 Gothenburg. T: (46 31) 13 12 97. Public education on acid rain, its effects in Sweden, and control measures.

World Wide Fund for Nature-Sweden, Ulriksdals Slott, S-171 71 Solna. T: (46 8) 85 01 20. Affiliate of the World Wide Fund for Nature (WWF International), listed in Part 6.

SWITZERLAND

Federal government:

Bundesamt für Umweltschutz/Office Fédéral de la Protection de l'Environnement (Federal Office for Environmental Protection), CH-3003 Bern. T: (41 31) 61 93 23. Tx: 911191. Fax: (41 31) 619981. Responsibilities include water, air quality, and fisheries.

Office Fédéral des Forêts et de la Protection du Paysage (Federal Office of Forests and Landscape Protection), Laupenstrasse 20, C.P. 1987, CH-3001 Berne. Includes a Division for Nature Conservation and Protection.

Federal Department of Foreign Affairs, Directorate of Development Cooperation and Humanitarian Aid, Eigerstrasse 73, CH-3003 Bern. T: (41 31) 61 34 75.

Cantonal governments:

The governments of the cantons have important responsibilities for environmental protection and natural resource management.

Other organizations:

Fonds Mondial pour la Nature (WWF-Suisse) (World Wide Fund for Nature-Switzerland), Forrlibuckstrasse 66, Postfach 749, CH-8037 Zurich. T: (41 1) 44 20 44. Affiliate of the World Wide Fund for Nature (WWF International), listed in Part 6.

Greenpeace Switzerland, Müllerstrasse 37, Postfach 4927, CH-8022 Zurich. National Office of Greenpeace International, listed in Part 6.

Ligue Suisse pour la Protection de la Nature (Swiss League for Protection of Nature), C.P. 73, CH-4020 Basel. T: (41 61) 42 74 42. Major association.

Swiss Academy of Sciences, Hirschengraben 11, C.P. 2535, CH-3001 Berne. T: (41 31) 22 33 75. ICSU national member.

Swiss Center for Appropriate Technology (SKAT), Varnbüelstrasse 14, CH-9000 St. Gallen. T: (41 71) 233481. Tx: 881000 txk ch attn. skat. Founded 1978. Provides an inquiry service and consulting in appropriate technology for developing countries; also conducts research and AT projects. Subject areas include energy and power; water and sanitation; and agriculture, forestry, and fisheries. Pub: Catalogs of information sources; manuals; bookshop.

SYRIA

Government:

Ministry of State for Environmental Affairs, Government House, Damascus. T: (963 11) 22 66 00. Tx: 411930.

TAIWAN

Government:

Environmental Protection Agency, Taipei

Ministry of the Interior. Includes:
■ National Park Department, 194, Section 3, Peihsin Road, Hsintein City, Taipei Hsien. T: (886 2) 9157610.

Other organizations:

Academy of Science, 128 Yen Chiu Yuan Road, Section 2, Nankang, Taipei 11529. ICSU national member. Includes the National Scientific Committee on Problems of the Environment.

Environmental Protection Society of the Republic of China, 10F 201, Back, Tung-Hua N Road, Taipei. T: (886 2) 7122083. Founded 1974. Research and public information. [83]

TANZANIA

Government:

Ministry of Lands, Housing, and Urban Development--National Environment Management Council, P.O. Box 20671, Dar es Salaam. T: (255 51) 21241. The Council is a small policy and coordination unit with broad responsibilities for resource and environmental matters.

Ministry of Natural Resources and Tourism, P.O. Box 9372, Dar es Salaam. T: (255 51) 27271. Includes:
■ Tanzania National Parks, P.O. Box 3134, Arusha. T: 3471.

Other organizations:

Chama cha Kuendeleza Mazingira na Viumbe Hai Tanzania (KAMAVITA) (Tanzanian Environmental Society) (TESO), P.O. Box 1309, Dar es Salaam. Founded 1985. Broad interests; research, public education, lobbying, and consulting. Affiliated with Friends of the Earth International, listed in Part 5.

THAILAND

Government:

National Environment Board, Soi Prachasumpun 4, Rama VI Road, Bangkok 10400. T: (66 2) 278-5467. Tx: 20838 moste. C: NEB. Policy development and coordination of government activities.

Department of Fisheries, Bangkok

Royal Forest Department, Phaholyothin Road, Bangkhen, Bangkok 10900. Includes a Wildlife Conservation Division and a National Park Division.

Royal Irrigation Department, Bangkok

Other organizations:

Ecological Society of Thailand, c/o Faculty of Environmental and Resource Studies, Mahidol University, R.S. Hotel, Larn Luang Road, Bangkok. T: (66 2) 281-8109. Research, education, and public information.

National Research Council of Thailand, c/o Research Project and Coordination Division, 196 Phahonyothin Road, Bangkhen, Bangkok 10900. T: (66 2) 579-2284. Tx: 82213 narecou th. ICSU national member.

Wildlife Fund Thailand, 255 Soi Asoke, Sukhumvit 21, Bangkok 10110. T: (66 2) 258 3004. Associate organization of the World Wide Fund for Nature (WWF International), listed in Part 5.

TOGO

Government:

Ministère de l'Environnement et du Tourisme (Ministry of Environment and Tourism), B.P. 355, Lomé

Ministère de l'Aménagement Rural (Ministry of Rural Planning), B.P. 1263, Lomé. T: (228) 21 33 90. Tx: 5268. Includes responsibility for forests and water matters.

Other organizations:

Conseil des Organismes Non Gouvernementaux en Activité au Togo (CONGAT) (Council of Non-Governmental Organizations Operating in Togo), B.P. 1857, Lomé. T: (228) 212489. Tx: 5327 congat. Founded 1976; 23 member groups. Education and development projects include soil conservation, forestry, watershed management, and environmental health.

TOKELAU
A New Zealand territory.

Government:

Office for Tokelau Affairs, Tokelau. Represents the New Zealand Ministry of Foreign Affairs.

TONGA

Government:

Ministry of Agriculture, Forests, and Fisheries, P.O. Box 14, Nuku'alofa

TRINIDAD AND TOBAGO

Government:

Ministry of Food Production, Marine Exploitation, Forestry, and Environment, Long Circular Road, St. James, Port-of-Spain. T: (1 809) 622-3217.

Ministry of Planning and Reconstruction, Town and Country Planning Department, Port-of-Spain

Other organizations:

Pointe-à-Pierre Wild Fowl Trust, 42 Sandown Road, Goodwood Park, Pt. Cumana. Operates reserve, research center, educational activities; works to protect wildlife throughout country.

TUNISIA

Government:

Ministère de l'Agriculture et de l'Environnement (Ministry of Agriculture and the Environment), 30 rue Alain Savary, Tunis. Includes:

■ Direction des Forêts (Directorate of Forests).
T: (216 1) 282-681.
■ Direction des Pêches (Directorate of Fisheries).
T: (216 1) 286-277.
■ Direction des Etudes et Grands Travaux Hydrauliques (Directorate of Water Studies and Major Works). T: (216 1) 280-647.

Ministere de l'Education, de l'Enseignement et de la Recherche Scientifique--Institut National de Recherche Scientifique et Technique (INRST) (Ministry of Education and Scientific Research--National Institute of Scientific and Technological Research), B.P. 95, Hammam-Lif. T: (216 3) 29 10 44. Research program focuses on natural resources and energy.

Other organizations:

Association Tunisienne pour la Protection de la Nature et de l'Environnement (Tunisian Association for Protection of Nature and the Environment), 12 rue Tantaoui el Jawhari el Omrane, Tunis 1005. T: (216 1) 288141. Founded 197. Focus is on student and public education on soils, forests, and wildlife.

Faculté des Sciences de Tunis, Campus Universitaire, Le Belvédère, Tunis 1060. T: (216 1) 51 10 20. Tx: 13162 facsit hn. ICSU national member.

Institut des Regions Arides (Institute of Arid Regions), Elfje, Medenine. T: (216 5) 40435. Program includes studies in resource management.

TURKEY

Government:

Prime Ministry, General Directorate of Environment, Atatürk Bulvari 143, Bakanliklar/Ankara. T: (90 41) 117 4455. Tx: 1844620. Fax: (90 41) 117 7971. Ministry of Agriculture, Forestry, and Rural Affairs. Includes:
■ General Directorate of Forestry, Ankara. Includes the Department of National Parks and Wildlife.

Other organizations:

Scientific and Technical Research Council of Turkey, Atatürk Bulvari Emek Is Hani Kat 15 Kizilay, Ankara. T: (90 41) 117 7123. Tx: 43186 btak tr. ICSU national member.

Dogal Hayati Koruma Dernegi (Turkish Society for the Protection of Wildlife), P.K. 18, Bebek, Istanbul. T: (90 1) 65 21 22.

Türkiye Cevre sorunlari Vakfi (Turkish Foundation for Environmental Problems), Kennedy Caddesi 33/7, Ankara. T: (90 41) 25 55 08.

Türkiye Tabiatini Koruma Dernegi (Turkish Association for the Conservation of Nature and Natural Resources), Menekse Sokak 29/4, Kizilay, Ankara. T: (90 41) 17 18 70. Major association.

TURKS AND CAICOS ISLANDS
British colony.

Government:

Ministry of Natural Resources, Cockburn Town, Grand Turk. Tx: 212.

TUVALU

Government:

Ministry for Commerce and Natural Resources, Vaiaku, Funafuti

UGANDA

Government:

Department of Town and Regional Planning, P.O. Box 1911, Kampala. T: (256 41) 34350. C: PLANNING.

Game Department, P.O. Box 4, Entebbe. T: (256 42) 20520. C: GAME. Wildlife management.

Uganda National Parks, 3 Shimoni Road, P.O. Box 3530, Kampala

National Water and Sewerage Corporation, P.O. Box 7053, Kampala. T: (256 41) 56761.

Other organizations:

Joint Energy and Environment Projects (JEEP), P.O. Box 1684, Jinja. T: (256 43) 20054. Tx: 64066 ugrain. Founded 1983. Action and public education; focuses on conservation and provision of fuelwood through cookstove and kiln development and reforestation; soil and water conservation.

Makerere University, Faculty of Agriculture and Forestry, P.O. Box 7062, Kampala. T: (256 41) 242271. Includes programs in forestry and soil science.

Uganda Nature Conservation Society (UNCS), P.O. Box 2259, Kampala. T: (256 41) 271556. Founded 1978. Research, training, and public education in forestry, pollution control, and water and soil conservation.

Wildlife Clubs of Uganda, P.O. Box 4596, Kampala. T: (256 41) 32971, ext. 19. Founded 1975; 252 member clubs with 20,000 members. Student and public education and lobbying; general conservation interests.

UNION OF SOVIET SOCIALIST REPUBLICS

Union Government:

USSR State Committee for Environmental Protection, Moscow. Established 1988. Coordinates governmental action; responsible for international relations in environmental affairs.

USSR State Committee for Nature Conservation (Goskompriroda), Nezhdanova ul. 11, 103009 Moscow

USSR State Committee for Forests, ul. Lesteva 18, Moscow. T: (7 95) 234 36 76.

Ministry of Agriculture and Tractor-Machine Building, Kuznetsky most 21/5, Moscow. T: (7 95) 925 11 32. Includes:
■ Main Administration of Nature Conservation, Game Preserves, Forestry, and Hunting, Orlikov per. 1-11, 107139 Moscow

Ministry of Atomic Energy, Staromonetny per. 26, Moscow

Ministry of Fisheries, Rozhdestvensky bul. 12, Moscow. T: (7 95) 923 76 34.

Ministry of the Forest Industry, Telegrapny per. 1, Moscow. T: (7 95) 208 00 56.

Ministry of Health, Rakhmanovsky per., Moscow. T: (7 95) 265 91 09.

Ministry of Land Reform and Water Resources, Novobasmannaya ul. 10, Moscow. T: (9 95) 265 91 09.

Republic governments:

The 15 constituent republics of the USSR are responsible for some important aspects of environmental protection and natural resource management.

Other organizations:

Academy of Sciences of the USSR, Leninsky prospekt 14, 117901 Moscow B-71. T: (7 95) 232 29 10. Tx: 411964. Includes:
■ Institute of State and Law, Sector on Environmental Law, 10 Frunze Street, Moscow
■ Vsesoyuznyi Naucho-issledovatel'ski Institut Okhrany Prirody i Zapovednogo Dela (All-Union Scientific Research Institute for Nature Conservation and Reserves), Znamenskoye-Sadki, 142790 P/O VILR, Leninskii raion, Moskovskaya Oblast M-628. Applied research in nature and natural resource conservation; maintains a computerized database of all natural areas in the USSR and is a major repository for research material.
■ Institute of Soil Science and Photosynthesis, 142292 Puschino, Moscow Region. Concerns include soil conservation and land reclamation.

■ Institut Evolyutsionnoi Morfologii i Ekologii Zhivotnykh Imeni A.M. Severtsova (All-Union Severtsov Institute of Evolutionary Animal Morphology and Ecology), Leninsky prospekt 33, 117071 Moscow V-71. Concerns include research on protection of natural areas.
■ Section of Chemistry, Chemical Technology, and Biology, Leninsky prospekt 14, 117901 Moscow. Includes the Commission on Conservation of Natural Waters.
■ Section of Earth Sciences, Leninsky prospekt 14, 117901 Moscow. Includes the Institute of Water Problems, Institute of Lake Conservation, and the Scientific Council on Caspian Sea Study.

Academy of Sciences of the Turkmen SSR, Desert Institute, Gogol Street 15, 744000 Ashkhabad, Turkmen SSR. Tx: 02 228116. Institute program includes research in desert natural resources.

Association for the Support of Ecological Initiatives, Apt. 111-19, Lomonosovski prospekt, Moscow

Eesti Roheline Liikkumine (Estonian Green Movement), P.O. Box 3207, 200080 Tallinn, Estonian SSR. Founded 1988. Popular movement for environmental protection in the Estonian Republic.
International Foundation for the Survival and Development of Humanity (IF). *See* listing in Part 5.

Rigas Ekologiskas Klubs (Riga Ecological Club), kr. Barona 4, 226050 Riga, Latvian SSR. Citizens' group in the capital of Latvia.

USSR Research Institute on Nature Conservation and Reserves, 113628 Moscow

VAK Environment Protection Club/The Greens of Latvia, c/o Liepajan Pedagogical Institute, Klaipedas 68-7, 229700 Liepaja, Latvian SSR. Focuses on pollution and nuclear power.

Vserossiiskoe Obshchestvo Okhrany Prirody (All-Russian Society for Nature Conservation), Kuibyshevskii prospekt 3, 103012 Moscow L-12. Founded 1924. Citizens' organization with a large membership in the Russian Republic; focuses largely on environmental education.
Zelenyi Swit (Green World), ul. Belgorodskaya 8, Apt. 55, 252137 Kiev, Ukrainian SSR. Founded 1988. Attached to the Ukrainian Peace Committee campaign against nuclear power plants. Promotes protection of nature.

UNITED ARAB EMIRATES

Government:

Higher Environmental Committee, c/o Ministry of Health, P.O. Box 1853, Dubai. T: (971 4) 23 30 21. Tx: 45678. Chaired by the Minister of Health. Conducts studies and makes policy recommendations; coordinates government activities.

Ministry of Agriculture and Fisheries, P.O. Box 1509, Dubai. Includes:
■ Arid Land Research Center, Sadiyat. Research in water and agricultural problems.

Ministry of Electricity and Water Resources, P.O. Box 629, Dubai

Abu Dhabi Fund for Arab Economic Development, P.O. Box 814, Abu Dhabi. T: (971) 82 2865. Tx: 22287 ah.

UNITED KINGDOM
Including adjacent islands. *See also* Bermuda, Cayman Islands, Falkland Islands (Islas Malvinas), Gibraltar, Hong Kong, Pitcairn Island, St. Helena and Dependencies, South Georgia and the South Sandwich Islands; Turks and Caicos Islands; and Virgin Isloands (British).

Directories: *Directory for the Environment: Organisations in Britain and Ireland* (Routledge and Kegan Paul, 11 New Fetter Lane, London EC4P 4EE, second edition 1986) describes some 1,400 governmental and private organizations.

Government:

Ministry of Agriculture, Fisheries, and Food (MAFF), Whitehall Place, London SW1A 2HH. T: (44 1) 233-3000. Responsible for agriculture and fisheries in England. There are separate agencies for Wales (see Welsh Office) and Scotland and Northern Ireland, listed below. Includes:
■ Royal Botanic Gardens, Kew, Richmond, Surrey TW9 3AB. T: (44 1) 940 1171. Tx: 296694 kewgar. C: KEWGAR. Established 1841. Major world center for the study of plant life; houses the Threatened Plants Unit of the IUCN World Conservation Monitoring Centre.

Department of Agriculture and Fisheries for Scotland (DAFS), 50 Gorgie Road, Edinburgh EH11 3AW. T: (44 31) 443 4020.

Department of Agriculture for Northern Ireland, Dundonald House, Upper Newtownards Road, Belfast, Northern Ireland BT4 3SB.

Department of Employment (DE), Caxton House, Tothill Street, London SW1H 9NF. T: (44 1) 213 3000. Concerns include air pollution, noise, and toxic substances in workplaces.

Department of Energy (DEn), Thames House South, Millbank, London SW1P 4QJ. T: (44 1) 211 3000. Broad responsibilities for energy, including offshore oil and gas and atomic energy.

Department of the Environment (DoE), 2 Marsham Street, London SW1P 3EB. T: (44 1) 212 3434. Tx: 2221. Fax: (44 1) 212 6635. The key environmental agency in the UK. Responsibilities environmental protection, town

and country planning, water resources, and rural conservation.

Department of the Environment for Northern Ireland, Stormont, Belfast, Northern Ireland BT4 3SS. T: (44 232) 63210. Broad responsibilities for environmental protection and natural resource management in Northern Ireland.

Scottish Development Department, New St. Andrew's House, St. James Centre, Edinburgh EH1 3SZ. T: (44 31) 556 8400. Responsibilities include environmental protection, water resources, and town and country planning in Scotland.
Welsh Development Agency (WDA), Treforest Industrial Estate, Pontypridd, Wales CF37 5UT. T: (44 44385) 2666. Responsibilities include reclaiming derelict land and otherwise improving the environment in Wales.

Welsh Office, Crown Buildings, Cathays Park, Cardiff, Wales CF1 3NQ. T: (44 222) 825111. Responsibilities include environmental protection, agriculture, town and country planning, and natural resource management in Wales.

Department of Transport (DTp), 2 Marsham Street, London SW1P 3EB. T: (44 1) 212 3434. Concerns include transportation planning and marine pollution.

Countryside Commission, John Dower House, Crescent Place, Cheltenham, Glos. GL50 3RA. T: (44 242) 521381. Works to conserve rural landscapes and develop and improve recreational facilities in the countryside in England and Wales. There is a separate Countryside Commission for Scotland.

Department of Education and Science. Includes:
■ Natural Environment Research Council (NERC), Plaris House, North Star Avenue, Swindon, Wiltshire SN2 1EU. T: (44 793) 40101. Carries out scientific research related to the natural environment and its resources; includes the following (at various locations): British Antarctic Survey, British Geological Survey, Institute for Marine Environmental Research, Institute of Hydrology, Institute of Marine Biochemistry, Institute of Oceanographic Sciences, Institute of Terrestrial Ecology, Sea Mammal Research Unit, and Unit of Comparative Plant Ecology.

Forestry Commission, 231 Corstorphine Road, Edinburgh EH12 7AT. T: (44 31) 334 0303. Responsible for forestry matters in England, Scotland, and Wales.

Health and Safety Executive (HSE), 1 Chepstow Place, Westbourne Grove, London W2 4TF. T: (44 1) 229 3456, ext. 6721. Responsibilities include protection from workplace hazards. Operates in England, Scotland, and Wales (see next entry for Northern Ireland). Includes H.M. Nuclear Installations Inspectorate.
Health and Safety Agency for Northern Ireland

(HSA), Canada House, 22 North Street, Belfast, Northern Ireland BT1 1NW. T: (44 232) 243249.

National Radiological Protection Board (NRPB), Chilton, Didcot, Oxon. OX11 0RQ. T: (44 235) 831600. Research and advice.

Nature Conservancy Council (NCC), Northminster House, Northminster Road, Peterborough, Cambridgeshire PE1 1UA. T: (44 733) 40345. Responsible for conservation of flora, fauna, and geological and physiographical features throughout Great Britain. Establishes and manages National Nature Reserves and other protected areas.

Nature Reserves Committee (Northern Ireland), Hut 6, Castle Grounds, Stormont, Belfast, Northern Ireland BT4 3ST. T: (44 232) 768716. Advises the government on nature conservation in Northern Ireland.

Overseas Development Administration (ODA), Eland House, Stag Place, London SW1E 5DH. T: (44 1) 213 3000. Provides development assistance overseas. Includes:
■ Land Resources Development Centre, Tolworth Tower, Surbiton, Surrey KT6 7DT. T: (44 1) 399 5281 Assists developing countries in assessment of land resources; training courses; information services.

Royal Commission on Environmental Pollution (RCEP), Church House, Great Smith Street, London SW1P 3BL. T: (44 1) 212 8620. Broad authority to inquire into and report independently on environmental matters, both in the UK and internationally.

Other organizations:

Agricultural and Food Research Council (AFRC), 160 Great Portland Street, London W1N 6DT. T: (44 1) 580-6655. Quasi-governmental body; scientific research related to agriculture.

Association for the Reduction of Aircraft Noise, 11 First Street, London SW3 2LB. T: (44 1) 584-1848.

Association of Professional Foresters (APF), Brokerswood House, Brokerswood, Westbury, Wiltshire BA13 4EH. T: (44 373) 822238.

Bio-Dynamic Agricultural Association (BDAA), Woodman Lane, Clent, Stourbridge, West Midlands DY9 9PX. T: (44 562) 884933. Promotes the "bio-dynamic gardening" originated by Rudolf Steiner in 1924, which emphasizes working with the formative forces active in nature, using natural preparations to enhance the vitality of soil and plants.

British Association for Shooting and Conservation, Marford Mill, Rossett, Wrexham, Clwyd, Wales LL12 0HL. T: (44 244) 570881. Hunters' organization that promotes conservation.

British Association of Nature Conservationists (BANC), Rectory Farm, Stanton St. John, Oxford OX9 1HF. T: (44 86735) 214. Forum for exchange of views on all aspects of nature conservation in seminars and in a quarterly journal, *Ecos*.

British Grassland Society (BGS), Grassland Research Institute, Hurley, Maidenhead, Berkshire SL6 5LR. T: (44 62882) 3626. Scientific society.

British Organic Farmers (BOF), Leggatts Park, Potters Bar, Hertfordshire EN6 1NZ. T: (44 707) 58561. Promotes organic agriculture.

British Waterfowl Association, 25 Dale Street, Haltwhistle, Northumberland NE49 9QB. T: (44 498) 21176. Purposes include conservation of waterfowl.

Buddhist Ecology Network (BecoN), 27 Devonshore Road, Bristol, Avon BS6 7NG. Forum for communication between Buddhists and environmentalists.

Business and Industry Panel for the Environment, Saxley Hill Barn, Meath Green Lane, Horley, Surrey RH6 8JA. T: (44 2934) 4903. Promotes and recognizes environmental responsibility on the part of businesses.

Centre for Economic and Environmental Development (CEED), 10 Belgrave Square, London SW1X 8PH. T: (44 1) 245 6440. Works to support and monitor implementation of the Conservation and Development Programme for the UK, which is the British response to the IUCN World Conservation Strategy. "The only NGO in the UK specifically devoted to reconciling the needs of both economic performance and environmental protection."

Centre for World Development Education (CWDE), 128 Buckingham Palace Road, London SW1W 9SH. T: (44 1) 730 8332. Teacher training and public education in the UK on Third-World problems and Britain's interdependence with developing countries.

Christian Ecology Group (CEG), 58 Quest Hills Road, Malvern, Worcestershire WR14 1RW. T: (44 6845) 2630. Activist and educational group that seeks to spread ecological insights among Christians and spread Christian insights in the Green movement.

Civic Trust, 17 Carlton House Terrace, London SW1Y 5AW. T: (44 1) 930 0914. Works in cooperation with some 1,000 local amenity societies throughout the UK to stimulate action for conservation and foster high standards of planning, design, and building.

Council for Environmental Conservation, 80 York Way, London N1 9AJ

Ecology Party, 36-38 Clapham Road, London SW9 0JQ. T: (44 1) 735 2485. Political party; the Green party of the UK. Over 250 local branches.

Ecoropa, Crickhowell, Powys, Wales NP8 1TA. T: (44 873) 810758. Promotes an ecological consciousness and a decentralized and regionalized Europe; facilitates communication among "Green" groups in Europe.

Farm and Food Society, 4 Willifield Way, London NW11 7XT. T: (44 1) 455 0634. Purposes include promoting sustainable agriculture.

Fauna and Flora Preservation Society (FFPS), 79-83 North Street, Brighton BN1 1ZA. T: (44 273) 820445. Founded 1903. Major wildlife preservation organization which works internationally in such areas as trade in endangered species, promotion of captive breeding, and protection of mountain gorillas. The Queen is Patron; officers have included such leading figures as Sir Peter Scott and Sir David Attenborough. Pub: *Oryx,* quarterly. Has established a branch in Boston, Massachusetts, to develop a U.S. membership.

Findhorn Foundation, The Park, Forres, Grampian, Scotland IV36 0TZ. T: (44 309) 30311. Works to foster a deeper understanding of man's relationship to nature through spiritually-oriented educational and work projects. Sponsors "Trees for Life" campaign, focused on tropical forests.

Fisheries Society of the British Isles, c/o Marine Biology Unit, CEGB, Fawley, Southampton SO4 1TW. Scientific society.

Friends of the Earth (FoE), 377 City Road, London EC1V 1NA (or 26-28 Underwood Street, London N1 7JQ). T: (44 1) 837 0731. Lobbying and public education; broad interests, including energy, pollution, transportation, wildlife, and countryside preservation issues. Some 250 local groups throughout England and Wales.

Friends of the Earth (Scotland), 53 George IV Bridge, Edinburgh EH1 1EJ. T: (44 31) 225 6906. Has some 15 local groups in Scotland. Grassland Research Institute, Hurley, Maidenhead, Berkshire SL6 5LR. T: (44 62882) 3631. Major program of research on management of grasslands.

Green Alliance, 60 Chandos Place, London WC2N 4HG. T: (44 1) 836 0341. Works to build a constituency within each political party to promote an ecological perspective; develops and analyzes the political dimensions of the environmental movement.

Green Deserts (GD), Geoff's House, Rougham, Bury St. Edmunds, Suffolk 1P30 9LY. T: (44 359) 70265. Promotes reclamation projects in arid zones and wasted areas. Public education; tree-planting in the Sudan.

Greenpeace U.K., 30-31 Islington Green, 3rd Floor, London N1 8XE. National office of Greenpeace International, listed in Part 5. Main focus is on wildlife protection.

Greenpeace (London), 6 Endsleigh Street, London WC1H 0DX. T: (44 1) 387-5370. Not connected to Greenpeace International.

Groundwork Foundation, 27 Mawdsley Street, Bolton, Lancashire BL1 1N. T: (44 204) 35155. Established by the Countryside Commission; links public, business, and voluntary interests to improve the remnant countryside around towns and cities.

Henry Doubleday Research Association (HDRA), National Centre for Organic Gardening, Ryton-on-Dunsmore, Coventry. Promotes organic gardening and agriculture.

Inland Waterways Protection Society, The Cottage, 69 Ivy Road, Macclesfield, Cheshire SK11 8QN. T: (44 625) 23595. Preservation and restoration of the UK's canal system.

Institute of Chartered Foresters (ICF), 22 Walker Street, Edinburgh EH3 7HR. T: (1 31) 225 2705. Professional society.

Institute of Development Studies (IDS), University of Sussex, Brighton BN1 9RE, England. T: (44 273) 606261. Tx: 877997 IDS BTN G. Cable: Development Brighton. Major center for research and short-term and postgraduate education in development; strong interest in environmental aspects of rural development.

Institute of Water Pollution Control, Ledson House, 53 London Road, Maidstone, Kent ME16 8JH. T: (44 0622) 62034. Professional association.

Institution of Environmental Sciences (IES), 14 Princes Gate, Hyde Park, London SW7 1PU. Professional association.

Intermediate Technology Development Group (ITDG), 9 King St., London WC2E 8HW, England. Alternative development projects in the Third World.

International Centre for Conservation Education (ICCE), Greenfield House, Guiting Power, Glos. GL54 5TZ. T: (44 4515) 549. Tx: 43670 eurocp g. Founded 1986 "to consolidate and expand work carried out since 1975 by the WWF/IUCN International Education Project." Provides advisory and consulting services on establishment and management of national conservation education programs; operates training courses for national of developing countries; produces audio-visual and printed educational materials; and designs and equips mobile conservation units to be shipped to developing countries. Projects are carried out in cooperation with international organizations and groups in many countries. ICCE is also the operational base for the WWF/IUCN International Education Project, Elsa Wild Animal Appeal (which was founded by the late Joy Adamson to support conservation work in East Africa), and the Wildlife Brass Rubbing Scheme.

International Society for the Prevention of Water Pollution, Little Orchard, Bentworth, Alton GU34 5RB. T: (44 420) 62225. Promotes research; public education.

Joint Committee for the Conservation of British Insects (JCCBI), c/o Institute of Terrestrial Ecology, Furzebrook Research Station, Wareham, Dorset BH20 5AS. T: (44 9295) 51518. Research; surveys of species; exchange of information.

Keep Britain Tidy Group (KBTG), Bostel House, 37 West Street, Brighton BN1 2RE. T: (44 273) 23585. Prevention and control of litter, mainly through public information and education.

Landscape Institute, 12 Carlton House Terrace, London SW1Y 5AH. T: (44 1) 839 4044. Founded 1929. The professional body for landscape architects, managers, and scientists in the UK.

Liberal Ecology Group (LEG), 77 Dresden Road, London N19 3BG. Works to encourage an environmental perspective in the Liberal Party.

London Green Belt Council, 52 Sharp's Lane, Ruislip, London HA4 7JQ. T: (44 8956) 34121. Protection of the Green Belt surrounding London.

London Wildlife Trust, 1 Thorpe Close, London W10 5XL. T: (44 1) 968 5368. Campaigns to protect natural areas and wildlife habitat within the Greater London area.

Marine Biological Association of the United Kingdom (MBA), The Laboratory, Citadel Hill, Plymouth, Devon PL1 2PB. T: (44 752) 21761. Promotes research; operates a Marine Pollution Information Centre.

Marine Conservation Society (MCS), 4 Gloucester Road, Ross-on-Wye, Herefordshire HR9 5BU. T: (44 989) 66017. Expeditions, courses, research, conferences, and lobbying.

National Association for Environmental Education (NAEE), West Midlands College of Higher Education, Gorway, Walsall, West Midlands WS1 3BD. T: (44 922) 31200. Promotes environmental education at all levels.

National Council for the Conservation of Plants and Gardens (NCCPG), c/o Royal Horticultural Gardens, Wisley, Woking, Surrey GU23 6QB. T: (44 483) 224234. Conservation of British gardens and garden plants.

National Energy Efficiency Forum (NEEF), 99 Midland Road, London NW1 2AH. T: (44 1) 387 4393. Exchange of information among groups concerned with energy policy, particularly energy conservation.

National Federation of Zoological Gardens of Great Britain and Ireland, c/o Zoological Gardens, Regent's Park, London NW1 4RY. T: (44 1) 586 0230. Has a Conservation and Animal Management Committee.

National Society for Clean Air (NSCA), 136 North Street, Brighton BN1 1RG. T: (44 273) 26313. Research and education on air pollution and noise control.

National Trust for Places of Historic Interest or Natural Beauty, 36 Queen Anne's Gate, London SW1H 9AS. T: (44 1) 222 9251. The National Trust owns and protects large areas of countryside and unspoiled coastline, as well as numerous historic houses. Nearly 1.2 million members.

Noise Abatement Society, P.O. Box 8, Bromley, Kent BR2 0UH. T: (44 1) 460 3146. Campaigns against excessive and unnecessary noise.

Open Spaces Society (OSS), 25A Bell Street, Henley-on-Thames, Oxon. RG9 2BA. T: (44 491) 573535. Works to protect common land, village greens, open spaces, and public paths through lobbying, advice to government, and land ownership.

Overseas Development Institute (ODI), Regent's College, Inner Circle, Regent's Park, London NW1 4NS. T: (44 1) 487 7413. Tx: 265451, quoting MAG 100474. Fax: (44 1) 487 7590. Founded 1960. Promotes "wise action" in the field of overseas development through research, discussion, and public education. Has a strong interest in environment-related development problems, including forestry and water resources. The Agricultural Administration Unit digests the findings of research in pastoral development, social forestry, and irrigation management and disseminates them to a network of interested professionals around the world.

Pedestrians Association, 1 Wandsworth Road, London SW8 2LJ. T: (44 1) 735 3270. Promotes the rights and mobility of those on foot.

People's Trust for Endangered Species, Hamble House, Meadrow, Godalming, Surrey GU7 3JX. T: (44 4868) 24848. Raises funds through direct-appeal letters; supports conservation projects.

Permaculture Association, P.O. Box 500, 8 Elm Avenue, Nottingham NG3 4GF. Promotes design and creation of productive landscapes for food, shelter, raw materials, and wildlife, which require a minimum of human intervention.

Population Concern, 231 Tottenham Court Road, London W1P 0HX. T: (44 1) 631 1546. Public education and fund-raising for population programs worldwide.

Professional Institutions Council for Conservation (PICC), 12 Great George Street, Parliament Square, London SW1P 3AD. T: (44 1) 222 7000. Liaison among professions concerned with planning, management, and development of natural resources; promotes ideas of conservation in these professions.

Ramblers' Association, 1-5 Wandsworth Road, London SW8 2LJ. T: (44 1) 582 6878. Major organization of ramblers (hikers); works to protect footpaths (trails) and access to open country, and defends outstanding landscapes.
Royal Forestry Society of England, Wales, and Northern Ireland, 102 High Street, Tring, Herts. HP23 4AH. T: (44 44282) 2028. Educational.

Royal Scottish Forestry Society, 1 Rothsay Terrace, Edinburgh EH3 7UP. T: (44 31) 225 1300. Educational.

Royal Society, 6 Carlton House Terrace, London SW1Y 5AG. T: (44 1) 839 5561. Tx: 917876. Learned society with broad scientific interests. ICSU national member.

Royal Society for Nature Conservation (RSNC), The Green, Nettleham, Lincoln LN2 2NR. T: (44 522) 752326. The national association of 46 regional Nature Conservation Trusts. Acquires and maintains nature reserves; works with landowners; education of youth and the general public.

Royal Society for the Protection of Birds (RSPB), The Lodge, Sandy, Beds. SG19 2DL. T: (44 767) 80551. Research; wildlife reserve acquisition and management; public education.

Royal Town Planning Institute (RTPI), 26 Portland Place, London W1N 4BE. T: (44 1) 636 9107. Professional society.

Sacred Trees Trust (STT), 31 Kings Avenue, Leeds LS6 1QP. T: (44 532) 459219. Founded 1983. Fosters the spiritual and metaphysical appreciation of indigenous broadleaved trees in the UK; works to reinstate ancient groves and locate and preserve legendary "Great Trees."

Schumacher Society, Ford House, Hartland, Bideford, Devon EX39 6EE. T: (44 2374) 293. Promotes a decentralized, ecological society according to the ideas of the late E.F. Schumacher, author of *Small is Beautiful*.

Scott Polar Research Institute, Lensfield Road, Cambridge CB2 1ER. T: (44 223) 36541. A leading center of research on polar zones.

Socialist Environment and Resources Association (SERA), 9 Poland Street, London W1V 3DG. T: (44 1) 439 3749. Formulates socialist policies on the environment; promotes environmental concerns within the political left.

Society Against Violation of the Environment (SAVE), 40 Kelvingrove Street, Glasgow G3 7RZ. T: (44 41) 332 4903. Formerly Sea Shepherd Fund. Activist group; concerns include marine wildlife and toxic waste.

Society for Radiological Protection (SRP), c/o NRPB, Chilton, Didcot, Oxon. OX11 0RQ. T: (44 235) 831600, ext. 348. Professional society.

Soil and Water Management Association (SaWMA), 22 Edgerton Grove Road, Huddersfield HD1 5QX. T: (44 484) 29417. Educational.

Soil Association, Walnut Tree Manor, Haughley, Stowmarket, Suffolk 1P14 3RS. T: (44 44970) 235. Promotes organic farming; discourages use of pesticides.

Survival International, 29 Craven Street, London WC2N 5NT. T: (44 1) 839 3267. Works to defend the rights of tribal peoples worldwide and their use of traditional lands.

Television Trust for the Environment (TVE), 46 Charlotte Street, London W1P 1LX. T: (44 1) 637 4602. Tx: 291721. Fax: (44 1) 580 7780. An "editorially-independent" television distribution service for new films on development and the environment, "concerned to promote issues, not organizations." Serves TV stations in the Third World free of charge; programs originate in many countries. Works in collaboration with UNEP, WWF, and other organizations.

Town and Country Planning Association (TCPA), 17 Carlton House Terrace, London SW1Y 5AS. T: (44 1) 930 8903. Campaigns for more effective planning and environmental protection.

UK National Committee for IUCN, c/o Nature Conservancy Council, Northminster House, Northminster Road, Peterborough, Cambridgeshire PE1 1UA. T: (44 733) 40345. Founded 1975. Coordinates the international work of IUCN member organizations in the UK. Pub: *The British Contribution to IUCN's Conservation Programme 1985-1987* (1988).

University College of North Wales, Centre for Arid Zone Studies, Gwynedd, Wales. T: (44 24) 835 1151, ext. 2345. Tx: 61100. Program includes research in environmental management, including field studies, focused on Africa and West Asia.

University of Aberdeen, Centre for Environmental Management and Planning (CEMP), 48 College Bounds, Aberdeen, Scotland AB9 1FX. T: (44 224) 272480. Tx: 73458 uniabn g. Fax: (44 224) 467658. A major center for consulting and training in environmental management, known especially for its work in environmental impact assessment.

University of East Anglia, Climatic Research Unit, Norwich NR4 7TJ. A leading center for the analysis of global climate change.

University of Oxford, Oxford Forestry Institute (OFI), South Parks Road, Oxford OX1 3RB. T: (44 865) 511431. Major center for education and research in forestry worldwide, with a strong interest in tropical forests.

Wadebridge Ecological Centre, Worthyvale Manor Farm, Camelford, Cornwall PL32 9TT. T: (44 840) 212711. Publishes *The Ecologist,* an important international journal of studies and opinion, emphasizing policy and philosophy, edited By Edward Goldsmith, Nicholas Hildyard, and Peter Bunyard.

Water Research Centre (WRC), P.O. Box 16, Marlow, Bucks. SL7 2HD. T: (44 491) 571531. Broad research program that includes water pollution control and protection of aquatic environments.

WaterAid, 1 Queen Anne's Gate, London SW1H 9BT. T: (44 1) 222 8111. Works to increase understanding and practical action concerning the water and sanitation needs of Third-World countries, particularly within the UK water industry.

Whale Conservation Society, 20 West Lea Road, Bath BA1 3RL. Protection of whales and dolphins.

Wildfowl Trust, Gatehouse, Slimbridge, Glos. GL2 7BT. T: (44 45389) 333, ext. 210. Promotes the study and conservation of wildfowl and wetlands in Britain.

World Tree Trust (WTT), La Capucine, 15 The Drive, Adel, Leeds LS16 6BG. T: (44 532) 673304. Promotes tree protection and planting everywhere.

World Wildlife Fund-United Kingdom, Panda House, Weyside Park, Godalming, Surrey GU7 1XR. T: (44 483) 426444. An affiliate of the World Wide Fund for Nature (WWF International), listed in Part 6.

UNITED STATES OF AMERICA

Overview: Entries for the USA are divided as follows: Federal government (subdivided into 4 numbered sections), state government; other organizations; Alaska; Hawaii. Coverage is selective; listings are restricted to major organizations, those with special expertise, those that are of special interest outside the U.S., and those particularly active in international affairs. (Note: Key organizations in Alaska and Hawaii are listed because they have special expertise in Arctic and tropical island problems, respectively.)

Directories: The *Conservation Directory,* published annually by the National Wildlife Federation, lists national government agencies and NGOs in some detail, as well as key state government agencies and selected state and regional NGOs. There are also detailed directories for several states and regions; a bibliography is included in the *Conservation Directory.* These include the *California Environmental Directory,* published by the California Institute of Public Affairs. The Institute has also published *The United States and the Global Environment: A Guide to American Organizations Concerned with International Environmental Issues* (first edition 1983), which provides in-depth profiles of some 100 organizations.

Federal government agencies:

(1) Offices of the Congress:

Office of Technology Assessment (OTA), 600 Pennsylvania Avenue SE, Washington, DC 20510. T: (1 202) 224-8713. Established 1974 to help the Congress anticipate and plan for the consequences of the uses of technology. Many of OTA's studies, which are available to the public, are related to the future of the global environment, e.g., alternative energy futures, world food supply, and effectiveness of development aid.

(2) Executive Office of the President:

Council on Environmental Quality (CEQ), 722 Jackson Place, NW, Washington, DC 20006. T: (1 202) 395-5700. Consists of 3 members appointed by the President; formulates and recommends national policies to promote environmental quality. In the 1970s, CEQ had an active concern with international resource problems, culminating in the 1980 *Global 2000 Report to the President* and a followup report recommending U.S. responses.

(3) Departments:

Department of Agriculture (USDA), Washington, DC 20250. Includes:
■ Agricultural Research Service (ARS), Beltville, Maryland 20705. T: (1 301) 344-2264. Fundamental and applied research on a wide range of environmental and resource conservation problems.
■ Forest Service (USFS), P.O. Box 2417, Washington, DC 20013. T: (1 202) 447-3760. Manages a system of National Forests and National Grasslands; research; assistance to private

forest operators. International Forestry Staff assists with USAID forestry projects. Two USFS research units are especially relevant to developing countries: Institute of Pacific Islands Forestry, 1151 Punchbowl Street, Honolulu, Hawaii 96813. T: (1 808) 546-5669. Institute of Tropical Forestry (see listing under Puerto Rico).
■ Soil Conservation Service (SCS), P.O. Box 2890, Washington, DC 20013. T: (1 202) 447-4543.

Department of Commerce:
■ National Atmospheric and Oceanic Administration (NOAA), Washington, DC 20230. T: (1 202) 377-2985. Includes the National Marine Fisheries Service (research, management, and regulation over commercial and all marine fisheries within the 200 nautical mile U.S. fisheries conservation zone, as well as authority over marine mammals; NMFS has an Office of International Fisheries Affairs); the Office of Ocean and Coastal Resource Management; National Ocean Service; National Weather Service; National Environmental Satellite, Data, and Information Service; and Office of Oceanic and Atmospheric Research.

Department of Energy, Washington, DC 20545. T: (1 202) 252-5000. Broad responsibilities for energy policy, supply, research, development, information, and conservation. Office of the Assistant Secretary for International Affairs is the focal point for international activities. The Department's Oak Ridge National Laboratory, Oak Ridge, Tennessee, includes a Global Environmental Studies Center whose concerns include global climate change.

Department of Health and Human Services (HHS). Includes:
■ National Institute of Environmental Health Sciences (NIEHS), P.O. Box 12233, Research Triangle Park, North Carolina 27709. T: (1 919) 541-2111. Research on toxic materials in the environment.
■ National Institute for Occupational Safety and Health (NIOSH), 5600 Fishers Lane, Rockville, Maryland 20852. T: (1 202) 472-7134. Research for preventing occupational diseases and injuries, including those from environmental hazards.

Department of Housing and Urban Development (HUD), 451 Seventh Street, NW, Washington, DC 20410. T: (1 202) 655-4000.
Department of the Interior, Washington, DC 20240. Includes:
■ Office of Territorial and International Affairs. T: (1 202) 343-4822. Responsible for U.S. external territories and for the Department's international relations.
■ Bureau of Indian Affairs (BIA), Washington, DC 20240. T: (1 202) 343-7445. Acts as trustee for native lands.
■ Bureau of Land Management (BLM). T: (1 202) 343-9435. Manages federal public lands that are located primarily in the Western states.

■ Bureau of Reclamation (BuRec). T: (1 202) 343-4662. Water resources development in the Western states.
■ Geological Survey (USGS), Reston, Virginia 22092. T: (1 703) 648-4460. Surveys and investigations on topography, geology, and mineral and water resources.
■ Minerals Management Service (MMS). T: (1 202) 343-3983. Management of offshore mineral resources.
■ National Park Service (NPS). T: (1 202) 434-7394. National Park System; national systems of trails, wild rivers, and other areas. Has an International Park Affairs Division, which provides technical assistance and training to park agencies of developing countries.
■ Office of Surface Mining Reclamation and Enforcement. T: (1 202) 343-4719.
■ U.S. Fish and Wildlife Service. T: (1 202) 343-5634. Management and protection of wild birds, mammals (except certain marine mammals), and inland sport fisheries. Maintains a system of National Wildlife Refuges. Has an International Affairs Staff concerned with bilateral conservation agreements, CITES, and assistance to developing countries.

Department of Labor. Includes:
■ Occupational Safety and Health Administration (OSHA), Washington, DC 20210. T: (1 202) 523-8017. Responsibilities include protection from environmental hazards in the workplace.

Department of State. Includes:
■ Bureau of Oceans and International Environmental and Scientific Affairs, Department of State, Washington, DC 20520. T: (1 202) 647-3529. Formation of U.S. policies concerning international actions on environmental and natural resource matters.
■ U.S. National Committee for Man and the Biosphere (MAB; see description under Unesco in Part 4). T: (1 202) 632-2816.

Department of Transportation, Washington, DC 20590. T: (1 202) 426-4000. Broad responsibilities for air, land, and water transportation; Coast Guard enforces federal conservation laws on U.S. waters and the high seas.

Department of the Treasury. Includes:
■ U.S. Customs Service, 1301 Constitution Avenue, NW, Washington, DC 20229. T: (1 202) 566-8195. Responsibilities include controlling imports of endangered wildlife species and their products.

(13) Independent federal agencies:

African Development Foundation, 1625 Massachusetts Avenue, NW, Washington, DC 20036. T: (1 202) 673-3916. Supports indigenous community-based, self-help African grassroots organizations in their efforts to solve their countries' development problems.

Agency for International Development (AID or USAID), Washington, DC 20523. T: (1 202) 647-1850. The principal U.S. government development assistance agency. AID's Environment and Natural Resources Division "promotes sustainable agriculture, natural resources management, and environmentally sound economic development." Projects focus on forestry, soil conservation and watershed management, resource inventories, environmental education, land use planning, water and wastewater treatment systems, improved industrial and urban pollution control, coastal resource management, and preserving biological diversity. Pub: *AID Policy Paper: Environment and Natural Resources* (1988); *Special Report: The Environment* (1987); numerous country reports, policy papers, and handbooks.

Environmental Protection Agency (EPA), Washington, DC 20460. T: (1 202) 382-2090. Air and water pollution control; solid waste management; regulation of pesticides, radiation, and toxic substances. Has an Office of International Activities.

Inter-American Foundation, 1515 Wilson Boulevard, Rosslyn, Virginia 22209. T: (1 703) 841-3800. Supports social and economic development in Latin America and the Caribbean; makes grants primarily to private, indigenous groups that carry out self-help projects.

Marine Mammal Commission, 1625 I Street, NW, Room 307, Washington, DC 20006. T: (1 202) 653-6237. Protection of marine mammals; research.

National Science Foundation (NSF), Washington, DC 20550. T: (1 202) 655-4000. Supports U.S. science and engineering research and education programs. Also conducts the U.S. Antarctic Program.

Nuclear Regulatory Commission (NRC), Washington, DC 20555. T: (1 202) 492-7000. Licenses and regulates the civilian use of nuclear energy.

Panama Canal Commission, 2000 L Street, Room 550, Washington, DC 20036. T: (1 202) 634-6441. Operates the Panama Canal and related areas in coordination with the Government of Panama; Panama is scheduled to assume full responsibility on December 31, 1999.

Peace Corps, Washington, DC 20526. T: (1 202) 254-5010. Volunteers serve in more than 60 developing countries; natural resource management and environmental protection are important elements of the program. Pub: Numerous training manuals and case studies of field projects (catalog available).

Smithsonian Institution, 1000 Jefferson Drive, SW, Washington, DC 20520. T: (1 202) 357-1300. Established 1846 "for the increase and diffusion of knowledge among men." Includes a complex array of museums, centers, laboratories, institutes, offices, and other organizations. Directorate of International Activities (T: (1 202) 357-4281) coordinates the Smithsonian's many international efforts. Office of Biological Conservation seeks to develop an awareness among Smithsonian staff and the general public of changes in the environment caused by human activity, and represents the Smithsonian in U.S. and international forums on world conservation issues; particular concerns are tropical forests and trade in endangered species. Pub: *Smithsonian* (monthly magazine); *Smithsonian Institution Research Reports* (3 times a year; news of current projects); yearbook; books, reports, papers, and periodicals (catalog available).
■ Smithsonian Tropical Research Institute. *See* listing under Panama.

State government agencies:

The governments of the 50 states have important responsibilities in all fields of environmental protection and natural resource management. For listings, see the National Wildlife Federation's *Conservation Directory*.

Other organizations:

Acid Rain Information Clearinghouse (ARIC), 33 S. Washington St., Rochester, New York 14608. T: (1 716) 546-3796. Information and educational services on acid rain.

Acid Rain Foundation, 1630 Blackhawk Hills, St. Paul, Minnesota 55122. T: (1 612) 455-7719. Founded 1981. Publishes public information and educational materials on acid deposition and other air pollutants.

Acoustical Society of America, 335 E. 45th Street, New York, New York 10017. T: (1 212) 661-9404. Founded 1929. Professional society. Concerns include control of noise pollution.

African Wildlife Foundation, 1717 Massachusetts Avenue, NW, Washington, DC 20036. T: (1 202) 265-8393. Founded 1961. Finances and operates wildlife conservation projects in Africa. Field office in Nairobi, Kenya.

Air and Waste Management Association, P.O. Box 2861, Pittsburg, Pennsylvania 15230. T: (1 412) 232-3444. Founded 1907; 8,300 members. Technical association. Formerly Air Pollution Control Association.

American Association for the Advancement of Science (AAAS), 1333 H Street, NW, Washington, DC 20005. T: (1 202) 326-6400. Founded 1848; 132,000 members. Federation of U.S. scientific and engineering societies; purposes include improving the effectiveness of science in promoting human welfare. Office of International Science (OIS) administers bilateral and multilateral cooperative projects and exchanges in such fields as arid lands and climate change.

American Association of Botanical Gardens and Arboreta, P.O. Box 206, Swarthmore, Pennsylvania 19081. T: (1 215) 328-9145. Founded 1949.

American Association of Zoological Parks and Aquariums (AAZPA), Oglebay Park, Wheeling, West Virginia 26003. T: (1 304) 242-2160. Founded 1924; 5,000 members. Includes programs for conservation of wildlife and preservation and propagation of endangered and rare species.

American Bar Association (ABA), 750 N. Lake Shore Drive, Chicago, Illinois 60611. T: (1 312) 988-5000. Professional association of lawyers. Maintains a Special Committee on International Environmental Law.

American Cave Conservation Association, P.O. Box 409, Horse Cave, Kentucky 42749. T: (1 502) 786-1466. Founded 1977. Preservation of caves and karstlands.

American Cetacean Society (ACS), P.O. Box 2369, San Pedro, California 90731. T: (1 213) 548-6279. Founded 1967. Conservation, education, and research on marine mammals, especially whales and dolphins.

American Committee for International Conservation (ACIC), c/o Roger McManus, Secretary, Center for Marine Conservation, 1725 DeSales Street, NW, Washington, DC 20036. T: (1 202) 429-5609. Members are U.S. organizations that are members of IUCN; works for exchange of information and coordination of activities.

American Farmland Trust (AFT), 1920 N Street, NW, Suite 400, Washington, DC 20036. T: (1 202) 659-5170. Founded 1980; 40,000 members. Protection of agricultural land from misuse and conversion to other uses.

American Fisheries Society, 5410 Grosvenor Lane, Bethesda, Maryland 20814. T: (1 301) 897-8616. Founded 1870; 8,500 members. Scientific society concerned with conservation, development, and wise use of fisheries.
American Littoral Society, Sandy Hook, Highlands, New Jersey 07732. T: (1 201) 291-0055. Founded 1961; 10,000 members. Study and conservation of coastal environments and resources.

American Lung Association, 1740 Broadway, New York, New York 10019. T: (1 212) 315-8700. Founded 1904. Major group concerned with pre-venting causes of lung disease, including air pollution. Has a National Air Conservation Commission.

American Medical Association, 535 N. Dearborn Street, Chicago, Illinois 60610. T: (1 312) 645-5000. Founded 1847. The major U.S. association of medical doctors. Has a Department of Environmental, Public, and Occupational Health.

American Planning Association (APA), 1776 Massachusetts Avenue, NW, Washington, DC 20036. T: (1 202) 872-0611. Professional society of urban and regional planners; 21,000 members.

American Psychological Association (APA), Division 34 (Population and Environmental Psychology), c/o Carol Werner, Department of Psychology, University of Utah, Salt lake City, Utah 84112

American Rivers, 801 Pennsylvania Avenue, NW, Suite 303, Washington, DC 20003. T: (1 202) 547-6900. Founded 1973. Preservation of remaining free-flowing rivers in the U.S.

American Society for Environmental History, Department of History, Oregon State University, Corvallis, Oregon 97331. T: (1 503) 754-3421. Founded 1976. Scholarly society that seeks to understand human ecology through the perspectives of history and the humanities in general.

American Society of Landscape Architects (ASLA), 1733 Connecticut Avenue, NW, Washington, DC 20009. T: (1 202) 466-7730. Founded 1899; 10,000 members. Professional society.

American Water Resources Association, 5410 Grosvenor Lane, Suite 220, Bethesda, Maryland 20814. T: (1 301) 493-8600. Founded 1964; 3,700 members. Exchange of information on water resources among scientists and engineers.

Americans for the Environment, 322 Fourth Street, NE, Washington, DC 20002. T: (1 202) 547-8000. The political skills training arm of the U.S. environmental activist community. Board of directors composed of representatives of major groups.

Antarctica Project, 218 D Street, SE, Washington, DC 20003. T: (1 202) 544-2600. Conducts scientific and policy research, acts as a consultant to major U.S. conservation groups, and presents policy proposals on protection of the Antarctic region, including the Falkland (Malvinas) Islands. Also serves as the headquarters of the Antarctic and Southern Ocean Coalition (ASOC), an international NGO listed in Part 6.

Arctic Institute of North America. See listing in Part 6.

Arctic International Wildlife Range Society. See listing in Part 6.

Arizona-Sonora Desert Museum, Route 9, Box 90, Tucson, Arizona 85704. T: (1 602) 883-1380. Museum and research focused on the natural resources of the Sonoran Desert region of northern Mexico and the Southwestern U.S.

Ashoka, 1200 N. Nash Street, Arlington, Virginia 22209. T: (1 202) 628-0370. Seeks out and funds "path-breaking innovators" who work for the public good in developing countries. Works in South Asia, Mexico, and Brazil.

Association of Arid Lands Studies (AALS), Box 4620, Texas Tech University, Lubbock, Texas 79409. T: (1 202) 742-2218. Founded 1977; 250 members. Scholarly association concerned with arid and semi-arid ecosystems worldwide and human impact upon them.

Association on American Indian Affairs (AAIA), 95 Madison Avenue, New York, New York 10016. T: (1 212) 689-8720. Founded 1923; 34,000 members. Major association concerned with welfare of native Americans; provides legal and technical assistance to Indian tribes.

Atlantic Center for the Environment, 39 S. Main Street, Ipswich, Massachusetts 01938. T: (1 508) 356-0038. Fax: (1 508) 356-7322. Education, policy, and research programs in Quebec and the Atlantic provinces of Canada, and northern New England in the U.S.

Atlantic Salmon Federation. *See* listing in Part 6.

Bio-Integral Resource Center, P.O. Box 7414, Berkeley, California 94707. T: (1 415) 524-2567. Founded 1979. Provides information on least-toxic pest control.

California Institute of Public Affairs (CIPA), P.O. Box 10, Claremont, California 91711. T: (1 714) 624-5212. Includes an international dimension in many of its projects on California environmental problems. Compiles and publishes information guides, including the *California Environmental Directory* and the *World Directory of Environmental Organizations*. An international project to promote collaborative approaches to environmental policy-making is being conducted in cooperation with IUCN.

Canada-United States Environmental Council. *See* listing in Part 6.

Center for Field Research (Earthwatch), P.O. Box 403, Watertown, Massachusetts 02272. T: (1 617) 926-8200. Tx: 5106006452. Matches scientists who need volunteers with amateurs interested in sharing the work and costs of field expeditions throughout the world. About 100 research projects are mobilized each year, many of them related to the natural environment. Examples: Tracking timber wolves in Minnesota, USA; ecological studies in a Costa Rican rain forest; collecting information needed to plan turtle beach reserves in Cyprus.

Center for Marine Conservation (CMC), 1725 DeSales Street, NW, Washington, DC 20036. T: (1 202) 429-5609. Founded 1972 as the Center for Environmental Education. Focuses on worldwide protection of marine wildlife and their habitats. Policy research; public awareness; citizen involvement.

Center for Plant Conservation, 125 Arborway, Jamaica Plain, Massachusetts 02130. T: (1 617) 524-6988. Network of botanic gardens dedicated to study and conservation of rare and endangered U.S. plants.

Cetacean Society International, 190 Stillwold Drive, Wethersfield, Connecticut 06109

Chelonia Institute, P.O. Box 9174, Arlington, Virginia 22209. T: (1 703) 524-4900. Founded 1977. Focuses on conservation of marine turtles through research, information, and land acquisition.

Chihuahuan Desert Research Institute (CDRI), P.O. Box 1334, Alpine, Texas 79831. T: (1 915) 837-8370. Founded 1974. Research and education on the Chihuahuan Desert of the southwestern U.S. and northern Mexico.

Children of the Green Earth, P.O. Box 95219, Seattle, Washington 98145. Founded 1980. Promotes tree-planting by young people worldwide.

Clark University, Program for International Development and Social Change, 950 Main Street, Worcester, Massachusetts 01610. Tx: 951-829. C: CENTED. Program founded 1973. Includes research and teaching about environmental and resource management in developing countries, particularly in Africa.

Clean Water Action Project, 317 Pennsylvania Avenue, SE, Washington, DC 20003. T: (1 202) 547-1196. Founded 1971; 400,000 members. Advocacy and education on water pollution and toxic chemicals.

Climate Institute, 316 Pennsylvania Avenue, Se, Suite 403, Washington, DC 20003. T: (1 202) 547-0104. Research and conferences on gloobal climate change.

Coastal Society, 5410 Grosvenor Lane, Suite 110, Bethesda, Maryland 20814. T: (1 301) 897-8616. Founded 1975. Works internationally to promote understanding and wise use of coastal resources.

The Conservation Foundation (CF), 1250 24th Street, NW, Washington, DC 20037. T: (1 202) 293-4800. Founded 1948. Affiliated with World Wildlife Fund-U.S. A major research and public education organization. Land, Heritage, and Wildlife Program focuses on U.S. land-use and public land management problems. Environmental Dispute Resolution Program brings together representatives of government, business, and public-interest groups to solve specific environmental conflicts, and develops and promotes the use of conflict resolution methods. Environmental Quality Program emphasizes pollution control, especially problems associated with toxic chemicals. International Environment Program provides technical assistance to governments and NGOs and conducts training programs in developing countries, and has projects on toxic chemicals in the Third World, alternatives to chlorofluorocarbons, impacts of climate change, U.S.-Mexico environmental relations, and population and environment. The Osborne Center for Economic Development, operated in cooperation with WWF-U.S., seeks to demonstrate the critical importance of integrating conservation and economic development in developing countries. The Center focuses on forestry and agriculture, as well as renewable energy resources; it sponsors pilot projects (the first to demonstrate improved forest management on Costa Rica's Osa Peninsula), conducts field research, and stimulates exchange of ideas and experience. Pub : *Conservation Foundation Letter; Resolve* (newsletter on dispute resolution); books and reports.

Conservation International (CI), 1015 18th Street, NW, Suite 1000, Washington, DC 20006. T: (1 202) 429-5660. Founded 1987. Acts as "a catalyst for conservation action" in Latin America, by "working with people and sovereign nations as partners within the context of local socio-political and economic realities." Main focus is on developing national conservation data centers, fellowships for conservation leaders, and creating and managing ecosystem reserves. CI is best-known for carrying out "debt-for-nature" trades in Bolivia and Costa Rica, in which CI purchased part of the countries' foreign debt at a discounted rate. In exchange for CI's agreement to cancel the debt, the governments agreed to establish legal protection for conservation areas. Pub: *Orion Nature Quarterly* (with the Myrin Institute).

Coolidge Center for Environmental Leadership, 1675 Massachusetts Avenue, Suite 4, Cambridge, Massachusetts 02138. T: (1 617) 864-5085. Founded 1983. Organizes programs on sustainable development for potential leaders from developing countries who are students at universities in the northeastern U.S.
Coordination in Development (CODEL), 475 Riverside Dr., Room 1842, New York, NY 10115. T: (1 212) 870-3000. Consortium of 42 U.S.-based, Christian-related groups that have development programs in Third-World countries; CODEL Environment and Development Program provides training in environmental concepts for home and field staff of member groups, as well as counterpart agencies and government officials in host countries. Focus has been on agriculture, agroforestry, and water resources.

Cornell University, Center for Religion, Ethics, and Social Policy, Ithaca, New York 14853. T: (1 607) 255-4225. Includes the Eco-Justice Project.

Cousteau Society, 930 W. 21st Street, Norfolk, Virginia 23517. T: (1 804) 627-1144. Founded 1973 by Captain Jacques-Yves Cousteau. Research and public education through films and TV, focusing on the oceans and water quality. Offices in Paris, New York, and Los Angeles.

Cultural Survival (CS), 11 Divinity Ave., Cambridge. MA 02138. T: (1 617) 495-2562. Founded 1972. "Supports projects on 5 continents which help indigenous peoples retain their rights and culture as they learn to live with the modern world." Examples: creating a center for traditional culture among the Chinchero in highland Peru; operating a cultural and educational center for the Sherpa in Nepal's Himalayan region. Also works to prevent cultural extinction through publicity and research. "Small, traditional societies are extinguished not by abstract historical processes but by greed and incomprehension." Pub: *Cultural Survival Quarterly;* reports.

Defenders of Wildlife, 1244 19th Street, NW, Washington, DC 20036. T: (1 202) 659-9510. Founded 1947; 80,000 members. Preservation of wildlife and habitat.

Ducks Unlimited, 1 Waterfowl Way, Long Grove, Illinois 60047. T: (1 312) 438-4300. Founded 1937. Protection of nesting, resting, and wintering areas of waterfowl in Canada, the U.S. and Mexico.

Earth Island Institute, 300 Broadway, Suite 28, San Francisco, California 94133. T: (1 415) 788-3666. Activist group founded by David Brower, formerly Executive Director of the Sierra Club and later President of Friends of the Earth. Works primarily through individual projects such as the Rain Forest Action Network. Pub: Project newsletters.

East-West Center, 1777 East-West Road, Honolulu, Hawaii 96848. T: (1 808) 944-7111. Tx: 989171 ewc ud. C: EASWESEN. Founded in 1960. National educational institution promoting better relations and understanding between the U.S. and countries of Asia and the Pacific through cooperative study, training, and research. Pub: Newsletters; books and reports. Two of the Center's 5 problem-oriented institutes deal with international environmental and resource issues:
■ East-West Environment and Policy Institute (EAPI). T: (1 808) 944-7555. Program focuses on resource utilization in rural areas, ocean governance, social responses to environmental change, economic analysis of natural resources, effectiveness of different management practices, and risk assessment.

■ East-West Resource Systems Institute (RSI). T: (1 808) 944-7555. Program focuses on energy, minerals policy, and development policy and international affairs.

Environmental Defense Fund (EDF), 257 Park Avenue South, New York, New York 10010. T: (1 212) 505-2100. Founded 1967; 60,000 members. Staff of lawyers, scientists, and economists conducts research, public education, litigation, and administrative and legislative advocacy on a broad range of issues, including energy and resource conservation, toxic chemicals, water resources, air quality, land use, and wildlife. International interests focus on the role of mulilateral development banks in "encouraging unsustainable over-exploitation of resources for export," particularly tropical forests. Pub: *EDF Letter;* reports.

Environmental Design Research Association (EDRA), c/o Setha Low, Environmental Psychology Program, City University of New York, 33 W. 42nd Street, New York, New York 10036

Environmental Law Institute (ELI), 1616 P Street, NW. Suite 200, Washington, DC 20036. T: (1 202) 328-5150. Founded 1969. Research and education in environmental law and policy.

Environmental Media Association (EMA), 10536 Culver Boulevard, Culver City, California 90232. T: (1 213) 559-9334. Founded 1989. "An entertainment industry response to the global environmental crisis." Led by a number of Hollywood figures including producer-director Norman Lear, EMA will encourage environmental themes in TV shows and feature films, sponsor educational forums for the entertainment community, institute an awards program, and provide communication expertise to environmentalists.

Environmental Policy Institute (EPI), 218 D Street, SE, Washington, DC 20003. T: (1 202) 544-2600. Founded 1972. Advocacy, focusing on energy, water, agriculture, toxics, and resource-national security issues.

Friends of Africa in America, 330 S. Broadway, Tarrytown, New York 10591. T: (1 914) 631-5168. Founded 1963. Promotes understanding of development problems of Africa; support for wildlife projects, primarily in East Africa.
Friends of the Earth (FOE), 530 Seventh Street, SE, Washington, DC 20003. T: (1 202) 543-4312. Founded 1969 by David Brower. Activist lobbying organization "committed to the preservation, restoration, and rational use" of the Earth. U.S. membership 15,000; affiliated FOE groups in several countries. International issues have been a major concern, particularly those related to nuclear power and alternative energy sources, marine mammals, the world oceans, and wilderness. Affiliated with Friends of the Earth International, listed in Part 6.

Friends of the United Nations Environment Programme (FUNEP), 2013 Q Street, NW, Washington, DC 20009. T: (1 202) 234-3600. Works to improve public awareness of global problems and UNEP's response to them.

Game Conservation International, P.O. Box 17444, San Antonio, Texas 78217. T: (1 512) 824-7509. Founded 1967; 1,500 members. Group of hunter-conservationists that participates in wildlife protection projects.

German Marshall Fund of the United States (GMF), 11 Dupont Circle, NW, Washington, DC 20036. T: (1 202) 745-3950. Tx: 197533. C: GMFUS. Fax: (1 202) 265-1662. Sponsors U.S.-based research and conferences on European environmental policies, as well as exchanges of U.S. and European professional environmentalists.

Global Tomorrow Coalition (GTC), 1325 G Street, NW, Suite 915, Washington, DC 20005. T: (1 202) 628-4016. Founded 1981. National alliance of 115 organizations with combined membership of 8 million, dedicated to broader public understanding in the U.S. of global trends in population, resources, environment, and development.

Grassland Heritage Foundation, 5450 Buena Vista, Shawnee Mission, Kansas 66205. T: (1 913) 677-3326. Founded 1976; 1,300 members. Promotes appreciation of native U.S. grassland; preserves representative areas.

Great Lakes United. *See* listing in Part 6.

Green Library, 1918 Bonita Avenue, Berkeley, California 94704. T: (1 415) 845-9975. Helps to establish environmental libraries in "areas hit by ecological crisis"; initial projects have been in Eastern Europe and Nepal.

Greenpeace USA. 1436 U Street, NW, Washington, DC 20009. T: (1 202) 462-1177. National office of Greenpeace International, listed in Part 6.

I*Kare Wildlife Trust. *See* International Wildlife Coalition

INFORM, 381 Park Avenue South, New York, New York 10016. T: (1 212) 689-4040. Founded 1973. Examines business practices that cause environmental problems and then evaluates practical, constructive steps that businesses can take. Focus has been on hazardous materials, solid waste, and water conservation.

Institute for Alternative Agriculture, 9200 Edmonstron Road, Suite 117, Greenbelt, Maryland 20770. T: (1 301) 441-8777. Founded 1983. Promotes sustainable agriculture in the U.S. through research and education, information dissemination, and contacts with farmer groups and policy-makers.

Institute for Alternative Futures (IAF), 1405 King Street, Alexandria, Virginia 22314. T: (1 703) 684-5880. Tx: 650 2154985. Fax: (1 703) 684-0640. Founded 1977. Assists governmental agencies, professional and voluntary organizations, and businesses in the U.S. to "more wisely choose their future."

Institute for Resource Management (IRM), 19 Exchange Place, Salt Lake City, Utah 84111. T: (1 901) 322-0530. Works to "anticipate problems and issues before the different viewpoints become polarized, provide a forum for discussion, and serve as a catalyst for active problem solving." Initial projects focused on American Indian lands and on electric power. President is actor Robert Redford.

Institute for 21st Century Studies, 1611 N. Kent Street, Arlington, Virginia 22209. T: (1 703) 841-0048. Counsels and assists countries interested in exploratory studies of their futures. Directed by Gerald O. Barney, who headed the Global 2000 Study in the Carter Administration.

International Conservation Institute, 45 Elm Street, Byfield, Massachusetts 01922. T: (1 617) 465-5389. Collaborative effort of several environmental organizations in northeastern North America to provide training and exchange opportunities for conservation professionals from other countries.

International Development Conference, 1401 New York Ave., NW, Suite 1100, Washington, DC 20005. T: (1 202) 638-3111. Coalition of U.S. organizations concerned with Third World development, including environment-development issues. Main activity is biennial conference. Founded 1952. Pub: *Ideas and Information about Development Education* (newsletter).

International Institute for Energy Conservation, 420 C Street, NE, Washington, DC 20002. T: (1 202) 546-3388. Works to encourage developing countries to create incentives for resource-efficient energy policies; helps them obtain appropriate technologies.

International Institute for Environment and Development-North America. *See* World Resources Institute

International Snow Leopard Trust, 16463 S.E. 35th Street, Bellevue, Washington 98008

International Society for the Preservation of the Tropical Rainforest, 3931 Camino de la Cumbre, Sherman Oaks, California 91423. T: (1 818) 788-2002. Tx: 650320411 mci uw. Activities include promoting cooperation between the USA and USSR on tropical forest protection.

International Studies Association (ISA), Byrnes International Center, University of South Carolina, Columbia, South Carolina 29208. T: (1 803) 777-2933. Professional association of scholars working in international affairs; members are mainly from the U.S. Maintains an Environmental Studies Section.

International Wildlife Coalition (IWC), 320 Gifford Street, Falmouth, Massachusetts 02540. T: (1 508) 540-8086. Incorporated as I*Kare Wildlife Trust. Solicits public contributions through mailings highlighting cruelty to wild animals; funds conservation projects in the field focusing on marine and terrestrial mammals. Branches in UK (Care for the Wild), Canada, and Brazil.

Island Resources Foundation. *See* listing under Virgin Islands of the U.S.

Izaak Walton League of America, 1401 Wilson Boulevard, Level B, Arlington, Virginia 22209. T: (1 703) 528-1818. National organization of 50,000 sportsfishermen; general conservation interests.

The Keystone Center, P.O. Box 606, Keystone, Colorado 80435. T: (1 303) 468-5822. Founded 1975. National center for negotiation of environmental disputes; also conducts training and education in such negotiation.

Land Trust Exchange, 1017 Duke Street, Alexandria, Virginia 22314. T: (1 703) 683-7778. Founded 1982. Assists local and regional private land-conservation groups which use innovative ways (such as easements) to preserve land of natural and cultural importance.

League of Conservation Voters (LCV), 2000 L Street, NW, Suite 804, Washington, DC 20036. T: (1 202) 785-8683. National, nonpartisan political campaign committee to promote election of public officials who will work for a healthy environment. Board includes representatives of many leading environmental organizations.

Legacy, 111 S. Patrick St., Alexandria, Virginia 22314. T: (1 703) 549-3630. Tx: 510600 1584 legacy. Founded 1977. An "educational organization fostering cross-cultural understanding and dialogue on critical global issues through training and action programs." Projects include Youths for Environment and Service (YES), which mobilizes people ages 20-35 to assume leadership roles in environmental protection (currently in the Mediterranean region and organizing in the USA); and sustainable development workshops (in North America).

Marine Technology Society (MTS), 2000 Florida Avenue, NW, Suite 500, Washington, DC 20009. T: (1 202) 462-7557. Professional society; promotes exchange of information on ocean-related subjects, mainly from a business standpoint, including coastal zone management, energy, minerals, and economic potential.

Monitor, 1506 19th Street, NW, Washington, DC 20036. T: (1 202) 234-6576. Founded 1972; consortium of 35 U.S. conservation and animal-welfare organizations. Information clearinghouse on endangered species and marine mammals worldwide. Works to achieve consensus positions among member groups; does not offer services or information directly to the public.

National Audubon Society, 950 Third Avenue, New York, New York 10022. T: (1 212) 832-3200. Founded 1905; 550,000 members. Originally devoted mainly to study of bird life, Audubon "has come to believe that all forms of life are interdependent." Broad interests and activities.

National Center for Atmospheric Research (NCAR), P.O. Box 3000, Boulder, Colorado 80307. T: (1 303) 494-5151. A major center for research on global climate change; has an Environmental and Social Impacts Group.

National Coalition Against the Misuse of Pesticides, 530 Seventh Street, SE, Washington, DC 20003. T: (1 202) 543-5450. Founded 1981. Information and public education.

National Coalition for Marine Conservation, P.O. Box 23298, Savannah, Georgia 31403. T: (1 912) 234-8062. Founded 1973. Conservation of ocean fish and the marine environment.

National Environmental Health Association (NEHA), 720 S. Colorado Boulevard, South Tower, Suite 970, Denver, Colorado 80222. T: (1 303) 756-9090. Founded 1937. Professional society of sanitarians.

National Institute for Urban Wildlife, 10921 Trotting Ridge Way, Columbia, Maryland 21044. T: (1 301) 596-3311. Founded 1973. Research and information on the relationship between man and wildlife in urban areas.

National Parks and Conservation Association (NPCA), 1015 31st Street, NW, Washington, DC 20007. T: (1 202) 944-8530. Founded 1919; 70,000 members. Focuses on promoting and improving the U.S. National Park System.

National Research Council (NRC), 2101 Constitution Avenue, NW, Washington, DC 20418. T: (1 202) 393-8100. Tx: 248664 nasw ur. C: NARECO. Fax: (1 202) 334-2854. Principal operating arm of the National Academy of Sciences, National Academy of Engineering, and Institute of Medicine. Includes:
■ Board of Environmental Studies and Toxicology. Carries out NRC's studies of environmental problems.
■ Office of International Affairs (OIA). Conducts NRC's international programs and examines

relevant science policy issues. A major unit of OIA is the:
■ Board on Science and Technology for International Development (BOSTID). Works to strengthen local science and technology capabilities in developing countries in various fields, including the environment and natural resources. Representative projects have focused on natural hazard mitigation, revegetation in the Sahel region of Africa, pesticides, and the role of science in foreign aid policy.

National Speleological Society, Cave Avenue, Huntsville, Alabama 35810. Founded 1941; 8,000 members. Exploration, study, and conservation of U.S. caves.

National Wildlife Federation (NWF), 1400 Sixteenth Street, NW, Washington, DC 20036. Founded 1936. Members and supporters number 5.1 million, including members of affiliated local rod-and-gun clubs. Broad interests, emphasizing public education. Maintains an International Affairs Committee.

Natural Resources Defense Council (NRDC), 122 E. 42nd Street, New York, New York 10168. T: (1 212) 949-0049. Founded 1970; 100,000 members. Uses an "interdisciplinary legal and scientific approach" to monitor government, disseminate information, and bring judicial action. Broad interests in domestic and international environmental policy. On global issues, priorities include an anti-greenhouse action strategy for the U.S., and protection of tropical forests in the U.S. and its territories. Pub: *The Amicus Journal;* books and reports.
■ International Program, NRDC, 1350 New York Avenue, NW, Suite 300, Washington, DC 20006. T: (1 202) 783-7800. "Encourages international policy-makers to develop environmentally sound policies and to consider long-term environmental factors as important as short-term political pressures." Focuses on U.S. foreign policy (especially on international development assistance) and the multilateral development banks.

The Nature Conservancy, 1815 N. Lynn Street, Arlington, Virginia 22209. T: (1 703) 841-5300. Fax: (1 703) 841-1283. Founded 1951; 436,000 members. The leading private sector organization working to preserve biological diversity in the U.S. by protecting natural lands and the life they harbor; operates a system of over 1,000 nature sanctuaries, "the largest private system of nature sanctuaries in the world." Latin America Program works with national agencies and NGOs, as well as international organizations, to protect critical natural areas. This is done by strengthening like-minded organizations, assisting to found national conservation organizations, supporting development of national conservation data centers, and helping to design national parks. The Nature Conservancy has also been active in negotiating "debt-for-nature swaps" which convert existing loans to Latin American countries into funds for conservation action in those countries. So far, these have been in Costa Rica and Ecuador; Peru, Brazil, and Jamaica may follow. Pub: *The Nature Conservancy Magazine,* bimonthly; *International News;* reports.

New York Zoological Society, The Zoological Park, Bronx, New York 10460. T: (1 212) 220-5100. Fax: (1 212) 220-7114. Founded 1895. Includes:
■ Wildlife Conservation International (WCI), a major international program of research, development of wildlife management plans, and establishment of parks and reserves. WCI is "unique among conservation organizations" in that it "emphasizes field biology as the first, vital step in saving a species. The field is the 'front line.'" Currently, WCI has 113 projects in 43 countries. Examples of projects: research on protection of pandas in China (conducted by WCI Director for Science George Schaller); control of disease spread between wild and domestic animals in East Africa; conservation of the Central American river turtle in Mexico, Belize, and Guatemala; flamingo habitat preservation in South America; start-up support for local groups in Papua New Guinea.

Nitrogen Fixing Tree Association, P.O. Box 680, Waimanalo, Hawaii 96795. T: (1 808) 948-7985. Founded 1980. Promotes development and use of nitrogen-fixing trees (which convert atmospheric nitrogen to soil nitrogen necessary for plant growth), particularly in the tropics.

North American Lake Management Society, 1000 Connecticut Avenue, NW, Suite 202, Washington, DC 20036. T: (1 202) 833-3382. Founded 1980. Protection, restoration, and management of lakes and reservoirs and their watersheds.

Oceanic Society, 1536 16th Street, NW, Washington, DC 20036. T: (1 202) 328-0098. Founded 1969; 40,000 members. Works to protect the marine environment through research, education, and conservation action. Most active groups are in California and New York.

Overseas Development Council (ODC), 1717 Massachusetts Avenue, NW, Washington, DC 20036. T: (1 202) 234-8701. Founded 1969. Policy research, seminars for professionals, and public education on the problems of Third-World development and the U.S. role.

Pacific Institute for Studies in Development, Environment, and Security, 1681 Shattuck Avenue, Suite H, Berkeley, California 94709. T: (1 415) 843-9550. Founded 1988. Conducts policy research and education on the connections between international security, global environmental change, and economic development; initial projects focus on the effects of large-scale environmental change resulting from global warming.

Pacific Whale Foundation, P.O. Box 1038, Kihei, Maui, Hawaii 96753. Founded 1980. Research, conservation, education, and action to protect whales and other marine mammals.

The Population Council, 1 Dag Hammarskjold Plaza, New York, New York 10017. T: (1 212) 644-1300. Founded 1952. Endeavors to advance knowledge in the broad field of population by fostering research, training, and technical consultation and assistance in the social and biomedical sciences. Pub: *Studies in Family Planning,* monthly; country reports; occasional bulletins; indexes and bibliographies.

Population Crisis Committee, 1120 19th Street, NW, Washington, DC 20036. T: (1 202) 659-1833. Founded 1965. Works to develop support worldwide for international population and family-planning programs through public education and liaison with leaders and organizations; direct funding of private family-planning projects.

Population Institute, 110 Maryland Avenue, NE, Washington, DC 20002. T: (1 202) 544-330. Founded 1969. Works to enlist and motivate key leadership groups in the U.S. to participate in the effort to bring population growth into balance with resources by means consistent with human dignity and freedom.

Population Reference Bureau, 777 14th Street, NW, Suite 800, Washington, DC 20005. T: (1 202) 639-8040. Founded 1929. Gathers, interprets, and publishes information on the social, economic, and environmental implications of U.S. and global population dynamics.

Population Resource Center, 500 E. 62nd Street, New York, New York 10021. T: (1 212) 888-2820. Founded 1975. Provides policy analyses and briefings to U.S. leaders that relate the impact of national and global population trends to public issues.

Program on Negotiation at Harvard Law School, 500 Pound Hall, Harvard Law School, Cambridge, Massachusetts 02138. T: (1 617) 495-1684. Founded 1983. An inter-university consortium to improve the theory and practice of conflict resolution. Has been a leader in developing the theory and practice of negotiation in environmental disputes, e.g., in land development and in cleaning up hazardous waste sites. Pub: *Negotiation Journal: On the Process of Dispute Settlement;* books and reports.

Programme for Belize, P.O. Box 385 M, Vineyard Haven, Massachusetts 02568. A temporary task force sponsored by national and international conservation NGOs with operations in Belize; is raising funds for research and conservation projects, including land purchases, in that country.

RARE, Inc., 19th and the Parkway, Philadelphia, Pennsylvania 19103. T: (1 215) 299-1182. "RARE" stands for Rare Animal Relief Effort." The conservation education affiliate of the World Wildlife Fund-U.S.; provides technical and financial aid to conservation education projects in developing countries. Focus is on rainforests and the oceans.

Renew America, 1001 Connecticut Avenue, NW, Suite 719, Washington, DC 20036. T: (1 202) 466-6880. An outgrowth of Solar Action, founded 1978. Monitors and reports on current developments in environmental protection in the 50 states of the USA.

Resources for the Future (RFF), 1616 P Street, NW, Washington, DC 20036. T: (1 202) 328-5000. Founded 1952. A major center for research and public education in resource conservation and environmental protection, emphasizing social scientific, particularly economic, approaches. Includes an Energy and Natural Resources Division, a Quality of the Environment Division, the National Center for Food and Agricultural Policy, and the Center for Risk Management. Areas of interest include forest economics, natural gas policy, multiple use of public lands, mineral economics, air and water pollution, energy and national security, hazardous waste, the economics of outer space, and climate. Emphasis is on the U.S., but some projects are international in scope (e.g., "Household Energy and the Poor in the Third World"; The Seventh Continent: Antarctica in a Resource Age"). Pub: *Resources* (newsletter); books and reports.

Rocky Mountain Institute, 1739 Snowmass Creek Road, Snowmass, Colorado 80654. T: (1 303) 927-3851. Fax: (1 303) 927-4178. Founded 1982 by energy analysts Amory and Hunter Lovins. Works to "foster the efficient and sustainable use of resources as a path to global security" through "transdiciplinary syntheses which harness the problem-solving power of market economies." Research focuses on energy, water, agriculture, community economic development, security, and their interconnections. International outreach includes exchanges with the USSR. Pub: Newsletter; reports.

Safari Club International, 4800 West Gates Pass Road, Tucson, Arizona 85745. T: (1 602) 620-1220. Organization of sportsmen-conservationists; supports wildlife conservation and research projects abroad, and conducts public education.

Safe Energy Communication Council, 1717 Massachusetts Avenue, NW, Washington, DC 20036. T: (1 202) 483-8491. Coalition of groups working to oppose nuclear power; works by providing information to the communications media.

Scientists' Institute for Public Information (SIPI), 355 Lexington Avenue, New York, New York 10017. T: (1 212) 661-9110. Founded 1963. Informs and enlists scientists in public information programs on a variety of issues, including environmental problems.

Sierra Club, 730 Polk Street, San Francisco, California 94109. T: (1 415) 567-6100; 408 C Street, NE, Washington, DC 20002. T: (1 202) 547-1144. Founded 1892 by John Muir; 500,000 members in 57 chapters and 340 groups throughout the U.S. and Canada. Works "to explore, enjoy, and protect the wild places of the earth; to practice and promote the responsible use of the earth's ecosystems and resources; and to educate and enlist humanity to protect and restore the quality of the natural and human environment." Broad interests. Pub: *Sierra* (bimonthly magazine); newsletters of topical and regional committees, chapters, and groups; policy reports; citizen action manuals; Sierra Club Books (including the Exhibit Format series, popular studies of environmental issues, and outdoor guides); publication catalog available.
■ International Program (at Washington office). Created in 1971. Focuses primarily on the policies and actions of the U.S. government, both at home and abroad, and the multilateral development banks (such as the World Bank) in which the U.S. plays a major role. Major international concerns include maintaining biological diversity, protection of tropical rainforests, promotion of sustainable agriculture, and protection of natural areas. The Club also forges cooperative links with NGOs in other countries through its Earthcare Network, "an informal network of like-minded groups who extend themselves to help each other when they are mounting major campaigns. There are no dues or obligations, but the network operates in the spirit that we can all help each other in our 'moments of need.'" Examples of issues handled by the Earthcare Network: flouting of wildlife laws in the Sudan; rare coral reefs threatened by a proposed airport in Japan; plans to dam a protected wild river in Costa Rica.

Society for Conservation Biology, Biology Department, Montana State University, Bozeman, Montana 59717. T: (1 406) 994-4548. Founded 1985. Professional society of biologists interested in applying their scientific knowledge to conservation.

Society for Marine Mammalogy, c/o Randall W. Davis, Secretary, Sea World Research Institute, 1700 South Shores Road, San Diego, California 92109. T: (1 619) 226-3877. Founded 1981. Scientific group whose purposes include promoting conservation of marine mammals.

Society for Range Management, 1839 York Street, Denver, Colorado 80206. T: (1 303) 355-7070. Founded 1948; 5,000 members. Professional society; promotes understanding of rangeland (livestock grazing land) ecosystems.

Society of American Foresters, 5400 Grosvenor Lane, Bethesda, Maryland 20814. T: (1 301) 897-8720. Founded 1900; 21,000 members. Professional society.

Soil and Water Conservation Society of America, 7515 N.E. Ankeny Road, Ankeny, Iowa 50021. T: (1 515) 289-2331. Founded 1945; 12,500 members. Formerly Soil Conservation Society of America. Professional and citizens' organization.

South and Central American Indian Information Center (SAIIC), P.O. Box 7550, Berkeley, California 94707. T: (1 415) 452-1235. Founded 1983. Disseminates information about the plight of indigenous people in South and Central America.

Stanford University. Includes:
■ Center for Conservation Biology, Stanford, California 94305. T: (1 415) 497-2300. International research and education in scientific aspects of preserving biological diversity; intensive short courses for professionals.
■ Morrison Institute for Population and Resource Studies, Stanford, California 94305. Conducts interdisciplinary research amnd postgraduate studies in world population and related problems.

Texas Tech University, International Center for Arid and Semiarid Land Studies (ICASALS), P.O. Box 4620, Lubbock, Texas 79409. T: (1 806) 742-2218. Center founded 1966. Conducts interdisciplinary studies of arid and semiarid environments and their management.

Threshold, International Center for Environmental Renewal, Drawer CU, Bisbee, Arizona 85603. T: (1 602) 432-7353. Founded 1972. Develops ecologically-sound practical alternatives related to protection of tropical forests, acid rain, solar energy, national park planning, community sacred parks, pollution control, bioregional education, and river basin studies. Works internationally.

TRAFFIC (U.S.A.), 1250 24th Street, NW, Washington, DC 20037. T: (1 202) 293-4800. Stands for Trade Records Analysis of Flora and Fauna in Commerce. A program of World Wildlife Fund-U.S. that monitors the international trade in wild animals and plants and their products; part of an international network of TRAFFIC offices.

TRANET, P.O. Box 567, Rangeley, Maine 04970. Transnational network for appropriate and alternative technology. An information source; publishes a newsletter and resource lists.

Tropical Forests Working Group, c/o Thomas Stoel, Natural Resources Defense Council, 1350 New York Avenue, NW, Washington, DC 20005. Brings together Washington-based representatives of national and international agencies and NGOs concerned with tropical forest issues.

Trumpeter Swan Society, 3800 County Road 24, Maple Plain, Minnesota 55359. T: (1 612) 476-4663. Founded 1968. Promotes research and information exchange internationally on the ecology and management of the trumpeter swan.

Trust for Public Land (TPL), 82 Second Street, San Francisco, California 94105. T: (1 415) 495-4014. Founded 1973. Major land conservation organization; acquires natural, scenic, and recreational lands in the U.S. through private acquisition.

University of Arizona, Office of Arid Lands Studies, Tucson, Arizona 85719. T: (1 602) 621-1955. Tx: 1561507. C: ARIDLANDS. Office founded 1964. Major center for research, education, and information dissemination on arid lands. Program includes field studies in West Africa and Mexico.

University of California, Scripps Institution of Oceanography, La Jolla, California 92093. T: (1 619) 534-2830. A leading center for oceanographic research, including coastal studies.

University of Michigan, School of Natural Resources, Ann Arbor, Michigan 48109. T: (1 313) 763-2200. Includes the Center for Strategic Wildland Management Studies, which conducts research and education in "important global issues involving the protection and use of wild species and natural ecosystems for sustainable development."

University of Minnesota, Hubert H. Humphrey Institute of Public Affairs, Minneapolis, Minnesota 55155. T: (1 612) 373-2653. Includes the Global Environmental Policy Project (directed by Dean E. Abrahamson), which "represents a major inquiry into the implications of the global warming of the atmosphere."

University of New Mexico, School of Law, Natural Resources Center, Albuquerque, New Mexico 87131. Publishes the *Natural Resources Journal*. Includes the International Transboundary Resources Center, which focuses on U.S-Mexico transboundary resources, and to a lesser degree on transboundary problems in other regions.

Water Pollution Control Federation, 601 Wythe Street, Alexandria, Virginia 22314. T: (1 703) 684-2400. Founded 1928; 34,000 members. Technical organization.

Whale Center, 3929 Piedmont Avenue, Oakland, California 94611. T: (1 415) 654-6621. Founded 1978. Research, education, and advocacy on whales and the oceans.

Wilderness Society, 1400 I Street, NW, 10th Floor, Washington, DC 20005. T: (1 202) 842-3400. Founded 1935; 220,000 members. Preservation of wilderness and wildlife in the U.S.

Wildlife Conservation International. *See* New York Zoological Society

Wildlife Society, 5410 Grosvenor Lane, Bethesda, Maryland 20814. T: (1 301) 897-9770. Founded 1937; 8,200 members. Organization of professionals in wildlife management.

Wild Wings and Underhill Foundations, 18 E. 74th Street, New York, New York 10021. Jointly operate a Tropical Conservation Program, created in 1983, which funds projects to protect and manage natural areas and related public education in developing countries.

Winrock International Institute for Agricultural Development, Route 3, Morrillton, Arkansas 72110. T: (1 501) 727-5435. Tx: 248589. C: WINROCK. Founded 1985 through a merger of several agricultural development groups. Program includes research, education, and extension work in natural resource management throughout the Third World. Regional office in Bangkok, Thailand. Office in Arlington, Virginia, T: (1 703) 525-9430, manages the USAID-funded Forestry/Fuelwood Research and Development (F/FRED) Project, which helps scientists in developing countries meet the need for fuelwood and other tree products.

Woods Hole Oceanographic Institution, Woods Hole, Massachusetts 02543. T: (1 617) 548-1400. A major center for ocean and coastal zone research and education; includes a Marine Policy and Ocean Management Program.

World Environment Center, 419 Park Avenue, Suite 1403, New York, New York 10016. T: (1 212) 683-4700. Founded 1974. Non-advocacy organization that serves as a bridge between industry and government to strengthen environmental management worldwide. Holds conferences and workshops.

World Forestry Center, 4033 S.W. Canyon Road, Portland, Oregon 97221. T: (1 503) 228-1367. Founded 1971. Research, demonstration, and public education on forests.

World Future Society, 4916 St. Elmo Avenue, Bethesda, Maryland 20814. T: (1 301) 656-8274. Produces publications and hold conferences that discuss future trends in popular terms. Pub: *The Futurist* (magazine).

World Nature Association, P.O. Box 673, Silver Spring, Maryland 20901. T: (1 301) 593-2522. Founded 1969. Funds small conservation projects in various parts of the world.

World Population Society, 1333 H Street, Suite 760, Washington, DC 20005. T: (1 202) 898-1303. Founded 1973. Organization of professionals working in population; concerned mainly with research and education.

World Resources Institute (WRI), 1735 New York Avenue, NW, Washington, DC 20006. T: (1 202) 683-6300. (The International Institute for Environment and Development-North America has become the Center for International development and Environment within WRI; IIED-London continues as a separate entity.) Founded 1982. A major policy research center "created to help answer a fundamental question: How can societies meet human needs and nurture economic growth while preserving natural resources and environmental integrity? Independent and nonpartisan, WRI brings together leading thinkers from many fields and countries to provide accurate information about global resources and environmental conditions, analyze emerging issues, and develop creative yet workable policy responses." Research programs focus on conservation of biological resources; sustainable agriculture; energy and climate; population and health; institutions and governance; and resource and environmental information. Examples of recent projects: "Public Policy and the Misuse of Forest Resources"; "Tropical Forests: A Call for Action"; "Improving Water Management in Mexico's Irrigated Agriculture." Pub: *World Resources Report* (biennial compendium of data in graphic form); annual *Journal* (report of activities with substantive articles); *NGO Networker* (quarterly newsletter for and about NGOs around the world concerned with environment and development; books, reports, and papers.

World Wildlife Fund-U.S., 1250 24th Street, NW, Washington, DC 20037. T: (1 202) 293-4800. Founded 1961. U.S. affiliate of the World Wide Fund for Nature (WWF International), described in Part 6; also affiliated with the Conservation Foundation.

Worldwatch Institute, 1776 Massachusetts Avenue, NW, Washington, DC 20036. T: (1 202) 452-1999. Founded 1974. Research and public education on emerging global problems and trends, many of which relate to resources and the environment. Publishes books, Worldwatch Papers, and a bimonthly magazine, *World Watch*.

Yale University, School of Forestry and Environmental Studies, 205 Prospect Street, New Haven, Connecticut 06511. T: (1 203) 432-5109. School founded 1900. A leading center for postgraduate education and research in conservation and natural resource management. Its Tropical Resources Institute (TRI) emphasizes integration of the biophysical and social sciences in research, education, and information dissemination on the natural resources of the tropics. Pub: School newsletter; *TRI News;* research reports.

Zero Population Growth (ZPG), 1601 Connecticut Avenue, NW, Washington, DC 20009. T: (1 202) 332-2200. Founded 1968; 15,000 members. Works to achieve a balance among people, resources, and the environment by advocating population stabilization in the U.S. and worldwide.

Alaska:
Note: Key Alaskan organizations are listed here because they offer special expertise on the environmental problems of the Arctic and sub-Arctic.

Alaska Department of Environmental Conservation, P.O. Box 0, Juneau, AK 99811. T: (1 907) 465-2600. State government agency responsible for environmental protection.

Alaska Department of Fish and Game, P.O. Box 3-2000, Juneau, AK 99802. T: (1 907) 465-4100. State government agency responsible for wildlife management.

Alaska Department of Natural Resources, 400 Willoughby, Juneau 99801. T: (1 907) 465-2400. State government agency responsible for forestry, agriculture, parks, energy, mining, and related resource issues.

Alaska Center for the Environment, 400 H Street, Sute 4, Anchorage, AK 99501. T: (1 907) 274-3621. Founded 1971. Advocacy and citizen organizing group.

Alaska Environmental Lobby, P.O. Box 22151, Juneau, AK 99802. Coalition of 19 environmental groups; lobbies the state Legislature.

Trustees for Alaska, 725 Christensen Drive, Suite 4, Anchorage 99501. T: (1 907) 276-4244. Public-interest law firm that works to protect Alaska's environment.

Hawaii:
Note: Key Hawaiian organizations are listed here because they offer special expertise on the problems of tropical oceanic islands.

Hawaii Office of Environmental Quality Control, 465 S. King Street, Room 104, Honolulu, HI 96813. T: (1 808) 548-6915. Coordinates state government environmental management activities; advises the state's governor.

Hawaii Department of Health, P.O. Box 3378, Honolulu, HI 96801. T: (1 808) 548-2211. State government agency whose responsibilities include environmental health.

Hawaii Department of Land and Natural Resources, P.O. Box 621, Honolulu, HI 96809. T: (1 808) 548-6550. State government agency with broad environmental and resource management responsibilities.

University of Hawaii, Institute of Tropical Agriculture and Human Resources, 3050 Maile Way, Honolulu, HI 96822. T: (1 808) 948-8131. Programs include research and assistance in natural resource management, with emphasis on the Pacific islands and Asia.

Conservation Council for Hawaii, P.O. Box 2923, Honolulu, HI 96802. T: (1 808) 941-4974. Citizens' group affiliated with the National Wildlife Federation.

Life of the Land, 19 Niolopa Place, Honolulu, HI 96817. T: (1 808) 595-3903. Citizens' group founded 1970. "Direct, aggressive action based on fact." Broad interests.

The Outdoor Circle, 200 N. Vineyard Boulevard, Room 506, Honolulu, HI 96817. T: (1 808) 521-0074. Citizens' group with broad interests.

URUGUAY

Directories: *See* "Directories" under Argentina.

Government:

Ministerio de Ganadería, Agricultura y Pesca--Dirección General de Recursos Naturales Renovables (Ministry of Livestock, Agriculture, and Fisheries--General Directorate of Renewable Natural Resources), Cerrito 322, 2º piso, Montevideo. T: (598 2) 95 98 78. Broad responsibilities for natural resource and environmental management. Includes a Wildlife Directorate and a Forestry Directorate.

Ministerio de Educación y Cultura, Instituto Nacional para la Preservación del Medio Ambiente (INPMA) (Ministry of Education and Culture, National Institute for Preservation of the Environment), Reconquista 535, piso 8, Montevideo. T: (598 2) 95 83 50. Assists in all areas of environmental and resource protection.

Other organizations:

Asociación Uruguaya de Derecho Ambiental (AUDA) (Uruguayan Association of Environmental Law), Echeverriarza 3396, Montevideo. T: (598 2) 72 10 24.

Centro de Estudios sobre Recursos y Medio Ambiente (CERMA) (Center for Studies on Resources and the Environment), Casilla de Correos 946, Monevideo. T: (598 2) 28 12 76. Promotes ecologically-sustainable development through research and education.

Centro de Estudios Uruguayos de Tecnologías Apropiadas (CEUTA) (Center for Uruguayan Studies of Appropriate Technology), Casilla de Correos 10958, Montevideo. Areas include energy, gardening, construction, and reforestation.

Centro de Investigación y Promoción Franciscano y Ecológico (CIPFE) (Franciscan Ecological Center for Research and Promotion), Casilla Postal 13125, Montevideo. T: (598 2) 90 76 48. Organization of Franciscan priests and brothers and others; training, information, and research.

Consejo Nacional de Investigaciones Científicas (CONICYT) (National Council of Scientific Research), Reconquista 535, piso 7, Casilla de Correo 1869, Montevideo. T: (598 2) 95 58 28. Tx: 23133. C: CONICYTUR. ICSU national member.

Sociedad de Conservación del Medio Ambiente (Society for Conservation of the Environment), Cerro Largo 1895, Montevideo. Founded 1986.

VANUATU

Government:

Ministry of Lands, Energy, and Water Supply, P.O. Box 151, Port Vila. Tx: 1040 vangov nh. Includes an Environment Unit.

VATICAN CITY
See Holy See

VENEZUELA

Government:

Ministerio de Ambiente y de los Recursos Naturales Renovables (Ministry of Environment and Renewable Natural Resources), Torre Norte, Centro Simón Bolivar, Caracas. T: (58 2) 483-3164. Tx: 22661. Broad responsibilities.

Instituto Nacional de Parques (INPARQUES) (National Institute of Parks), Parte Sur, Museo de Transporte, Urbanización Santa Cecilia, 1010 Caracas. T: (58 2) 355-533. Tx: 24362 inap. Autonomous agency responsible for national park system.

Other organizations:

BIOMA: Fundación Venezolana para la Conservación de la Diversidad (BIOMA: Venezuelan Foundation for Conservation of Diversity), Apartado 1968, 1010-A Caracas. T: (58 2) 571-8831. Founded 1986. Works to protect natural areas.

Consejo Nacional de Investigaciones Científicas y Tecnológicas (CONICIT) (National Council of Scientific and Technological Research), Apartado de Correos 70.617, Caracas 1071-A. T: (58 2) 239 7791. Tx: 25205. ICSU national member. Fundación para la Defensa de la Naturaleza (FUDENA) (Foundation for the Defense of Nature), Apartado 70376, 1071-A Caracas. T: (58 2) 239-6547. Tx: 23280 hidecvc. Major organization.

Sociedad Conservacionista Audubon de Venezuela (Audubon Conservation Society of Venezuela), Apartado 80450, 108 Caracas. T: (58 2) 91-3813.

VIET-NAM

Government:

Comité d'Etat des Sciences et Techniques (State Committee for Science and Technology), 39 rue Tran Hung Dao, Hanoi. T: 52731. Tx: 287. ICSU national member. Includes Natural Resources, Pollution Control, Water Resources, and Environmental Planning and Management units.

VIRGIN ISLANDS, BRITISH
British dependent territory.

Government:

Ministry of Natural Resources and Labour, Road Town, Tortola. T: (1 809) 43701.

Ministry of Health, Education, and Welfare, Road Town, Tortola. T: (1 909) 43701.

VIRGIN ISLANDS OF THE UNITED STATES
Territory of the U.S.

Government:

Department of Planning and Natural Resources, P.O. Box 4399, St. Thomas, VI 00801, USA. T: (1 809) 774-3320. Broad environmental and natural resource management responsibilities.

Department of Health, St. Thomas, VI 00801, USA

Other organizations:

Island Resources Foundation, P.O. Box 33, St. Thomas, VI 00802. T: (1 809) 775-6225. Founded 1972. Conducts research on resource systems of various islands for improved resource management and comprehensive eco-development planning.

Virgin Islands Conservation Society, P.O. Box 12379, St. Thomas, VI 00801. Affiliated with the National Wildlife Federation (USA).

WAKE ISLAND
U.S. possession.

Government:

Under jurisdiction of the U.S. Department of the Air Force, Washington, DC 20380, USA. T: (1 202) 694-8010.

WALLIS AND FUTUNA
A French possession.

Government:

Chief Administrator, Government Offices, Mata-Uta, Wallis Island

Ministère des Départements et Territoires d'Outre Mer (Ministry of Overseas Departments and Territories, 27 rue Oudinot, F-75700 Paris, France. T: (33 1) 47 83 01 23.

WESTERN SAMOA

Government:

Department of Agriculture, P.O. Box 206, Apia. T: 22561. Tx: 221. Responsibilities include fisheries.

Department of Health, Private Bag, Apia. T: 21212. Tx: 277.

YEMEN ARAB REPUBLIC (NORTH YEMEN)

Government:

Ministry of Municipalities and Housing, Environment Department, P.O. Box 1445, Sana'a. T: (967 2) 21 56 58. Tx: 2526 muhaws ye. Broad environmental responsibilities.

Ministry of Agriculture and Fisheries, Sana'a

Ministry of Electricity and Water Resources, Sana'a

Ministry of Health, Sana'a. Environmental health.

YEMEN, PEOPLE'S DEMOCRATIC REPUBLIC OF (SOUTH YEMEN)

Government:

Ministry of Fisheries, Aden

Ministry of Agriculture and Agrarian Reform, Aden

Ministry of Public Health, P.O. Box 4200, Khormaksar, Aden. Environmental health.

YUGOSLAVIA

Federal government:

Savez za Zastitu Covekoves Sredine (Federal Agency for the Human Environment), 2 boulevar Lenjina, YU-11000 Belgrade

Zavod za Zastitu Spomenika Kulture i Prirode BiH (Federal Committee for Natural and Cultural Patrimony), 27 Julia 11a, YU-71000 Sarajevo

Republic governments:

The governments of the 6 constituent republics have important responsibilities for environmental protection and natural resource management.

Other organizations:

Centar za Istrazivanje Mora (Marine Research Institute), Bijenicka 54, YU-41000 Zagreb. Focuses on the Adriatic Sea.

Association of Scientific Unions, c/o Referral Centre, University of Zagreb, Trg Marsala Tita 3, P.O. Box 327, YU-41000 Zagreb. T: (38 41) 422965. Tx: 22486 rcszgh yu. ICSU national member.

Ekoloski Zbor (Ecological Assembly), Moste 34, YU-64274 Zirovnica

Jugoslavenska Akademija Znanosti i Umjetnosti (Yugoslav Academy of Sciences and Arts), Zrinski trg. 11, YU-41000 Zagreb

Jugoslovensko Drustve za Cistocu Vazduha (Yugoslav Society for Clean Air), Masinski Fakultet, YU-71001 Sarajevo

ZAIRE

Government:

Departement de l'Environnement, Conservation de la Nature et Tourisme (Department of the Environment, Conservation of Nature, and Tourism), B.P. 12348, Kinshasa 1. T: (243 12) 31252. Broad responsibilities for resource management and environmental protection.

Other organizations:

Agriculture et Bois: Société Africaine d'Etude sur l'Environnement (AGRIBO) (Agriculture and Wood: African Society for Study of the Environment), N.R.C. 9914 KIN, B.P. 5698, Kinshasa-Gombe. Conducts research aimed at the sustainable utilization and conservation of natural resources.

Centre d'Etudes pour l'Action Sociale (CEPAS) (Study Center for Social Action), B.P. 5717, Kinshasa-Gombe. Includes projects on energy conservation and waste recycling.

ZAMBIA

Government:

Ministry of Lands and Natural Resources, P.O. Box 50694, Lusaka. T: (260 1) 214988. Includes the Department of National Parks and Wildlife Services.

Ministry of Agriculture and Water Development, P.O. Box 50291, Lusaka. T: (260 1) 213551. Ministry of Health, P.O. Box 30205, Lusaka

Ministry of Higher Education, National Council for Scientific Research, P.O. Box CH 158, Lusaka. T: (260 1) 281081. Tx: 40005 nacsir za. C: NACSIR. Program includes research in natural resource management.

Other organizations:

Chongololo and Conservation Club of Zambia (CCCZ), P.O. Box 30255, Lusaka. Environmental youth organization with 900 clubs comprised of 31,000 members. Clubs are of 3 types: Chongololo Clubs, in primary schools; Conservation Clubs, in secondary schools; and the Chongololo Club of the Air, built around a radio program. Education, training, and tree-planting.

Wildlife Conservation Society of Zambia, P.O. Box 30255, Lusaka

Zambia Forestry Association, P.O. Box 22099, Kitwe, Copper Belt Province. T: (260 2) 210456. Tx: 52051 za. Founded 1974. Education, information, and action projects in forestry, wood use, and natural resources generally.

ZIMBABWE

Directories: *Zimbabwe NGO Directory* (1988), VOICE, P.O. Box 8465, Causeway, Harare. 120 pages.

Government:

Ministry of Natural Resources and Tourism, Private Bag 7753, Causeway, Harare. T: (263 0) 794455. Tx: 4435. Includes a Department of Natural Resources and a Department of National Parks and Wildlife Management.

Ministry of Health, P.O. Box 8204, Causeway, Harare

Other organizations:

The Zambezi Society, P.O. Box UA 334, Union Avenue, Harare

The Zimbabwe National Conservation Trust (ZNCT), P.O. Box 8575, Causeway, Harare. T: (263 0) 700300. C: SABLES. Founded 1974. Coordinates conservation projects in the NGO sector and functions as a link between NGOs and the government. Broad interests, ranging from wildlife habitat and pesticide regulation to educational TV programs.

Appendix
Directories & Databases

The directories and databases listed here are sources of information about organizations concerned with the environment and natural resources. Addresses of publishers, if not listed here, can be found elsewhere in this book (see the index) or in directories of commercial publishers. Directories for individual countries are listed by country in Part 7. The UNEP *World Directory of Environmental Expertise* (see below), includes a discussion and list of major environmental libraries and databases.

ACCIS Guide to United Nations Information Sources on the Environment. New York: Advisory Committee for the Co-ordination of Information Systems, United Nations, 1988.

Annotated Directory of Organizations Dealing with Desertification Control and Dryland Development. Nairobi: Desertification Control Programme Activity Centre, United Nations Environment Programme, 1986.

Annual Report of the Executive Director, United Nations Environment Programme. Nairobi: UNEP, annual. Includes brief descriptions of numerous projects which UNEP undertakes in cooperation with other organizations within and outside the UN system, thus serving as a useful guide to organizational interrelationships.

Arid Lands Research Institutions: A World Directory. By Barbara S. Hutchinson and Robert G. Varady. Office of Arid Lands Studies, University of Arizona. New York: Allerton Press, 3rd ed., 1988.

Catalogs of environmental protection organizations in developing countries. Bundesministerium für Wirtschaftliche Zusammenarbeit (German Federal Ministry for Economic Cooperation), Karl-Marx-Strasse 4-6, D-5300 Bonn, Federal Republic of Germany. Consists of individual catalogs on some 50 countries (as of 1987); comments are in German. Available from: INFU-Dortmund, P.O. Box 50 05 00, D-4600 Dortmund 50. T: (49 231) 7554096.

Directorio Preliminar de Organismos No Gubernamentales de América Latina y el Caribe Relacionado con Asuntos Ambientales. Mexico City: Centro de Documentación e Información, UNEP Office for Latin America and the Caribbean, 1983. Out of print; not updated as of 1989.

A Directory: NGOs in the Forest Sector: 2nd Africa Edition. New York: International Tree Project Clearinghouse, Non-Governmental Liaison Service, United Nations, 1987. Describes over 200 groups.

Directory of Environmental NGOs in the Asia-Pacific Region. Penang: Sahabat Alam Malaysia (Friends of the Earth Malaysia), 1983. Describes some 200 organizations in 20 countries.

Directory of Institutions and Individuals Active in Environmentally-Sound and Appropriate Technology. Published for the United Nations Environment Programme (UNEP Reference Series, vol. 1). Oxford, England: Pergamon Press, 1979. 2,000 organizations are given brief descriptions and coded by subject.

A Directory of Natural Resource Management Organizations in Latin America and the Caribbean. Edited by Julie Buckley-Ess. Washington and New York: Partners of the Americas and The Tinker Foundation, 1988. Describes over 400 governmental agencies and NGOs.

Directory of Non Governmental Conservation Organizations in the Wider Caribbean. Gland, Switzerland: IUCN, 1983.

Directory of Nongovernmental Organizations in Official Relations with the World Health Organization. Geneva, Switzerland: WHO, periodically updated.

Directory of Principal Governmental Bodies Dealing with the Environment. Nairobi: UNEP, periodically revised. A list of agency names, addresses, and communication services. Coverage is not complete.

Directory of Technical and Scientific Directories. Edited by A.P. Harvey. Harlow, England: Longman Group, 6th ed., 1987. Describes 1,200 reference works, many of which include listings of organizations concerned with scientific aspects of environmental problems.

Directory of U.S. Foundations and Private Organizations Working on Conservation and Development Issues in the Third World. By Rita Feiberg. Washington, D.C: International Institute of Environment and Development, 1984.

Environment Liaison Centre NGO Database. Covers activities of some 6,000 citizen environmental groups around the world; updated every two years. Several directories have been generated from this database, including lists of NGOs working on energy, pesticide, and wildlife issues. Environment Liaison Centre International, Nairobi, Kenya.

Environmental Information Sources. Edited by Thomas F.P. Sullivan and Richard F. Hill. Rockville, Maryland: Governmental Institutes, Inc. (966 Hungerford Drive, Suite 24, Rockville 20850), 1986. Includes a fairly lengthy section on periodical publications (journals, newsletters, magazines) published outside, as well as within, the U.S.

Environmental NGOs in Developing Countries: Information about Environmental Non-Governmental Organizations (NGOs); Suggestions for Cooperation. Leiden, Netherlands: Centre for Environmental Studies, (State University of Leiden, P.O. Box 9518, 2300 RA Leiden), 1985.

Environmental Programmes of Intergovernmental Organizations, with Special Reference to the Sphere of Interest of the Chemical Industry. By P.L. de Reeder. The Hague, Netherlands: Martinus Nijhoff, The Hague, 1977.

Global Action Guide: A Handbook for NGO Cooperation on Environment and Development. Edited by Ronald A. Kingham. Nairobi: Environment Liaison Centre International, 1987.

Guide to Information on Research in Marine Science and Engineering. Washington, D.C.: Office of Ocean Engineering, U.S. National Oceanic and Atmospheric Administration, 1978. *Guide to International Marine Environmental Data Services.* Paris: Unesco, 1975.

Human Ecology: A Survey of Courses Offered at Institutions of Higher Education in the Commonwealth. London: Commonwealth Human Ecology Council, 2nd ed., 1988.

Information Sources on Biotechnology. By A. Crafts-Lighty. London: Macmillan, 2nd ed., 1986. Includes a section on organizations.

International Directory of Botanical Gardens II. International Association of Plant Taxonomy, 1969.

International Directory of Sources. Nairobi: INFOTERRA, UNEP, periodically revised. A massive compilation derived from INFOTERRA's computerized database of over 6,000 sources of environmental information. An abridgement has been published as *World Directory of Environmental Expertise* (listed below).

Life Sciences Organizations and Agencies Directory. Detroit: Gale Research Co., 1st ed., 1988. Lists about 8,000 organizations in the agricultural and biological sciences, mainly in the U.S. but including many international organizations and groups elsewhere.

NGO Directory, Tropical Forest and Multilateral Development Bank Campaigns. Washington, D.C.: Environmental Policy Institute, 1988. Printout of a mailing list with some 600 contacts.

NGO Networker. Washington: World Resources Institute, quarterly. A newsletter targeted at non-governmental organizations (NGOs) primarily in the Third-World. This is an excellent source of information on organizations and new projects concerned with environmental problems in developing countries.

Status of Multilateral Conventions related to the Environment. A database maintained by the IUCN International Law Centre, Bonn, Federal Republic of Germany.

The United States and the Global Environment: A Guide to American Organizations Concerned with International Environmental Issues. Edited by Thaddeus C. Trzyna and Nancy Matsumoto. Claremont: California Institute of Public Affairs, 1983. Detailed descriptions of over a hundred organizations.

World Directory of Environmental Expertise. Nairobi: INFOTERRA, UNEP, 1987. An abridgement of INFOTERRA's more comprehensive *International Directory of Sources*. Describes sources of environmental information by country. Includes a useful section on "Major Environmental Libraries, Databases, and Database Hosts."

World Directory of Environmental Organizations. Claremont: California Institute of Public Affairs, 3rd ed., 1989. Published in cooperation with the Sierra Club and IUCN.

The World Environment Handbook: A Directory of Government Natural Resource Management Agencies and Non-Governmental Environment Organizations in 145 Countries. By Mark Baker and others. New York: World Environment Center, 1985. Out of print. Lists some key governmental agencies and a few NGOs by country; no systematic listings of international organizations.

World Environmental Directory. Silver Spring, Maryland: Business Publishers, Inc., 951 Pershing Drive, Silver Spring 20910), 4th ed. 1980; 5th ed. announced for 1989. The title is somewhat of a misnomer: the book concentrates mainly on U.S. and Canadian organizations. (US $125.00.)

Worldwide Directory of National Earth Science Agencies and Related International Organizations. Reston, Virginia: U.S. Geological Survey, periodically revised.

Yearbook of International Organizations. Brussels: Union of International Associations, biennual. Describes thousands of international organizations, many of which are concerned with environmental and natural resource problems.

Yearbook, International Council of Scientific Unions. Paris: ICSU, annual. Includes directory information for national and international science organizations affiliated with ICSU.

NOTES

NOTES

INDEX

This is an index of organizations and major programs. All of the international organizations listed in Parts 4, 5, and 6 are indexed. National organizations are indexed selectively; if a national organization is not listed here, check the country entries in Part 7. If you are searching for groups concerned with a particular *topic*, see Part 2, Who's Doing What: Problems, Resources, and Biomes. If you are looking for organizations concerned with a particular *region* of the world, see Part 3: The World Regions: Key Organizations.